THE ROAD TO THE WHITE HOUSE 2016

The Politics of Presidential Elections

THE ROAD TO THE WHITE HOUSE 2016

The Politics of Presidential Elections

TENTH EDITION

Stephen J. Wayne
Georgetown University

CENGAGE
Learning·

Australia • Brazil • Mexico • Singapore • United Kingdom • United States

CENGAGE
Learning®

The Road to the White House 2016: The Politics of Presidential Elections, Tenth Edition

Stephen J. Wayne

Product Director: Paul Banks

Product Manager: Carolyn Merrill

Content Developer: Stephanie Laird

Associate Content Developer: Amy Bither

Product Assistant: Michelle Forbes

Marketing Manager: Valerie Hartman

Content Project Manager: Corinna Dibble

Art Director: Linda May

Manufacturing Planner: Fola Orekoya

IP Analyst: Alexandra Ricciardi

IP Project Manager: Betsy Hathaway

Production Service and Compositor: Lumina Datamatics, Inc.

Cover Designer: Travis Hoffman

Cover Images: © Gary Blakeley/Shutterstock.com
© Gutzemberg/shutterstock.com
© Mike McDonald/shutterstock.com
© Shelby Allison/Shutterstock.com
© Terri Francis/Shutterstock.Com

Unless otherwise noted, all items © Cengage Learning

Library of Congress Control Number: 2015934739

ISBN: 978-1-285-86520-1

Cengage Learning
20 Channel Center Street
Boston, MA 02210
USA

Cengage Learning is a leading provider of customized learning solutions with employees residing in nearly 40 different countries and sales in more than 125 countries around the world. Find your local representative at **www.cengage.com**.

Cengage Learning products are represented in Canada by Nelson Education, Ltd.

To learn more about Cengage Learning Solutions, visit **www.cengage.com**.

Purchase any of our products at your local college store or at our preferred online store **www.cengagebrain.com**.

Printed in the United States of America
Print Number: 01 Print Year: 2015

PREFACE

We are in another presidential election cycle. It follows the most costly and one of the most contentious elections in U.S. history in 2012. The new electoral cycle occurs within an economic environment in which the income gap between rich and poor has widened, costs of education have risen, and controversy over minimum wages remains a hot political issue; it occurs within a social environment in which allegations over racial, ethnic, and gender discrimination persist; immigration reform and enforcement continues to divide the nation as does the role of government in providing social services; and it occurs within a polarized, partisan environment in which both parties have unfavorable images, the proportion of Independents has grown, and government has become more contentious. Add to these problems a chaotic world in which national, sectarian, and tribal conflicts; state and nonstate-based terrorism; nuclear proliferation; and world health issues threaten to drag an America weary of the human and material costs of war and other forms of international involvement into a continuous cycle of decisions and actions that affect the country's interests, reputation, and security. The 2016 campaign will be framed by these conditions, these issues, and the electorate's evaluation of how well the Obama administration and Republican-controlled Congress have dealt with them.

The campaign will last about two years. By the end of it, the electorate will be weary to the point of numbness; the presidential candidates will be exhausted and, with the exception of one, disappointed; and the costs of the campaigns will be in the billions of dollars. Is it really necessary to have such an extended election period, to spend so much money, and to go through such a vigorous, oftentimes nasty, public debate? Perhaps not, but free and frequent elections are critical for a democracy. They are a means by which the people can judge the candidates, keep the winners accountable, and hold them responsible for the policy decisions they make.

Elections tie citizens to their government. But for the voters to make an intelligent judgment, they need information about the qualities of the candidates, the policies they propose, and the partisan labels they wear. Does the current presidential electoral system encourage the most qualified candidates to run? Does it force them to discuss the most important issues, present feasible policy solutions, and talk candidly with the American people? Does the electorate get the kind of information it needs to make an enlightened voting decision? Will the results of the election fairly and accurately reflect the opinions, interests, and needs of the population as a whole? Is the system consistent with principles and practices of a democratic electoral process?

A primary goal of this book is to answer these questions. It does so by describing and evaluating the presidential election system from the perspectives of the candidates, the parties, and the American people. As with its previous editions, *The Road to the White House 2016* discusses the legal, political, and financial framework in which the election occurs; the process by which the parties nominate their standard-bearers and position themselves for the general election; the strategies, tactics, and operations of the presidential campaigns themselves; the news media's role; and the attitudes, opinions, and decisions of the voters and what those decisions augur for policy and government once the election is over.

This edition emphasizes the changes that have revolutionized electoral politics in recent years: the flood of money to and from Super PACs, instantaneous communications, digital campaigning, and microtargeting messaging; and the principal continuities: the nomination and Electoral College systems, news coverage, television debates, political commercials, partisan appeals, voting patterns, and election analysis.

OUTLINE

The book is organized into four parts. Part I discusses the arena in which presidential elections occur. Its three chapters examine the electoral system, campaign finance, and the political environment. Chapter 1 provides a historical overview of nominations as well as elections with an extended discussion of the Florida vote controversy in 2000 and its consequences. Chapter 2 examines recent developments in campaign finance, the Supreme Court's decision on independent spending by individuals and groups, the explosion of revenues and expenditures, and the apparent demise of public funding. The chapter will also describe the ways in which campaign finance rules have been circumvented by the candidates and parties and the impact of that circumvention on a democratic electoral system. In the third chapter, continuities and changes in the political environment serve as the principal focus and provide a perspective on how the environment in which the elections occur affects the turnout of voters, the attitudes of the electorate, and the composition of partisan electoral coalitions.

Part II describes and analyzes the presidential nomination process from its early beginning through the national nominating conventions. Chapter 4 discusses the reforms that the parties have made in the way they select their standard-bearers, the legal issues that have arisen from these reforms, and the impact the reforms have had on the partisan electorate, the parties, and the candidates. Chapter 5 continues this discussion through the competitive stage of the caucuses and primaries until the nominee is effectively determined. This chapter pays particular attention to the strategies the candidates adopt and the hurdles they must overcome, illustrating these strategies with case studies from the 2008 and 2012 nomination campaigns. Chapter 6 describes the period after the nominees have been effectively determined through the conventions that officially anoint them and launch their general election campaigns. It describes how the candidates attempt to heal divisions within the party; improve their leadership image, which may have been damaged during the nomination process; and begin to challenge their partisan opposition and launch their general election campaigns . It also discusses the impact of the conventions on the voters' knowledge and partisan preferences.

Part III examines the general election. Chapter 7 describes the strategies, tactics, and field operations of the campaigns. It assesses the new communication technologies that have been used to identify voters, target appeals to them, and measure their impact. The discussion is illustrated with case studies from recent presidential campaigns. Chapter 8 turns to the news media: how the press covers the election and how the candidates try to affect that coverage with paid advertising, scripted public performances, and participation in the presidential debates as well as circumvent it with digital technology. Throughout, the chapter evaluates the impact that media-driven forces can have on the turnout and voting behavior of the electorate.

Part IV looks at and beyond the elections. Chapter 9 discusses and evaluates the vote: Who is going to win? Why? And what difference it makes for governance and public policy. What are the difficulties of moving from campaign promises to presidential performance? Chapter 10 considers problems in the electoral system and possible reforms to alleviate these problems. It examines some of the major difficulties that have affected the political system from party rules to campaign finance to media coverage. The chapter also looks at proposals being discussed for improving the electoral process, making it more equitable to the citizenry, more responsive to popular choice, less prone to human error and fraud, and more likely to guide those in government and facilitate their policy-making responsibilities.

PURPOSE

Elections link the people with their public officials, a vital component of a functioning democracy. However, that link is far from perfect. Voting is individualized, yet governing is a collective undertaking. Everyone does not participate in elections, but government makes rules for all the people, including those who are not eligible to vote. Presidential candidates regularly overpromise and underdeliver. They create unrealistic expectations that are impossible to achieve by the president alone in a system of shared powers and divided government and also to accomplish as quickly as the public demands. As a consequence, the hopefulness that a campaign generates frequently fades into disillusionment, apathy, and cynicism as an administration progresses.

How can we improve elections? How can we encourage more of the citizenry to participate? How can we persuade the most qualified people to run? How can we level the electoral playing field? How can we ensure that the mood of the voters will be reflected in the results of the election and that government officials will pursue the public's interest as reflected in the vote? In other words, how can we make sure that elections achieve their principal goals: to select the most qualified people, to provide them with a blueprint for governing, and to hold them individually and collectively accountable for their decisions and actions in office?

Without information on how the system works, that is, whether it is functioning properly and meeting its objectives, we cannot answer these questions and assess the merits of our electoral democracy. We cannot cajole the citizenry to meet its civic responsibilities and vote; we cannot recruit the best and the brightest to give up their privacy, shift their family responsibilities to others, and, in many cases, sacrifice financially to run for office; we cannot improve the people–government–public policy connection for which elections are the critical link. In the case of presidential politics, ignorance is definitely not bliss, nor is the norm always or usually the ideal.

The road to the White House is long and arduous. In fact, it has now become more difficult to travel than in the past. Yet, surprisingly, given all the criticism, there continue to be many would-be travelers. Evaluating their journey is essential to rendering an intelligent judgment on election day. However, more is at stake than simply choosing the occupant of the Oval Office. The system itself is on trial in every presidential election. That is why it is so important to understand and appreciate the intricacies of the process and to participate in it. Only an informed and active citizenry can determine whether the nation is being well served by the way we go about choosing our president and have some say in determining who that president will be and what he or she will do in office.

ACKNOWLEDGMENTS

Few books are written alone, and this one was no exception. For the 2016 edition, I was fortunate to have an excellent editorial and publishing team at Cengage Learning: Carolyn Merrill, Product Manager; Stephanie Laird, Content Developer; Amy Bither, Associate Content Developer; Michelle Forbes, Product Assistant; Corinna Dibble, Content Project Manager.

I would also like to express my thanks to the political scientists who have reviewed one or more of the ten editions of this book: John Bruce, University of Mississippi; Richard L. Cole, University of Texas at Arlington; Anthony Corrado Jr., Colby College; Stephen C. Craig, University of Florida at Gainesville; James W. Davis, Washington University; Gordon Friedman, Southwest Missouri State University; Jay S. Goodman, Wheaton College; Anne Griffin, the Cooper Union; Marjorie Randon Hershey, Indiana University; Hugh L. LeBlanc, George Washington University; Kuo-Wei Lee, Pan-American University; Robert T. Nakamura, State University of New York at Albany; Richard G. Niemi, University of Rochester; Diana Owen, Georgetown University; Charles Prysby, the University of North Carolina at Greensboro; Michael Robinson, Georgetown University; Lester Seligman, University of Illinois; Earl Shaw, Northern Arizona University; John W. Sloan, University of Houston; Priscilla Southwell, University of Oregon at Eugene; William H. Steward, University of Alabama; Edward J. Weissman, Washington College; and Clyde Wilcox, Georgetown University.

Finally, everyone makes personal sacrifices in writing a book. I want to thank my wife, Cheryl, for her patience and understanding and for allowing me to enjoy Vermont summers and Marlboro Music without the other obligations of family life while I worked on the book.

Stephen J. Wayne
Georgetown University

DEDICATION

*To the memory of my parents and grandparents,
who encouraged my interests in politics and
my pursuit of higher education; to my wife,
Cheryl, who has tolerated my passion for politics
and keeps me pointed in the right political
direction; and to my Georgetown students,
whose questions, comments, and, in some cases,
careers have strengthened my understanding and
appreciation of American politics.*

About the Author

Stephen J. Wayne has been a professor of government at Georgetown University since 1989. A Washington-based expert on the American presidency, he has authored or edited 12 books in multiple editions and more than 100 articles, chapters, and book reviews. In addition to *The Road to the White House,* he has coauthored *Presidential Leadership* (with George Edwards), *Conflict and Consensus in American Politics,* and *The Politics of American Democracy* (both with G. Calvin Mackenzie and Richard L. Cole), all published by Cengage Learning, plus two books on democratic elections and governance, and a more recent study of the Obama presidency.

A much-quoted source for journalists covering the White House, he frequently appears on television and radio news and discussion programs and has consulted for television documentaries. He has testified before Congress on presidential elections, appeared before both Democratic and Republican advisory committees on the presidential nomination process, directed a presidential transition project for the National Academy of Public Administration, and participated in the White House transition projects conducted by the Presidency Research Group. Professor Wayne lectures widely throughout the United States and abroad on the contemporary presidency, personality and politics, and presidential elections.

CONTENTS

LIST OF FIGURES AND TABLES

FIGURES

TABLES

THE ELECTORAL ARENA

PART | I

Stephen J. Wayne

1 CHAPTER | PRESIDENTIAL SELECTION: A HISTORICAL OVERVIEW

INTRODUCTION

The road to the White House is long, circuitous, and bumpy. It contains numerous hazards and potential dead ends. Those who choose to traverse it—and there are many who do so—need considerable skill, perseverance, and luck to be successful. They also need substantial amounts of time, money, and effort. For most candidates, there is no such thing as a free or easy ride to the presidency.

The framers of the Constitution worked for several months on the presidential selection system, and their plan has since undergone a number of constitutional, statutory, and precedent-setting changes. Modified by the development of parties, the expansion of suffrage, the growth of the news media, and the revolution in communications technology, the electoral system has become more open and participatory but also more contentious, complex, and expensive. It has "turned off" many people who, for a variety of reasons, have chosen not to participate. This chapter is about that system: why it was created; what it was supposed to do; the compromises that were incorporated in the original plan; its initial operation and the changes that have subsequently affected it; the groups that have benefited from these changes; and the overall effect on the parties, the electorate, and American democracy.

In addressing these questions, I have organized the chapter into four sections. The first section discusses the creation of the presidential election process. It explores the motives and intentions of the delegates at Philadelphia and describes the procedures for selecting the president within the context of the constitutional and political issues of that day.

The second section examines the development of nominating systems. It explores the three principal methods that have been used to nominate presidential candidates: partisan congressional caucuses, brokered national conventions, and state primaries and caucuses. It also describes the political forces that helped to shape these modes of nomination and, in the case of the first two, destroyed them.

The third section discusses presidential elections. It focuses on the most controversial ones, those determined by the House of Representatives (1800 and 1824), influenced by Congress (1876), and decided by the Supreme Court (2000). The chapter also examines elections in the twentieth and twenty-first centuries in which the shift of a relatively small number of votes could have changed the outcome (1960, 1968, 1976, and 2004). In doing so, this section highlights the strengths and weaknesses of the Electoral College and assesses its consistency with the principles of a democratic electoral process.

The final section of the chapter examines the current operation of the electoral system. It describes its geographic and demographic biases and how they affect the national character of the presidential elections. The section also discusses the Electoral College's major-party orientation and its adverse impact on third-party and independent candidacies.

THE CREATION OF THE ELECTORAL COLLEGE

Of the many issues facing the delegates at the Constitutional Convention of 1787 in Philadelphia, the selection of the president was one of the toughest. Seven times during the course of the convention the method for choosing the executive was altered. The framers' difficulty in designing electoral provisions for the president stemmed from their need to guarantee the institution's independence and, at the same time, to create a technically sound, politically effective mechanism that would be consistent with a republican form of government. They wanted a representative government based on consent, but not a direct democracy in which every citizen had an opportunity to participate in the formulation of public policy. Their goal was an electoral system that would choose the most qualified person, but not necessarily the most popular. There seemed to be no precise model to follow; heredity was out of the question, and a direct popular vote was viewed as impractical and undesirable.

Three methods of election had been proposed. The Virginia Plan, a series of resolutions designed by James Madison and introduced by Governor Edmund Randolph of Virginia, provided for legislative selection. Eight states chose their governors in this fashion at that time. Having Congress choose the president would be practical and politically expedient. Moreover, members of Congress could be expected to exercise a considered judgment, more considered than that of the general public.

The difficulty with legislative selection was the threat it posed to the institution of the presidency. How could the executive's independence be preserved if the election of the president hinged on popularity with Congress and reelection depended on the legislature's appraisal of the president's performance in office? Only if the president were to serve a long term and not be eligible for reelection, it was thought, could the institution's independence be guaranteed so long as Congress was the electoral body. But ineligibility also posed problems, as it provided little incentive for performance in office and denied the country the possibility of reelecting a person whose experience and success demonstrated qualifications that were superior to others.

Reflecting on these concerns, Gouverneur Morris urged the removal of the ineligibility clause on the grounds that it tended to destroy the great motive to good behavior, the hope of being rewarded by a reappointment.[1] Delegates for a majority of the states agreed. Once the ineligibility clause was deleted, however, the term of office had to be shortened to prevent what the framers feared might become unlimited tenure or, in the words of Thomas Jefferson, "an elective monarchy." With a shorter term of office and permanent reeligibility, legislative selection was not nearly as desirable because it could make the president beholden to the legislature. Moreover, there was still the issue of whether the Congress would vote as one body or as two separate legislative houses. The large states favored a joint vote; the small states wanted separate votes by the House and Senate (since they had equal representation in the upper chamber).

Popular election did not generate a great deal of enthusiasm. It was twice rejected in the convention by overwhelming votes.[2] Lacking confidence in the public's ability to choose the best-qualified candidate, many delegates also believed that the size of the country and the relatively primitive state of its communications and transportation in the eighteenth century precluded a national campaign and election. The geographic expanse was simply too large to allow for proper supervision and administration of the election. Sectional distrust and rivalry also contributed to the difficulty of holding a national election.

A third option, indirect election, in which popular sentiment could be expressed but would not dictate the outcome, was proposed by James Wilson after he failed to generate much support for a direct popular vote. Luther Martin, Gouverneur Morris, and Alexander Hamilton also suggested an indirect popular election through intermediaries. It was not until the debate over legislative selection divided and eventually deadlocked the delegates, however, that election by electors was seriously considered. Proposed initially as a compromise that incorporated previous convention agreements by a Committee on Unfinished Business, the Electoral College design was viewed as acceptable by weary delegates eager to return home and get the Constitution ratified.

The debate over the Electoral College system was short and to the point. Viewed as a safe, workable solution to the election dilemma, it was deemed consistent with the constitutional and political features of the new government and resistant to the kind of cabal and corruption that might tinge a popular vote. How the electors were to be selected was left to the states to determine. To ensure their independence, the electors could not simultaneously hold a federal government position.

The number of electors was to equal the number of senators and representatives from each state. At a designated time, they would meet, vote, and send the results to Congress, where they would be announced to a joint session by the president of the Senate, the vice president. Each elector had two votes since a president and vice president were to be selected separately. The only limitations on voting were that the electors could not cast both their ballots for inhabitants of their own states[3] nor designate which of the candidates they preferred to be president and which one vice president.[4]

Under the initial plan, the person who received a majority of votes cast by the Electoral College was elected president, and the one with the second-highest total, vice president. In the event that no one received a majority, the House of Representatives would choose from among the five candidates with the most electoral votes, with each state delegation casting one vote. If two or more individuals were tied for second, then the Senate would select one as vice president. Both of these provisions were subsequently modified by the Twelfth Amendment to the Constitution.

The electoral system was a dual compromise that incorporated provisions of the big–small state and North–South compromises. Both dealt with representation. The first provided for one legislative body to be based on population (the House of Representatives) and one in which the states were equally represented (the Senate); the other compromise allowed three-fifths of the slave population to be counted in the determination of a state's popular representation. Both compromises protected slave owners in the South by making it difficult for the representatives of the more populous North to determine public policy on their own.

Designating the number of electors to be equal to a state's congressional delegation gave the larger states an advantage in the initial voting for president; casting ballots by state delegations in the House, if the Electoral College was not decisive, benefited the smaller states. It was anticipated that this two-step process would occur most of the time since there would probably not be a consensus national leader other than George Washington. In effect, the large states would nominate, much like the state primaries and caucuses do today, and the small states would exercise equal influence in the final election.[5]

The other compromise between the proponents of a federal system and those who favored a more centralized, national government allowed state legislatures to establish the procedures for choosing electors but had a national legislative body, the House of Representatives, decide among the candidates if there was no Electoral College majority. Finally, limiting the vote to the electors was intended to reduce intrigue, fraud, and cabal, fears that were expressed about the undesirability of state-based, popular voting.

THE DEVELOPMENT OF NOMINATING SYSTEMS

Although the Constitution prescribed a system for electing a president, it made no reference to the nomination of candidates. Political parties had not emerged prior to the Constitutional Convention. Factions existed, and the framers of the Constitution were concerned about them, but the development of a party system was not anticipated. Rather, it was assumed that electors, whose interests were not tied to the national government, would make an independent judgment, and it was hoped they would choose the person they felt was best suited for the job.

In the first two elections, the system worked as intended. George Washington was the unanimous choice of the electors. There was, however, no consensus on the vice president. The eventual winner, John Adams, benefited from some informal lobbying by prominent individuals prior to the vote.[6] A more organized effort to agree on candidates for the presidency and vice presidency was undertaken in 1792. Partisan alliances were beginning to develop in Congress. Members of the two principal groups, the Federalists and the Anti-Federalists, met separately to recommend individuals for whom to vote in addition to Washington. The Federalists chose Vice President John Adams (Massachusetts); the Anti-Federalists picked Governor George Clinton of New York.

With political parties evolving during the 1790s, the selection of electors quickly became a partisan contest. In 1792 and 1796, a majority of the state legislatures chose them directly. Thus, the political group that controlled the legislature also determined the selection of electors. Appointed for their political views, electors were expected to exercise a partisan judgment. When in 1796 a Pennsylvania elector did not do so, he was accused of faithless behavior. Wrote one critic in a Philadelphia newspaper: "What, do I chuse Samuel Miles to determine for me whether John Adams or Thomas Jefferson shall be President? No! I chuse him to act, not to think."[7]

Washington's decision not to serve a third term forced Federalist and Anti-Federalist members of Congress to recommend the candidates in 1796. Meeting separately, party leaders agreed among themselves on the tickets. The Federalists urged their electors to support John Adams and Thomas Pinckney(South Carolina), while the Anti-Federalists (or Democratic-Republicans, as they began to be called) suggested Thomas Jefferson (Virginia) and Aaron Burr (New York). Since it was not possible to specify presidential and vice presidential choices on the ballot, Federalist electors, primarily from New England, decided to withhold votes from Pinckney to make certain that he did not receive the same number as Adams. This strategy enabled Jefferson with sixty-eight votes to finish ahead of Pinckney with fifty-nine, but behind Adams, who had seventy-one. Four years of partisan differences followed between a president who, though he disclaimed a political affiliation, clearly favored the Federalists in appointments, ideology, and policy, and a vice president who was the acknowledged leader of the opposition party.

PARTISAN CONGRESSIONAL CAUCUSES

Beginning in 1800, partisan caucuses, composed of members of Congress, met for the purpose of recommending their party's nominees. The Democratic-Republicans continued to choose candidates in this manner until 1824; the Federalists did so only until 1808. In the final two presidential elections in which the Federalists ran candidates, 1812 and 1816, top party leaders, meeting in secret, decided on the nominees.[8] "King Caucus," as the partisan congressional caucuses were called, violated the spirit of the Constitution. Caucuses effectively allowed members of Congress to pick the nominees. After the decline of the Federalists, the nominees of the Democratic-Republicans, or simply Republicans as they became known, were, in fact, assured of victory— a product of the dominance of that party in the Congress and the country.

There were competing candidates within the Republican congressional caucus, however. In 1808, Madison prevailed over James Monroe and George Clinton. In 1816, Monroe overcame a strong challenge from William Crawford. In both cases, the electors united behind the successful nominee. In 1820, however, they did not. Disparate elements within the party selected their own candidates.

Although the caucus was the principal mode of candidate selection during the first part of the nineteenth century, it was never formally institutionalized. How the meetings were called, who called them, and when they were held all varied from election to election, as did attendance. A sizable number of representatives chose not to participate at all. Some stayed away on principle; others did so because of the particular choices they would have to make. In 1816, less than half of the Republican members of Congress were at their party's caucus. In 1820, only 20 percent attended, and the caucus had to adjourn without formally supporting President Monroe and Vice President Daniel D. Tompkins for reelection. In 1824, almost three-fourths of the members boycotted the session.

The 1824 caucus did nominate candidates. But with representatives from only four states constituting two-thirds of those attending, the nominee, William Crawford, failed to receive unified party support. Other candidates were nominated by state legislatures and conventions, and the electoral vote was divided. Since no candidate obtained a majority, the House of Representatives had to make the final decision. John Quincy Adams was selected on the first ballot. He received the votes of thirteen of the twenty-four state delegations.

The caucus system was never resumed. In the end, it was a victim of the Federalist Party's decline, the decentralization of political power within the country, and Andrew Jackson's strong opposition to this method of nomination. As the Republican Party grew from being the majority to the only party, factions developed within it, the two principal ones being the National Republicans and the Democratic-Republicans. In the absence of a viable opposition party, there was little to hold these factions together. By 1830, they had split into two separate groups, one supporting and one opposing President Jackson.

Political leadership was changing as well. A relatively small number of individuals had dominated national politics for the first three decades following the ratification of the Constitution. Their common experience in the Revolutionary War, the Constitutional Convention, and the early government produced personal contacts, political influence, and public respect that contributed to their ability to agree on candidates and to generate public support for them.[9] Those who followed them in office had neither the tradition nor the national orientation with which to affect the presidential selection process nor the national recognition to build support across the country for their candidates. Most of this new generation of political leaders owed their prominence and political influence to states and regions, and their loyalties reflected these bases of support.

The growth of party organizations at the state and local level affected the nomination system. In 1820 and 1824, it evolved into a decentralized mode of selection, with state legislatures, caucuses, and conventions nominating their own candidates. Support was also mobilized on regional levels. Whereas the congressional caucus had become unrepresentative, state-based nominations suffered from precisely the opposite problem. They were too sensitive to sectional interests and produced too many candidates. Unifying these diverse elements behind a single national ticket proved extremely difficult, although Jackson was successful in doing so in 1828. Nonetheless, a system that was more broadly based than the old caucus and could provide a more decisive and mobilizing mechanism was needed. National nominating conventions filled the void.

NATIONAL NOMINATING CONVENTIONS

The first such convention was held in 1831 by the Anti-Masons. A small but relatively active third party, it had virtually no congressional representation. Unable to utilize a congressional caucus, the party turned instead to a general meeting, which was held in a saloon in Baltimore, with 116 delegates from thirteen states attending. These delegates decided on the nominees as well as on an address to the people that contained the party's position on the dominant issues of the day. Three months later, a second convention was held in the same saloon by opponents of President Jackson. The National Republicans (or Whigs, as they later became known) also nominated candidates and agreed on a platform critical of the Jackson administration.

The following year, the Democratic-Republicans (or Democrats, as they were later called) also met in Baltimore. The impetus for their convention was Jackson's desire to demonstrate popular support for his presidency as well as to ensure the selection of Martin Van Buren as his running mate. In 1836, Jackson resorted to another convention—this time to handpick Van Buren as his successor. The Whigs did not hold a convention in 1836. Believing that they would have more success in the House of Representatives than in the nation as a whole, they ran three regional candidates, nominated by the states, who competed against Van Buren in their areas of strength. The plan, however, failed to deny Van Buren an electoral majority. He ended up with 170 votes compared with a total of 124 for the other principal contenders.

Thereafter, the Democrats and their opponents, first the Whigs and then their Republican successors, held nominating conventions to select their candidates. The early conventions were informal and rowdy by contemporary standards, but they also set the precedents for later meetings. The delegates decided on the procedures for conducting the convention, developed policy statements (addresses to the people), and chose nominees. Rules for apportioning the number of delegates were established before the meetings were held. Generally speaking, states were accorded as many votes as their congressional representation merited, regardless of the number of actual participants.

Party leaders within the states controlled the delegate selection process. Their influence depended on their ability to deliver votes, which in turn required that the convention delegates not exercise their own independent judgment but support their state leader's choice. Much of the bartering was conducted behind closed doors. Actions on the convention floor often had little to do with the wheeling and dealing that occurred in the smaller "smoke-filled" rooms. Since there was little public preconvention activity, many ballots were often necessary to reach the number that was required to win the party's nomination, usually two-thirds of the delegates. The winner owed his selection to the heads of the powerful state organizations, not to his own political prominence and organizational support. But the price he had to pay for the nomination, when calculated in terms of patronage and other political payoffs, was often quite high.

Nonetheless, nineteenth-century conventions served a number of purposes. They provided a forum for party leaders, particularly at the state level. They constituted a mechanism by which agreements could be negotiated and support mobilized. By brokering interests, conventions helped unify the disparate elements within a party, thereby converting an organization of state parties into a national coalition for the purpose of conducting a presidential campaign.

POPULAR PRIMARIES AND CAUCUSES

Demands for reform began to be heard at the beginning of the twentieth century. The Progressive movement, led by Robert La Follette of Wisconsin and Hiram Johnson of California, aimed to break the power of state bosses and their machines through the direct election of convention delegates or, alternatively, through the expression of a popular choice by the electorate. Florida became the first state to provide its political parties with such an option. In 1904, the Democrats took advantage of it and held a statewide vote for convention delegates. One year later, Wisconsin enacted a law for the direct election of delegates to nominating conventions. Others followed suit. By 1912, fifteen states provided for some type of primary election. Oregon was the first to permit a preference vote for the candidates themselves.

The year 1912 was also the first in which a candidate sought to use primaries as a way to obtain the nomination. With almost 42 percent of the Republican delegates selected in primaries, former President Theodore Roosevelt challenged incumbent William Howard Taft. Roosevelt won nine primaries to Taft's one, yet lost the nomination. Taft's support among regular party leaders who delivered their delegations and controlled the convention was sufficient to win renomination. He received one-third of his support from southern delegations, although the Republican Party had won only a small percentage of the southern vote in the previous election.

Partially in reaction to the unrepresentative, "boss-dominated" convention of 1912, additional states adopted primaries. By 1916, more than half of them held a Republican or Democratic contest. Although a majority of the delegates in that year were chosen by some type of primary, most of them were not bound to support specific candidates. As a consequence, the primary vote did not control the outcome of the conventions.

The movement toward popular participation was short-lived, however. Following World War I, the number of primaries declined. State party leaders, who saw primaries as a threat to their own influence, argued against them on three grounds: they were expensive; they did not attract many voters; and major candidates tended to avoid them. Moreover, primaries frequently encouraged factionalism, thereby weakening a party's organization. In response to this criticism, the reformers that supported primaries could not claim that their principal goal, rank-and-file control over the selection of party nominees, had been achieved. Public involvement was disappointing. Primaries rarely attracted more than 50 percent of those who voted in the general election, and usually much less. The minority party, in particular, suffered from low turnout for an obvious reason—its candidates stood little chance of winning the general election. In some states, rank-and-file influence was further diluted by the participation of Independents.

As a consequence of these factors, some states that had enacted new primary laws reverted to their former method of selection. Others made their primaries advisory rather than mandatory. Fewer convention delegates were elected in them. By 1936, only fourteen states held Democratic primaries, and twelve held Republican ones. Less than 40 percent of the delegates to each convention that year were chosen in this manner. For the next twenty years, the number of primaries and the percentage of delegates hovered around this level.

Theodore Roosevelt's failure in 1912 and the decline in primaries thereafter made them at best an auxiliary route to the nomination. Although some presidential aspirants became embroiled in primaries, none who depended on them won. In 1920, a spirited contest among three Republicans (General Leonard Wood, Governor Frank Lowden of Illinois, and Senator Hiram Johnson) failed to produce a convention majority for any of these candidates and resulted in party leaders choosing Warren Harding as the standard-bearer. Similarly, in 1952, Senator Estes Kefauver, who chaired the highly publicized and televised Senate hearings on organized crime, entered thirteen of seventeen presidential primaries, won twelve of them, and became the most popular Democratic contender but failed to win his party's nomination.

The reason Kefauver could not parlay his primary victories into a convention victory was that a majority of the delegates were not selected in primaries in 1952. Of those who were, many were chosen separately from the presidential preference vote. Kefauver did not contest these separate delegate elections. As a consequence, he obtained only 50 percent of the delegates in states in which he actually won the presidential preference vote. Moreover, the fact that most of his wins occurred against little or no opposition undercut Kefauver's claim to being the most popular and electable Democrat. He had avoided primaries in four states in which he feared that he might either lose or do poorly.

Not only were primaries not considered to be an essential road to the nomination but running in too many of them was interpreted as a sign of weakness, not strength. It indicated a lack of national recognition, a failure to obtain the support of party leaders, or both. For these reasons, leading candidates tended to choose their primaries carefully, and the primaries, in turn, tended to reinforce the position of the leading candidates. Those who entered primaries did so mainly to test their popularity rather than to win convention votes. Dwight D. Eisenhower in 1952, John F. Kennedy in 1960, and Richard M. Nixon in 1968 had to demonstrate that being a general, a Catholic, or a once-defeated presidential candidate would not be fatal to their chances. In other words, they needed to prove they could win the general election if nominated by their party.

With the possible exception of John Kennedy's victories in West Virginia and Wisconsin, primaries were neither crucial nor decisive for winning the nomination until the 1970s. When there was a provisional consensus within the party, primaries helped confirm it; when there was not, primaries could not produce it.[10] In short, they had little to do with whether the party was unified or divided at the time of the convention.

Primary results tended to be self-fulfilling in the sense that they confirmed the front-runner's status. Between 1936 and 1968, the preconvention leader, the candidate who was ahead in the Gallup Poll before the first primary, won the nomination seventeen out of nineteen times. The only exceptions were Thomas E. Dewey, who was defeated by Wendell Willkie in 1940, and Kefauver, who lost his race for the nomination to Adlai Stevenson in 1952. Willkie, however, had become the leader in public opinion by the time the Republican convention met. Even when leading candidates lost a primary, they had time to recoup. Dewey and Stevenson, defeated in early primaries in 1948 and 1956, respectively, went on to reestablish their credibility as front-runners by winning later primaries.

This situation in which the primaries were not the essential route to the nomination changed dramatically after 1968. Largely as a consequence of the tumultuous Democratic convention of that year, in which the party's nominees and platform were allegedly dictated by party "bosses," demands for a larger voice for rank-and-file partisans increased. In reaction to these demands, the Democratic Party began to look into the matter of delegate selection. The party enacted a series of reforms designed to ensure broader representation at its convention. To avoid challenges to their delegations, a number of states that had used caucus and convention systems changed to primaries. The number of primaries began to increase as did the percentage of convention delegates chosen from them.

New finance laws, which provided for government subsidies for preconvention campaigning, and increased news media coverage, particularly by television, also added to the incentive to enter primaries. By 1972, primaries had become decisive. In that year, Senator Edmund Muskie, the leading Democratic contender at the beginning of the process, was forced to withdraw after doing poorly in the early contests. In 1976, President Gerald Ford came close to being the first incumbent president since Chester A. Arthur in 1884 to be denied his party's nomination because of a primary challenge by Ronald Reagan. In 1980, President Jimmy Carter was also challenged for renomination by Senator Edward Kennedy, as was George H. W. Bush by Pat Buchanan in 1992. Bill Clinton, George W. Bush, and Barack Obama were not challenged for renomination, in part because they raised millions to ensure that a credible candidate would not oppose them. But the threat of a challenge kept them sensitized to the needs and interests of their partisan supporters.

Since the 1970s, primaries have revolutionized the presidential nomination process. They have been used to build popularity rather than simply reflect it. Challengers can no longer hope to succeed without entering them; incumbents can no longer ignore them. The impact of primaries has been significant, affecting the strategies and tactics of the candidates, the composition and behavior of the convention delegates, and the decision-making process at the national conventions. The contests for the nomination have shifted power within the parties. They have enlarged the selection zone of potential nominees, but still advantage establishment, well-funded candidates.

An extended, divisive nomination process can also adversely affect the party's standard bearer in the election by depleting the winning candidate's war chest, damaging his or her leadership image, and forcing that nominee to have taken extreme policy positions, more popular with the base than with the electorate as a whole. Each of these developments will be discussed in subsequent chapters.

THE EVOLUTION OF THE GENERAL ELECTION

The general election has changed as well. The Electoral College no longer operates in the manner in which it was designed. It now has a partisan coloration. There is greater opportunity for the general public to participate, but the campaign is not geared to obtaining the most popular votes. Although the system bears a resemblance to its past form, it has become more subject to democratic influences while continuing to contain many electoral biases.

The electoral system for president and vice president was one of the few innovative features of the Constitution. It had no immediate precedent, although it bore some relationship to the way Maryland selected its state senators.

In essence, it was invented by the framers, not synthesized from British and American experience, and it is one aspect of the constitutional system that has rarely worked as intended.

Initially, the method by which the states chose their electors varied. Some provided for direct election in a statewide vote. Others had the legislatures do the choosing. Two states used a combination of popular and legislative selection. As political parties emerged at the beginning of the nineteenth century, state legislatures maneuvered the selection process to benefit the party in power. This maneuvering resulted in the selection of more cohesive groups of electors who shared similar partisan views. Gradually, the trend evolved into a winner-take-all system, with most electors chosen on a statewide basis by popular vote. South Carolina was the last state to move to popular selection after the Civil War.

PARTISAN ELECTORS

The development of the party system changed the character of the Electoral College. Only in the first two elections, when Washington was the unanimous choice, did the electors exercise a nonpartisan and presumably independent judgment. Within ten years from the time the federal government began to operate, electors quickly became the captives of their party and were expected to vote for its candidates. The outcome of the election of 1800 vividly illustrates this new pattern of partisan voting.

The Federalist Party supported President John Adams of Massachusetts and Charles C. Pinckney of South Carolina. Democratic-Republicans, who had emerged to oppose the Federalists' policies, backed Thomas Jefferson of Virginia and Aaron Burr of New York. The Democratic-Republican candidates won, but, unexpectedly, Jefferson and Burr received the same number of votes. All electors who had cast ballots for Jefferson also cast them for Burr. Since it was not possible in those days to differentiate the candidates for the presidency and vice presidency on the ballot, the results had to be considered a tie, though Jefferson was clearly his party's choice for president. Under the terms of the Constitution, the House of Representatives, voting by state, had to choose the winner.

CONGRESSIONAL DECISIONS

On February 11, 1801, after the results of the Electoral College vote were announced by the vice president, who happened to be Jefferson, a Federalist-controlled House convened to resolve the dilemma. Since the winners of the 1800 election did not take office until March 4, 1801, representatives from a "lame-duck" Congress would have to choose the next president.[11] A majority of Federalists supported Burr, whom they regarded as the more pragmatic politician, a person with whom they could deal. Jefferson, on the other hand, was perceived as a dangerous, uncompromising radical by many Federalists. Alexander Hamilton, however, was outspoken in his opposition to Burr, a political rival from New York, whom Hamilton regarded as "the most unfit man in the United States for the office of President."[12]

On the first ballot taken on February 11, Burr received a majority of the total votes, but Jefferson won the support of more state delegations.[13] Eight states voted for Jefferson, six backed Burr, and two were evenly divided. This result left Jefferson one short of the needed majority. The House took nineteen ballots on its first day of deliberations and a total of thirty-six before it finally elected Jefferson. Had Burr promised to be a Federalist president, it is conceivable that he could have won.

The first amendment to reform voting procedures in the Electoral College was enacted by the new Congress, controlled by Jefferson's party, in 1803 and ratified by the states in 1804. This amendment to the Constitution, the twelfth, provided for separate voting for president and vice president. It also refined the selection procedures in the event that the president or vice president did not receive a majority of the electoral vote. The House of Representatives, still voting by state delegation, was to choose from among the three presidential candidates with the most electoral votes, and the Senate, voting by individual senator, was to choose from the top two vice presidential candidates. If the House could not make a decision by March 4, the amendment provided for the new vice president to assume the presidency until such time as the House could render a judgment.

The next nondecisive presidential vote did not occur until 1824. That year, four people received electoral votes for president: Andrew Jackson (ninety-nine votes), John Quincy Adams (eighty-four), William Crawford (forty-one), and Henry Clay (thirty-seven). According to the Twelfth Amendment, the House of Representatives had to decide from among the top three, since no one had a majority. Eliminated from the contest was Henry Clay, who happened to be Speaker of the House. Clay threw his support to Adams, who won. It was alleged that Clay did so in exchange for appointment as secretary of state, a charge that Clay vigorously denied. After Adams became president, however, he nominated Clay for secretary of state, a position Clay readily accepted.[14]

Jackson was the winner of the popular vote in 1824. In eighteen of the twenty-four states that chose electors by this method, he received 192,933 votes compared with 115,696 for Adams, 47,136 for Clay, and 46,979 for Crawford. Adams, however, had the backing of more state delegations. A Massachusetts resident, he enjoyed the support of the six New England states, and with Clay's help, the representatives of six others backed his candidacy. The votes of thirteen states, however, were needed for a majority. New York seemed to be the pivotal state and Stephen Van Rensselaer, a Revolutionary War general, the swing representative. On the morning of the vote, Speaker Clay and Representative Daniel Webster tried to persuade Van Rensselaer to vote for Adams. It was said that they were unsuccessful.[15] As the voting began, Van Rensselaer bowed his head as if in prayer. On the floor he saw a piece of paper with "Adams" written on it. Interpreting this as a sign from on high, he dropped the paper in the box. New York went for Adams by only one vote, providing him with the barest majority.[16]

Jackson, outraged at the turn of events, urged the abolition of the Electoral College. His claim of a popular mandate, however, was open to question. The most populous state at the time, New York, did not permit its electorate to choose electors. Moreover, in three of the states in which Jackson won the electoral vote but lost in the House of Representatives, he had fewer popular votes than Adams.[17]

Opposition to the system mounted, however, and a gradual democratization of the electoral process occurred. More states began to choose their electors directly by popular vote. In 1800, ten of the fifteen states used legislative selection. By 1832, only South Carolina retained this practice. The trend was also toward statewide election of an entire slate of electors. States that had chosen their electors within legislative districts converted to a winner-take-all system to maximize their voting power in the Electoral College. This change, in turn, created the possibility that there could be a disparity between the popular and electoral vote.

The next disputed election did not occur until 1876. In that election, Democrat Samuel J. Tilden received the most votes. He had 250,000 more popular votes and 19 more electoral votes than his Republican rival, Rutherford B. Hayes. Nonetheless, Tilden fell one vote short of a majority in the Electoral College. Twenty electoral votes were in dispute. Dual election returns were received from Florida (4 votes), Louisiana (8 votes), and South Carolina (7 votes). Charges of fraud and voting irregularities were made by both parties. The Republicans, who controlled the three state legislatures, contended that Democrats had forcibly prevented newly freed slaves from voting. The Democrats, on the other hand, alleged that many nonstate residents participated as did people who were not registered to vote. The other disputed electoral vote occurred in Oregon where a single Republican elector was challenged on the grounds that he held another federal position (assistant postmaster) and thus was ineligible to be an elector.

Three days before the Electoral College vote was to be officially counted, Congress established a commission to examine and try to resolve the dispute. The electoral commission was to consist of fifteen members: ten from Congress (five Republicans and five Democrats) and five from the Supreme Court. Four of the Supreme Court justices were designated by the act (two Republicans and two Democrats), and they were to choose the fifth. Their choice, Justice David Davis, a political independent, was expected to become a member of the commission, but on the day it was created, Davis was appointed by the Illinois legislature to the U.S. Senate. The Supreme Court justices then picked Joseph Bradley, an independent Republican from New Jersey. Bradley sided with his party on every issue. By a strictly partisan vote, the commission validated the credentials of all the Republican electors, thereby giving Hayes a one-vote margin of victory in the Electoral College.[18]

Prior to the election of 2000, the only other one in which the winner of the popular vote was beaten in an undisputed Electoral College vote occurred in 1888. Democrat Grover Cleveland had a plurality of 95,096 popular votes, but only 168 electoral votes compared with 233 for Republican Benjamin Harrison.

JUDICIAL DETERMINATION

The 2000 election was different. Not only was the popular vote very close but the electoral vote was close as well. Al Gore was ahead in twenty states plus the District of Columbia with a total of 267 electoral votes. George W. Bush led in twenty-nine states with a total of 238 electoral votes. The vote in one state, Florida, was in dispute. Out of more than 5.9 million votes cast in that state, only 537 votes separated the two candidates. Both sides alleged procedural irregularities, voter eligibility issues, and ballot counting errors.

Four legal issues had marred the Florida election: voter confusion over the design of the ballot in one county, disagreement over eligible voters and absentee ballots in several others, tabulation problems in counties that used punch-card ballots, and the date when the official results had to be certified by the secretary of state.

Voter confusion stemmed from a "butterfly ballot" used in Palm Beach County, where many retirees live. Designed by a Democratic campaign official, the ballot was intended to help senior citizens read the names of the candidates more clearly by using larger type. To fit all the names on a single punch card, however, two columns had to be used, with the punch holes for voting, or "chads" as they are called, between them. Although Democrats Al Gore and Joe Lieberman were listed second on the left-hand column, their chad was positioned third, after the chad of the candidates on the right-hand column, Pat Buchanan and Ezola Foster of the Reform Party. (See Figure 1. 1.)

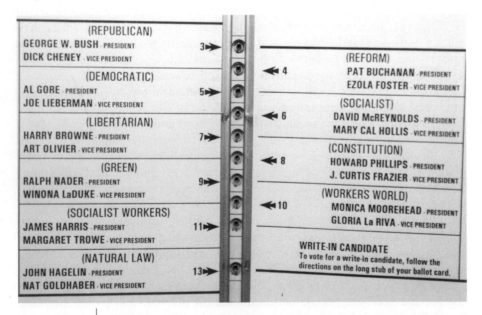

FIGURE 1.1 | THE PALM BEACH BALLOT

Source: AP Images/Gary I. Rothstein

Some voters, who claimed that they intended to vote for the Democratic candidates, punched out the second rather than the third chad, which registered as a vote for Buchanan. Others, in confusion, pushed out both the second and third chads, automatically voiding their ballots.[19] Aggrieved Democrats in the county immediately filed a lawsuit to contest the election and demand a new vote. A Florida state court, however, rejected their request, effectively terminating the revote option.

The second legal issue concerned ballots that were not properly included in the machine count. Many counties in Florida used a punch-card system of voting in which chads, a small perforated box on the card, must be removed with a specially designed instrument for the vote to be properly cast. The holes in the card were then tabulated by machine. However, if a chad was not completely removed, the vote may not have been recorded by the voting machine. The Gore campaign alleged that thousands of presidential votes in three Democratic counties—Miami-Dade, Broward, and Palm Beach—were not counted because part or all of a chad was still attached to the ballot. In other words, voters had not completely punched through the card. Democrats appealed to county officials for a hand count of these ballots.

One county, Palm Beach, began such a count; another, Miami-Dade, initiated a sample count to see whether a hand count was merited; the third, Broward, initially chose not to recount at all. Gore's representatives put pressure on the reluctant counties to proceed with a hand count of these uncounted ballots while Bush's attorneys went to federal court to stop it, arguing that a selective hand count in some counties was unfair to people in the other counties. Before the courts had rendered a judgment, however, Florida's secretary of state, a Republican appointee, certified the original county vote as the official one to which only absentee ballots, postmarked no later than election day and received by the counties within one week of the election, could be added. The secretary of state's certification prompted Gore's legal team to go to state court to force the secretary to accept hand-counted votes and an amended vote total submitted after the certification.

A Florida circuit court ruled that the secretary had discretion to accept or reject additional vote counts submitted by counties as long as she did not exercise that discretion arbitrarily. The secretary then asked the counties to justify why they wished to amend their original submission with an additional hand count of some votes. After they did so, however, she rejected their arguments, thereby forcing Gore's attorneys to take the entire matter to the Florida Supreme Court.

In an extraordinary session, televised across the country, lawyers for both sides debated the hand-count and vote deadline issues within the context of state and federal law and the U.S. Constitution. The Gore side claimed that the only way to ensure a "full, fair, and accurate" vote that represented the will of the Florida electorate would be to tabulate the disputed ballots by hand. But Bush's legal counsel contended that a hand count was blatantly unfair to those who had voted in accordance with the established rules and procedures of the state. Besides, they contended, extending the deadline for certified results violated an 1887 federal law that requires states to choose their electors by laws that are enacted *prior* to Election Day. The Florida Supreme Court, consisting of eight judges, all but one of whom were appointed by Democratic governors, sided with Gore and proceeded to give the counties an additional six days to submit a revised vote that included hand-counted ballots. Bush's lawyers appealed the Florida Supreme Court's decision to the U.S. Supreme Court.

What followed was a frantic hand count in two counties while a third, Miami-Dade, decided not to go ahead with one, in part because officials believed that they could not do so within the time frame established by the court. Meanwhile, in another part of the state, Democrats filed suit to exclude all absentee ballots from certain counties because Republicans had been given an opportunity to add required voter registration numbers to the forms, omitted erroneously by a glitch in the software program that printed the request forms. Democrats had not been given a chance to add the numbers. However, a circuit judge ruled against the Democrats' claim.

On Monday, December 4, nearly a month after the presidential election, the U.S. Supreme Court vacated the Florida Supreme Court's verdict that had extended the deadline for hand-counted ballots in the three Florida counties on the grounds that its legal basis for this decision was unclear. The Court remanded the case back to the Florida Supreme Court for clarification and judgment. After reviewing the ruling that the U.S. Supreme Court returned to it, the Court in Florida again sided with Gore, ordering an immediate recount of ballots that had not been included in the machine tabulation in all the state's counties. Bush's lawyers immediately appealed that decision to the U.S. Supreme Court.

The final legal maneuvering ended on December 11, 2000, one day before Florida law required the designation of its electors. The Supreme Court heard oral arguments in the case known as *Bush v. Gore*, 531 U.S. 93 (2000), and announced its ruling the next evening. The majority opinion reversed the Florida Supreme Court's judgment that ordered the hand count to be resumed. The U.S. Supreme Court stated that the absence of a single standard to be used throughout the state by election officials violated the Fourteenth Amendment, which requires states to provide all their residents with equal protection under the laws. A majority of the Court also went on to conclude that there was not sufficient time, given the state legislature's intent to designate Florida's electors by December 12, to establish such a standard. Hence, the certified vote that had Bush leading by 537 was final.

Four justices dissented from the decision that time had run out on the Florida Supreme Court. Two of these justices believed that the deadline for the designation of electors specified by U.S. law, the first Monday following the second Wednesday in December (the 18th in 2000), took precedence over the state legislature's date of December 12 and thus provided sufficient time for the state supreme court to establish a single statewide standard for recounting the votes. The two other dissenters felt that the Florida Supreme

Court had acted properly, that the vote count was legal, and that it should not have been halted by the U.S. Supreme Court.

Following the disputed election, changes in the election laws occurred on both state and national levels. Florida enacted electoral reforms to prevent a repetition of the problems that occurred in 2000. In 2002, Congress passed The Help America Vote Act which, provided federal funds to the states to help them consolidate and computerize their voter registration lists.[20] Although electoral problems have persisted, none has been of the magnitude to question to the outcome of the presidential Electoral College vote.

OTHER CLOSE ELECTIONS

There have been other close elections, however, in which the switch of a relatively small number of people would have altered the results. In 1860, a shift of 25,000 in New York from Abraham Lincoln to Stephen Douglas would have denied Lincoln a majority in the Electoral College. A change of less than 30,000 in three states in 1892 would have given Benjamin Harrison another victory over Cleveland. In 1916, Charles Evans Hughes needed only 3,807 more votes in California to have beaten Woodrow Wilson. Similarly, Thomas E. Dewey could have denied Harry S Truman a majority in the Electoral College with 12,487 more California votes in 1948. A change in the votes of fewer than 9,000 people in Illinois and Missouri in 1960 would have meant that John F. Kennedy would have lacked an Electoral College majority. In 1968, a shift of only 55,000 votes from Richard M. Nixon to Hubert H. Humphrey in three states would have thrown the election into the House of Representatives, which at that time was controlled by the Democrats. In 1976, a shift of only 3,687 in Hawaii and 5,559 in Ohio would have cost Jimmy Carter the election.[21] In 2004, George W. Bush received only .02 percent more votes (120,000 out of 5.6 million) than John Kerry did in Ohio; had Kerry won Ohio, he would have had an Electoral College majority.

Not only could the results of these elections have been affected by very small shifts in voter preferences, but in 1948, 1960, 1968, and 1992, there was the added possibility that the Electoral College vote would not be decisive. In each of these elections, third-party or independent candidates threatened to secure enough votes to prevent either majority-party candidate from gaining a majority. In 1948, Henry Wallace (Progressive Party) and Strom Thurmond (States' Rights Party) received almost 5 percent of the total popular vote, and Thurmond won 39 electoral votes. In 1960, fourteen unpledged electors were chosen in Alabama and Mississippi. In 1968, George Wallace of Alabama, running under the American Independent Party label, received almost 10 million popular votes and 46 electoral votes, and in 1992, H. Ross Perot received 19.7 million popular votes (almost 19 percent of the total) but none in the Electoral College. Four years later, he got 8.1 million popular votes but, again, no electoral votes. Ralph Nader received less than 3 percent of the popular vote in

2000, but his 97,488 votes in Florida undoubtedly cost Gore that state and an overall election victory.

It is clear that close competition between the two major parties combined with a strong third-party or independent candidate provides the Electoral College with its most difficult test.

THE POLITICS OF ELECTORAL COLLEGE VOTING

The presidential campaign and election is shaped by the Electoral College. The strategies the candidates pursue, the resources they utilize, and the states in which they place their major efforts are all calculated on the basis of Electoral College politics, not the popular vote.

The Electoral College is not neutral. No system of election can be. The way votes are aggregated does make a difference. It benefits some at the expense of others. The Electoral College usually works to the advantage of the candidate who wins the most popular votes. More often than not, it tends to exaggerate that candidate's margin of victory. (See Appendix.)

Why does the Electoral College usually enhance the margin of the popular vote winner? The reason has to do with the winner-take-all system of voting that has developed in most states. In almost every instance, the presidential and vice presidential candidates who receive a plurality of the popular vote within the state get all its electoral votes.[22] This translates into a larger percentage of the Electoral College vote than it would have had with a direct popular vote.[23]

Advocates of the system see this enlarged Electoral College vote as an advantage for the new or reelected president. They claim that it increases the president's mandate for governing as well as the coalition of supporters on whom the president can rely. Most states also perceive a benefit from casting their votes as a unit. They believe that it enhances their political clout. In 2004, voters in Colorado soundly defeated a constitutional amendment that would have allocated their state's electoral vote in proportion to the popular vote that the candidates received. Such an amendment would have decreased that state's importance to the presidential candidates and the state's impact on the Electoral College vote. Following the 2012 election, Republicans in Virginia suggested the state's electors be chosen by congressional districts rather than the state as a whole, but the governor, a Republican, opposed the plan, and it died.

The large states, theoretically, gain more influence in the Electoral College by winner-take-all voting. The very smallest states do so as well because they receive a minimum of three electoral votes regardless of the size of their population. As a consequence, their citizens have greater voting power than they would have in a direct election system. To illustrate, if Wyoming's population of approximately 570,000 in 2012 were divided by its three electoral votes, there would be one elector for every 190,000 people. Dividing California's estimated 2012 population of about 38,000,000 by its fifty-five electoral votes yields one elector for every 690,000 persons.[24] Medium-sized states are comparatively disadvantaged.[25]

But the advantage that the largest and smallest states reap from the current Electoral College system pales by comparison to the benefit that the most competitive states receive regardless of their size. Since the advent of frequent public opinion polling during the election period, candidates concentrated their time, efforts, and resources in those states that seemed to be up for grabs, according to the polls. Noncompetitive states, large or small, see little of the presidential campaign. The candidates rarely visit them; they spend little, if any, money in them; they run few, if any, political advertisements in their major media markets; and they mount little, if any, grassroots efforts. They are essentially ignored because their Electoral College vote is predictable.

And at the presidential level, the number of competitive states had been declining. In 1960, about half the states were deemed competitive; either of the major-party candidates had a realistic chance to win them. In the twenty-first century, only about one-third of the states have been seen as competitive at the beginning of the general election campaign and less than one-fifth at the end.[26] In 2012, the presidential and vice presidential candidates only visited 12 of the 50 states.[27] In short, the one national election in the United States has been reduced to a contest fought in a small number of states.

Not only does the Electoral College in practice give disproportionate influence to the most competitive states, but it also advantages cohesive groups that live in them. The increase in Hispanic proportion of the electorate in the Southwest and Florida has aided the Democrats; the relatively small minority populations in some of the traditional Midwest battleground states have helped the Republicans.

The Electoral College also benefits the two major parties at the expense of third parties and independent candidates.[28] The reason it does so is that the winner-take-all system of voting by states when combined with the need for a majority of the total electoral vote makes it difficult for third parties to accumulate enough votes to win an election. To have any effect, minor-party candidates must have support that is geographically concentrated, as Strom Thurmond's was in 1948 and George Wallace's was in 1968, rather than more broadly distributed across the country, as Henry Wallace's was in 1948 and H. Ross Perot's was in 1992 and 1996.

Given the limitations on third parties, their most realistic electoral objectives would seem to be to defeat one of the major contenders rather than to elect their own candidate. In 1912, Theodore Roosevelt's Bull Moose campaign split the Republican Party, thereby aiding the Democratic Party candidate, Woodrow Wilson. In 2000, Nader's vote in Florida probably cost Gore the election.[29]

Which of the major parties is advantaged by the Electoral College? Today, the answer seems to be the Democrats. Although the major parties have been at or near parity since the late 1980s, the large states tilt Democratic. Of the seven largest (with 209 of the 538 electoral votes), only one (Texas) trends Republican, four (California, Illinois, New York, and Pennsylvania) lean Democratic, with only two (Florida and Ohio) remaining highly competitive. The Democrats' demographic advantage has also been growing.

SUMMARY

The quest for the presidency has been and continues to be influenced by the system designed in Philadelphia in 1787. The objectives of that system were to protect the independence of the institution, ensure the selection of a well-qualified, national candidate, and do so in a way that was politically expedient and technologically feasible, given the state of communications and transportation at the end of the eighteenth century. The Electoral College was also thought to be consistent with the tenets of a republican form of government.

Although many of the objectives remain the same, the system has changed significantly over the years. Of all the factors that have influenced these changes, none has been more important than the advent of political parties. Their development created an additional first step in the process, the nomination, which has influenced the selection and behavior of electors ever since.

The nomination process is necessary to the parties, whose principal interest is to get their candidates elected. At first, members of Congress, meeting in partisan caucuses, decided on the nominees. After the caucus method broke down, a more decentralized mode of selection, reflective of the increasing sectional composition of the parties, emerged. Controlled by state leaders, the nominations were decided at brokered-operated national conventions.

Demands for greater public participation eventually opened up the nomination process and reduced but did not eliminate the influence of party elites, interest group leaders, and wealthy donors. Today, candidates compete for their party's nomination in primaries and caucuses. They effectively choose the slates of electors that will vote for them if they win a plurality of the state vote. Thus, the Electoral College reflects the popular vote but does so within the states rather than the nation as a whole.

Winner-take-all voting at the state level distorts the national vote. In most elections, it has magnified that vote; in four elections, it has reversed it. Critics contend that the system is undemocratic, unequal, and unwise. They argue that it does not encourage candidates to campaign nationwide, does not encourage turnout in less competitive states, and does not produce a mandate or electoral coalition for governing. Considering that a substantial portion of the people do not vote, and the popular vote itself may be close, the winner rarely gains the support of one-third of the population, hardly the popular backing one might expect or desire in a democratic political system, nor one sufficient for governing effectively most of the time.

Defenders of the Electoral College, on the other hand, say that it is consistent with the country's constitutional design and political tradition, reflects the federal character of the system, minimizes the extent to which fraudulent electoral activity at the state level affects the overall national results, and produces a quick and conclusive outcome for an extended presidential campaign.

 **WHERE ON THE WEB?**

General Sites

All of the major search engines and news web sites will have information on the next presidential campaign in addition to the following web sites:

- 270towin.com
  www.270towin.com
    Contains an interactive electoral map for current and past presidential elections.
- Fivethirtyeight.com
  www.fivethirtyeight.com
    A web site that contains a wealth of data on elections.
- C-SPAN: Road to the White House 2012
  www.cspan.org
    Provides up-to-date information about the campaign.
- Center for Voting and Democracy
  www.fairvote.org
    An organization that promotes voter education and outreach, the center supports a national popular vote for president.
- Democracy in Action
  www.P2016.org
    A site that contains a wealth of up-to-date information on recent presidential campaigns with links to other sources.
- ElectionLine
  www.electionline.org
    A nonpartisan, non-advocacy site for election reform news and information.
- Politics 1
  www.politics1.com
    An online guide to current politics with links to other relevant sites for the 2016 campaign.

Government Sources

- Election Assistance Commission
  www.eac.gov
    The commission set up by Congress in the 2002 Help America Vote Act to facilitate voter registration and voting procedures in U.S. elections.
- Federal Election Commission
  www.fec.gov
    This commission collects and disseminates data on election turnout, voting, and most importantly, candidate, party, and nonparty group revenues and expenditures. It publishes the official results.
- National Archives and Records Administration; Office of the Federal Register
  www.archives.gov/federal-register/electoral-college
    Provides access to federal laws and presidential documents as well as statistics on past presidential elections and information on the Electoral College.

- The White House
  www.whitehouse.gov
    Provides information on the activities of the president and vice president: what
    they say, who they meet, and their positions on current issues.

EXERCISES

1. Prior to the completion of the next nomination process, obtain the most
   recent schedule of primaries and caucuses for the selection of delegates to the
   Democratic and Republican national nominating conventions for the year of the
   presidential election. You can do this on most major news organizations' web
   sites, thegreenpapers.com, or at the Federal Election Commission. Try to figure
   out which of the declared and undeclared candidates for each party's nomination
   is most and least advantaged by this schedule.

2. Get up to speed on the Electoral College by accessing and reviewing the material
   on the Electoral College at the National Archives and Records Administration site
   (www.archives.gov/federal-register/electoral-college). Use the links available at
   this site to find out how the electors in your state are selected and the dates and
   procedures by which they will vote in 2016.

3. Access the web site www.270towin.com. Explain how the Electoral College maps
   for the 2008 and 2012 elections differed. Then construct a winning Electoral
   College strategy for the Democratic or Republican candidate you prefer in 2016.
   Focus on the likely swing states in your analysis. Why do you think these states
   may go Democratic or Republican in 2016?

SELECTED READINGS

Amar, Vikram David. "The 2004 Presidential Election and the Electoral College: How
    the Results Debunk Some Defenses of the Current System" (Nov. 12, 2004). www
    .writ.news.findlaw.com/amar/20041112.html.
Bennett, Robert W. *Taming the Electoral College*. Stanford, CA: Stanford University
    Press, 2006.
Best, Judith. "Presidential Selection: Complex Problems and Simple Solutions." *The
    Political Science Quarterly*, 119 (Spring 2004): 39–59.
Edwards, George C., III. *Why the Electoral College Is Bad for America*. 2nd ed. New
    Haven: Yale University Press, 2011.
Fortier, John C., ed. *After the People Vote: A Guide to the Electoral College*.
    Washington, DC: The AEI Press, 2004.
Issacharoff, Samuel. "Law, Rules, and Presidential Selection." *Political Science
    Quarterly*, 120 (Spring 2005): 113–129.
Levinson, Sanford, Daniel Lowenstein, and John McGinnis. "Should We Dispense
    with the Electoral College?" *University of Pennsylvania Law Review*, 156 (2007):
    10–37.
Longley, Lawrence D., and James D. Dana, Jr. "The Biases of the Electoral College in
    the 1990s," *Polity*, 25 (Fall 1992): 123–145.
Panagopoulos, Costas. "Electoral Reform." *Public Opinion Quarterly*, 68 (Winter
    2004): 623–640.
Presidential Election Inequality: The Electoral College in the 21st Century. Center for
    Voting and Democracy. (www.fairvote.org/asststs/presidentialinequality.pdf)

Rakove, Jack. "Presidential Selection: Electoral Fallacies." *The Political Science Quarterly*, 119 (Spring 2004): 21–38.
Troy, Gil. *See How They Ran: The Changing Role of the Presidential Candidate.* New York: Free Press, 2012.

NOTES

1. Gouverneur Morris, *Records of the Federal Convention*, ed. Max Farrand (New Haven: Yale University Press, 1921), vol. II, pp. 2, 33.
2. The first proposal for direct election was introduced in a very timid fashion by James Wilson, delegate from Pennsylvania. James Madison's *Journal* describes Wilson's presentation as follows: "Mr. Wilson said he was almost unwilling to declare the mode which he wished to take place, being apprehensive that it might appear chimerical. He would say however at least that in theory he was for an election by the people; Experience, particularly in N. York & Massts, shewed that an election of the first magistrate by the people at large, was both convenient & successful mode." Farrand, *Records of the Federal Convention*, vol. I, p. 68.
3. This provision was intended to decrease parochialism and facilitate the selection of a national candidate. It forced Dick Cheney, George W. Bush's choice to be his vice presidential running mate in 2000, to move his official residence from Texas to Wyoming so that Texas's electors could vote for the entire Republican ticket if Bush and Cheney won the popular vote in that state, which they did.
4. So great was the sectional rivalry, so competitive the states, so limited the number of people with national reputations, that it was feared electors would tend to vote primarily for residents of their own states. To prevent the same states, particularly the largest ones, from exercising undue influence in the selection of both the president and vice president, this provision was included.
5. George Mason declared, "Nineteen times out of twenty, the President would be chosen by the Senate." Farrand, *Records of the Federal Convention,* vol. II, 500. The original proposal of the Committee on Unfinished Business was that the Senate should select the president. The delegates substituted the House of Representatives, fearing that the Senate was too powerful with its appointment and treaty-making powers. The principle of equal state representation was retained. Choosing the president is the only occasion on which the House of Representatives votes by state.
6. Thomas R. Marshall, *Presidential Nominations in a Reform Age* (New York: Praeger, 1981), p. 19.
7. Neal R. Peirce and Lawrence D. Longley, *The People's President* (New Haven, CT: Yale University Press, 1981), p. 36.
8. Marshall *Presidential Nominations*, p. 20.
9. Ibid., p. 21.
10. Louis Maisel and Gerald J. Lieberman, "The Impact of Electoral Rules on Primary Elections: The Democratic Presidential Primaries in 1976," in *The Impact of the Electoral Process*, eds. Louis Maisel and Joseph Cooper (Beverly Hills, CA: Sage, 1977), p. 68.
11. Until the passage of the Twentieth Amendment, which made January 3 the date when members of Congress took their oaths of office and convened, it was the second session of the preelection Congress that met after the election.
12. Lucius Wilmerding, *The Electoral College* (New Brunswick, NJ: Rutgers University Press, 1953), p. 32.

13. There were 106 members of the House (58 Federalists and 48 Republicans). On the first ballot, the vote of those present was for Burr, 53–51.

14. In those days, being secretary of state was considered a stepping-stone to the presidency. With the exception of Washington and John Adams, all the people who became president prior to Andrew Jackson had first held appointment as secretary of state.

15. Peirce and Longley, *People's President*, p. 51.

16. Marquis James, *The Life of Andrew Jackson* (Indianapolis: Bobbs-Merrill, 1938), p. 439.

17. He captured the majority of electoral votes in two of these states because the electors were chosen on a district rather than on a statewide basis. William R. Keech, "Background Paper," in *Winner Take All: Report of the Twentieth Century Fund Task Force on Reform of the Presidential Election Process* (New York: Holmes & Meier, 1978), p. 50.

18. The act that created the commission specified that its decision would be final unless overturned by both houses of Congress. The House of Representatives, controlled by the Democrats, opposed every one of the commission's findings. The Republican Senate, however, concurred. A Democratic filibuster in the Senate was averted by Hayes's promise of concessions to the South, including the withdrawal of federal troops. Tilden could have challenged the findings of the commission in court but chose not to do so.

19. The vote tabulated in this county provided some evidence of the confusion. Buchanan's vote was larger in Palm Beach than in any other Florida county. Palm Beach had a large, elderly Jewish population unlikely to have supported Buchanan. Moreover, Palm Beach had a larger percentage of ballots in which no presidential vote was recorded than all but two of the other sixty-seven counties in the state.

20. The money ($4.1 billion) was also used to buy more modern, touch-screen voting machines and make voting places more accessible to the disabled and ballots more understandable to non-English speakers. The law required states to allow provisional voting for people who believe that they were properly registered but who were not listed as registered at the precinct at which they voted.

21. Richard M. Scammon and Alice V. McGillivray, *America Votes 12* (Washington DC: Congressional Quarterly, 1977), p. 15.

22. Two states, Maine and Nebraska, do not always vote as a bloc because they do not select all their electors on an at-large basis. Two are chosen at large and the remaining ones are elected in each of the states' congressional districts. In 2008, Nebraska's electoral vote was divided, with Republican John McCain winning four and Democrat Barack Obama one. McCain won the popular statewide vote as well as the vote in two of the state's three congressional districts. Obama won the other congressional district. In 2012, a plurality in all of Nebraska's electoral districts voted for Republican Mitt Romney. The Maine vote has not been divided.

23. Thomas Brunell and Bernard Grofman, "The 1992 and 1996 Presidential Elections: Whatever Happened to the Republican Electoral College Lock?" *Presidential Studies Quarterly*, 112 (Winter 1997): pp. 134–138.

24. The 2012 population estimates are from the Census Bureau. www.census.gov /popest/data/state/totals/2012/index/html.

25. Lawrence D. Longley and James D. Dana, "The Biases of the Electoral College in the 1990s," *Polity,* 25 (Fall 1992): p. 134. There are two other, less obvious, biases in the Electoral College. The distribution of electoral votes is calculated on the basis of the census, which occurs every ten years. Thus, the Electoral College does not mirror population shifts within this period. Nor does it take into account the number of people who actually cast ballots. It is a state's population, not its turn-out, that determines the number of electoral votes it receives, over and above the automatic three.

26. Rob Richie and Andrea Levien, "Presidential Elections State-by-State Hardening Partisanship," Center for Voting and Democracy, February 5, 2013. http://www .fairvote.org/presidential-elections-state-by-state-hardening-partisanship

27. "2012 Presidential Tracker," Center for Voting and Democracy, November 16, 2012. http://www.fairvote.org/presidential-tracker.

28. James C. Garand and T. Wayne Parent, "Representation, Swing, and Bias in U.S. Presidential Elections, 1872–1988," *American Journal of Political Science* 35 (Nov. 1991): pp. 1024, 1029.

29. In 2012, Mayor Michael Blumenthal of New York City was persuaded not to launch an independent candidacy because of the disadvantages he would face in the Electoral College.

2 CHAPTER | CAMPAIGN FINANCE

INTRODUCTION

Running for president is very expensive. In the 2011–2012 election cycle, about $1.3 billion was spent by candidates for the presidency, almost twice as much as for 2004 and four times as much as 2000.[1] When party, group, and independent spending are added, total spending exceeded $2.3 billion. And that's just for the race for the presidency. According to the Center for Responsive Politics, a public interest research organization, about $6.3 billion was spent on all federal elections in 2012.[2]

The magnitude of these expenditures poses serious problems for presidential candidates who must raise considerable sums, closely watch their expenses, make important allocation decisions, and conform to the intricacies of finance laws during both the nomination and general election campaigns. In addition, the candidates must coordinate their financial activities with party leaders who must also solicit, distribute, and spend millions on behalf of their nominees for national office. Such large expenditures raise important issues for a democratic selection process. This chapter explores some of these problems and those issues.

The chapter is organized into four sections. The first details the rising costs of running for president. The next section discusses Congress's attempts to regulate federal elections and the supreme court's decisions on these regulations. In the third section, the explosion of money in the form of candidate contributions and expenditures as well as the activities of party and nonparty groups are examined. In the fourth and final section, the relationship between money and electoral success is explored.

THE RISING COSTS OF RUNNING FOR PRESIDENT

Candidates have always spent money in their quest for the presidency, but it was not until they started personal campaigning across the country that these costs began to increase sharply.

When electioneering was conducted within a highly partisan press environment before the Civil War, there were few expenses other than for the occasional biography and campaign pamphlet printed by the party and sold to the public at less than cost. With the advent of more active public campaigning toward the middle of the nineteenth century, candidate organizations turned to buttons, billboards, banners, and pictures to symbolize and illustrate their campaigns. By the beginning of the twentieth century, the cost of this type of advertising in each election exceeded $150,000, a lot of money then but a minuscule amount by contemporary standards.[3]

In 1924, radio was employed for the first time in presidential campaigns. The Republicans spent approximately $120,000 that year, whereas the Democrats spent only $40,000.[4] Four years later, however, the two parties together spent more than $1 million. Radio expenses continued to equal or exceed a million dollars per election for the next 20 years.[5]

Television emerged as a vehicle for presidential campaigning in 1952. Both national party conventions were broadcast on television as well as on radio. Although there were only 19 million television sets in the United States at that time, almost one-third of Americans were regular TV viewers. The number of households with television sets rose dramatically over the next four years. By 1956, an estimated 71 percent had television, and by 1968, the figure was close to 95 percent; today, it exceeds 98 percent, with most homes having two or more sets.[6]

The first commercials for presidential candidates appeared in 1952. They became regular fare thereafter, contributing substantially to campaign costs. Film biographies, interview shows, political rallies, town meetings, and other campaign-related events have all been seen with increasing frequency.

In 1948, no money was spent on television by either party's candidate. Twenty years later, $13 million was expended for television advertising, approximately one-fourth of the total cost of the 1968 campaign. Forty years later in 2008, about $600 million was spent; in 2012, it was $896 million.[7]

The advent of the electronic campaign following World War II was the principal reason campaign costs skyrocketed. In 1960, John Kennedy and Richard Nixon each spent a hundred times the amount Lincoln had spent 100 years earlier. In the 12 years following the 1960 general election, expenditures increased from about $20 million to over $90 million, an amount that far outstripped the inflation rate during that period. Table 2.1 lists the costs of the major party candidates in presidential elections from 1860 to 1972, the last general election before Congress enacted legislation to regulate campaign finance.

TABLE 2.1 | COSTS OF PRESIDENTIAL GENERAL ELECTIONS, MAJOR PARTY CANDIDATES, 1860–1972

Year	Democratic	Cost	Republican	Cost
1860	Stephen Douglas	$50,000	Abraham Lincoln*	$100,000
1864	George McClellan	50,000	Abraham Lincoln*	125,000
1868	Horatio Segmous	75,000	Ulysses Grant*	150,000
1872	Horace Greeley	50,000	Ulysses Grant*	250,000
1876	Samuel Tilden	900,000	Rutherford Hayes*	950,000
1880	Winfield Hancock	335,000	James Garfield*	1,100,000
1884	Grover Cleveland*	1,400,000	James Blaine	1,300,000
1888	Grover Cleveland	855,000	Benjamin Harrison*	1,350,000
1892	Grover Cleveland*	2,350,000	Benjamin Harrison	1,700,000
1896	William Jennings Bryan	675,000	William McKinley*	3,350,000
1900	William Jennings Bryan	425,000	William McKinley*	3,000,000
1904	Alton Parker	700,000	Theodore Roosevelt*	2,096,000
1908	William Jennings Bryan	629,341	William Taft*	1,655,518
1912	Woodrow Wilson*	1,134,848	William Taft	1,071,549
1916	Woodrow Wilson*	2,284,950	Charles Evans Hughes	2,441,565
1920	James Cox	1,470,371	Warren Harding*	5,417,501
1924	John Davis	1,108,836	Calvin Coolidge*	4,020,478
1928	Alfred Smith	5,342,350	Herbert Hoover*	6,256,111
1932	Franklin Roosevelt*	2,245,975	Herbert Hoover	2,900,052
1936	Franklin Roosevelt*	5,194,751	Alfred Landon	8,892,972
1940	Franklin Roosevelt*	2,783,654	Wendell Willkie	3,451,310
1944	Franklin Roosevelt*	2,169,077	Thomas Dewey	2,828,652
1948	Harry Truman*	2,736,334	Thomas Dewey	2,127,296
1952	Adlai Stevenson	5,032,926	Dwight Eisenhower*	6,608,623
1956	Adlai Stevenson	5,106,651	Dwight Eisenhower*	7,778,702
1960	John Kennedy*	9,797,000	Richard Nixon	10,128,000
1964	Lyndon Johnson*	8,757,000	Barry Goldwater	16,026,000
1968†	Hubert Humphrey	11,594,000	Richard Nixon*	25,042,000
1972	George McGovern	30,000,000	Richard Nixon*	61,400,000

*Indicates winner.

†George Wallace spent an estimated $7 million as the candidate of the American Independent Party in 1968.

Source: Data based on *Financing Politics: Money, Elections, and Political Reform*, 3rd ed. By Herbert E. Alexander. Copyright 1984 by Congressional Quarterly.

Prenomination costs have risen even more rapidly than those in the general election. Until the 1960s, large expenditures were the exception, not the rule, for gaining the party's nomination. General Leonard Wood spent an estimated $2 million in an unsuccessful quest to head the Republican ticket in 1920. The contest between General Dwight D. Eisenhower and Senator Robert A. Taft in 1952 cost about $5 million, a total that was not exceeded until 1964, when Nelson Rockefeller and Barry Goldwater together spent approximately twice that amount. The increasing number of primaries, caucuses, and candidates, combined with the willingness of recent candidates for their party's nomination to rely solely on private funds with no expenditure limits, have been largely responsible for the rise.

In the 1950s, the preconvention contests were optional; since the 1970s, they have been mandatory. Even incumbent presidents have to enter them, and they spend money even when they are not challenged. In 1984, the Reagan campaign committee spent almost $28 million during the nomination period, much of it on voter registration drives for the general election; in 1992, George H. W. Bush spent over $27 million in defeating Pat Buchanan, a conservative newspaper columnist who had not previously sought public office. In 1996, Bill Clinton spent almost $35 million running unopposed for the Democratic nomination; eight years later, George W. Bush spent over $250 million without a nomination opponent; Barack Obama spent $211 million in 2012, also without a challenger for the Democratic nomination. Table 2.2 lists the costs of major party nominations from 1964 through 2012.

Throughout most of U.S. electoral history, parties and candidates depended on large contributions. In the midst of the industrial boom at the end of the nineteenth century, the Republicans were able to count on the support of the Astors, Harrimans, and Vanderbilts, while the Democrats looked to financier August Belmont (American representative of the Rothschild banking interests) and inventor and industrialist Cyrus McCormick. Corporations, banks, and life insurance companies soon became prime targets of party fund-raisers. The most notorious and probably most adroit fund-raiser of this period was Mark Hanna. A leading official of the Republican Party, Hanna owed most of his influence to his ability to obtain substantial political contributions. He set quotas, personally assessing the amount that businesses and corporations should give. In 1896 and again in 1900, he was able to obtain contributions of $250,000 from Standard Oil. Theodore Roosevelt personally ordered the return of some of the Standard Oil money in 1904 but accepted large gifts from magnates E. H. Harriman and Henry C. Frick. Roosevelt's trust-busting activities during his presidency led Frick to remark, "We bought the son of a bitch and then he did not stay bought."[8]

Sizable private gifts remained the principal source of party and candidate support until the mid-1970s. In 1972, the last year when the size of contributions was not restricted, Richard Nixon and George McGovern raised an estimated $27 million from fewer than 200 individual contributors.[9] In general, the Republicans benefited more than the Democrats from wealthy contributors, known in the campaign vernacular as "fat cats." Only in 1964

TABLE 2.2 | COSTS OF PRESIDENTIAL NOMINATIONS, 1964–2012 (IN MILLIONS)

Year	Expenditures	
	Democrats	Republicans
1964	(uncontested)	$10.0
1968	$25.0	20.0
1972	33.1	*
1976	40.7	26.1
1980	41.7	86.1
1984	107.7	28.0
1988	94.0	114.6
1992	66.0†	51.0
1996	41.8	182.0
2000	95.8	247.2
2008	1,043.9	450.2
2012	211.4	283.2

*During a primary in which Richard M. Nixon's renomination was virtually assured, Representative John M. Ashbrook spent $740,000 and Representative Paul N. McCloskey spent $550,000 in challenging Nixon.

†Estimates based on Alexander and Corrado, *Financing the 1992 Elections*, Tables 2.1 and 2.4.

Sources: 1964–1972, Herbert E. Alexander, *Financing Politics* (Washington, DC: Congressional Quarterly, 1976), pp. 45–47, Copyright © 1984 by Congressional Quarterly Press, a Division of SAGE Publications, Inc. Reprinted by permission; 1976–1984, Federal Election Commission, "Reports on Financial Activity, 1987–88," *Presidential Pre-Nomination Campaigns* (August 1989), Table A.7, p. 10; Herbert E. Alexander, "Financing the Presidential Elections" (paper presented at the Institute for Political Studies in Tokyo, Japan, September 8–10, 1989), pp. 4, 10; 1988–1992, Herbert E. Alexander and Anthony Corrado, *Financing the 1992 Elections* (Armonk, NY: Sharpe, 1995), Copyright © 1995 by M. E. Sharpe, Inc. Reprinted with permission of the publisher.; 1996–2012, updated by author from data published by the Federal Election Commission, "Presidential Pre-Nomination Campaign Disbursements." (www.fec.gov).

was a Democrat, incumbent president, Lyndon B. Johnson, who enjoyed a large lead in the preelection polls, able to raise more money from large donors than his Republican opponent, Barry Goldwater. The reluctance of regular Republican contributors to support the Goldwater candidacy forced his organization to appeal to thousands of potential supporters through direct mail. The success of this effort, raising $5.8 million from approximately 651,000 people, showed the potential of a popular appeal for funds and shattered what had been an unwritten rule of politics that money could not be raised by a mass appeal.

Despite the use of postal mailings and party telethons to broaden the base of political contributors in the 1960s, dependence on large donors continued. In 1964, more than $2 million was raised in contributions of $10,000 or more. Eight years later, approximately $51 million was collected in gifts of this size or larger. Some gifts were in the million-dollar range. The magnitude of these contributions, combined with the heavy-handed tactics of the Nixon fund-raisers in 1971–1972, brought into sharp focus the difficulty of maintaining a democratic selection process that was dependent on private funding from a relatively small number of donors.[10]

Reliance on large contributors who did not want to be identified, the inequality of funding between parties and candidates, and the high cost of campaigning, especially in the mass media, all raised serious questions. Were there assumptions implicit in giving and receiving? Could elected officials be responsive to individual benefactors and to the general public at the same time? Was the need to gain large contributors and keep them happy consistent with the tenets of a democratic society that all people have equal influence on the selection of and access to public officials? Did the high cost of campaigning, in and of itself, eliminate otherwise qualified candidates from running? Were certain political parties, interest groups, or individuals consistently advantaged or disadvantaged by the distribution of funding sources? Had the presidency become an office that only the wealthy could afford or that only those with wealthy supporters could seek?

THE REGULATION OF CAMPAIGN FINANCE

Reacting to these issues, Congress in the 1970s enacted far-reaching legislation designed to reduce dependence on large donors, discourage illegal contributions, broaden the base of public giving, and control escalating costs at the presidential level. Additionally, the Democratic Congress that passed these laws wanted to equalize the funds available to the Republican and Democratic nominees. Finally, the legislation was designed to increase the transparency of the entire process and buttress the two-party system.

THE FEDERAL ELECTION CAMPAIGN ACT

The Federal Election Campaign Act (FECA), enacted in 1971, set ceilings on the amount of money presidential and vice presidential candidates and their families could contribute to their own campaigns.[11] It allowed unions and corporations, which had been prohibited from contributing, to form political action committees (PACs), consisting of their members, employees, and stockholders, to solicit voluntary contributions for candidates or parties and to fund the group's election activities. The FECA also established procedures for public disclosure of contributions over a certain amount. A second statute, the Revenue Act of 1971, created tax credits and deductions to encourage private contributions. It also provided for public funding by creating a presidential election campaign fund. Financed by an income tax checkoff provision, the fund initially allowed taxpayers to designate one dollar of their federal income taxes to a special presidential election account.

These laws began a period of federal government regulation of national elections that has continued into the twenty-first century. The history of that regulation is a history of good intentions built on political compromise but marred by unintended consequences of the legislation and its implementation as candidates, parties, and nonparty groups have circumvented the letter and spirit of the law to gain electoral advantage.

Partisan compromises in the enactment of campaign finance legislation were evident from the outset. Although the original funding provision was enacted in 1971, it did not go into effect until the 1976 presidential election. Most Republicans, including President Nixon, opposed the policy of government financial support and regulation. In addition to conflicting with their general ideological belief that the national government's role in the conduct of elections be limited, the legislation offset their party's traditional fund-raising advantage. President Nixon was persuaded to sign the public funding bill, however, after Democrats agreed to delay the date when the legislation would go into effect until after his likely reelection.[12]

The 1972 election was marked by heavy-handed fund-raising tactics. The Nixon campaign in that election cycle raised more money than in any other previous presidential campaign. In addition to aggressive solicitation, the expenditures of the Nixon reelection effort also became an issue, albeit after the election. Investigative reporting by the *Washington Post* and hearings conducted by a Senate committee revealed that the Committee to Reelect the President, referred to by Nixon's opponents as CREEP, had spent some of its funds on "dirty tricks" and other unethical and illegal activities, such as the break-in at the Democratic National Committee's headquarters at the Watergate office building. These revelations aroused public ire and created the incentive for a Democratic Congress to enact new and even more stringent legislation.

In 1974, the FECA was amended to include public disclosure provisions, contribution ceilings for individuals and groups, spending limits for the campaigns, federal subsidies for major party candidates in the nomination process, and complete funding for them in the general election. The law also restricted the amount candidates could contribute to their own campaign and the amount that others could spend independently on their behalf. Finally, it established a six-person commission, the Federal Election Commission (FEC), to implement and enforce the law.

The 1974 amendments were highly controversial. Critics immediately charged a federal giveaway, a raid on the Treasury. Opponents of the legislation also argued that the limits on contributions and spending violated their constitutionally guaranteed right to freedom of speech, that the funding provisions unfairly discriminated against third-party and independent candidates, and that Congress's appointment of some of the commissioners violated the separation of powers.

BUCKLEY V. VALEO DECISION

In 1976 in the landmark case of *Buckley v. Valeo*, 424 U.S. 1 (1976),[13] the Supreme Court upheld the right of Congress to regulate campaign contributions and expenditures but negated the overall limits on spending by individuals and nonparty groups and the appointment by Congress of four of the six election commissioners. The majority opinion in that case contended that by placing restrictions on the amount of money a person or organization could spend during a campaign, the law directly and substantially restrained freedom of speech, a freedom protected by the First Amendment to the Constitution. The Supreme Court did allow limits on contributions to candidates for federal office, however, and limits on expenditures of those candidates who accepted public funds but not those who refused these funds. By holding that contributions to and expenditures of presidential candidates could be limited, the justices acknowledged that large, often secret contributions and rapidly increasingly expenditures did pose problems for a democracy, problems that Congress could address.

The Court's decision required that the election law be amended once again. It took Congress several months to do so. In the spring of 1976, during the presidential primaries of that year, amendments were enacted that continued public funding of the presidential nomination and election campaigns, based on a figure of $10 million in 1974 to be adjusted for inflation, but did so on a voluntary basis. Candidates did not have to accept government funds, but if they did, they were limited in how much they and others could contribute to their own campaigns and how much those campaigns could spend. The FEC was reconstituted with all six members to be nominated by the president and appointed subject to the advice and consent of the Senate. The law required that three commissioners be Democrats and three be Republicans to ensure that the commission would be fair to both major parties.

With limited amounts of money available, the candidates opted to spend most of it on television advertising. Gone were the buttons, bumper stickers, and other election paraphernalia that had characterized previous campaigns. Fewer resources were directed toward grassroots organizing. Turnout fell. The national parties lost influence. Congress was concerned.

The Soft Money Loophole and Other Amendments

In 1979, additional amendments to the FECA were enacted to rectify these problems. To encourage voluntary activities and higher voter turnout, the amendments allowed party committees at the national, state, and local levels to raise and spend unlimited amounts of money for party-building activities such as registration and getting out the vote. Known as the *soft money provision*, this amendment, as interpreted by the FEC, created a gigantic loophole in the law.[14] It permitted, even encouraged, the major parties to solicit large contributions and distribute the money to their state and local affiliates as they saw fit. Pandora's Box had been opened, although it took another decade and a half to exploit it fully.[15] Later amendments to the FECA increased the base grant for nominating conventions of the major parties to $3 million in 1979 and $4 million in 1984 (adjusted to inflation). Congress eliminated this grant entirely in 2014.

It was not until 1993 that the law was amended again to increase the amount of money in the fund used to subsidize candidates for their party's presidential nomination and provide general election grants. Congres's failure to tie the amount of money taxpayers could designate for the fund to inflation, the decline in the percentage of taxpayers making such a designation, and the increasing number of candidates vying for party nominations all contributed to a treasury shortfall that was only expected to get worse in the years ahead. To rectify the problem, Congress increased the income tax checkoff from $1 to $3, a little less than the cost-of-living adjustment since the provision had originally gone into effect. However, the portion of taxpayers designating a payment to the fund had fallen significantly from its high of 28.7 percent in 1980. For the tax year of 2012, only 6.4 percent of taxpayers contributed to the fund.[16]

A new problem of a very different magnitude emerged in 1996—the exploitation of the soft money loophole to circumvent the law's intended contribution and expenditure limits. This exploitation resulted from a very creative interpretation of the 1979 amendments by President Clinton's political advisers, the major parties, subsequently the FEC, and finally, the courts. Here's what happened.

In 1995, Clinton and his advisers began planning for the president's reelection campaign. Their strategy was to position Clinton as a centrist by airing a series of advertisements that touted his record and favorably contrasted it with that of the congressional Republicans. The ad campaign was costly. After $2 million was spent by the president's reelection committee in the summer of 1995, the president's advisers feared that there would not be sufficient funds left to handle a challenge for the Democratic nomination if one developed and also respond to a strong Republican opponent prior to the nominating conventions. They resolved this dilemma by turning to soft money. Since the commercials that the Clinton administration aired were policy-oriented and did not specifically and directly urge the president's reelection, the president's advisers (and Democratic Party lawyers) argued that the party could pay for the ads with soft money, which the president would help raise.

What followed was a frantic, no-holds-barred fund-raising effort in which the president and the vice president actively participated. Inducements to contribute included dinners with the president and vice president at expensive Washington hotels, sleepovers in the Lincoln bedroom in the White House, state dinners with world leaders, rounds of golf with Clinton, trips on Air Force One, VIP treatment at Democratic Party functions such as its 1996 nominating convention, even invitations to join the commerce secretary on official U.S. trade missions abroad. Naturally, Republicans were outraged by these activities, particularly the use of public office for partisan purposes. Their party officials and elected leadership protested and congressional investigations followed, but to no avail. In the end, the Republicans resorted to the same tactics as the Democrats, using their control of Congress as leverage to raise soft money. They eventually netted more of it than did the Democrats.

THE BIPARTISAN CAMPAIGN REFORM ACT

The soft money issue reemerged during the 2000 nomination campaign. Republican candidate John McCain and Democrat Bill Bradley promised, if elected, to support a ban on soft money. Although neither candidate's bid for their party's nomination was successful, the campaign finance issue remained salient; it put presidential candidates Bush and Gore on the defensive and led to cries for reform. In April 2001, the Senate enacted the Bipartisan Campaign Reform Act (BCRA), also known by the name of its sponsors as the McCain–Feingold bill, to close the soft money loophole. The legislation also restricted the use of the principal instrument by which nonparty advocacy groups had tried to affect the election's outcome—issue advocacy advertising. Nine months later, the House of Representatives followed suit, and in March 2002, the legislation became law.

The BCRA banned the national party committees from raising soft money, but to compensate, the new law also raised individual and overall federal contribution limits to candidates and parties and restricted the use of issue advocacy ads, in which candidates were cited by name, to periods that exceeded thirty days before a primary and sixty days before the general election. Exemptions, however, remained for tax-exempt organizations.

Opponents of the law immediately questioned its constitutionality. Such disparate groups as the National Rifle Association, the American Civil Liberties Union, and the Christian Coalition argued that the ban on issue advocacy advertising in the final days of the campaign violated the First Amendment's protection of freedom of speech and freedom of the press. The Republican National Committee claimed that the prohibition on soft money violated the state parties' right to raise money to organize and mobilize voters in elections, while groups representing poorer Americans contended that the increase in amount of money that could be contributed by individual donors violated the rights of less wealthy people under the Fifth Amendment's equal protection clause. In contrast, the bill's sponsors, the FEC, Common Cause and other public interest groups, and twenty-one state attorneys general supported the new law.

Anticipating a constitutional challenge, the drafters of the legislation included a provision for a quick judicial review. One year later, on December 10, 2003, as the Democratic nomination process was underway, the Court issued its ruling in the case of *McConnell v. FEC*, 540 U.S. 93 (2003). By a 5-to-4 vote, the justices upheld most of the provisions of the BCRA, including the ban on soft money solicitation by the national parties and the limits placed on issue advocacy ads that identified specific candidates in the closing month of primaries and sixty days or less in the general election.[17] It was left to the FEC to regulate enforcement.[18]

The FEC issued a series of regulations, some of which were very contentious.[19] New legal challenges to these regulations immediately ensued. In the end, the courts invalidated a number of the FEC's regulations. One of the most controversial involved "nonpolitical" organizations, which the FEC had indicated were not subject to the soft money restrictions. But how was nonpolitical to be defined? Did it mean that the group could not engage in political activities, or that most of its expenditures could not be devoted to electioneering, or that its primary purpose could not be to elect a specific candidate?

The question was more than a theoretical one. It had very practical and immediate consequences. The reason is that Democrats, fearing that the prohibition on soft money would place their party at a competitive disadvantage, had turned to nonprofit, nonpartisan groups to raise unlimited amounts of money and spend it on election-related activities.[20] Sponsors of the BCRA and their supporters urged the FEC to regulate these groups in accordance with the intent of the law to prohibit soft money in national elections. Republicans who had previously opposed the law also urged the FEC to issue new regulations that prohibited nonparty groups from engaging in these activities. However, the commission voted 4 to 2 not to do so.

After the election, and with prodding from a federal judge, the commission said that it would regulate these groups on an ad hoc basis rather than prescribe general rules for all of them. It fined four of the groups, two Democratic and two Republican, a total of $1.38 million for not registering with the FEC as political organizations and for accepting contributions that exceeded the legal amount.[21] Since the groups raised millions, the fines were considered minimal—the cost of doing business. It has not deterred similar groups from large-scale fund-raising during subsequent presidential campaigns.[22]

Although the Supreme Court upheld Congres's right to prohibit advocacy ads in which candidates are identified by name in the final days before the election, the issue came up again in 2006 after a pro-life group in Wisconsin sued the FEC for ruling that the group's advocacy ads violated the sixty-day rule. During the fall of 2006, the pro-life group had urged people to write to their senators opposing the confirmation delay of several of President Bush's judicial nominations. Mentioned in the ad were the names of the state's two senators, Russell Feingold and Herbert Kohl, but not their voting records on nomination or abortion-related issues. Feingold was running for reelection in that year. A three-judge federal court reversed the FEC's ruling on the grounds that the group's freedom of speech was violated. In 2007, the Supreme Court agreed to review the lower court ruling.

THE COURT'S *CITIZENS UNITED* DECISION

One year later, during the 2008 nomination campaign, a conservative, nonprofit corporation, Citizens United, produced a documentary film attacking Hillary Rodham Clinton. The film was made available to movie theaters and sold as a DVD. The Citizens United organization, also wanted to distribute it on cable television as a paid-for video; it intended to run advertisements informing the public of the film's availability. The FEC, however, ruled that a movie produced by a corporation at its expense violated the ban on corporate spending in federal elections. The commission also indicated that advertising for the film would be subject to the disclosure provision of the BCRA. A lower court that considered the controversy also ruled against Citizens United, prompting the corporation to appeal the case to the Supreme Court.

The Court heard oral arguments on both cases, the Wisconsin Pro-life group and Citizens United, which was a corporation, in March 2009. The Court then asked the parties to reargue the case in September of that year. Solicitor General Elena Kagan, later nominated by President Obama to the Supreme Court, defended the government's position validating the election law. In January 2010, the Supreme Court issued its decision in the case of landmark *Citizens United v. Federal Election Commission*, 130 S. Ct.876 (2010).

A 5-to-4 majority concluded that corporations have free speech rights that are protected by the First Amendment. In the words of the justice who wrote the majority opinion, Anthony Kennedy, "If the First Amendment has any force, it prohibits Congress from fining or jailing citizens, or associations of citizens, for simply engaging in political speech."[23] Justice John Paul Stevens, author of the dissent, retorted, "At bottom, the Court's opinion is … a rejection of the common sense of the American people who have recognized a need to prevent corporations from undermining self-government since the founding, and who have fought against the distinctive corrupting potential of corporation electioneering since the days of Theodore Roosevelt."[24] The Court did not invalidate the BCRA's disclosure requirements or the limits that the law placed on the size of contributions to candidates in federal elections.

Following the Court's decision, a unanimous Court of Appeals ruled that the *Citizens United* judgment also applied to other nonparty groups.[25] This Court of Appeals decision enabled the candidates, or more precisely their aides, friends, and financial backers, to establish their own, candidate-oriented Super PACs. As a consequence, money poured into the 2012 campaign.

The *Citizens United* decision was criticized by Democrats who feared that groups with access to large amounts of money would be able to exercise undue influence on American elections. In his 2010 State of the Union Address, President Obama said, "The Supreme Court reversed a century of law to open the flood gates for special interests—including foreign corporations—to spend without limit in our elections."[26] Republicans responded that freedom of speech, a basic right of Americans, individually and collectively, had been preserved. In response to the Court's decision, Democrats introduced legislation to prevent corporations that received $50,000 or more in government contracts and foreign corporations from spending in U.S. elections. The legislation was not enacted, however.

In 2014, the Court went further. In the case of *McCutcheon v. FEC*, 134 S. Ct. 1434 (2014), another 5-to-4 majority ruled that the aggregate limits the law placed on individual contributions to all federal candidates,

TABLE 2.3 | CONTRIBUTION LIMITS, 2015–2016

	To Each Candidate or Candidate Committee Per Election	To National Party Committee Per Calendar Year	To State, District & Local Party Committee Per Calendar Year	To Any Other Political Committee Per Calendar Year
Individual may give	$2,700*	$33,400*	$10,000 (combined limit)	$5,000
National Party Committee	$5,000	No limit	No limit	$5,000
State, District & Local Party Committee	$5,000 (combined limit)	No limit	No limit	$5,000 (combined limit)
PAC (multicandidate)	$5,000	$15,000	$5,000 (combined limit)	$5,000
PAC (not multicandidate)	$2,700*	$33,400*	$10,000 (combined limit)	$5,000
Authorized Campaign Committee	$2,000	No limit	No limit	$5,000

*These contributions are indexed for inflation

†Legislation enacted in 2014 allows national party committees to establish separate accounts to help defray the costs of their national nominating conventions, election recounts, and headquarter buildings. These accounts may accept $45,000 per year from multicandidate committees and up to $100,200 from other contributors for the 2015–2016 election cycle.

Source: "Contribution Limits for 2015–2016." Federal Election Commission, (Feb. 3, 2015). http://www.fec.gov/pages/fecrecord/2015/february/contriblimits20152016.shtml

party committees, and nonparty groups abridged freedom of speech and was thus unconstitutional.[27] This decision raised the question about whether the Court might revisit (and revise) its 1976 *Buckley v. Valeo* judgment that permitted Congress to limit the amounts contributed to candidates for federal office.

THE MONEY EXPLOSION

The BCRA, the *Citizens United* decision, and the revolution in communications technology have significantly affected campaign finance. They have the amount of money raised and spent by candidates as well as the number of donors, both large and small to these campaigns. The rise in individual contribution limits (from $1 to $3 and adjusted for inflation) increased the incentive for campaigns to expand their fund-raising activities among the general public. The development of the Internet provided the communications tool to do so. As a consequence, the amount of revenue have grown.

CANDIDATE REVENUES

Private Donors

Candidates for their party's nomination in 2004 were the first to benefit from the change. In that competitive Democratic nomination, $347.5 million was received from 338,735 individual donors. President George W. Bush, running unopposed for the Republican nomination, took in $257.4 million from 190,332 contributors.[28] In 2008, with campaigns in both parties, Republican candidates raised a total of $405.1 million and Democrats $689.9 million prior to their party's political conventions.[29] In 2012, with no opposition, Obama raised $409 million prior to the Democratic convention and $337 million after it (a total of $746 million); Romney raised almost $90 before and during the competitive phase of the Republican caucuses and primaries and a little more than $500 million after it (a total of $596).[30]

The number of small donors has increased dramatically in recent elections. In 2012, Obama received 28 percent of his total revenue in contributions of $200 or less, the minimum amount that must be itemized (with the name, address, and profession of the donors) and reported to the Federal Election Commission. The Romney campaign received 12 percent of its funds from small donors. On the other hand, Obama received 22 percent and Romney 49 percent from donors that gave the maximum amount, $2,500.[31]

There were also gender differences in the candidates' donor bases. Obama had a higher percentage of female donors (44 percent) than Romney (28 percent).[32] Lawyers, educators, and people in the communications/electronic industries gave more to Obama; those in finance, insurance, and real estate gave more to Romney.[33] In total, the Obama campaign listed 800,000 individual, itemized donors and Romney's 400,000.[34]

The large donor base has been due primarily to the Internet. Obama was not the first presidential candidate to use it for fund-raising. In 2000, Republican John McCain supplemented his campaign treasury by raising about $7 million online, much of it after his surprising victory over George W. Bush in the New Hampshire primary. Similarly, Howard Dean used the web during 2003 to gain money and attention in his quest for the 2004 Democratic nomination. A web site with a blog for communication among Dean's supporters and officials of the campaign netted about $30 million from almost 1 million contributors, making the campaign look like a spontaneous grassroots operation. The news media took notice.

Obama expanded the Dean model in 2008 and 2012. His campaigns assembled an experienced group of Internet entrepreneurs to maximize the use of this new communications technology. They created multipurpose sites that directed prospective donors from major social networks to make a contribution on line and charge it to their credit card. Supporters were encouraged to make monthly donations and ask their friends to do the same as well. In 2012, Obama's donors averaged more than five contributions each and Romney's more than two.

Personal Gifts, Loans, and Money Left Over from Previous Campaigns

In addition to gifts from others, candidates can provide some of their own personal funds. There is no restriction on the amount of their own money they can contribute prior to their official candidacy and a $50,000 limit after they file with the FEC, but only if they accept public funds. Of the major party candidates, the single largest personal contributors to their own nomination campaigns have been Republicans Steve Forbes ($38 million in 1996 and $48 million in 2000) and Mitt Romney ($42.4 million in 2008). In 1992, H. Ross Perot spent $63 million of his own fortune in the general election.

Borrowing money is also allowed. John Kerry and Hillary Rodham Clinton lent their nomination campaigns $6.4 million and $20 million, respectively. Kerry's success in winning the Democratic nomination in 2004 enabled his campaign to repay him; Hillary Clinton's campaign was unable to do so although Obama promised to help her retire some of it. Mitt Romney's campaign had to borrow money after he had effectively won the Republican nomination just to keep his campaign afloat until his treasury replenished the funds it spent during the caucuses and primaries.

Funds raised but not spent by candidates in their campaigns for other federal offices can be used in their quest for the presidential nomination. John McCain transferred $2 million from his Senate account to fund the initial stages of his 2000 campaign for the Republican nomination and $22 million in 2008. Hillary Clinton transferred $10 million in unspent funds from her 2006 Senate race for her presidential bid two years later. The ability to tap funds raised in other federal campaigns encourages potential candidates in the House and Senate to raise as much money as they can prior to an anticipated bid for their party's presidential nomination.

Federal Funds

The FECA had provided for public funding of presidential elections, matching grants for the nomination process, and a general grant for the general election. Box 2.1 summarizes these funding provisions. Table 2.4 indicates the amount of government funding of presidential elections since the campaign finance legislation went into effect. Note how that funding has dramatically declined in recent elections.

Why the decline? The reason is simple. Candidates that can raise a large amount of money from private sources gain a strategic advantage. The legislation that established government grants also set limits on spending for those who accepted federal funds.

| BOX 2.1 | PUBLIC FUNDING PROVISIONS OF THE LAW |

Matching Funds   Candidates for their party's presidential nomination can match any individual contributions they receive in the election year or the year before up to $250 with an equal amount from the federal election fund. To be eligible for such a match, they must raise $5,000 in twenty states in contributions of $250 or less, a total of $100,000. To remain eligible, candidates must receive at least 10 percent of the vote in two consecutive primaries in which they are entered, a rule that disadvantages lesser-known candidates.[35] The funds are distributed in the calendar year of the election.

Minor party candidates may also receive matching funds if they seek their party's nomination.

Convention Grants   Federal funding was also given to the major parties for their national nominating conventions. The convention grant in 2012 was $18.2 million; in 2014, with tight budgets and across-the-board cutbacks, Congress eliminated this grant. Parties also seek substantial amounts from individual donors, large organizations, and the states and cities in which the conventions occur. The private sector also provides goods and services.[36]

General Election Funds   Once the major party candidates have been officially nominated, they are eligible for a direct grant. In 2008, $84.1 million was given to Republican John McCain. In 2012, it would have been $91.2 million had Obama and Romney accepted federal funds, which they did not.

TABLE 2.4 | GOVERNMENT FUNDING OF THE PRESIDENTIAL ELECTION CYCLES 1976–2012 (IN MILLIONS)

Year	Matching Funds	Convention Grants	General Election	Total
1976	$24.8	$4.1	$43.6	$73.6
1980	31.3	8.8	63.1	103.3
1984	36.5	16.1	80.8	133.5
1988	67.5	18.4	92.2	178.2
1992	42.9	22.1	110.5	175.4
1996	58.5*	24.7	152.7	236.0
2000	62.3	29.5	147.7	239.5
2004	28.4	29.8	149.2	207.5
2008	21.7	33.6	84.1	139.4
2012	0.9	36.5	---	37.5

Source: "Presidential Public Funding Fact Sheet (Updated September 2012)," Federal Election Commission. http://www.fec.gov/press/bkgnd/pres_cf/Pres_Public_Funding.pdf

During the nomination process there is an individual state and overall spending restriction for candidates that accept federal funds. In 2012, the state limits ranged from a low of $912,400 in the smallest ones—a real problem in Iowa and New Hampshire—to a high of $20.7 million in the largest, California. The overall preconvention limit was $45.6 million. The three to five months that separates the contested phase of the nominations from the national nominating conventions put the primary winner at a considerable financial disadvantage during this period, dependent on the support of the party and nonparty groups. George W. Bush was the first non-self-funded, major party candidate to refuse preconvention funds for these reasons.[37] Beginning in 2004, it became standard practice for nominees of the major parties who believed that they could raise sufficient funds on their own to reject matching grants.

The law also restricts general election funding to the size of the federal grant. In 2012 that grant would have been $91.2 million. It cannot be supplemented by private contributions. Barack Obama was the first major party candidate in the general election not to accept federal funds. John McCain did but only received $84.1 million compared to the $337 million that Obama raised after the Democratic convention.

Unless the law is changed, spending limits increased, and supplementary private contributions allowed, the only major party candidates likely to accept public funds in the future will be those who have no other viable options.

Minor party candidates are also eligible to receive federal funds in the general election, but only an amount equal to their proportion of the popular vote, provided it is 5 percent or more. They get this grant after the election unless their party received the minimum percentage or more in the previous election. Using his own wealth to fund his 1992 presidential campaign, H. Ross Perot, a candidate of his newly created Reform Party, received 19 percent of the popular vote, making his party eligible for $29 million in the next election. Perot accepted these funds for his 1996 campaign. The Reform Party candidate in 2000, Pat Buchanan, received $12.6 million in 2000, but fell short of the 5 percent threshold need to be eligible for automatic federal funds thereafter.

CANDIDATE EXPENDITURES

According to the Center for Responsive Politics, $2.3 billion was spent on the 2012 presidential campaign. Approximately half that amount was spent by the candidates' campaigns, the other half by outside groups.[38] For the candidates, the largest single item on which money was spent was mass media. About 59 percent of total campaign expenditures was directed toward the production and airing of advertisements on radio, television, and the Internet, plus the cost of media consultants and their firms. (Consultants generally work on a percentage basis, with their firms getting a proportion of the costs of the advertising they place on local and national cable and broadcast media.)

Fund-raising was the next largest expenditure (14 percent) followed by administrative costs, such as salaries, travel, and office rentals.[39]

Most expenses for outside groups were spent on broadcast television advertising.[40] They also had to pay for fund-raising, salaries, and administrative costs.

SUPPLEMENTAL PRESIDENTIAL CAMPAIGNS

In addition to the campaign run by the presidential candidate, party and non-party groups are also active in presidential elections.

Political Parties
The national party organizations tend to remain neutral during the primaries and caucuses. They impose the rules that frame the process, but their leadership remains on the sideline until the nominee has been effectively decided. State party leaders, on the other hand, frequently endorse individual candidates and help bolster their campaigns with organizational support and access to financial resources.

Once the nominee is effectively determined, the national party gets involved. It coordinates fund-raising with its future standard bearer, a coordination that is necessary because both presidential campaign and party solicit contributions from the same base of donors. Although national parties can no longer accept soft money, they can accept individual and group contributions that are indexed to inflation. (See Table 2.3) In addition, each party's House and Senate campaign committees raise money as do state and local party organizations. These funds can be considerable.

Once a candidate has been officially nominated, the political party can spend a limited amount of coordinated activities with their presidential candidate's campaigns as well as spend unlimited money independently on its nominee's behalf. The national party committees have raised and spent record amounts during the last three presidential election cycles. Table 2.5 lists their revenues in recent election cycles.

Nonparty Groups
Until the Supreme Court's *Citizens United* decision, corporations and labor unions were prohibited from making direct contributions to political

TABLE 2.5 | NATIONAL PARTY REVENUES IN RECENT PRESIDENTIAL ELECTIONS (IN MILLIONS)

	2003–2004	2007–2008	2011–2012
Democrats	$678.8	$763.3	$805.6
Republicans	782.4	792.9	806.9

Source: "Federal Financial Activity of Party Committees," Federal Election Commission. http://www.fec.gov/press/summaries/2012/tables/party/Prty1_2012_24m.pdf

candidates. Unions got around this restriction in 1944 by asking their members to make voluntary contributions into a separate political fund to help reelect Franklin D. Roosevelt. The fund maintained its own bank account and administrative structure. It was the first political action committee (PAC) that operated in the presidential electoral process.

PACs. The campaign finance legislation enacted in the 1970s and revised in 2002 opened this activity to corporation employees and stockholders, people associated with trade associations, and other nonconnected groups, those that did not have a formal business or labor tie. The legislation also placed limits on the size of the contributions they could make ($5,000 per candidate; $15,000 per party) and receive ($5,000 from an individual donor). PACs had to register with the FEC and file periodic reports.

Because of the limited size of the contributions they could provide, PACS did not become a major source of funding for presidential candidates. In 2012, they contributed only $1.6 million.[41] However, they do help presidential campaigns in a variety of other ways by holding fund-raisers and by communicating with their members and the public. In general, corporate, labor, trade PACs have been more important to members of Congress than they are to presidential candidates.

Prospective presidential candidates regularly set up their own Leadership and Advocacy PACs to fund their preelection activity to pay for staff and travel as well as make contributions to other candidates whose support they hope to gain for a presidential campaign. These PACs help establish a donor base and generate visibility for their ideas and policy positions.

527s and 501c Groups. When the soft-money spigot was turned off in 2002 by the BCRA, party activists and interest group leaders looked for other ways to solicit large contributions from the wealthy individuals and groups to use in federal campaigns. They turned to nonpolitical groups, such as social welfare and nonprofit organizations, to do so. These groups are allowed to accept unrestricted contributions and involve themselves in political activities as long as their primary purpose is not political. They must spend less than half their budget on political activities.

Organized under provisions 527 and 501c of the Internal Revenue code, the groups must receive government approval for tax-exempt status. IRS review became a partisan issue in 2013. Republicans accused the agency of targeting conservative groups, a charge that the Obama White House denied and the IRS attributed to a few overzealous and overworked employees.

The 527 organizations can raise unrestricted amounts of money for election activities, such as voter mobilization and issue advocacy, but they cannot specifically advocate the election or defeat of a particular candidate. In 2003, Congress also required them to identify their donors; 501c groups do not have to do so. 527s were most active in the 2004 election, raising and spending over $400 million.[42] Their spending levels have decreased since then. Spending by 501c groups, however, has increased, exceeding $300 million in the 2011–2012 election cycle.[43]

Super PACS. Although 521 and 501c groups were allowed to accept unlimited contributions, the Supreme Court's *Citizens United* decision allowed corporations, labor unions, and candidate-centered groups to do the same. Super PACs are independent expenditure groups. They cannot contribute to a candidate's campaign nor coordinate their electoral activities with those campaigns, but they can raise and spend unlimited amounts of money. They do have to identify their donors, a reason why many Super PACs have established their own 501c groups to provide anonymity to donors who want it.

Super PACs played a major role in the 2012 federal election. They raised and spent more than $600 million, most of it for the presidential campaign. Mitt Romney was the principal beneficiary. Almost half the money spent on his campaign came from Super PACs, his own, and other Republican-oriented groups. Most of it was spent on negative political commercials. Table 2.6 lists the top 10 nonparty groups that spent the most during the 2011–2012 election cycle.

Of the contributions reported by Super PACs to the FEC, more than half came from a relatively small number of donors; 156 contributed $1 million or more; seven individuals and two groups gave $10 million or more.[44]

The proliferation of Super PACs and the disproportion contributions from a small number of wealthy donors have contributed to the public perception that wealthy interests exercise undue influence on candidates, election outcomes, and governance. Big contributors gain more access to elected officials, receive more invitations to government briefings and social events,[45] and more appointments to office.[46]

TABLE 2.6 | TOP SUPER PAC SPENDERS IN THE 2012 ELECTION

Group	Total (in millions)	Ideological Orientation Conservative (C)/ Liberal (L)
American Crossroads/Crossroads GPS	$176.4	C
Restore Our Future (Romney's Super PAC)	$142.1	C
Priorities USA/Priorities USA Action (Obama's Super PAC)	$65.2	L
Americans for Prosperity	$36.4	C
US Chamber of Commerce	$35.7	C
American Future Fund	$25.4	C
Service Employees International Association	$23.0	L
National Rifle Association	$19.8	C
Freedom Works	$19.6	C
American Federation of State, County, and Municipal Employees	$18.0	L

Source: "Outside Spending, by Group," Center for Responsive Politics. http://www.opensecrets.org/outsidespending/summ.php?disp=O2012

The growing importance of Super PACs has reduced the control candidates and their managers exercise over presidential campaigns. Their agenda, narrative, even geographic emphasis may be affected by Super PAC activity.[47]

Super PACs, however, have gotten less bang for their bucks than do the candidate campaigns; the law requires the media to charge candidates the lowest rate; Super PACs do not enjoy the same preferential treatment. Thus in 2012, the Obama campaign ran more ads than did Romney and the Super PACs supporting him but spent less money on advertising.[48]

MONEY AND ELECTORAL SUCCESS

The relationship between money and electoral success has spurred considerable debate in recent years and generated much anger from those who believe unequal resources undermine the democratic character of the U.S. electoral process. Is the conventional wisdom correct? Do those with more money have an advantage? Do they usually win? The simple answer is usually yes, but the longer answer is more complicated. First, who has or gets the money? Second, what difference does the money make in the election?

Two types of candidates tend to have disproportionate resources at their disposal: those who are personally wealthy and those who are well-known and well-connected public figures. Money can buy recognition, as it did for Ross Perot in 1992 and 1996, Steve Forbes in 1996 and 2000, and Mitt Romney in 2008; it gave them a chance that they might not otherwise have had. But obviously, money cannot, in and of itself, buy an electoral victory, as Perot, Forbes, and Romney found out. Similarly, party front-runners, incumbents such as Bill Clinton in 1996, George W. Bush in 2004, and Barack Obama in 2008, can raise more money because they are perceived likely to win their party's nomination. That money, in turn, contributes to their success.

Money matters most when the candidates are least known to the voters, when they do not receive a lot of news coverage, and when paid advertising, which, of course, is expensive, can bring recognition and enhance images, factors more prevalent during the nomination process than during the presidential election.[49] As the race begins, money buys name recognition, organizational support, and campaign consultants; over the course of the campaign, it purchases advertising, digital outreach, and a grassroots operation.

The need to develop a digital infrastructure, collect and integrate the data to support it, and hire the experts to operate it also gives advantage to candidates that begin with a large war chest. As Romney was spending the money he raised in the first 15 months of the election cycle to secure the Republican nomination, Obama was using to structure and staff his Internet operation.

Have the candidates with the largest bankrolls generally been victorious in the general election? The answer again seems to be yes, although as in the nomination process, it is difficult to determine precisely whether money contributed to victory or simply flowed to the likely winner. Between 1860 and 1972, the winner outspent the loser twenty-one out of twenty-nine times. Republican candidates have spent more than their Democratic opponents in twenty-five out of twenty-nine elections during this period. The four times they did not, the Democrats won.

The correlation between money and electoral success has continued in the contemporary period even though the major party candidates who accept federal funds are offered the same amount of money. Independent spending by party and nonparty groups can make a difference. In the 1980s, considerably more was spent on behalf of Republican nominees than on their Democratic opponents, and the GOP won each presidential election during this period. In the 1990s, the Democrats benefited from substantial expenditures by organized labor and the impact of the Perot campaign, although their total spending was still less than the Republicans'. George W. Bush was the financial as well as electoral victor in 2000; in 2004, however, the amount of money each side had in the general election was about equal and the results of the vote were very close. In 2008, Obama had a significant financial advantage and probably enlarged his general election victory by using his superior resources effectively. In 2012, the Obama campaign raised more money than did Romney's, but outside groups spent more on the Romney campaign. Although more was spent by and for Romney, Obama exercised more control over how the money was spent by getting lower advertising rates than the nonparty groups that supported Romney could obtain.

What do all these trends suggest? According to political scientist Larry Bartels, "campaign spending has had a significant electoral impact in presidential elections over the past half century [1952–2004]."[50] It has benefited the party that has spent the most, the Republicans. Bartels concludes that campaign spending increases the probability of voter support, particularly among the most affluent voters.[51]

The pattern of greater spending and electoral victories indicates that money contributes to success; potential success also attracts money. Having more funds is an advantage, but it does not explain all outcomes. The fact that heavily favored incumbent Richard Nixon outspent rival George McGovern more than 2 to 1 in 1972 does not explain McGovern's huge defeat, although it probably portended it. On the other hand, Hubert Humphrey's much narrower defeat by Nixon four years earlier was partially influenced by Humphrey spending less than $12 million, compared with more than $25 million spent by Nixon. The closer the election, the more the disparity in funds can make a difference.

SUMMARY

Campaign finance became an important aspect of presidential elections by the end of the nineteenth and the beginning of the twentieth centuries. In recent years, however, it has become even more important as costs have escalated and legal restrictions have limited large gifts to candidates and their political parties but not to outside groups. As a consequence, more money donated by more people to more groups has supplemented presidential campaigns but have also magnified the difficulty of candidates controlling those campaigns.

In the early- and mid-twentieth century, candidates of both major parties turned to large contributors for financial support. Their dependence on a relatively small number of large donors, combined with spiraling costs, created serious problems for a democratic selection process. The 1972 presidential election, with its high expenditures, "dirty tricks," and illegal campaign contributions, vividly illustrated these problems and generated public and congressional support for rectifying them.

In the 1970s, Congress enacted and amended the Federal Election Campaign Act to bring donors into the open, to limit the size of their contributions, and to provide government subsidies to reduce the burdens of fund-raising. These reforms were designed to produce a less costly, more equitable, more visible, and candidate-centered presidential selection process. A Federal Election Commission was also established to monitor election activities and oversee compliance.

But the legislation was only partially successful. It increased the importance of having a large base of contributors during the preconvention period but did not reduce the time and energy spent on fund-raising nor the incentive to "max-out" donors. For candidates who accepted federal funds, it limited their expenditures but did not reduce the amount of money spent on presidential elections. It produced greater equity by limiting contributions and by providing federal subsidies but did not level the playing field among the candidates. During the nomination stage, well-known and well-funded candidates were still advantaged.

The FECA also contributed to fractionalization of parties by providing financial incentives for candidates who might otherwise not have had opportunities to run to do so. Moreover, it has encouraged the formation and involvement of nonparty groups, which supplement the campaigns of the major party candidates but cannot coordinate their efforts with the candidates and their parties. Finally, the law has increased public information about campaign finance but has also forced campaigns to engage in additional bookkeeping and reporting procedures, which in turn have increased the costs of their campaigns.

In the 1980s, Congress amended the law to allow the parties to solicit unlimited contributions for party-building activities. This loophole undermined the equity goal of the original legislation and generated a "no-holds-barred" race to tap the wealthy. The Bipartisan Campaign Reform Act sought to end this race by banning the national parties from soliciting soft money. To compensate, the 2002 law doubled individual contribution limits and indexed them to inflation. Along with the development of the Internet as a cheap, quick, and broad-based fund-raising tool, the candidates were incentivized to rely on private funding solely rather than accept federal funds and the limits those funds imposed.

The Supreme Court's decision in the *Citizens United* case opened the door further to large individual and group nonparty contributions and expenditures, reigniting the debate over the influence of the wealthy on campaigns and elections. Although the results of the 2012 election has not resolved that debate, it did set trends expected to continue in the 2015–2016 election cycle: the increasing amount of money raised and spent on presidential nominations and elections, the increasing proportion of the electorate that contributes to campaigns, the explosion of Super PACs and the expansion of their election activities, and the demise of federal funding.

WHERE ON THE WEB?

- **Campaign Finance Information Center**
  www.campaignfinance.org
  > A source that lists news media stories on campaign finance issues.

- **The Campaign Finance Institute**
  www.cfinst.org
  > A nonprofit institute that collects and analyzes current information on campaign finance, reviews the impact of legislation on election giving and spending, and makes recommendations for legal reforms.

- **Center for Public Integrity**
  www.publicintegrity.org
  > Evaluates the impact of public service, government accountability, and various ethical issues on democratic governance. Has also been concerned with campaign finance reform.

- **Center for Responsive Politics**
  www.opensecrets.org
  > A nonpartisan, public interest group that is concerned with providing the public with information on the conduct of federal elections, particularly how money is raised and spent. Publishes alerts, press releases, and major studies on campaign finance.

- **Common Cause**
  www.commoncause.org
  > Another public interest group that is concerned with large and unreported contributions and expenditures and has continually urged campaign finance reform.

- **Democracy 21**
  www.democracy21.org
  > Still another public interest group interested in campaign finance reform, especially to reduce the influence of money on elections and government.

- **Federal Election Commission**
  www.fec.gov
  > The first stop for any study of campaign finance; the FEC collects and disseminates data on contributions to and expenditures of candidates seeking federal office as well as money donated to and spent by parties, PACs, and other nonparty groups.

- **Public Campaign**
  www.publicampaign.org
  > A public interest organization devoted to campaign reform to reduce the role of special interest money and large contributors in American politics.

- **Sunlight Foundation**
  www.sunlightfoundation.com
  > A nonpartisan, nonprofit foundation that is devoted to openness and transparency in politics and government. It releases reports and detailed analyses of campaign finance issues.

EXERCISES

1. During the preelection period, see if you can identify the leadership and Super PACs that potential candidates on the Republican and Democratic sides have created for their presidential campaigns. You can find these groups on the web site of the Center for Responsive Politics (www.opensecrets.org). Some of them are also listed in the "Where on the Web?" section in Chapter 5. Note the amount of money these groups have raised and how they have spent it.

2. Compile a running summary of revenue and expenditures as filed with the FEC (www.fec.gov) by candidates who have officially declared themselves for their party's 2016 presidential nomination. Does the differential in their war chests explain their respective campaign activities and/or their position in the public opinion polls?

3. List the funds raised and spent by the major party candidates in the 2016 general election. Note how the news media have reported these revenues and expenditures as part of their narrative on status of the candidates in the preelection polls and the election outcome.

SELECTED READINGS

Christenson, Dino P. and Corwin D. Smidt, "Following the Money: Super PACs and the 2012 Presidential Nomination," *Presidential Studies Quarterly*, 44 (September 2014): 410–430.

Corrado, Anthony. "Party Finance in the Wake of BCRA: An Overview," in Michael J.Malbin, ed. *The Election after Reform: Money, Politics and the Bipartisan Campaign Reform Act*. Lanham, MD: Rowman and Littlefield, 2006.

Corrado, Anthony, Michael J.Malbin, Thomas E. Mann, and Norman J.Ornstein. *Reform in an Age of Networked Campaigns*. Washington, DC: Campaign Finance Institute, Brookings Institution, and the American Enterprise Institute, 2010. cfinst.org/Press/PReleases/10-01-14/Reform_in_an_Age_of_Networked _Campaigns.aspx

Drutman, Lee. "The Political 1% of the 1% in 2012." Sunlight Foundation, June 24, 2013. http://sunlightfoundation.com/blog/2013/06/24/1pct_of_the_1pct/

Haynes, Audrey A., Paul-Henri Gurian, and Stephen Nichols. "The Role of Candidate Spending in Presidential Nomination Campaigns." *Journal of Politics* (Feb. 1997): 213–235.

Magleby, David B., ed. *Financing the 2012 Elections*. Washington, DC: Brookings Institution, 2014.

Malbin, Michael J., ed. *The Election after Reform: Money, Politics and the Bipartisan Campaign Reform Act*. Lanham, MD: Rowman and Littlefield, 2006.

Malbin, Michael J. "Small Donors, Large Donors and the Internet," Campaign Finance Institute (March 25, 2010). cfinst.org/Press/Releases_tags/10-03-25 /Small_and_Large_Donors_to_National_Political_Parties_and_Candidates.aspx

Mann, Thomas E. and Anthony Corrado, "Party Polarization and Campaign Finance," Brookings Institution, July 2014. http://www.brookings.edu/~/media /research/files/papers/2014/07/polarization and campaign finance/mann and corrad_party polarization and campaign finance.pdf

NOTES

1. "Presidential Campaign Disbursements through December 31, 2012," Federal Election Commission. www.fec.gov/press/summaries/2012/tables/presidential /Pres2_2012_24m.pdf. "2012 Presidential Race," Center for Responsive Politics. www.opensecrets.org/pres12/index.php#out.
2. Russ Choma, "The 2012 Election: Our Price Tag (Finally) for the Whole Ball of Wax," Center for Responsive Politics, March 13, 2013. http://www.opensecrets .org/news/2013/03/the-2012-election-our-price-tag-fin.html
3. Herbert E. Alexander, "Making Sense about Dollars in the 1980 Presidential Campaigns," in Michael J. Malbin, ed., *Money and Politics in the United States* (Washington, DC: American Enterprise Institute/Chatham House, 1984), p. 24.
4. Edward W. Chester, *Radio, Television, and American Politics* (New York: Sheed & Ward, 1969), p. 21.
5. Herbert E. Alexander, *Financing Politics: Money, Elections, and Political Reform*, 3rd ed. (Washington DC: Congressional Quarterly, 1984), pp. 11–12.
6. For a summary of household media usage see "Utilization of Number and Selected Media, 2000–2009," *Statistical Abstract of the United States*, Table 1132. (Washington DC: Bureau of the Census, 2012). www.census.gov /prod/2011pubs/12statab/infocommun.pdf
7. "Mad Money: TV Ads in the 2012 Presidential Campaign," *Washington Post* (updated November 14, 2014). http://www.washingtonpost.com/wp-srv/special /politics/track-presidential-campaign-ads-2012/
8. Jasper B. Shannon, *Money and Politics* (New York: Random House, 1959), p. 35.
9. Herbert E. Alexander and Brian Haggerty, *Financing the 1984 Election* (Lexington, MA: Lexington Books, 1987), p. 148.
10. In 1972, the chief fund-raiser for the Nixon campaign, Maurice Stans, and Richard Nixon's private attorney, Herbert Kalmbach, collected contributions, some of them illegal, on behalf of the president. They exerted strong pressure on corporate executives, despite the prohibition on corporate giving at that time. Secret contributions totaling millions of dollars were received, and three special secured funds were established. It was from these funds that the "dirty tricks" of the 1972 campaign and the Watergate burglary were financed.
11. The 1971 act also limited the amount that could be spent on media advertising, but that limit was eliminated in 1974.
12. There was also a short but critical delay in the effective date for the disclosure provision of the other 1971 campaign finance act. Signed by the president on February 14, 1972, it was scheduled to take effect in sixty days. This delay precipitated a frantic attempt by both parties to tap major donors who wanted to remain anonymous. During this period, the Republicans collected an estimated $20 million, much of it pledged beforehand and some of it in forms that could not even be traced.
13. James Buckley, one of the opponents of the legislation, was a Republican senator from New York. Francis Valeo was secretary of the United States Senate.
14. The FEC defined these activities broadly. It permitted parties to engage in a variety of public-oriented communications with one proviso: they could not expressly advocate the election of a specific candidate for federal office. Express advocacy included such words as "vote for," "support," and "elect." If these magic words were not included in the communication, then soft money could be used to pay for it.

15. It was not until 1992 that the FEC imposed reporting requirements on this soft money.
16. "Presidential Election Campaign Fund," Federal Election Commission, April 9, 2014. http://www.fec.gov/press/bkgnd/fund.shtml#search=public funds in 2012 presidential election. R. Samuel Garrett, "Proposals to Eliminate Public Financing of Presidential Campaigns," Congressional Research Service, Library of Congress, December 9, 2013. http://assets.opencrs.com/rpts/R41604_20131209.pdf
17. The Court did strike down a provision of the law that prohibited minors from making contributions on the grounds that it violated their freedom of speech. It also held that a requirement that prevented the national parties from independent spending if they coordinated their campaign activities with their candidates was unconstitutional.
18. Even here there was controversy. The bill's sponsors objected to many of the regulations that the FEC issued, claiming that they undermined the objectives of the law. In September 2004 during the general election campaign, a district court sided with the critics of the FEC rules and voided some of them.
19. For an extended discussion of the FEC's rulings, see Anthony Corrado, "The Regulatory Environment: Uncertainty in the Wake of Change," in David Magleby, Anthony Corrado, and Kelley D. Patterson, eds., *Financing the 2004 Election* (Washington DC: Brookings Institution, 2006), pp. 48–53.
20. The Supreme Court had defined political organizations in its *Buckley v. Valeo* decision as a group controlled by a candidate or created for the purpose of nominating or electing a specific candidate. The nonprofit, nonpartisan groups claimed that their primary purpose was not the election of a specific candidate, so they did not have to file with the FEC nor were they subject to the soft money restrictions.
21. R. Jeffrey Smith, "FEC Fines 3 '527' Groups for Use of Large Donations in '04'," *The Washington Post* (Dec. 14, 2006), p. A5. "FEC to Collect $750,000 Civil Penalty from Progress for America Fund," FEC, Feb. 28, 2007. www.fec.gov /press/press2007/20070228MUR.html.
22. According to the Campaign Finance Institute, two types of groups permitted to accept soft money under the IRS codes 501c and 527 spent about $400 million in the 2007–2008 election cycle. "Soft Money Political Spending by 501c Nonprofits Tripled in 2008," Campaign Finance Institute. www.cfinst.org/Press /PReleases/09-02-25/Soft_Money_Political_Spending_by_Nonprofits_Tripled _in_2008.aspx.
23. *Citizens United v. Federal Election Commission*, 130 S. Ct.876 (2010).
24. Ibid.
25. *SpeechNow v. Federal Election Commission*, United States Court of Appeals for the District of Columbia circuit, No. 08-5223, decided on March 26, 2010. http://www.fec.gov/law/litigation/speechnow_ac_opinion.pdf.)
26. Barack Obama, "State of the Union Address," January 27, 2010. www .whitehouse.gov
27. *McCutcheon v. Federal Election Commission*, 134 S.Ct. 1434 (2014).
28. "Individual Donors to Presidential Candidates," Campaign Finance Institute, January 6, 2010. 2004. http://www.cfinst.org/pdf/federal/president/2010_0106 _Table2.pdf
29. "Sources of Funds for the Presidential Candidates, 2007–2008 Pre-Nomination," Campaign Finance Institute, January 6, 2010. http://www.cfinst.org/pdf/federal /president/2010_0106_Table1.pdf

30. 2012 Presidential Campaign Finance," Federal Election Commission. (http://fec .gov/disclosurep/pnational.do)

31. "Aggregated Individual Contributions by Donors to 2012 Presidential Candidates, Cumulative through December 31, 2012," Campaign Finance Institute. http://cfinst.org/pdf/federal/president/2012/Pres12Tables_YE12 _AggIndivDonors.pdf

32. "Donor Demographics by Gender," Center for Responsive Politics, www .opensecrets.org/pres12/donordemCID_compare.php?cycle2012

33. "2012 Presidential Race, "Center for Responsive Politics. www.opensecrets.org /pres12/index.php

34. Micah, Sifry, "Presidential Campaign 2012, By the Numbers," *Tech President*, November 26, 2012. http://techpresident.com/news/23178 /presidential-campaign-2012-numbers

35. Twice during the 1984 campaign, Democrat Jesse Jackson lost his eligibility for matching funds, only to regain it later. Similarly in 2004, Al Sharpton and Dennis Kucinich lost their eligibility early in the process and thus could not benefit from the multiplier effect that federal funds provide.

36. These supplements can be substantial. In 2008, the Democratic and Republican national committees raised a total of $118 million, $61 million for the Democrats and $57 million for the Republicans. "Heavy Hitters ($250,000 to $3 Million Donors) Supplied 80% of Private Financing for 2008 Party Conventions," Campaign Finance Institute, December 10, 2008. www.cfinst.org /Press/PReleases/08-12-10/Heavy_Hitters_Supplied_Bulk_of_Private.

37. Steve Forbes used his own money to fund his quest for the 1996 Republican nomination. He did so again in 2000.

38. "2012 Presidential Race," Center for Responsive Politics. http://www.opensecrets .org/pres12/index.php

39. "Presidential Expenditures," Center for Responsive Politics. http://www .opensecrets.org/pres12/expenditures.php.

40. Fowler and Ridout, "Negative, Angry, and Ubiquitous." http://www.degruyter .com/view/j/for.2012.10.issue-4/forum-2013-0004/forum-2013-0004.xml? format=INT

41. "2012 Presidential Campaign Finance," Federal Election Commission. http://fec .gov/disclosurep/pnational.do

42. "527s: Advocacy Group Spending," Center for Responsive Politics. http://www .opensecrets.org/527s/#tots

43. "Political Nonprofits," Center for Responsive Politics. http://www.opensecrets .org/outsidespending/nonprof_summ.php

44. The top donors in 2012 included Sheldon Adelson ($49.8 million), Miriam Adelson ($42.0 million), Harold Simmons ($25.7 million), Bob Perry ($23.5 million), Fred Eychaner ($14.0 million), J. Joe Rickets ($13.5 million), International Union of the United Auto Workers ($11.4 million), and Michael Bloomberg ($10.0 million). Most of the money was spent for Republican candidates. Keenan Steiner and Jacob Fenton, "The 2012 Super PAC Million Club," Sunlight Foundation Reporting Group, December 7, 2012. http://reporting .sunlightfoundation.com/2012/2012-super-pac-million-dollar-club

45. In an examination of visitor logs to the Obama White House, two *New York Times* reporters found "those who donated the most to Mr. Obama and the Democratic Party since he started running for president were far more likely

to visit the White House than others. Among donors who gave $30,000 or less, about 20 percent visited the White House, … among those who donated $100,000 or more, the figure rises to about 75 percent. Approximately two-thirds of the president's top fund-raisers in the 2008 campaign visited the White House at least once, some of them numerous times." Mike McIntire and Michael Luo, "White House Opens Door to Big Donors, and Lobbyists Slip In," *New York Times*, April 14, 2021. http://www.nytimes.com/2012/04/15/us/politics/white-house-doors-open-for-big-donors.html?pagewanted=all&_r=0

46. For an up-to-date list of donors who received transition appointments or appointments as ambassadors in the Obama administration, see "Obama Administration," Center for Responsive Politics. http://www.opensecrets.org/obama/index.php

47. Dino P. Christenson and Corwin D. Smidt, "Following the Money: Super PACs and the 2012 Presidential Nomination," *Presidential Studies Quarterly*, 44 (September 2014), p. 428.

48. Erika Franklin Fowler and Travis N. Ridout, "Negative, Angry, and Ubiquitous: Political Advertising in 2012," *The Forum*. Volume 10, Issue 4 (February 2013), pp. 51–61. http://www.degruyter.com/view/j/for.2012.10.issue-4/forum-2013-0004/forum-2013-0004.xml?format=INT

49. Michael Robinson, Clyde Wilcox, and Paul Marshall, "The Presidency: Not for Sale," *Public Opinion* II (March/April 1989), p. 51.

50. Larry M. Bartels, *Unequal Democracy: The Political Economy of the New Gilded Age* (Princeton, NJ: Princeton University Press, 2008), p. 120.

51. Ibid., pp. 120–122.

The Political
Environment

CHAPTER 3

INTRODUCTION

The nature of the electorate influences the content, images, and strategies of the campaign and affects the outcome of the election—an obvious conclusion to be sure, but one that is not always appreciated. Campaigns are not conducted in ignorance of the voters. Rather, they are calculated to appeal to the needs and desires, attitudes and opinions, and associations and interactions of the electorate within the environment in which the election occurs.

Voters do not come to the election with completely open minds. They come with preexisting views. They do not see and hear the campaign in isolation. They observe it and absorb it as part of their daily lives. In other words, people's attitudes and associations affect their perceptions and influence their behavior. Preexisting beliefs and opinions make it important for students of presidential elections to examine the formation of political attitudes and the patterns of social interaction.

Who votes and who does not? Why do people vote for certain candidates and not others? Do campaign appeals affect voting behavior? Are the responses of the electorate predictable? Political scientists have been interested in these questions for some time. Politicians have been interested in them for even longer. A great deal of social science research and political savvy has gone into finding the answers to these questions. Spurred by the development of sophisticated survey techniques, methods of data analysis, and experimental research, political scientists, sociologists, and social psychologists have uncovered a wealth of information about public reactions and the electorate's behavior during a campaign. They have examined correlations between demographic characteristics and voter turnout. They have explored psychological motivations, social influences, and political pressures that contribute to voting behavior. They have even done research on the genetic components of attitudes, participation, and voting. This chapter discusses some of their findings.

It is organized into three parts. The first looks at who votes. After describing the expansion of suffrage in the nineteenth and twentieth centuries, the section turns to recent voting trends in the late twentieth and early twenty-first centuries. Turnout is influenced by personal feelings and beliefs, especially partisanship; social factors such as age, education, and group associations; and situational variables such as the state of domestic and foreign affairs, the competitiveness of the election, the weather, and the efforts by candidate campaigns, parties, and nonparty groups to get out the vote. Turnout is also affected by state and national laws that govern elections, especially registration requirements, early and absentee voting, and the locations and hours of polling places, especially the time it takes to vote. The impact of these variables, singularly and together, on the decision of whether or not to cast a ballot is the principal focus of this section.

The second and third parts of the chapter study influences on the vote. First, it examines the partisan basis of politics. How have political attitudes changed over the years, and how do they affect the ways people evaluate the candidates and their campaigns and shape their actual voting decisions? Models of voting behavior are presented and then used to help explain contemporary voting patterns.

Next, the chapter analyzes the social basis of politics. Here we look at the electorate's demography, its socioeconomic divisions, and the public's various beliefs and the values upon which those beliefs are based. Our objective is to discuss the relationship between groups within the electorate and their voting behavior. Primary emphasis is placed on the formation of party coalitions and their evolution. The chapter concludes with a description of the groups that comprise contemporary Republican and Democratic electoral coalitions.

TURNOUT

Who votes? In one sense, this is a simple question to answer. Official election returns indicate the number of voters and the states, even the precincts, in which people voted. By easy calculation, the percentage of the voting-age population (VAP) that actually cast ballots for president can be determined: 50.0 percent (2000), 55.4 percent (2004), 56.9 percent (2008), and 53.6 percent (2012).[1]

But there is a problem with using the VAP as a basis for determining voting turnout. The VAP includes people who are old enough to vote but may not be eligible to do so: noncitizens; most of the people who are currently incarcerated in penal institutions; in some states, ex-felons and ex-military who were dishonorably discharged from the armed forces; citizens who do not meet their state's residence requirements; and people who are not registered to vote.[2] If these people are excluded, then the percentage voting increases by about 4 to 5 percent.[3] Professor Michael P. McDonald, a political scientist who studies turnout figures, concluded that 60.1 percent of the voting-eligible population (VEP) actually did so in 2004, 61.6 percent in 2008, and 58.7 percent in 2012.[4]

More people say they vote than actually do so. They realize that it is a responsibility of citizenship and do not like to admit that they have not met that responsibility. Pollsters anticipate inflated positive responses to the question, "Did you vote in the last election?" To get at a more accurate figure, they often ask questions about past voting practices: Are you currently registered to vote? Did you vote in the last election? By the way, where do people vote around here? After the election, survey researchers weigh the responses they receive on the basis of the official results, knowing full well that approximately 15 to 20 percent more people will claim that they voted than actually cast ballots.[5]

VOTING IN AMERICAN ELECTIONS

Voting turnout in the United States has varied markedly over the years. A number of legal, social, and political factors have contributed to this variation. The next section documents these shifts and explains them within the context of the political environment of the times.

Turnout Before the Twentieth Century
The Constitution empowers the state legislatures to determine the time, place, and manner of holding elections for national office. Although it also gives Congress the authority to alter such regulations, Congress did not do so until after the Civil War. Thus, states were free to restrict suffrage, and most did. In some of them, property ownership was a requirement for exercising the franchise; in others, a particular religious belief was necessary. In most, it was essential to be white, male, and over twenty-one.[6]

Only about 11 percent of the adult population participated in the first national election. The percentage voting for president was even lower since most of the electors were designated by the state legislatures and not chosen directly by the people. Prior to 1824, voters remained a relatively small percentage of the eligible population, in the range of 20 to 25 percent. Without a tradition of participation in politics or a well-entrenched party system during this period, the general public deferred to the more politically prominent members of the society in choosing their state's elected officials.[7]

Turnout began to increase in the 1820s, spurred by a political reform movement known as Jacksonian Democracy. This movement advocated a greater role for the public in the electoral process. By the 1830s, most states had eliminated property and religious restrictions, thereby extending suffrage to approximately 80 percent of the adult white male population. Turnout expanded accordingly.[8] The rise of competitive, popular-based parties in the 1840s, along with campaigns directed at the entire electorate, boosted participation. Professor Walter Dean Burnham estimated turnout in the range of 70 to 80 percent of eligible voters throughout the remainder of the nineteenth century, although these percentages may be misleading because of the coercive and sometimes fraudulent practices that occurred during the era of machine party politics, a period during which the parties ran the elections, provided the ballots (distinguished by color), oversaw the voting, mobilized their partisans, and got them to the polls early, and sometimes repeatedly.[9]

Reforms at the end of the nineteenth and beginning of the twentieth centuries, however, reduced some of the more flagrant attempts to influence election outcomes. States began to monitor the conduct of elections more closely and more impartially. They adopted the Australian ballot and instituted secret voting; no longer could party poll watchers know how people voted by looking at the color of the ballot they dropped into the box. Registration procedures were introduced to prevent nonresidents and noncitizens from voting. These reforms improved the integrity of the electoral process, but they also reduced the percentage of the population that voted.

Following the Civil War, the growth of one-party politics in the South and the removal of federal troops contributed to declining turnout in that region of the country. Despite the ratification of the Fifteenth Amendment in 1870, which removed race and color as qualifications for voting, the size of the southern electorate actually decreased after the Civil War. A series of restrictive state laws, such as poll taxes, literacy tests, and "private" primaries in which only whites could participate, plus the imposition of more restrictive residence requirements, substantially reduced the proportion of adults in the South that could vote.

Turnout During and After the Twentieth Century

Decreasing competition between the major parties in the North and West at the end of the nineteenth century had much the same effect. It reduced the percentage of the population that voted, as did the extension of suffrage to women in 1919. Although the size of the eligible electorate doubled in the 1920s, turnout declined because newly enfranchised citizens do not vote with the same regularity as do people who have been exercising the franchise for years. In 1924, only 44 percent of the voting-age population cast ballots. Within a period of thirty years, turnout had declined almost 40 percent.[10]

Although voter participation grew moderately during Franklin Roosevelt's presidency and the post–World War II era, it decreased again following the 1960 presidential election, an election in which 64 percent of the adult population voted. Part of the decline had to do with the expanding base of the electorate, especially among the young and new immigrants; part with growing voter disillusionment, heightened by the war in Vietnam, the Watergate scandal, and a series of lackluster presidential candidates; and part with the weakening of the major parties' grassroots organizations and their increased dependence on television advertising for mobilizing the vote.

Beginning in the 1960s, suffrage rights were expanded. In 1961, the District of Columbia was granted three electoral votes, thereby extending to its residents the right to vote in presidential elections (Twenty-third Amendment); in 1964, the collection of a poll tax was prohibited for national elections (Twenty-fourth Amendment); in 1971, the right to vote was extended to all citizens eighteen years of age and older (Twenty-sixth Amendment).

Moreover, the Supreme Court and Congress began to eliminate the legal and institutional barriers to voting. In 1944, the Court outlawed the white-only primary.[11] In the mid-1960s, Congress passed the Civil Rights Act (1964) and the Voting Rights Act (1965). The latter banned literacy tests in federal elections for all citizens who had at least a sixth-grade education in a U.S. school. Federal officials were sent to facilitate registration in districts in which less than 50 percent of the population was registered to vote. Amendments to the Voting Rights Act have also reduced the residence requirement for presidential elections to a maximum of thirty days. In 2002, The Help Americans Vote Act, designed to improve the accuracy of registration lists and allow provisional voting in cases in which controversies over registration occurred at the time of voting, was enacted. The legislation also created the Election Assistance Commission to facilitate registration by providing people with information on where and how to do so.

These legal initiatives broadened the opportunities for people, particularly minority ethnic and racial groups, to participate in the electoral process. However, those initiatives also engendered pushback from state officials fearing that fraudulent voting practices could result. Following the 2004 presidential election, a number of states, controlled by Republican legislators and governors, enacted laws that required citizens to show government-issued identification cards in order to vote. In 2008, the Supreme Court, in the case of *Crawford vs. Marion Election Board*, 533 U.S. 181 (2008), upheld the state of Indiana's right to do so. These laws have since proliferated.

Democrats perceive these state laws as discriminatory, designed to reduce the vote of racial and ethnic minorities and lower-income citizens, people that are more apt to lack these credentials. Many states have also eliminated or restricted weekend and evening voting, ostensibly to save money. However, Democrats contend that these restrictions also disproportionately affect minorities and people with lower incomes who find it easier to vote during nonworking days and hours. Data reported by the Brennan Center for Justice in 2014 indicates that states that have enacted such restrictions tend to have larger minority populations and are more likely to have histories of racial discrimination:

> Of the 11 states with the highest African American turnout in 2008, 7 have new restrictions in place. Of the 12 states with the largest Hispanic population growth between 2000 and 2010, 9 passed laws making it harder to vote. And nearly two-thirds of states, or 9 out of 15, previously covered in whole or in part by Section 5 of the Voting Rights Act because of a history of race discrimination in voting have new restrictions since the 2010 election.[12]

Democratic Party officials, citizen advocacy groups, and the Obama administration have challenged the new state election laws, arguing that the Voting Rights

Act required election law preclearance by the Department of Justice. The suits reached the Supreme Court, in 2012. In the case of *Shelby County v. Holder*, 570 U.S. 2 (2013), the Court held that the 1965 preclearance requirement for states that had engaged in racial discrimination, mostly in the South, was outdated; Congress needed to establish new criteria for determining discrimination. The battle over state voting regulations on voting continues within both the political and judicial arenas.

Table 3.1 indicates turnout levels in recent presidential elections based on voting-age population (VAP).

TABLE 3.1 | SUFFRAGE AND TURNOUT IN THE TWENTIETH AND TWENTY-FIRST CENTURIES

Year	Voting-Age Population (VAP)	Turnout	Percent of the VAP
1900	40,753,000	13,974,188	35.0
1920	60,581,000	26,768,613	44.0
1932	75,768,000	39,732,000	52.4
1940	84,728,000	49,900,000	58.9
1952	99,929,000	61,551,000	61.6
1960	109,672,000	68,838,000	62.8
1964	114,090,000	70,645,000	61.9
1968	120,285,000	73,212,000	60.9
1972	140,777,000	77,719,000	55.5
1976	152,308,000	81,556,000	53.5
1980	164,595,000	86,515,000	52.6
1984	174,447,000	92,653,000	53.1
1988	182,600,000	91,602,291	50.2
1992	189,044,000	104,426,659	55.2
1996	196,507,000	96,277,564	49.1
2000	205,815,000	105,586,284	51.3
2004	215,694,000	122,295,345	56.7
2008	230,898,029	132,645,504	56.9
2012	240,926,957	130,292,355	53.6

Sources: Population figures for 1900 and 1920 are based on estimates and early census figures that appear in Neal R. Peirce, *The People's President* (New York: Simon & Schuster, 1968), p. 206; copyright renewed © 1979 by Neal R. Peirce. Reprinted by permission of Yale University Press. Population figures from 1932 to 1984 are from the U.S. Department of Commerce, Bureau of the Census, *Statistical Abstract of the United States* (Washington, DC: Government Printing Office, 1987), p. 250. Figures from 1988 to 2004 were compiled from official election returns supplied by the Federal Election Commission (www.fec.gov); 2008 and 2012 data from Michael P. McDonald, "2008 General Election Turnout Rates" (Updated March 13, 2010) and "2012 General Election Turnout Rates" (Updated September 3, 2014). www.electproject.org/2012g

COMPARATIVE TURNOUT IN WESTERN DEMOCRACIES

As the percentages in Table 3.1 reveal, turnout has been mediocre at best. A smaller percentage of Americans votes than in many other democratic countries (see Table 3.2).

TABLE 3.2 | INTERNATIONAL VOTER TURNOUT (IN PERCENTAGES)

Country	Year	Type of Election	Turnout of Eligible Voters
Argentina	2011	Parliamentary	77.2
	2011	Presidential	79.4
Australia	2010	Parliamentary	93.2
Austria	2008	Parliamentary	74.9
Belgium	2010	Parliamentary	88.2
Brazil	2010	Parliamentary	81.9
Canada	2008	Parliamentary	61.4
	2013	Presidential	59.1
Czech Republic	2013	Parliamentary	59.5
Ecuador	2013	Parliamentary	80.8
France	2012	Parliamentary	55.4
	2012	Presidential	80.4
Germany	2013	Parliamentary	71.6
Greece	2012	Parliamentary	62.5
India	2009	Parliamentary	58.2
Ireland	2011	Parliamentary	70.1
	2011	Presidential	59.1
Israel	2012	Parliamentary	67.8
Italy	2013	Parliamentary	75.2
Japan	2012	Parliamentary	59.3
Korea	2012	Parliamentary	54.3
	2012	Presidential	75.8
Mexico	2012	Parliamentary	62.5
	2012	Presidential	63.1
Pakistan	2013	Parliamentary	55.0
Poland	2011	Parliamentary	48.9
	2010	Presidential	55.3
Russia	2011	Parliamentary	60.1
	2012	Presidential	65.3
South Africa	2009	Parliamentary	77.3

continued

TABLE 3.2 | INTERNATIONAL VOTER TURNOUT (IN PERCENTAGES) *continued*

Country	Year	Type of Election	Turnout of Eligible Voters
Spain	2011	Parliamentary	68.9
Switzerland	2011	Parliamentary	49.1
Turkey	2011	Parliamentary	87.6
Ukraine	2012	Parliamentary	57.4
	2010	Presidential	69.7
United Kingdom	2010	Parliamentary	65.8
United States	2012	Presidential	58.2
	2014	Congressional	36.1

Sources: Institute for Democracy and Election Assistance. www.idea.int/vt/viewdata.cfm#; Michael P. McDonald, "General Election Turnout Rates" (updated September 3, 2014). www.electproject.org/2012g; www.electproject.org/2014g

Why is turnout in U.S. elections lower than in many other democracies? Unlike some countries, the United States does not impose penalties on those who fail to register and vote, nor does it have a national system for automatic registration as do other democracies. Moreover, the day of the election is a workday in the United States, whereas in most other countries, it is Sunday or a holiday. Another factor that contributes to a lower turnout percentage in the United States is the winner-take-all system of voting, which discourages participation in noncompetitive electoral districts and states.

INFLUENCES ON TURNOUT

Why don't people vote? Does low turnout indicate voter satisfaction or alienation? Does it contribute to stability or create conditions for instability within the democratic political system? What party and which programs benefit or suffer when so many people do not vote? The next part of the chapter answers these questions.

Legal Constraints

Some citizens have lost their right to vote. In 48 of the 50 states—Vermont and Maine are the exceptions—people who are incarcerated cannot vote. Other states have laws that prohibit from voting those on parole or probation, convicted of a felony, or dishonorably discharged from the military, thereby preventing almost 6 million people from voting. The felony restrictions have disproportionately impacted African Americans, particularly men. One out of 13 African Americans (7.7 percent) cannot vote because of this restriction compared to 1.8 percent of the rest of the population.[13]

Congress tried to deal with registration problems in 1993 with its enactment of the "Motor-Voter" bill. The legislation requires states to permit registration by mail and provide registration forms at convenient statewide offices such as motor vehicle registries, military recruitment offices,

| BOX 3.1 | REGISTERING TO VOTE |

It is easy to register to vote. All you have to do is go to the web site of the Election Assistance Commission and download the National Voter Registration form: www .eac.gov/voter_resources/register_to_vote.aspx. The booklet containing the form also lists the location to which the form should be sent in each state.

You can also do any of the following to register:

- Contact your state's election office and follow instructions for registering to vote.
- Go to your nearest department of motor vehicles, military recruitment, or public assistance office to obtain a copy of the registration form. Complete it, and give it to the appropriate person at the office where you obtained the form.
- Access the web site of an organization called Rock-the-Vote at www.rockthe vote.org, which will help facilitate your online registration.

and welfare services. Ten states and the District of Columbia have even implemented election-day registration that allows residents to register and then vote at the same time and place; almost half the states now permit online registration.[14]

After the Motor-Voter law took effect in 1995, the youngest group of eligible voters was expected to increase their electoral participation the most. Although eighteen- to twenty-four-year-olds have traditionally had the lowest registration rates (in the range of 30 to 40 percent), they have much higher driving rates (85 percent have driver's licenses). By making registration available at the same time and place where people get or renew their driver's licenses, it was thought that the law would increase the number of registered voters in the lowest age cohort. It did, but the youngest group of voters still has the lowest rate of turnout of all age groups (see Table 3.4).

Voter registration has continued to increase but not rapidly. The Election Assistance Commission reported that 194.2 million people were registered to vote in 2012, about 80 percent of the voting-age population and 87.4 percent of eligible voters.[15] States that permitted same-day registration had the largest increase in the percentage of registered voters. The bottom line is that the higher the registration, the larger the turnout is likely to be.

Convenience Issues

In addition to the registration requirements of most states, the availability of absentee ballots and early voting—about 32 million people voted early in 2012—are also factors that can affect turnout. The distribution of ballots by mail (Oregon requires mail voting and Colorado permits it), the length of the period for voting, and the accessibility of voting precincts facilitate voting and naturally enhance turnout. The easier it is to vote, the more likely people will do so.

Geographic mobility can be an impediment to voting. Elections are conducted by state and local officials and official residence is the principal factor in determining where people vote. Being away at college makes voting more difficult. Students need to return home, obtain absentee ballots, or change their official residences. Moreover, many young people have not yet developed the habit of voting. Peer pressure to do so may be low as well because so many in this younger age group have not voted or even registered. Thus, it is the older generation with whom young people interact as they move into voting age—parents, teachers, community, and religious leaders—that exercises greater influence on who votes. Older voters provide the critical information and model civic behavior that affects the initial decision of many young people, whether or not to vote.

The act of voting, however, increases the likelihood of doing it again and again.[16] Finding the correct location, getting to the polls, and figuring out how to use the machines or punch cards are no longer major obstacles once a person has voted. However, for people who have limited English language skills, various mental and physical handicaps, and those that lack required identification, voting can still be difficult.

Psychological and Political Attitudes

Personal feelings and beliefs are important in motivating people to vote. Interest in the election, concern over the outcome, feelings of civic pride, and political efficacy (the belief that one's vote really counts) are factors that affect how regularly people vote.[17] A recent experimental study found that social pressure also contributes to voting. People who received mail promising to publicize the fact that they voted to their family and community turned out at a higher level than those who did not receive the mailing.[18]

Naturally, those who feel more strongly about the election and who have the most interest in it are more likely to participate in the campaign and vote. Anger seems to be a greater motivator for voting than satisfaction with the candidates and their parties.[19] Engaging supporters and making them feel as if they were part of the campaign has been a basic component of the Obama's two presidential campaign strategies, a component likely to be followed by others in forthcoming elections.

Since the mid-1960s, the proportion of people identifying themselves as Republicans and Democrats has declined while the percentage of Independents has gotten larger. Because party loyalties are a motivation for voting, the decline in partisan identification has contributed to lower turnout. Independents are less likely to vote than partisans. However, more people say that they are independent than actually vote independently. Moreover, the emphasis on partisanship in an electorate nearly evenly divided between Republicans and Democrats has increased the influence of party loyalties on turnout and voting behavior.

Another factor that has reduced turnout is lower voter efficacy, the belief that one can make a difference and that voters can change the way government works or public officials behave. Political efficacy has declined since the late 1960s. Mistrust of government has increased. Critical perceptions of politicians and government also contribute to nonvoting.

Nonetheless, for many, voting is a civic responsibility; for others, it is a matter a personal conviction; and as we have mentioned, it can even become a habit, one reason that turnout tends to increase with age. With advances in medicine, the point at which senior citizens stay informed and involved has been extended to their mid to late seventies with correspondingly higher voting rates for people ages sixty-five and over.

Social and Economic Factors

Several social and economic variables correlate with turnout. They include education, income, and occupational status, which also correlate with one another. As people become more educated, as they move up the socioeconomic ladder, and as they gain more professional jobs, higher in status and income, they are more likely to vote.

Education has a larger impact than any other single social characteristic on voting.[20] The reason education is so important is that it provides people with the skills for processing and evaluating information; for perceiving differences among the parties, candidates, and issues; and for relating these differences to personal values and behavior. Education also increases a person's stake in the system, interest in the election, and concern over the outcome. Since the lesson that voting is a civic responsibility is usually learned in the classroom, schooling may also contribute to a more highly developed sense of responsibility about the importance of voting in a democracy.[21]

Given the relationship of education to turnout, why did the rate of turnout decline from the 1960s through most of the 1990s as the general level of education increased in the United States during this period? The answer is that the attitudinal factors of weakening partisanship in the 1970s and declining efficacy during most of this time frame countered the increase in education. Had educational levels not increased, turnout would have been even lower.[22]

Another contributing factor may be the growing gap in incomes and assets between the rich and the poor that has widened since the 1980s. People with lower levels of income tend to have a lower sense of personal efficacy. They either do not see or are pessimistic about how the outcome of the election will affect them, so why vote?

Environmental Factors

In addition to legal, attitudinal, and social factors, the environment in which elections occur also affects the level of voter participation. Competition stimulates turnout. It does so directly because people believe that their vote can make a difference in the outcome. If the public perception is that the election is not likely to be close, then motivation for voting tends to be reduced.

The candidates or issues can also affect the competitive climate. In 2004, Republican state officials purposely put initiatives opposing the marriage of same-sex partners on the ballot in eleven states. They believed that the people who felt most strongly about these issues, fundamentalist and evangelical Christians, would also be more likely to vote for George W. Bush if they voted at all, hence the reason for the ballot initiative bait.

To the extent that presidential strategies are targeted to the Electoral College, not to the general population, overall turnout suffers in those states that the presidential campaign neglects. In 2004, turnout increased almost twice as much in the battleground states (8.3 percent) than in nonbattleground ones (4.7 percent).[23] In 2008 and 2012, similar patterns emerged. Turnout in the ten battleground states averaged 65.9 percent VEP compared with 61.9 for the nonbattleground states in 2008;[24] in 2012, it averaged 65 percent in the top ten battleground states compared to 58 percent in the others.[25] Moreover, turnout was up in most states in which Obama waged the strongest challenge in 2008 and 2012, states that had previously been considered safely Republican, such as Virginia and Colorado, and it decreased in states that lost their battleground status.

Competition encourages more extensive mobilization efforts by the candidates. More people are contacted and personal contact increases the rate of voting. The recent gains in turnout have been associated with larger and more effective on-the-ground party and candidate mobilization efforts, as is evident from the larger percentage of the population reporting that they have been contacted in 2012 by phone (53 percent), home or personal visits (16 percent), or email or text messages (25 percent).[26] The Obama campaign claimed that it contacted one out of every 2.5 people in the country during the 2011–2012 election cycle, making over 125 million personal phone calls and visits.[27]

The weather may also be a factor. Three political scientists—Brad T. Gomez, Thomas G. Hansford, and George A. Krause—examined the impact of weather on turnout and found that rain reduces turnout by 1 percent per inch of precipitation. Snow also decreases participation, primarily in rural areas.[28]

Finally, situational variables help explain fluctuations in the vote. In 2004, the highly polarizing candidacy of George W. Bush, the controversy over the war in Iraq, and the domestic environment—the threat of terrorism and the spike in gas prices—energized both Republicans and Democrats and got them out to vote. In 2008, it was the increasing dissatisfaction of the electorate as the recession worsened plus the charisma of Barack Obama.

Turnout and Democracy

What difference does it make that some people do not vote? A great deal!

Turnout affects perceptions of how well the democratic electoral system is functioning. Low turnout suggests that people may be alienated, lack faith in the candidates and parties, think that the government is and will remain unresponsive to their needs and interests, and, most importantly, believe that they cannot achieve change through the electoral process.[29]

Low turnout also impacts representation and public policy decisions. "Who gets what" relates in large part to the influence some people and groups have on election outcomes and government decisions. The connection between low economic status and not voting results in a class bias that undercuts the democratic character of the American political system by widening the participation gap between the haves and have-nots.[30] This gap has produced an electorate that is not representative of the population as a whole, an electorate that is better educated and has higher incomes than the general public. To the extent that government responds to the electorate rather than to the general population, government policies take on a "have" rather than "have-not" coloration.

This class bias in voting produces a tragic irony in American politics. Those who are most disadvantaged, who have the least education and who need to change conditions the most, actually vote the least. Those who are the most advantaged, who benefit from existing conditions and presumably from the public policy that contributes to those conditions, vote more often.

TURNOUT AND PARTISANSHIP

Obviously, turnout has partisan implications as well. Since the Democratic Party draws more of its electoral support from those in the lower socioeconomic groups—people with less formal education and fewer professional opportunities—lower turnout tends to hurt that party more than the GOP (see Table 3.3 for demographic trends in turnout).

The common wisdom is that, all things being equal, the larger the turnout, the better the Democrats will do. In 1960 and 1976, increases in turnout did favor the Democrats and resulted in two very close victories. The relatively high Democratic turnout in these two elections overcame the advantage the Republicans usually gain from having a larger proportion of their rank-and-file vote.[31] Similarly, in the 2000 presidential election, a late surge of support for Gore gave him a popular vote victory although he lost in the Electoral College. Republican strategists, surprised by the larger turnout the Gore campaign generated, studied the election day tactics, particularly the efforts of organized labor and leadership within the African American community to increase the Democratic vote in that election. Determined not to be outmaneuvered again, the Republicans devised a turnout strategy for 2004 in which potential Republican voters were targeted, canvassed, and contacted by local volunteers within seventy-two hours before the vote. The strategy was successful; Republican turnout increased more than Democratic turnout in 2004.

Obama's campaign advisers studied the Republican turnout effort in 2004 as they prepared for the 2008 campaign. They devised an even more sophisticated effort in 2012, using social networks to identify and connect potential voters. They set up almost 700 field offices in the battleground states, and contacted millions of potential supporters by phone, home visits, and on the Internet. These turnout strategies confirmed the findings of political scientists that personal contact, strong feelings, and partisan allegiances are keys to maximizing the vote.

Not only does partisan orientation affect turnout, but it also has a major impact on voting behavior. The next part of the chapter examines the role of political identity, the ebbs and flows of partisan feelings, and the impact of ideology on partisanship and voting behavior.

TABLE 3.3 | TURNOUT IN PRESIDENTIAL ELECTIONS, 2000–2012
(TOTAL PERCENTAGE OF CITIZEN POPULATION OF VOTING
AGE WHO REPORTED THAT THEY VOTED)

Population Characteristics	Year			
	2012	2008	2004	2000
Total	61.8	63.6	63.8	59.5
Race				
White (non-Hispanic)	64.1	66.1	67.2	61.8
Black	66.2	64.7	60.0	56.8
Hispanic	48.0	49.9	47.2	45.1
Asian	47.3	44.1	43.4	45.0
Gender				
Male	59.7	54.4	55.7	56.3
Female	63.7	58.5	60.4	60.1
Age				
18 to 24 years	41.2	48.5	46.7	NA+
25 to 44 years	57.3	60.0	60.1	NA
45 to 65 years	67.9	69.2	70.4	NA
65 years and over	73.5	72.0	71.0	NA
Education				
Less than 9th grade	21.6	23.4	23.6	26.8
9–12th grade	32.2	33.7	34.6	33.6
High school diploma	48.7	50.9	52.4	49.4
Some college	61.5	65	66.1	60.3
College graduate	71.7	73.3	74.2	72.0
Region				
Northeast	56.6	57.4	58.6	55.2
Midwest	62.3	63.4	65.0	60.9
South	55.7	57.7	56.4	53.5
West	52.3	54.6	54.4	49.9

+Not Applicable

Source: U.S. Census Bureau, Current Population Reports, "Voting and Registration," February 2012. Table A-1. Reported Voting and Registration by Race, Hispanic Origin, Sex, and Age Groups: November 1964 to 2012; Table A-2. Reported Voting and Registration by Region, Educational Attainment, and Labor Force: November 1964 to 2012. http://www.census.gov/hhes/www/socdemo/voting/publications/historical/index.html

THE PARTISAN BASIS OF POLITICS

Why do people vote as they do? Considerable research has been conducted to answer this question. Initially, much of it has been done under the direction of the Center for Political Studies at the University of Michigan. Beginning in 1952, that center conducted nationwide surveys during presidential elections, surveys now called American National Election Studies (ANES).[32] To identify the major influences on voting behavior, a random sample of the electorate is interviewed before and after each election. Respondents are asked a series of questions designed to reveal their attitudes toward the parties, candidates, and issues. On the basis of their answers to these questions, researchers have amassed a wealth of data to explain the voting behavior of the U.S. electorate.

Voting Behavior

One of the earliest and most influential theories of voting behavior based on the Michigan survey data was presented in a book titled *The American Voter* (1960).[33] The model on which the theory was based assumed that individuals are influenced by their partisan attitudes and social relationships in addition to the political environment in which the election takes place. In fact, these attitudes and those relationships condition the impact of that environment on individual voting behavior. According to the theory, people develop attitudes early in life, largely as a consequence of interacting with their families, particularly their parents and other significant elders. These attitudes, in turn, tend to be reinforced by neighborhood, school, and religious associations.

Psychologically, it is more pleasing to have beliefs and attitudes supported than challenged. Socially, it is more comfortable and safer to associate with "nice," like-minded people, people with similar cultural, educational, and religious backgrounds, than with others who do not share the same values, beliefs, and experiences. This desire to increase one's "comfort level" in social relationships explains why the environment for most people reinforces rather than challenges their values and beliefs most of the time. Attitudes mature and harden over time. The older people become, the less amenable they are to change. They are more set in their ways and their beliefs. Consequently, their behavior is more predictable.

Although scholars have offered modifications to the Michigan model of attitude development, most of the political science literature has remained focused on external factors within the environment that shape how people think and behave politically. A newer line of research, however, has taken a different approach, a biological one. This research postulates that the genes people inherit from their biological parents affect the beliefs they develop and the behavior they exercise within the electoral arena.[34] Two researchers have gone so far as to identify specific genes that they believe affect turnout.[35] Their findings, however, have been difficult to replicate.[36]

At this relatively early stage of genetic research, neuroscience, and biological politics, postulating causal relationships based on genetic sequencing is a difficult and even a dubious task. Although the nature–nurture debate is likely to continue, the impact of socialization on how political attitudes are shaped over time is clearer.

Partisanship
Of all the external factors that contribute to the development of a political attitude, identifying with a political party seems to be the most important. It affects how people see campaigns, how they evaluate candidates and issues (and also elected officials), and how they vote on election day. Party identification operates as a conceptual framework, a mindset, a lens through which the campaign is understood and the candidates evaluated. Partisan allegiances provide cues for interpreting the issues, for judging the candidates, and for deciding whether or not to vote.

If the decision is to vote, partisanship influences for whom the vote is cast. The stronger these attitudes, the more compelling the cues; conversely, the weaker the attitudes, the less likely they will affect perceptions during the campaign and influence voting.[37] When identification with a party is weak or nonexistent, other factors, such as the personalities of the candidates and their issue positions, are correspondingly more important.

Partisanship is stable but can be modified or even changed over time. Although partisan allegiances affect perceptions of the candidates and issues, perceptions of the candidates and issues also affect allegiances toward the parties.[38] It is a two-way street in which people's perceptions can be reinforced or challenged by what happens before, during, and after campaigns. To summarize, partisanship is stable but not static; it can vary in intensity.[39]

Partisan orientation may even be a factor for those who identify themselves as independent. There are more people in the electorate who claim that they are independent than vote in an independent manner. In fact, political scientists have found more independents that lean toward one of the major parties than independents that do not.[40] So then, why would so many people claim to be independent? Some may have a negative view of both parties and even of partisanship in general; others like the idea of thinking and saying that they vote for the best candidate regardless of party because it creates the impression that they think on their own and that they can make an enlightened and rational judgment, one that will be in the public interest rather than some narrower partisan or parochial one. The empirical evidence, however, indicates that there are patterns of partisan voting behavior, even among Independents.

Perceptions of Candidates and Issues
People form general impressions on the basis of what they know about candidate qualifications, experience, and character. Challengers are judged primarily on their potential for office and incumbents on their performance in office. Even when incumbents are not running, their record usually affects their party's standard-bearer. Reagan's positive evaluations in 1988 helped Republican George H. W. Bush while George W. Bush's negative ones hurt Republican John McCain in 2008.[41]

Personal attributes, such as trustworthiness, integrity, empathy, and candor, may also be relevant, depending on the nature of the times. In the aftermath of a presidency besmirched by scandal or lacking in candor, integrity and honesty assume more importance than at other times when the problem has been weak or indecisive leadership.

Candidates' stands on the issues, unless misinformed, politically incorrect, or in other ways out of the mainstream, seem less critical than their partisan affiliation and leadership capabilities. To be important, issues must be salient. They must attract attention; they must hit home. Without personal impact, they are unlikely to be primary motivating factors for voting.

In addition, candidates must discuss a multitude of issues over the course of the election cycle. To the extent that their policy positions are not known or clearly indistinguishable from one another, voters tend to rely more on their partisanship and perceptions of their personal character in making a voting decision.

Ironically, that portion of the electorate that can be more easily persuaded, weak partisans and Independents, tends to have the least political information.[42] Conversely, the most committed also tend to be the most informed. They use their information to support their partisanship.

The relationship between partisan loyalties and political knowledge has significant implications for a democratic society. The traditional view of a democracy holds that information and awareness are necessary to make an enlightened voting decision. However, the finding that those who have the most information are also the most committed, and that those who lack this commitment also lack the incentive to get more information, has upset some of the assumptions about the motivation for acquiring information and using it to vote intelligently.

Do people think and vote rationally? According to political scientist Morris Fiorina, they do. In his study *Retrospective Voting in American National Elections* (1981), Fiorina used a rational choice model adopted from economics to argue that voting decisions are calculations people make on the basis of their accumulated political experience. They make these calculations by assessing the past performance of the parties and their elected officials in light of the promises they made, positions they took, and actions in office. Fiorina called this a retrospective judgment.[43]

Retrospective judgments are not only important for influencing voting in a given election, they are also important for shaping partisan attitudes, which Fiorina defined as "a running tally of retrospective evaluations of party promises and performance."[44] In other words, the running tally is a summary judgment of how well the parties and their leaders have done. Over time, that judgment can change, which in turn affects people's evaluations of the parties. How have these partisan attitudes evolved over the past several decades, and how have they impacted voting behavior?

SHIFTS IN PARTISANSHIP

When the first studies on voting behavior were published in the middle of the twentieth century, about three-fourths of the electorate identified with one of the major parties, half of them strongly (see Table 3.4). Both major parties were heterogeneous. Although they differed on economic and social issues, the divide was not as deep as it is today. The Democrats had been in the majority since the 1930s, and controlled government for the most of the period from 1932 to 1968. Much has changed in the political environment since then.

Television and the Internet have become primary communication links between candidates and the electorate. Public opinion polls are more accurate, dependable, and frequent, a major source of information for the candidates in tailoring and targeting their messages to voters.

Accompanying the communication revolution have been significant international and domestic developments. The war in Southeast Asia and the civil rights movement at home divided the country and hurt the Democrats, beginning in the mid 1960s. The Watergate scandal, culminating in President Nixon's resignation and his pardon by President Ford, adversely affected the Republicans in the 1970s. During this period, partisan intensity and identification declined. More people claimed to be Independents.

Elections became more candidate-oriented with candidate organizations competing with party committees for money, staff, and influence. More emphasis was placed on personal imagery with television used to project it. Media gurus began to replace grassroots organizers as key campaign staff.

Not only were campaigns more candidate-focused, but they also became more issue-oriented. Ideological differences between the parties began to emerge on social issues in the 1960s in addition to the economic ones that already existed. These divisions carried over into the 1980s.

In the short run, the Republicans benefited. Weakening support for the dominant party, the Democrats, and the greater emphasis put on personal qualifications and experience of the candidates allowed Republicans to run for office without hiding their political affiliation. The GOP's more conservative policies, and especially its opposition to preferential treatment for minorities, coincided with the views of many Americans, especially those living in the South. As the country prospered and the middle class grew, people became more conservative. They evidenced less sympathy for policies that trumpeted social, economic, and political reform, if not in theory, then in practice. They also became more leery of legislating social and economic policy.

The Democrats lost their status as the majority party by the end of the 1970s and their partisan plurality began to shrink in the mid-1980s. By the 1990s, the parties were at rough parity with one another. Although more people still identified themselves as Democrats, that advantage was offset by higher turnout by Republicans. The electorate was and remained at or near parity since then with economic conditions at home and international conflicts abroad affecting electoral outcomes.

Despite the shifts in partisan advantage and the growth in the proportion of the population that identifies itself as Independent (see Figure 3.1), partisan loyalties and leanings have remained a strong influence on voting behavior. If anything, that influence has increased as a consequence of the parties and their presidential candidates becoming more ideological.

As the partisan policy differences became clearer in the 1980s, two distinct governing philosophies emerged. The Republican blueprint, articulated by

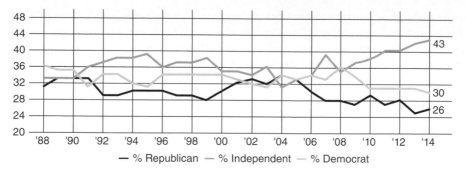

Based on multiple day polls conducted by telephone

FIGURE 3.1 | PARTY IDENTIFICATION (INCLUDING INDEPENDENT
LEANINGS) ANNUAL AVERAGES, GALLUP POLLS, 1988–2014

Source: Jeffrey M. Jones, "In U.S. New Record 43% Are Political Independents," Gallup Poll, January 7,
2015. http://www.gallup.com/poll/180440/new-record-political-independents.aspx

Ronald Reagan in his presidential campaigns and, Newt Gingrich in the
House Republican's "Contract with America" in 1994, President George W.
Bush, and Tea Party activists during the Obama administration, contends that
the national government has gotten too large, too expensive, and too invasive.
They believe that it should play a smaller and less regulatory role in the economic and social spheres while focusing more on domestic order and national
security issues. In contrast, the Democrats' position is that government is an
important instrument for addressing social and economic inequities and for
redistributing resources, for closing the gap between the rich and the poor.
The New Deal and Great Society programs of Franklin D. Roosevelt and
Lyndon B. Johnson embodied these beliefs. So did the legislative activism of
the first two years of the Obama administration, evident in the enactment of
the Recovery and Reinvestment Act, health care reform, and the Frank-Dodd
bill that increased regulation of the banking and investment industry.

The differences are less pronounced in foreign and national security policy. Democrats agreed with Republicans on the need for a strong defense during the Cold War. After the Cold War ended, the Democrats have been more
reluctant than Republicans to use military force although they have supported
the fight against domestic and international terrorism. In general, Democrats
place greater emphasis on diplomacy, international organizations, and multi-
lateral agreements in the conduct of U.S. foreign policy, whereas Republicans
have been more willing to act unilaterally and, if necessary, forcefully to promote American national interests.

These diverging domestic and foreign perspectives have contributed to
an aligning of partisan attitudes along ideological lines, with the Democrats
the more liberal party and the Republicans the more conservative. The
convergence of ideology and partisanship has made the two major parties
more internally cohesive and externally distinctive from one another.

Partisan cleavages within government have also become much more pronounced. There is more party-line voting in Congress, more partisan divisions

over judicial appointments, more strident partisan rhetoric, and less civility in government. The number of moderates elected to Congress has declined. Conservative Southern Democrats, who frequently sided with the Republicans on budget and tax matters, were replaced by even more conservative Republicans, while moderate Republicans, especially from the Northeast, who sided with the Democrats on some social issues, have been replaced by liberal Democrats.

Not only has political polarization deeply divided elected officials, but it has also divided the American electorate, although political scientists disagree on how deep and wide that division is. There are two schools of thought on this question. One, put forth by Professor Morris Fiorina and some of his colleagues at Stanford University, argues that the polarization is not nearly as extensive or as deep within the general population as it is among those in power.[45] The Fiorina School attributes the shift of public policy issues along ideological lines to elite sorting, to the diverse political choices the public faces. Put simply, candidates and elected officials are taking more divergent policy position from which the electorate has to choose.[46]

In contrast, the polarization school believes that the ideological divisions run deep within the body politic.[47] They point to the persistence of partisan voting patterns and partisan presidential evaluations since the end of the 1980s and the effectiveness of base-oriented campaign strategies since 2004 in maximizing the vote.[48] They also rely on empirical findings of recent surveys that the partisan gap on values and issues has doubled over the last 25 years.[49]

The debate over the degree of polarization in America has serious implications for politics and government. For the parties, it calls into question the extent to which they can accommodate the diversity of views and interests within the country as a whole. Can parties claim to be big tents, large enough to attract and welcome all those who choose to enter? At its core, the issue is the ability of the two-party system to sustain itself in an increasingly heterogeneous society.

For candidates, the dilemma is whether to moderate their policy views and appeal to those in the middle of the political spectrum by taking more centrist positions or direct their messages to core supporters who tend to be more ideological. With the most ideological partisans dominating the nomination processes of both major parties, candidates and elected officials tend to reflect the beliefs of the activists who supported them.

For those in government, the issue is pragmatic as well as representational. Should elected officials compromise or adhere to their partisan political beliefs? Should they represent the views of the body politic or the people that voted for them? In 2008, Barack Obama campaigned on changing politics as usual, reducing the strident ideological rhetoric, and finding common ground, but he found it difficult to achieve these goals as president.

In summary, partisan orientation remains a strong influence on how people evaluate candidates and issues, on how they vote and how they assess government. Table 3.4 indicates partisan preferences of the American people since 1952 and Figure 3.1 graphs the proportion of the population identifying as Republican, Democratic, and Independent since 1988.

Table 3.4 | Party Identification, 1952–2012 (in Percentages)

Party Identification	1952	1956	1960	1964	1968	1972	1976	1980	1984	1988	1992	1996	2000	2004	2008	2012
Strong Democrat	23	22	21	27	20	15	15	18	17	18	18	18	19	17	19	20
Weak Democrat	26	24	26	25	26	25	25	23	20	18	17	19	15	16	15	13
Independent Democrat	10	7	6	9	10	11	12	11	11	12	14	14	15	17	17	16
Independent Independent	5	9	10	8	11	15	16	15	13	12	13	10	13	10	11	10
Independent Republican	8	9	7	6	9	10	10	10	12	13	12	12	13	12	12	17
Weak Republican	14	15	14	14	15	13	14	14	15	14	14	15	12	12	13	11
Strong Republican	14	16	16	11	10	10	9	9	12	14	11	12	12	16	13	13
N	1689	1690	1864	1536	1531	2695	2833	1612	2228	2026	2473	1706	1790	1194	2293	2039

QUESTION TEXT:

"Generally speaking, do you usually think of yourself as a Republican, a Democrat, an Independent, or what?" (IF REPUBLICAN OR DEMOCRAT) "Would you call yourself a strong (REPUBLICAN/DEMOCRAT) or a not very strong (REPUBLICAN/DEMOCRAT)?" (IF INDEPENDENT, OTHER [1966 and later: OR NO PREFERENCE]) "Do you think of yourself as closer to the Republican or Democratic party?"

Sources: "The ANES Guide to Public Opinion and Electoral Behavior," American National Election Studies. http://electionstudies.org/nesguide/toptable/tab2a_1.htm; updated from ANES 2012 Preelection data by author.

THE SOCIAL BASIS OF POLITICS

Attitudes and opinions are also influenced by the associations people have with others and by the groups with which they are affiliated.[50]

Although more attention has been given to the effect of partisanship on voting since the publication of *The American Voter* in 1960, recent studies by political scientists also indicate that the social context in which elections occur matters. Intermediaries between the candidates and voters—individuals, media, and groups—provide information that contributes to voters' decisions. Communicating information and conveying enthusiasm about candidates, parties, and issues informs and energizes the electorate; it brings into the electoral arena people who might otherwise have avoided it.[51]

As we have emphasized in this chapter, personal contact is important in turning out voters. Politicians have believed this proposition for a long time, and more recently experimental and field research by political scientists Donald P. Green and Alan Gerber has confirmed it. ". . . as a rule of thumb," they write, "one additional vote is produced for every fourteen people who are successfully contacted by canvassers."[52]

We now turn to these intermediaries and their influences on voting behavior, specifically to the demographic and social groups that are part of the major parties' electoral coalitions. Three primary factors, the group's size, cohesiveness, and voting orientation, affect its impact on the party's electoral base.

THE NEW DEAL REALIGNMENT

Political coalitions form during periods of partisan realignment. The last time a classic realignment occurred was in the 1930s. Largely as a consequence of the Great Depression, the Democrats emerged as the dominant party.[53] Their electoral coalition, held together by a common belief that the government should play a more active role in addressing the nation's economic problems, supported Franklin Roosevelt's New Deal program. Those in more dire economic circumstances generally subscribed to this view; they had few other options. On the other hand, many of the owners and executives of still solvent businesses saw government intervention in the private sector as a threat to the capitalist system. They opposed much of Roosevelt's domestic legislation and remained Republican in attitude and vote.

The Democrats became the majority party during this period by expanding their base. Since the Civil War and the withdrawal of federal troops, the Democrats had enjoyed solid support in the South. White Protestants living in rural areas dominated the southern electorate; African Americans were largely excluded. Only in the election of 1928 when Al Smith, the Catholic governor of New York, ran as the Democratic candidate was there a sizable southern vote for a Republican presidential candidate. As a Catholic and an opponent of prohibition, Smith was unacceptable to many southern, white Protestants.

Catholics, living primarily in the urban centers of the North, became an increasingly important component of the Democrats' electoral coalition in the 1930s. Facing difficult economic circumstances, social discrimination, and, for many, language barriers, Catholic immigrants turned to big-city bosses for help; in return, they were expected to support the boss and the candidates that his organization ran for office. In 1928, for the first time, a majority of voters living in cities voted Democratic, and for Al Smith for president.

The harsh economic realities of the Great Depression enabled Roosevelt to expand his Democratic base even further, especially among people in the lower socioeconomic strata. Outside the South, Roosevelt's political coalition was differentiated along class lines. It attracted people with less education and income and those who were unemployed, underemployed, or had lower-paying jobs. Organized labor, in particular, became reliably Democratic.

In addition to establishing a broad-based, blue-collar, working-class coalition, Roosevelt also lured specific racial and ethnic groups, such as African Americans and Jewish Americans, from their former Republican roots. African Americans who lived outside of the South voted increasingly Democratic for economic reasons, whereas Jewish Americans supported Roosevelt's liberal domestic programs and his anti-Nazi foreign policy. Neither of these groups provided the Democratic Party of the 1930s with a large number of votes, but their long-term allegiances have given the party a secure and dependable core of voters.

In contrast, during the same period, the Republican Party shrank. Not only were Republicans unable to attract new groups, they were unable to prevent the defection of people whose economic plight made Democratic policies more appealing as well. Although the Republicans did retain the backing of the business and professional classes, which grew after World War II, their working-class base eroded. Republican strength remained concentrated in the Northeast.

EVOLVING POLITICAL COALITIONS: 1950S–1970S

The coalitions that were restructured during the 1930s and 1940s held together for another twenty years. During this period, African Americans and Jewish Americans increased their identification with and support of the Democratic Party and its candidates. Although Catholics, for the most part, stayed Democratic, their vote fluctuated more at the presidential level, reaching its highest level in 1960 when the first Catholic president, John F. Kennedy, was elected.

Protestants remained Republican with the exception of less-educated, lower-income fundamentalist and evangelical groups that voted Democratic, largely for economic reasons. Concentrated in the South and the states that border it, these fundamentalist and evangelical Christians overwhelmingly supported Jimmy Carter, a born-again Christian, in 1976.

Prior to the 1980s, there were no major partisan distinctions in gender preferences although some cleavages among different age cohorts were evident. Younger voters, attracted by the liberal policies of Democratic candidates and older Americans who had benefited from these policies, particularly Social Security, backed the Democrats during this decade, while newly affluent, more conservative voters became increasingly Republican.

Socioeconomic Shifts

The changes that did take place in the 1950s and early 1960s emanated primarily from the growth of a larger and more populous middle class and its movement from the cities to the suburbs. In the short run, the nation's postwar prosperity did not result in a complete partisan realignment. People who gained in economic and social status did not, as a general rule, discard their partisan loyalties unless and until they objected to some of the social changes that were occurring during this period: democratically initiated civil rights legislation followed by affirmative action policies, Supreme Court decisions on abortion and school prayer, and the movement by feminists for greater equality in the workplace. Over time, however, rising economic prosperity made the Republicans' policy positions more attractive to a growing middle class. Coincidentally, the Democrats' labor base began to shrink. In 1952, organized labor represented about 25 percent of the American electorate. Today, it constitutes less than half that amount.

Regional Shifts

More dramatic than this economic erosion of the Democrats' electoral coalition has been the defection of Southerners, a group that had been solidly Democratic since the end of the Civil War. The political attitudes and partisan allegiances of whites in the South began to change as a consequence of the Democratic Party's support of civil rights. Harry Truman's order to integrate the military and his backing of the 1948 Democratic Convention platform's civil rights plank led to a walkout of southern delegates at the party's nominating convention, the third-party candidacy of Strom Thurmond, and a decline in the Democratic presidential vote in the South. In 1948, Harry Truman won 52 percent of the southern vote, compared with Roosevelt's 69 percent four years earlier. Although Adlai Stevenson and John Kennedy carried the South by reduced margins, the southern white Protestant vote for president went Republican for the first time in 1960 and has continued, for the most part, to do so since then.

The enfranchisement of African Americans in the South following the enactment of the Voting Rights Act of 1965, however, has made the southern vote less homogeneous. During this period, the Republicans also gained strength in the Southwest with the movement of population to this area of the country; in contrast, the coastal areas in the Northeast and on the Pacific Coast were becoming more Democratic.

CONTEMPORARY ELECTORAL COALITIONS

The 1980s saw the end of Democratic dominance and the growth of the Republican Party to near parity with the Democrats.

The Republicans

President Ronald Reagan gave voice and structure to a rejuvenated conservative Republican coalition that included southern whites, Protestant fundamentalists and evangelicals, and other economic and national security conservatives. The coalition, disproportionately white and male, has aged. The women who tend to be part of the coalition are also older and married.

Since the 1980s, southern whites have continued to shift their political allegiances from the Democrats to the GOP. In fact, the South has been the most Republican area of the country, more apt to vote for the Republican presidential nominee than any other region. In the 1994 midterm elections, Republican congressional candidates won a majority of the southern vote for the first time since Reconstruction. In subsequent elections, the Republicans enlarged their congressional southern majority. And even though the Democrats ran two southern candidates in 1992 and 1996 (Bill Clinton and Al Gore), the white vote in the South remained Republican. Barack Obama did make inroads in the South—he won the electoral vote of three southern states (Florida, North Carolina, and Virginia) in 2008 and two of them (Florida and Virginia) in 2012

Beginning in the 1980s, Protestant fundamentalists and evangelical Christians shifted their political allegiances to the Republican Party, largely because of that party's position on social issues. Mainline Protestants remained Republican but have not been as supportive of Republican candidates as their fundamentalist and evangelical brethren. This "traditionalist–modernist" distinction within the Protestant religious community extends to other religion groups. In general, people who have the greatest involvement in religious activities, who attend church services regularly, and who subscribe to more literal readings and interpretations of the Bible are more likely to vote Republican than those whose theological views are more nuanced, who are less engaged in church-related activities, and who attend services less often.[54]

The sectarian–secular divide, evident for the past three decades, is applicable to white America. It does not extend to racial minority groups whose loyalties to the Democrats are more deeply rooted in that party's economic and social policy positions than they are in its attitude toward religious values and practices.

In summary, the Republican electoral coalition has become whiter, older, more rural, more male, more religious, and more conservative. The party has become more homogeneous and its geographic base more insular. Republicans have maintained their support in the South and most of the Rocky Mountain states but not in the Northeast, the Pacific Coast, and those states in which the Hispanic population has grown most rapidly.

The Democrats

The Democrats' electoral coalition has frayed from its New Deal days. No longer a majority of the electorate, their base remains more diverse than the Republicans'. The party receives about 40 percent of its support from ethnic and racial minorities. Women, younger people, and secularists constitute core constituencies. Democrats still receive overwhelming support from those with the lowest incomes and those who live in the cities. However, the relatively small size of the latter two groups within the electorate makes them a less important voting bloc than they used to be.

The Democratic electoral coalition has retained and even increased its support among African Americans and Hispanics. Today, at least 90 percent of African Americans consider themselves Democrats compared to the late 1950s when only about 75 percent did.[55] With their increased loyalty to the Democrats and their election turnout now equal or higher than whites,[56] African Americans have become a larger and more important component in the Democrats' core constituency, contributing between 20 and 25 percent of the party's total vote. Hispanic voters have become another increasingly important component of the Democrats' electoral coalition with a large majority identifying or leaning in a Democratic direction.[57]

Women, particularly younger, unmarried women, have also become more Democratic as have younger voters. The latter's support for Democrats has long-term implications since partisan attitudes tend to hard over time.

Regionally, the Northeast has become more Democratic but not primarily as a consequence of population movement. The Republican Party's increasing ideological rigidity, particularly its social agenda, has alienated some of old-line moderate Republicans from this area. New Hampshire, the last bastion of GOP strength, went Democratic at the presidential level in 2004 and has stayed that way since then. The mid-Atlantic and Pacific Coast states have also remained Democratic. Competition between the parties tends to be greatest in the Midwest and parts of the South and southwest, particularly in states in which Hispanic population has been expanding.

The movement of Protestant fundamentalists to the Republican Party has left the Democrats with a more secular base. With the exception of the Jewish community, which has retained its allegiances to the party, Muslims and other non-Christians, and Hispanic Catholics, the party lacks the strong religious support it had in past.[58]

Democratic voting trends are also evident on the basis of gender and sexual orientation. With more women in the electorate, the gender gap has probably helped Democrats more than the Republicans as has the support of homosexuals and lesbians (although a relatively small percentage of voters, about 4 to 5 percent of those surveyed in public opinion polls, admit to being gay).

In summary, the Democrats have become a party of racial, ethnic, and religious minorities; women, particularly unmarried women; those in the younger-aged groups; people who are most and least educated; and those living in metropolitan areas, primarily on the East and West coasts, and in areas in which minority groups, are concentrated. Gallup Poll data on group voting patterns in the presidential election since 2000 are presented in Table 3.5.

What conclusions can we draw about the social basis of politics today? It is clear that the old party coalitions have evolved. The class divisions evident during the New Deal era have faded, although income, and to a lesser extent education levels continue to distinguish partisan voting behavior, as do race, gender, gender orientation, and religion and religious activity. Population shifts are also affecting partisan voting patterns and the Electoral College map.

TABLE 3.5 | VOTE BY GROUPS IN PRESIDENTIAL ELECTIONS, 2000–2012 (IN PERCENTAGES)

	2000			2004		2008		2012	
	Gore 48.7	Bush 48.6	Nader 2.7	Kerry 48.5	Bush 51.5	Obama 53.0	McCain 46.0	Obama 52.0	Romney 48
National									
Sex									
Men	45	52	3	44	56	50	50	47	53
Women	53	45	2	52	48	57	43	57	43
Race									
White (incl. Hispanics)	43	55	3	44	56	45	55	44	56
Nonwhite	87	9	4	83	17	90	10	89	11
Non-Hispanic white	42	56	2	43	57	44	56	43	57
Nonwhite (incl. Hispanics)	80	17	3	78	22	86	14	82	18
Black	95	3	2	93	7	99	1	95	5
Age									
Under 30 years	47	47	6	60	40	61	39	62	38
30–49 years	45	53	2	43	57	53	47	53	47
50–64 years old	50	48	2	48	52	54	46	50	50
65 years and older	56	42	2	52	48	46	54	46	54

continued

TABLE 3.5 | VOTE BY GROUPS IN PRESIDENTIAL ELECTIONS, 2000–2012 (IN PERCENTAGES) *continued*

	2000			2004		2008		2012	
	Gore	Bush	Nader	Kerry	Bush	Obama	McCain	Obama	Romney
Education									
Grade school	55	42	3	69	31	67	33	48	52
High school	52	46	2	54	46	47	53	54	45
College	46	51	3	48	52	55	45	53	47
Postgraduate	53	43	4	53	47	65	35	62	38
Region									
East	55	42	3	58	42	57	43	63	37
Midwest	48	49	3	48	52	53	47	51	49
South	45	54	1	43	57	50	50	47	53
West	48	47	5	48	52	55	45	50	50
Politics									
Republicans	7	92	1	5	95	7	93	3	97
Democrats	89	10	2	93	7	93	7	95	5
Independents	44	49	7	52	48	51	49	53	47
Ideology									
Conservative	27	71	2	20	80	23	77	18	82
Moderate	57	41	2	63	37	63	37	67	33
Liberal	84	9	7	88	12	94	6	92	8

	2000			2004		2008		2012	
	Gore	Bush	Nader	Kerry	Bush	Obama	McCain	Obama	Romney
Protestants	42	55	3	38	62	47	53	45	55
Catholics	52	46	2	52	48	53	47	56	44
Attend weekly	41	56	2	37	63	45	55	40	60
Attend monthly	47	51	2	45	55	51	49	53	47
Seldom/never attend	52	41	7	50	40	62	38	63	37
Marital status									
Married	40	57	2	40	60	44	56	45	55
Not married	59	36	3	60	40	65	35	66	34
Married men	37	59	3	39	61	42	58	41	59
Married women	41	56	2	42	58	47	53	48	52
Unmarried men	49	42	5	55	45	63	37	60	40
Unmarried women	66	31	2	64	36	66	34	71	29
Labor union									
Union families	68	31	2	67	33	64	36	–	–

National figures are based on actual election outcomes, repercentaged to exclude minor third-party candidates.

Demographic data are based on Gallup Poll final preelection surveys, repercentaged to exclude "no opinions" and support for minor third-party candidates; results are then weighted to conform with actual election results.

Source: Gallup Poll, "Election Polls: Presidential Vote by Groups." http://www.gallup.com/poll/139880/Election-Polls-Vote-Groups-2012.aspx.

SUMMARY

The electorate is not neutral. People do not come to campaigns with completely open minds. Rather, they come with preexisting attitudes and accumulated experiences that color their perceptions and affect their judgments. Stimuli from the campaign tend to reinforce rather than challenge those attitudes and experiences.

Of the political beliefs people possess, partisanship has the strongest impact on turnout and voting behavior. It provides a perspective for evaluating the campaign and for deciding whether and how to vote. It is also a motive for being informed and getting involved.

Toward the end of the 1960s, there was a decline in the proportion of the population that identified with a political party. This decline, a product of disillusionment with both major parties, contributed to lower voter turnout. It also increased the importance of short-term factors on voting behavior. During this period, more people identified themselves as Independent; there was more candidate and issue voting; and, as a consequence, more split-ticket ballots.

The use of television as the primary channel through which candidates and parties communicated to the electorate, the weakening of the major parties' grassroots organizations, and the creation of separate candidate and party organizations required by the Federal Election Campaign Act all worked to reduce the influence of the parties on voting behavior. By the 1980s, however, that influence was strengthening again even though the proportion of the population identifying themselves as political partisans had declined.

Since the 1980s, the parties have also become more ideological, with the Republicans more conservative and the Democrats still liberal. Their diverse ideologies have divided the electorate and deeply divided the government. How wide and deep these divisions are within the body politic has been debatable, although the growth in the proportion of self-identified Independents suggests that many people may be "turned off" by the extreme beliefs and behavior of party leaders and elected officials.

Nonetheless, the parties remain close to electoral parity. That parity has been reflected in relatively close elections with frequent shifts in the control of the White House and Congress.

Group ties to the parties have shifted as well. The Democratic Party has lost the support of a majority of southern whites, non-Hispanic Catholics, and Protestant fundamentalists and evangelicals. The Democratic labor base shrunk as union laborers decline as a proportion of the population. Racial minorities, however, such as African Americans, Hispanics, and Asian Americans, have increased their loyalty to the Democrats, and Jewish Americans have retained theirs. Women have become much more supportive of Democratic candidates, as have people with secular views and younger voters. The party has improved its proportion of the vote in the Northeast, Pacific Coast, and more recently, the Southwest—the latter a result of Hispanic immigration.

The Republicans have made inroads among the growing middle- and upper-middle classes, older people who came of age after the New Deal, and people with sectarian beliefs that are the most active within their religious communities. The Republicans' emphasis on family and traditional values has attracted more support from married heterosexuals, white men, and older voters. In addition to the South, the GOP has maintained its support in most of the Mountain states and some of the Midwest.

The changes within the political environment have important implications for presidential politics. They have produced a more ideologically based party system, but they have also alienated moderate voters who find it difficult to identify with the policies and candidates of either major party. They have also produced a more divided government in which Republicans and Democrats find it difficult to work together, much less agree, on national public policy.

 # WHERE ON THE WEB?

- **Democratic National Committee**
  www.democrats.org
  > Provides information on Democratic Party history, rules, conventions, and campaigns with links to Democratic youth and state party affiliates.

- **Green Party**
  www.gp.org
  > Information on the Green Party, its rules, conventions, and candidates.

- **League of Women Voters**
  www.lwv.org
  > A nonpartisan organization, it provides information on candidates, their positions, and how to register and vote.

- **Reform Party**
  www.reformparty.org
  > Information on the Reform Party, its rules, conventions, and candidates.

- **Republican National Committee**
  www.rnc.org
  > Information on Republican Party history, rules, conventions, and campaigns with links to Republican youth and state party affiliates.

- **Rock-the-Vote**
  www.rockthevote.com
  > An organization whose goal is to encourage young people to register and vote by providing a registration form online, as well as details about how to obtain an absentee ballot.

- **Project Vote Smart**
  www.votesmart.org
  > An organization that provides a wealth of information on candidates and their issue positions and evaluates their performance in office.

EXERCISES

1. If you are a U.S. citizen, eighteen years of age or older, and haven't already done so, begin your registration process by accessing the Election Assistance Commission's web site at www.eac.gov and downloading the national voter registration form, completing it, and sending it to your state election officials. Alternately, access Rock-the-Vote at www.rockthevote.com and provide that organization with information to begin the registration process.

2. How can the differences between the voting-age population (VAP) and eligible voters (VEP) be reduced? Is higher turnout feasible? Is it desirable? Does higher turnout make for a more representative electorate, a more informed one, and greater legitimacy in the outcome? Would it produce a more or less effective government?

3. Go to the web sites of the candidates who are running for president in the next election to determine what they are doing to mobilize their supporters. On the basis of what you can determine from their web sites, which candidates seem to have the most comprehensive and creative turnout campaigns? Which of them do you think will be able to turn out the most supporters to vote?

4. Describe the composition of the major parties' electoral coalitions. On the basis of your description, locate interest groups that represent groups of supporters. Access the web sites of these groups and note what they have done or plan to do to mobilize their supporters in the election.

SELECTED READINGS

Abramowitz, Alan I. *The Disappearing Center: Engaged Citizens, Polarization, and American Democracy*. New Haven, CT: Yale University Press, 2010.

Abramson, Paul R., John H. Aldrich, and David W. Rohde. *Change and Continuity in the 2012 Elections*. Washington, DC: Sage/CQ Press, 2014.

Berinsky, Adam J. "The Perverse Consequences of Electoral Reform in the United States," *American Politics Research*, 33 (July 2005): 471–491.

Burnham, Walter D. "The Turnout Problem," in *Elections American Style*, A. James Reichley, ed. Washington, DC: Brookings Institution, 1987, 97–133.

Campbell, Angus, Philip E. Converse, Warren E. Miller, and Donald E. Stokes. *The American Voter*. New York: Wiley, 1960.

Fiorina, Morris, Samuel J. Abrams, and Jeremy C. Pope. *Culture War? The Myth of a Polarized America*. New York: Longman, 2006.

Gerber, Alan S., Donald P. Green, and Christopher W. Larimer. "Social Pressure and Voter Turnout: Evidence from a Large-Scale Field Experiment," *American Political Science Review*, 102 (Feb. 2008): 33–48.

Green, Donald P., and Alan S. Gerber. *Get Out the Vote! How to Increase Voter Turnout*. Washington, DC: Brookings Institution, 2004.

Green, Donald P., Bradley Palmquist, and Eric Schickler. *Partisan Hearts and Minds: Political Parties and the Social Identities of Voters*. New Haven, CT: Yale University Press, 2002.

Highton, Benjamin. "Voter Registration and Turnout in the United States," *Perspectives on Politics*, 2 (Sept. 2004): 507–515.

Holbrook, Thomas M., and Scott D. McClurg. "The Mobilization of Core Supporters: Campaigns, Turnout, and Electoral Composition in United States Presidential Campaigns," *American Journal of Political Science*, 49 (Oct. 2005): 689–703.

Keith, Bruce E., David B. Magleby, Candice Nelson, and Elizabeth Orr. *The Myth of the Independent Voter*. Berkeley: University of California Press, 1992.

Lewis-Beck, Michael S., William G. Jacoby, Helmut Norpoth, and Herbert F. Weisberg. *The American Voter Revisited*. Ann Arbor: University of Michigan Press, 2008.

Martinez, Michael D., and Jeff Gill. "The Effects of Turnout on Partisan Outcomes in U.S. Presidential Elections, 1960–2000," *Journal of Politics*, 67 (Nov. 2005): 1248–1274.

Nivola, Pietro S., and David W. Brady, eds. *Red and Blue Nation? Characteristics and Causes of America's Polarized Politics*. Washington, DC: Brookings Institution, 2006.

Patterson, Thomas E. *The Vanishing Voter*. New York: Knopf, 2002.

Stanley, Harold W., and Richard G. Niemi. "Partisanship, Party Coalitions, and Group Support, 1952–2004," *Presidential Studies Quarterly*, 36 (June 2006): 172–188.

Tate, Katherine. *From Protest to Politics: The New Black Voters in American Elections*. Cambridge, MA: Harvard University Press, 1994.

Wald, Kenneth D., and Allison Calhoun-Brown. *Religion and Politics in the United States*. 6th ed. Lanham, MD: Roman and Littlefield, 2011.

Wattenberg, Martin P. *The Decline of American Political Parties: 1952–1996*. Cambridge, MA: Harvard University Press, 1998.

NOTES

1. Michael P. McDonald, "2012 General Election Turnout Rates" (Updated September 3, 2014). www.electproject.org/2012g

2. "The Diversifying Electorate—Voting Rates by Race and Hispanic Origin in 2012 (and Other Recent Elections)," U.S. Census Bureau, May 2013. http://www .census.gov/prod/2013pubs/p20-568.pdf

3. Michael P. McDonald and Samuel L. Popkin, "The Myth of the Vanishing Voter," *American Political Science Review,* 95 (Dec. 2001), pp. 963–974; Samuel L. Popkin and Michael McDonald, "Turnout's Not as Bad as You Think," *The Washington Post,* (Nov. 5, 2000), pp. B1, B2; Michael P. McDonald, "The Return of the Voter: Voter Turnout in the 2008 Presidential Election," *The Forum,* 6, issue 4, article 4 (2008). www.bepress.com/forum/vol6/iss4/art4. See also Michael P. McDonald, "2012 General Election Turnout Rates" (Updated September 3, 2014). www.electproject.org/2012g

4. The gap between the voting-age population and the voting-eligible population has increased over the last fifty years. There are more immigrants, legal and illegal, in the United States today. There are also more people who are or have been incarcerated and as a consequence have lost their right to vote on a temporary or permanent basis. See Michael P. McDonald, "Up, Up and Away! Voter Participation in the 2004 Presidential Election," *The Forum, II* (Post Election) (2004). www.bepress.com/forum/vol2/iss4.; Michael P. McDonald, "The Return of the Voter," *The Forum* 6 (2008), pp. 1–10. See also Michael P. McDonald, "2008 General Election Turnout Rates" (Updated March 13, 2010); "2012 General Election Turnout Rates" (Updated September 3, 2014). www .electproject.org/2012g

5. Pollsters use screens, a set of questions that indicate past voting behavior, current feelings about the parties and candidates, and knowledge about voting procedures

and places. These screens are designed to differentiate people on the basis of their likelihood to vote. In 2012, several large commercial polling organizations, such as the Gallup Poll and Rasmussen Reports, wrongly predicted the outcome of the presidential election by basing their estimate on most "likely voters." The Obama organization expanded the number of less likely voters. Romney's own proprietary polls made the same mistake, prompting him to write a victory statement on election night, a statement that he never gave.

6. Although some states initially permitted all landowners to vote, including women, by 1807, every state limited voting to men. Michael X. Delli Carpini and Ester R. Fuchs, "The Year of the Woman: Candidates, Voters, and the 1992 Election," *Political Science Quarterly*, 108 (Spring 1993), p. 30.

7. Ronald P. Formisane, "Deferential-Participant Politics: The Early Republic's Political Culture, 1789," *American Political Science Review*, 68 (June 1974), pp. 473–487.

8. Delli Carpini and Fuchs, "The Year of the Woman," p. 30.

9. Despite these allegations, Walter Dean Burnham still maintains that the high turnout percentages were real, "not artifacts of either census error or universal ballot stuffing." (p. 117). Walter Dean Burnham, "The Turnout Problem," in A. James Reichley, ed., *Elections American Style* (Washington, DC: Brookings Institution, 1987), pp. 112–116.

10. Peter F. Nardulli, Jon K. Dalager, and Donald E. Greco, "Voter Turnout in U.S. Presidential Elections: An Historical View and Some Speculation," *PS: Political Science and Politics* (Sept. 1996), p. 480.

11. In the case of *Smith v. Allwright*, 321 U.S. 649 (1944), the Supreme Court declared the white primary to be unconstitutional. In its opinion, the Court rejected the argument that parties were private associations and thus could restrict participation in their selection process.

12. Wendy R. Weiser and Erik Opsal, "The State of Voting in 2014," Brennan Center for Justice, June 17, 2014. http://www.brennancenter.org/analysis/state-voting-2014

13. Ibid.

14. "Online Voter Registration," National Conference of State Legislatures, June 30, 2012. http://www.ncsl.org/research/elections-and-campaigns/electronic-or-online-voter-registration.aspx

15. "The Impact of the National Voter Registration Act of 1993 on the Administration of Elections for Federal Office, 2011–2012," Election Assistance Commission, June 30, 2013. www.eac.gov/assests/1/Documents/EAC_NVRA

16. Eric Plutzer, "Becoming a Habitual Voter: Inertia, Resources, and Growth in Young Adulthood," *American Political Science Review*, 96 (March 2002), pp. 41–56.

17. Angus Campbell, Philip E. Converse, Warren E. Miller, and Donald E. Stokes, *The American Voter* (New York: Wiley, 1960), p. 102.

18. Alan S. Gerber, Donald P. Green, and Christopher W. Larimer, "Social Pressures and Voter Turnout: Evidence from a Large-Scale Field Experiment," *American Political Science Review*, 102 (Feb. 2008), pp. 233–248.

19. Nicholas A. Valentine, Ted Brader, Eric W. Groenendyk, Krysha Gregorowicz, and Vincent L. Hutchings, "Election Night's Alright for Fighting: The Role of Emotions in Political Participation," *Journal of Politics*, 73 (Jan. 2011), pp. 156–170.

20. Raymond E. Wolfinger and Steven J. Rosenstone, *Who Votes?* (New Haven, CT: Yale University Press, 1980), pp. 13–26; Rachel Milstein Sondheimer and Donald P. Green, "Using Experiments to Estimate the Effects of Education on Voter Turnout," *American Journal of Political Science*, 54 (Jan. 2010), pp. 174–189.

21. Wolfinger and Rosenstone, *Who Votes?*; pp. 18–20, 35–36.
22. Estimates range from 16 to 19 percent for the decline in turnout if educational levels had not increased. Abramson, Aldrich, and Rohde, *Change and Continuity in 2008*, p. 103; Steven J. Rosenstone and John Mark Hansen, *Mobilization, Participation, and Democracy in America* (New York: Macmillan, 1993), pp. 214–215.
23. McDonald, *Up, Up and Away!* p. 2.
24. McDonald, "The Return of the Voter," *The Forum* 6 (2008), p. 1.
25. Juliet Lapidos, "Voter Turnout," *New York Times* (March 13, 2013). http://takingnote.blogs.nytimes.com/2013/03/13/voter-turnout/?_r=0&pagewanted=print.
26. "Low Marks for the 2012 Election: Voters Pessimistic About Partisan Cooperation," Pew Research Center for the People and the Press, November 11, 2012.http://www.people-press.org/2012/11/15/section-1-campaign-report-card/
27. A memo posted by the field directors of the Obama campaign claimed: "At the start of GOTV weekend, our volunteers have made 125,646,479 personal phone calls or door knocks that resulted in conversations with voters—not counting robo calls on auto-dialers, mail, literature drops or any other nonvolunteer, non-personal contacts." Sam Stein, "Obama Campaign: We've Contacted One Out of Every 2.5 People in the Country," *Huffington Post* (November 3, 2012). http://www.huffingtonpost.com/2012/11/03/obama-voter-contact_n_2069289.html
28. Brad T. Gomez, Thomas G. Hansford, and George A. Krause, "The Republicans Should Pray for Rain: Weather, Turnout, and Voting in U.S. Presidential Elections," *Journal of Politics*, 69 (Aug. 2007), pp. 649–663.
29. On the other hand, low turnout can also indicate a level of satisfaction since citizens are more likely to vote when they are angry than when they are content.
30. Another related factor is the increasing percentage of single people and single parents in the voting-age population over the past fifty years. For a variety of reasons, from time constraints to lower income levels, single adults do not turn out to vote as regularly as do married adults.
31. Michael D. Martinez and Jeff Gill, "The Effects of Turnout on Partisan Outcomes in U.S. Presidential Elections 1960–2000," *Journal of Politics*, 67 (Nov. 2005), pp. 1248–1274.
32. Actually, a small interview/reinterview survey was conducted in 1948, but the results were never published. In contrast to the emphasis on political attitudes of the large-scale interview projects in the 1950s, the project in 1948 had a sociological orientation.
33. Campbell, Converse, Miller, and Stokes, *The American Voter*.
34. John R. Alford, Carolyn L. Funk, and John R. Hibbing, "Are Political Orientations Genetically Transmitted?" *American Political Science Review*, 99 (May 2005), pp. 153–167.
35. J. H. Fowler and C. T. Dawes, "Two Genes Predict Voter Turnout," *Journal of Politics*, 70 (3):579–594.
36. Evan Charney and William English, "Genopolitics and the Science of Genetics," *American Political Science Review*, 107 (May 2013): 382–395.
37. In examining the concept of party identification, Michigan analysts have stressed two dimensions: direction and strength. Others, however, have criticized the Michigan model for overemphasizing party and underemphasizing other factors, such as social class, political ideology, and issue positions. For a thoughtful critique, see Jerrold G. Rusk, "The Michigan Election Studies: A Critical

Evaluation." Paper presented at the annual meeting of the American Political Science Association, New York (Sept. 3–6, 1981).

38. See Benjamin Highton and Cindy D. Kam, "The Long-Term Dynamics of Partisanship and Issue Orientations," *Journal of Politics*, 73 (Jan. 2011): 202–215.

39. Janet M. Box-Steffensmeier and Renee M. Smith, "The Dynamic of Aggregate Partisanship," *American Political Science Review* (Sept. 1996), pp. 567–580; Ronald B. Rapoport, "Partisanship Change in a Candidate-Centered Era," *Journal of Politics* (Feb. 1997), pp. 185–199.

40. Bruce E. Keith, David B. Magleby, Candice J. Nelson, Elizabeth Orr, Mark C. Westlye, and Raymond E. Wolfinger, *The Myth of the Independent Voter* (Berkeley University of California Press, 1992). See also Alan I. Abramowitz, "Setting the Record Straight: Correcting Myths About Independent Voters," Center for Politics, University of Virginia. http://www.centerforpolitics.org/crystalball/articles/aia2011070702/; Morris P. Fiorina, "If I Could Hold a Seminar for Political Journalists," *The Forum* 10 (4) (2013): 2–10.

41. Aware of the public's view of President Bush, McCain tried to distance himself from the administration by emphasizing that he was an independent thinker and a maverick; Obama's theme was also change.

42. Campbell, Converse, Miller, and Stokes, *The American Voter*, pp. 143, 547. Independents that lean in a partisan direction tend to be better informed than those who do not. These independent leaners have many of the characteristics of party identifiers, including loyalty to the party's candidates. They do not, however, identify themselves as Republicans or Democrats.

43. Morris P. Fiorina, *Retrospective Voting in American National Elections* (New Haven, CT: Yale University Press, 1981), pp. 65–83.

44. Ibid., p. 84.

45. Morris Fiorina, Samuel J. Abrams, and Jeremy C. Pope, *Culture War? The Myth of a Polarized America* (New York: Longman, 2006).

46. Morris P. Fiorina and Matthew S. Levendusky, "Disconnected: The Political Class versus the People," in Peitro S. Nivola and David W. Brady, eds., *Red and Blue Nation? Characteristics and Causes of America's Polarized Politics* (Washington, DC: Brookings Institution, 2006), pp. 49–71; pp. 95–111.

47. See Alan I. Abramowitz, "Disconnected or Joined at the Hip?" in Nivola and Brady, eds., *Red and Blue Nation?* pp. 72–85, and Gary C. Jacobson, "Comment," Ibid. pp. 85–95.

48. According to data in recent American National Election Studies, the level of participation in elections has increased. More people have given money; contacted more friends, neighbors, or acquaintances; attended rallies or other campaign events; and volunteered to work for candidates than in the past. The expansion of turnout in 2004 by both parties, and in 2008 by the Democrats, illustrates this increased activity. American National Election Studies. www.electionstudies.org/nesguide/gd-index.htm#6.

49. "Partisan Polarization Surges in Bush, Obama Years, Trends in American Values: 1987–2012." Pew Research Center for the People and the Press, June 4, 2012. http://www.people-press.org/files/legacy-pdf/06-04-12 Values Release.pdf; Jeffrey M. Jones, "Obama's Fifth Year Job Approval Ratings Among Most Polarized," Gallup Poll, January 23, 2012. http://www.gallup.com/poll/167006/obama-fifth-year-job-approval-ratings-among-polarized.aspx

50. That social influences can affect voting behavior is a theory first postulated by Paul F. Lazarsfeld, Bernard R. Berelson, and others who examined the sociology of electoral politics more than sixty years ago. Paul F. Lazarsfeld, Bernard R. Berelson, and Hazel Gaudet, *The People's Choice: How the Voter Makes Up His Mind in a Presidential Campaign* (New York: Columbia University Press, 1948); Bernard R. Berelson, Paul F. Lazarsfeld, and William N. McPhee, *Voting: A Study of Opinion Formation in a Presidential Campaign* (Chicago: University of Chicago Press, 1954).

51. Paul Allen Beck, Russell J. Dalton, Steven Greene, and Robert Huckfeldt, "The Social Calculus of Voting: Interpersonal, Media, and Organizational Influences on Presidential Choices," *American Political Science Review*, 96 (March 2002), pp. 67–69.

52. Donald P. Green and Alan S. Gerber, *Get Out the Vote; How to Increase Voter Turnout* (Washington, DC: Brookings Institution, 2004), p. 34.

53. This description of the New Deal realignment is based primarily on the discussion in Everett Carll Ladd, Jr., with Charles D. Hadley, *Transformations of the American Party System* (New York: Norton, 1975), pp. 31–87.

54. David Leege C. and Lyman A. Kellstedt, eds., *Rediscovering the Religious Factor in American Politics* (Armonk, NY: M. E. Sharpe. 1993); John C. Green, "The American Religious Landscape and Political Attitudes: A Baseline for 2004," Ray C. Bliss Institute of Applied Politics, University of Akron. www.uakron.edu /bliss/docs/Religious_Landscape_2004.pdf. Lauren E. Smith and Lee Demetrius Walker, "Belonging, Believing, and Group Behavior: Religiosity and Voting in American Presidential Elections," *Political Research Quarterly*, 66 (May 2012). http://prq.sagepub.com/content/66/2/399.

55. Andrew Dugan, "Democrats Enjoy 2–1 Advantage over GOP among Hispanics," Gallup Poll, February 25, 2013. www.gallup.com/poll/160706/democrats-enjoy-advanatge-gop-among-hispanics.aspx?version=print

56. The turnout of African Americans was actually higher than white turnout in 2008 and 2012.

57. Dugan, "Democrats Enjoy Advantage." www.gallup.com/poll/160706/democrats-enjoy-advanatge-gop-among-hispanics.aspx?version=print

58. Jeffrey M. Jones, "U.S. Muslims Most Approving of Obama, Mormons Least," Gallup Poll, July 11, 2014. http://www.gallup.com/poll/172442/muslims -approving-obama-mormons-least.aspx

THE NOMINATION

PART II

Stephen J. Wayne

95

4

PARTY RULES AND THEIR IMPACT: THE LEGAL ENVIRONMENT

INTRODUCTION

Presidential nominees are selected by the delegates who attend their party's national nominating convention. The manner in which these delegates are chosen, however, influences the choice of nominees and also affects the influence of the state and its party leaders.

State law determines the procedures for delegate selection. Today, these procedures also have to conform to the general guidelines and rules established by the national parties. Prior to the 1970s, they did not. Under the old system, statutes passed by a state legislature reflected the needs and desires of state party leaders. Naturally, these laws were designed to buttress that leadership and extend its clout. Although primary elections were held, many of them were advisory; the actual selection of the delegates was left to caucuses, conventions, or committees, which were more easily controlled by party officials. The selection of favorite-son candidates, tapped by state party leaders, prevented meaningful contests in many states. There were also impediments to delegates getting on the ballot: high fees, lengthy petitions, and early filing dates. Winner-take-all provisions gave a great advantage to candidates backed by the party organization, as did rules requiring delegates to vote as a unit.

Popular participation in the selection of convention delegates has been a relatively recent phenomenon in the history of national nominating conventions. It began in the 1970s when the Democratic Party adopted a series of reforms that affected the period during which delegates could be selected, the procedures for choosing them, and ultimately their actions at the party's national nominating convention. Although these Democratic rules limited the states' discretion, they did not result in uniform voting practices in primaries and caucuses. Considerable variation still exists in how delegates are chosen, how the vote is apportioned, and who participates in the selection.

This chapter explores these rules and their consequences for the nomination process. It is organized into three sections: the first section details the changes in party rules, the second section considers the legal challenges to those rules and the Supreme Court's decisions on them, and the third section examines the impact of the rules changes on the parties, their leaders, and their electorates.

REFORMING THE NOMINATION PROCESS: DEMOCRATIC RULE CHANGES

The catalyst for the changes in the delegate selection rules was the tumultuous Democratic convention of 1968, a convention in which Senator Hubert Humphrey won the nomination without actively campaigning in the party's primaries. Yet the primaries of that year were very important. They had become the vehicle by which Democrats could protest the Johnson administration's conduct of the war in Vietnam. Senator Eugene McCarthy, the first of the antiwar candidates, had challenged Lyndon Johnson in the New Hampshire primary. To the surprise of many political observers, McCarthy received 42.4 percent of the vote, almost as much as the president, who got 49.5 percent.[1]

Four days after McCarthy's unexpectedly strong showing, Senator Robert Kennedy, brother of the late president and a political rival of Johnson, declared his candidacy for the nation's highest office. With protests against the war mounting across the country and divisions within the Democratic Party intensifying, Johnson bowed out, declaring that he did not want the nation's involvement in Southeast Asia to become a divisive political issue.

Johnson's withdrawal cleared the way for Hubert Humphrey, the vice president, to run. Humphrey, however, waited almost a month to announce his candidacy. His late entrance into the Democratic nomination process intentionally precluded a primary campaign since filing deadlines had expired in most of the states. Like Johnson, Humphrey did not want to become the focal point of antiwar opposition, nor did he have a grassroots organization to match McCarthy's and Kennedy's. What he did have was the support of most national and state Democratic leaders, including the president.

The last big-state primary in 1968 was California's. In it, Kennedy scored a significant win, but during the celebration that followed, he was assassinated. His death left McCarthy as the principal anti-establishment, antiwar candidate, but he was far short of a convention majority. Despite the last-minute entrance of Senator George McGovern, who hoped to rally Kennedy delegates to his candidacy, Humphrey easily won the nomination.

To make matters worse for those who opposed Humphrey and the administration's war efforts, an amendment to the party platform calling for an unconditional end to the bombing of North Vietnam was defeated. McCarthy and Kennedy delegates felt victimized by the nomination process and the resulting Humphrey victory. They were angry.

Compounding the divisions within the convention were demonstrations outside of it. Thousands of youthful protesters, calling for an end to the war, congregated in the streets of Chicago. To maintain order, the police, under direction from Mayor Richard Daley, used strong-arm tactics to disperse the crowds. Clashes between police and protesters followed. Television news crews filmed these confrontations, and the networks showed them during their convention coverage. The spectacle of police beating demonstrators further inflamed emotions and led to calls for party reform, not only from those who attended the convention but also from those who watched it on television.

To try to unify a divided party, Humphrey and his supporters agreed to the demands of dissident delegates to establish a commission to study procedures for electing and seating convention delegates and to propose ways of improving the selection process. Initially chaired by Senator George McGovern, the commission recommended a series of reforms aimed at encouraging greater rank-and-file participation during the nomination stage and the selection of convention delegates who were more representative of the party's electorate. They also desired the process to be timely, to occur in the year of the general election, and to be accessible to a wider range of candidates.

To achieve these objectives, the commission proposed that delegate selection be a *fair reflection* of Democratic sentiment within the state and, implicitly, less closely tied to the wishes of state party leaders. Rules were approved by the party to make it easier for individuals to run as delegates, to limit the size of the districts from which they could be chosen, and to require that the number of delegates elected be proportional to the popular vote that they, or the candidates to whom they were pledged, received. A requirement that delegates be chosen no earlier than the calendar year of the election was also established.

Additionally, Democrats tried to prevent Independents, and especially partisans of other parties, from participating in the selection of Democratic delegates. The difficulty, however, was to determine who was a Democrat since some states did not require or even permit registration by party. When implementing this rule, the national party adopted a very broad interpretation of partisan affiliation. People that identified themselves as Democrats at the time of voting, or those requesting Democratic ballots, were considered to be Democrats for the purpose of participating in the primaries. Self-identification by voters allowed Republicans and Independents to cross over and vote in the Democratic primaries in some states. The only primaries that the Democratic rules effectively prohibited were those that were open, primaries in which voters were given the ballots of both major parties, told to discard one and vote on the other.

In addition to translating public preferences into delegate selection, another major objective of the reforms was to improve representation of the party's rank and file in the delegations themselves. Three groups in particular—African Americans, women, and people under thirty—had protested their underrepresentation on party councils and at the nominating conventions. Their representatives and others sympathetic to their plight pressed the party for greater equity. The reform commission reacted to these pressures by proposing a rule requiring that all states represent these particular groups in reasonable relationship to their presence in the state's population. Failure to do so was viewed as *prima facie* evidence of discrimination. In point of fact, the party had established quotas. Considerable opposition developed to the application of this rule during the 1972 nomination process, and it was subsequently modified to require only that states implement affirmative action plans for groups that had been subject to past discrimination.[2]

Still another goal of the reforms, to involve more Democrats in the selection process, was achieved not only by the fair reflection rule but also by making primaries the preferred method of delegate selection. To avoid a challenge to the composition of their delegation, many states switched to primary elections.

Caucuses in which party regulars selected the delegates were still permitted, but they, too, were redesigned to encourage more rank-and-file involvement. No longer could state party leaders vote a large number of proxies for the delegates of their choice. Caucuses had to be publicly announced with adequate time given for campaigning. Moreover, they had to be conducted in stages, and three-fourths of the delegates had to be chosen in districts no larger than those for members of Congress.

The rules changes, which were approved by the Democratic National Committee, achieved some of these initial objectives. Turnout increased; representation of the Democratic electorate at the party's convention improved; more candidates sought the nomination; and two candidates not associated with the national Democratic Party leadership, George McGovern (1972) and Jimmy Carter (1976), won their party's nomination.

Problems remained, however. Rank-and-file participation in the primaries was not as large as anticipated; the states that held their contest early received disproportionate attention from the candidates and news media, had higher turnouts, and exercised more influence on the selection of the nominee. It took longer than in the past to determine a winner, which, in turn, extended divisions within the party that became harder to heal for the general election. The amount of money needed to run for the nomination increased substantially. In addition, tensions emerged between the winning candidate and the national party organization on policy priorities, staffing, and financial needs.

Finally, and most importantly, even though the Democrats constituted a partisan plurality in the 1970s, they lost two of three presidential elections by large amounts after the reforms were implemented and had difficulty governing when they were in power from 1977 through 1980. From the perspective of the party leadership, the new delegate selection rules needed to be modified.

There were three principal problems: the disproportionate influence of the early states, the continuing representation inequality at the national conventions, and the decreasing clout of party leaders over the selection of the nominee.

FIXING THE CALENDAR

The nomination calendar was becoming front-loaded. The attention given to the states that held their contests early by the candidates and the press created incentives for other states to schedule their primary or caucus toward the beginning of the nomination period. In 1996, almost two-thirds of all the Democratic convention delegates were chosen by the end of March; in 2000 and 2004, two-thirds were chosen by mid-March; in 2008, almost 60 percent were chosen by the first Tuesday in February although the process did not end until June when the last state delegates were chosen.

From the party's perspective, front-loading was undesirable for several reasons. Some states separated their presidential primary from the primaries for other state-wide and national offices, thereby increasing election costs and potentially damaging party unity.

Partisan learning suffered. The sequential nature of the nomination process facilitates information acquisition more than a compressed process does. In recent nominations, by the time people turn their attention to the presidential nomination campaign, the field of candidates has been narrowed and much of the issue debate has already occurred. Moreover, once a front-runner emerges with a sizable delegate lead, turnout declines, thereby reducing the proportion of partisans who have a voice and vote in the selection of the party's standard-bearer.

A front-loaded nomination process reinforces and magnifies resource inequality among the candidates. It gives those candidates who have the most money a strategic advantage. They can wage media-oriented, multistate campaigns, while others, less well known and funded, have to focus on a few early states. And even if these non-front-runners are successful, they have less time to take advantage of their good fortune to raise additional funds in a highly compressed nomination calendar. In addition, the front-loaded calendar forces all candidates to begin running a year or two before the nomination in order to raise the money and gain the visibility they need to compete.

To gain greater involvement of rank-and-file partisans, achieve better representation of all groups within the party, and provide more opportunities for a larger field of candidates, the Democrats have tried to impose a "window" during which primaries and caucuses could be held; they also instituted a bonus delegate system to reward states that schedule their caucuses and primaries later in the spring.

Initially, the Democrats allowed states to hold their presidential nominations from the second Tuesday in March to the second Tuesday in June. In 2008, they began a month earlier but have since reverted to the first Tuesday in March.

What to do with those states, such as Iowa and New Hampshire, whose laws require them to start earlier than others, has been a perennial issue.[3] Conceding that its national party could not conduct the selection process in these states, the Democrats decided that the best they could do was grant Iowa and New Hampshire exceptions to its calendar. Naturally, Democrats in other states complained, noting that Iowa and New Hampshire were not representative of African Americans and Hispanics that comprised much of the party's electoral base. To improve these groups' representation, the party also granted calendar exceptions to Nevada to hold its caucus after Iowa's and South Carolina to hold its primary after New Hampshire's.

When Michigan and Florida also scheduled their primaries before the official beginning of the Democrats' calendar in 2008, the party pressured candidates for the nomination not to campaign in these states and initially indicated that they would not seat delegates chosen in elections that violated party rules. After the nomination was decided, however, the party recanted, giving Michigan and Florida half their allocated delegates. Both states were deemed critical in the general election.

In addition to imposing sanctions, the party also tried to encourage states to hold their nomination contests later by offering them more convention delegates if they did so—the later the date, the more delegates they would receive.[4] However, only a small number of states have taken advantage of this opportunity for additional delegates.

Beginning in 2012, the Democratic National Committee has established its official nomination calendar from the first Tuesday in March to the second Tuesday in June with exceptions given to Iowa, New Hampshire, Nevada, and South Carolina to hold their contests earlier.

IMPROVING REPRESENTATION

A second problem concerns the fair reflection principle and its application. The formulas states initially used in converting the popular vote into delegate votes did not always reflect the wishes of most partisan voters, in part because state officials feared that straight proportionality would reduce their collective influence on the outcome of the state primary.

The issue of proportionality came to a head in the 1980s when Democratic front-runners, Walter Mondale (1984) and Michael Dukakis (1988), each received a larger proportion of the delegates than the popular vote. Jesse Jackson, another candidate in those elections, in contrast, won less than his popular support would have merited. Jackson's complaints led the national party to impose strict proportionality in applying the fair reflection rule. Today, candidates receive delegates in proportion to the vote they receive, provided they get at least 15 percent of the total. This percentage, referred to as a *threshold*, is designed to discourage frivolous candidates from running and keeping the party divided for an extended period.

Democratic rules also specify that no more than 25 percent of the delegates can be selected on a state-wide basis. The rest are chosen in districts that can be no larger than congressional districts. The allocation of at-large and district delegates is based on the population and the Democratic vote in the last three presidential elections. This allocation formula advantages the most Democratic areas, which tend to be districts with large proportions of minority voters. Barack Obama designed a strategy in 2008 to take advantage of higher concentrations of Democratic delegates in urban districts that increased the number of convention delegates he eventually won.

Another representational problem with which the Democrats had to contend initially was the selection of more men than women as delegates.

BOX 4.1 | THE IOWA CAUCUS: HOW IT WORKS

STAGES

Step 1 Caucuses are held in about 1,700 precincts within the state to choose approximately 2,500 delegates to 99 county conventions.

Step 2 One month later, conventions are held in counties to elect delegates to the five congressional district conventions.

Step 3 Conventions are held in congressional districts to elect district-level delegates to national party conventions. The same delegates also attend the state convention.

Step 4 State conventions elect at-large delegates to the national party convention.

Democrats also designate their state party and elected official delegates.

PROCEDURES FOR THE FIRST-ROUND PRECINCT CAUCUSES

Democrats   Only registered Democrats who live in the precinct and can vote may participate. Attendees are asked to join preference groups for candidates. A group must consist of at least 15 percent of those present to be viable. Nonviable groups are dissolved, and people in these groups are free to join other viable groups. Much lobbying occurs at this stage of the meeting. Delegates are allocated to candidates strictly on the basis of each group's proportion to the caucus as a whole.

Republicans   Attendees, who must be eligible to vote but do not have to be registered as Republicans—they can register at the caucus—cast a presidential preference vote by secret ballot, which is tabulated on a state-wide basis. Delegates to the county conventions are then selected by whatever method the caucus chooses—either by direct election or proportionally on the basis of a straw vote.

To rectify the balance and achieve gender equality, the Democrats now require the elected delegates to consist of equal proportions of men and women. This requirement forces the candidates to choose approximately the same number of men and women for their slates of pledged delegates.

Despite the changes designed to reflect more accurately partisan voting preferences during the nomination process, inequities still exist. Hillary Rodham Clinton received a higher proportion of the popular vote in the 2008 Democratic primaries, including Florida and Michigan, than the proportion of pledged delegates she received. There were less discrepancy in her caucus popular and delegate vote.[5]

Box 4.1 describes how the Iowa caucus works.

EMPOWERING THE LEADERSHIP

The third unintended consequence of the Democratic rule changes that the party revisited was the decreasing number of party leaders and elected officials who were chosen as delegates. Unhappy about their loss of influence over the presidential selection process as well as their decreasing visibility and notoriety at the nominating conventions, state and national party leaders convinced the party to establish a new category of delegates known as "superdelegates."[6]

To facilitate closer ties between the nominees and the party, the Democrats established a category of add-on delegates to be composed of political leaders and elected officials (PLEOs). Included in this group were all members of the Democratic National Committee, all Democratic governors and members of Congress, plus a number of other national, state, and local officials. These PLEOs were to be unpledged. It was thought that this group of distinguished Democrats might be in a position to hold the balance of power if the primaries did not produce a winner, a situation that has not occurred since the rules were changed.[7]

Although these superdelegates have not been in a position to broker a divided convention, they have had an impact on delegate selection by their endorsement of candidates. These endorsements, which have tended to go disproportionately to front-runners, have led to the criticism that the PLEOs made the Democratic selection process more elitist and less democratic than it was intended to be. There was also a fear that the superdelegates could reverse the results of a popular-based nomination process. This fear was expressed by senior staffers in the Obama campaign during the final months of the 2008 nomination. Hillary Clinton, the Democratic front-runner, initially received the endorsements of a majority of the superdelegates, eager to back the candidate then deemed the "inevitable" nominee. Barack Obama's early victories and his growing lead in the number of pledged delegates created a potential problem for these Clinton backers as well as for the democratic character of the party's nomination process. The problem did not materialize, however, because the superdelegates, politicians and political leaders, were sensitive to the preferences of voters of their states. Thus, as Obama neared a majority of convention delegates, party leaders and elected officials jumped on his bandwagon.

Nonetheless, the possibility of superdelegates upsetting the state's electoral results prompted the Democrats to change their status to that of pledged delegates that also made them part of their state's delegation to reflect the results of its caucus or primary.

Technically, all Democratic delegates can still vote for whom they want at the national convention because in 1980 the Democrats adopted a rule that allows delegates to vote their consciences rather than simply redeem their campaign pledges. However, the requirement that people who want to be convention delegates indicate their presidential preference in writing before they are put on candidate slates in the caucuses and primaries makes it highly unlikely that many of them will change their minds at the convention, unless the candidate to whom they are pledged encourages them to do so.

REPUBLICAN REFORMS

Although the Republicans initially did not alter their rules as quickly or as extensively as the Democrats, they still were affected by the Democratic rules changes. Since state legislatures enact laws governing party nominations, and since the Democrats controlled many of these legislatures in the 1970s and 1980s when the reforms were initiated, some of the rules were literally forced on the Republicans by Democratic state legislatures. Subsequently, the Republicans did modify their own rules to eliminate discrimination and prevent a small group from controlling the nomination process. Nonetheless, it has been the philosophy of the GOP to give states more discretion in determining their delegate selection procedures than the Democrats; the GOP practice is to abide by nondiscriminatory state rules that do not violate its nomination calendar.

It is the Republican convention that formally approves the rules for choosing delegates for the next Republican convention. This practice has effectively prevented rules changes between convention years. In 2008, however, the rules adopted by the Republican National Convention authorized the creation of a committee to examine the schedule and process for delegate selection and to make recommendations to the Republican National Committee, which was given authority to adopt new recommendations without amendment by virtue of a two-thirds vote.

Beginning in the 2011–2012 election cycle, the party approved a revised calendar that designates the first Tuesday in March as the official starting time. Exceptions were granted to Iowa, New Hampshire, Nevada, and South Carolina, to hold their contests in February. The penalty for violating the calendar was the loss of half a state's convention delegates, a penalty that has not been sufficient to prevent some states, such as Florida, Michigan, and Arizona, from holding their primaries before the window officially opened.

The calendar that the party has established for its 2016 nomination process is February 1 for the Iowa caucus, February 9 for the New Hampshire primary, with contests in Nevada and South Carolina to follow in February and the remaining states may hold their contest from March first until the second Tuesday in June. The Republicans have also increased the penalties for violating this calendar.[8]

Another change, which the Republicans implemented prior to its 2012 nomination process, was a proportional voting rule for states that held their selection process prior to April. Intended to discourage early winner-take-all primaries that greatly advantaged front-runners in previous nomination processes, the rule slowed but did not threaten Mitt Romney's win in 2012.[9] In 2016, the proportional voting requirement only applies to states that hold caucuses and primaries between March 1 and March 14. After that date, states may decide for themselves on the method they wish to use to select their convention delegates. The reason for the change was to encourage states to hold their elections later in the calendar year by giving them the opportunity to enhance their clout by adopting a winner-take-all nomination system.

Whereas the Democrats prescribe a minimum threshold to receive delegate support, the Republicans do not. Their threshold varies from state to state.[10] Nor do Republicans have special categories of delegates for party leaders and elected officials, although GOP state and national leaders traditionally attend their party's convention. The Republicans also do not have a requirement for gender equality. Since the 1980s, the proportion of women delegates at Republican conventions has ranged from 29 percent to 44 percent.

A summary of delegate selection rules for the 2016 nomination appears in Table 4.1.

TABLE 4.1 | DELEGATE SELECTION RULES

	Democrats	Republicans
Rank-and-file participation	Open to all voters who want to participate as Democrats.	No national rule.*
Apportionment of delegates within states	75 percent of base delegation elected at congressional district level or lower; 25 percent elected at large on a proportional basis.	No national rule; may be chosen at large.
Apportionment of delegates to states	Democratic delegate counts are determined by the jurisdiction's presidential vote in 2004, 2008, and 2012, along with the jurisdiction's electoral vote allocation based on 2010 census.	Republican delegate counts are based on the number of Republicans elected to the state legislatures, governors, and to the U.S. House and Senate through December 31, 2015.
Allocation of delegates	By proportional vote in both caucuses and primaries.	By proportional vote only for primaries and caucuses held between March 1 and March 14. Other times at state party's discretion.
Party leaders and elected officials	DNC members, Democratic members of the U.S. House and Senate, Democratic governors, and distinguished party leaders are all allocated proportionally according to the state-wide vote and are pledged delegates.	None.
Composition of delegations	Equal gender division; no discrimination; affirmative action plan required with goals and timetables for specified groups (African Americans, Native Americans, and Asian/ Pacific Americans).	No gender rule, but each state is asked to try to achieve equal gender representation; "positive action" to achieve broadest possible participation required.
Time frame	Prewindow for Iowa, Nevada, New Hampshire, and South Carolina opens February 1, 2016; all others may hold caucuses and primaries on or after the first Tuesday in March.	Prewindow for Iowa, Nevada, New Hampshire, and South Carolina opens February 1, 2016; all others may hold caucuses and primaries on or after the first Tuesday in March.
Threshold	15 percent.	No national rule, but state threshold cannot exceed 20 percent.
Delegate voting	May vote their conscience.	No national rule.
Enforcement and penalties	Automatic reduction in state delegation size for violation of time frames, allocation, or threshold rules.	Reduction of delegation size by more than half for violating time frame and proportional voting rules.

*Republican national rules prescribe that selection procedures accord with the laws of the state.

THE LEGALITY OF PARTY RULES

As previously mentioned, party reforms, to be effective, must be enacted into law. Most states have complied with the new rules. A few have not, sometimes resulting in confrontation between these states and the national party. When New Hampshire and Iowa refused to move the dates of their respective primary and caucuses into the Democrats' window period in 1984, the national party backed down. But previously, when Illinois chose its 1972 delegates in a manner that conflicted with new Democratic rules, the party sought to impose its rules on the state.

In addition to the political controversy that was engendered in that case, the conflict between the Democratic National Committee and Illinois also presented an important legal question: Which body—the national party or the state—has the higher authority on delegate selection? In its landmark decision *Cousins v. Wigoda*, 419 U.S. 477 (1975), the Supreme Court sided with the national party. The Court stated that political parties were private organizations with rights of association protected by the Constitution. Moreover, choosing presidential candidates was a national requirement that states could not abridge unless there were compelling constitutional reasons to do so. Although states could establish their own primary laws, the party could determine the criteria for representation at its national convention.

Crossover voting in open primaries prompted still another court challenge between the rights of parties to prescribe rules for delegate selection and the rights of states to establish their own election laws. Democratic rules prohibit open primaries. Four states had conducted this type of election in 1976. Three voluntarily changed their law; a fourth, Wisconsin, did not. It permitted voters who participated in the primary to request the ballot of either party. The Democrats' Compliance Review Commission ordered the state party to design an alternative process. It refused. The case went to court. Citing the precedent of *Cousins v. Wigoda*, the Supreme Court held in the case of *Democratic Party of the U.S. v. Wisconsin ex. rel. La Follette*, 450 U.S. 107 (1981) that a state had no right to interfere with the party's delegate selection process unless it demonstrated a compelling reason to do so. It ruled that Wisconsin had not demonstrated such a reason; hence, the Democratic Party could refuse to seat delegates who were selected in a manner that violated its rules.[11]

In the case of *California Democratic Party v. Jones*, 530 U.S. 567 (2000), the Supreme Court reiterated its judgment by invalidating California's "blanket" primary system, which voters had approved in a 1996 ballot initiative. The initiative required state officials to provide a uniform ballot in which voters, regardless of their partisan affiliation, could vote for any candidate of any party for any elected position. Naturally, the parties were upset by the possibility that their nominees could be decided by the votes of Independents and partisans of the opposition party. Four California state parties, including the Democrats and Republicans, went to court to challenge the constitutionality of the initiative, claiming that it violated their First Amendment right to freedom of association. The Supreme Court agreed. Its majority opinion held that the blanket primary system represented "a clear and present danger" to the parties and was therefore unconstitutional.

Although these Court decisions have given the political parties the legal authority to design and enforce their own rules, the practicality of doing so is another matter. Other than going to court if a state refuses to change its election law, a party, particularly a national party, has only two viable options: require the state party to conduct its own delegate selection process in conformity with national rules and penalize it if it does not do so, or grant the state party an exemption so that it can abide by the law of the state.

The rule for allocating a specific number of delegates to the states has also generated legal controversy, but in this case, within the Republican Party. The formula that the Republicans use contains a bonus for states that voted Republican in the previous presidential election.[12] Opponents of this rule contend that it discriminates against the large states because bonuses are allocated regardless of size. Moreover, they argue that the large states are apt to be more competitive and thus less likely to receive a bonus. Particularly hard hit are states in the Northeast and on the Pacific Coast, which have gone Democratic in recent elections. The Ripon Society, a moderate Republican group, has twice challenged the constitutionality of this apportionment rule, but it has not been successful. The Democratic apportionment formula, which results in larger conventions than the Republicans, has also been subject to some controversy, although not in recent years.[13]

THE IMPACT OF THE RULES CHANGES

The reforms to the nomination process have produced some of their desired results. They have opened up the process by allowing more people to participate. They have broadened representation at the conventions. And they have weakened the ability of state party leaders to determine the delegates and control their voting at the nominating conventions, but party elites and nonparty group leaders still exercise disproportionate influence in the process and on its outcome.

TURNOUT

One objective of the reforms was to involve more of the party's rank and file in the delegate selection process. This goal has been partially achieved. In 1968, before the reforms, only 12 million people participated in primaries, approximately 11 percent of the voting-age population (VAP). In 1972, the first nomination contest held after the changes were made, that number rose to 22 million. For the next three decades, turnout rose and fell depending on the level of competition within the major parties and the number of weeks or months it took to effectively determine a winner.

In 2004, only the Democrats had a competitive nomination and it was settled early. Less than 10 percent of eligible voters, 16.3 million people, participated.[14] In 2008, it was another story. With competitive contests in both parties, almost 58 million people, approximately one-quarter of the voting-age population participated (37.2 million in the Democratic nomination process and 20.8 million in the Republican one).[15] Turnout declined in 2012. The Republican contest attracted approximately 19 million voters, and the uncontested Democratic nomination, 8.3 million. Turnout of eligible voters in the primaries exceeded 30 percent in only two states, New Hampshire and Montana.[16]

The level of participation in presidential nominations varies with the type of election. It has always been greater in primaries than in caucuses. In Iowa, which traditionally holds the first caucus, only 6.1 percent participated in 2004 when only the Democrats had a contested race; in 2008, with competition in both parties, 16.1 percent of eligible voters came to the caucuses: 108,000 (5 percent) Republicans and 239,000 (11.1 percent) Democrats; in 2012, Republican turnout in Iowa increased slightly to 121,000 (approximately 19 percent of registered Republicans).[17]

Primary turnout is much larger than that of caucuses, especially for the early contests. New Hampshire, which has the first primary, usually has the highest percentage. In 2008, 53.6 percent of those eligible voted in the New Hampshire primary; in 2012, with only one party participating in a contested nomination, 31.1 percent of eligible voters turned out.[18] The key to primary turnout is the date and competitiveness of the election.

Not only does turnout vary among states, but it also varies among population groups within the states. People who are better educated, have higher incomes, and are older vote more often than do younger, less-educated, and poorer people.[19] In general, the lower the turnout, the greater the demographic differences between voters and nonvoters.

Primary voters tend to be more ideologically extreme in their political beliefs than the average party voter, with Democrats being more liberal and Republicans more conservative than their party as a whole.

Finally, higher turnout in the nomination process tends to benefit a party because it informs and energizes more partisans, priming them for the general election. The long gap between the primaries and the beginning of the general election campaign, however, reduces that priming effect.

REPRESENTATION

Another goal of the reforms was to improve the representative character of the nomination process both with respect to the electorate that participated in the caucuses and primaries and the delegates who represented them at the national nominating conventions. In theory, the more representative the party's electorate during the nomination, the more likely that its standard-bearers and platform will reflect the wishes of rank-and-file partisans. One of the criticisms of the reforms that the major parties initiated in the 1970s was that they gave organized groups and party activists greater opportunities to affect the outcome of the nominations.

Prior to the reforms, the people who voted in the nomination contests were not representative of their party's rank and file. Part of the rationale for the Democratic rules changes, which added one caucus after Iowa (Nevada) and one primary after New Hampshire (South Carolina), was to better represent Hispanics and African Americans, two groups that constitute major components of the Democrats' electoral coalition. African Americans, 20 to 25 percent of the Democratic vote in recent presidential elections, make up 55 percent of that party's electorate in South Carolina and 15 percent in Nevada.[20] Hispanics constitute 27 percent of the population in Nevada.[21]

A related issue is whether those participating in the caucuses and primaries are representative of rank-and-file partisans in that state. Two recent studies of voters in the 2008 and 2012 Iowa caucuses indicated that they were, demographically and ideologically.[22]

The demographic composition of each party's convention delegates still do not accurately reflect its rank and file, much less the general electorate. Ideologically, Democratic delegates have overrepresented liberals and moderates within their party's electoral coalition; Republican delegates have overrepresented conservatives. Regular churchgoers were overrepresented at both major party conventions, although the greater religiosity of the Republican delegates was also indicative of voters in that party's electoral base. Although the Democrats better represent women and minorities than do the Republicans, these two groups also constitute a much larger proportion of the Democrats' vote.

PARTY ORGANIZATION AND LEADERSHIP

Weakening the state party organizations and their leadership was not a goal of party reforms, but to some extent it has been a product of it, at least initially. The proliferation of candidates along with the requirements of the campaign finance legislation has produced separate electoral organizations, run by candidates and now their Super PAC supporters that can rival the regular party organization.

Party leaders can still use their influence with their state legislatures to help determine the date on which their nomination contest occurs and the rules by which it is conducted, but they can no longer dictate the composition of their state delegation and their votes at the national nominating convention. State leaders also can work with interest group leaders, party donors, and partisan-oriented media to endorse candidates and mobilize support for them during the nomination.

Referred to as party elites, the leaders and their activist supporters band together to pursue a range of overlapping and disparate policy goals.[23] Their influence is greatest in the first stage of the contest, the so-called invisible primary, when political endorsements and resources effectively narrow the field, identify the front-runners, gain media attention for them, and begin to shape public opinion.

Do partisan divisions, created and inflated by the nomination process, adversely affect the party's chance in the general election? Some political scientists have argued that they do, claiming that the longer and more divisive the nomination process, the more likely that it will hurt the party's nominee in the general election.[24] Yet the election of Bill Clinton in 1992 and of Barack Obama in 2008, both after extended nomination battles, suggests that there is more that unifies partisans in the general election than divides them.

The passage of time, the healing efforts of the winning candidates, and shared political beliefs and perspectives of the candidate and their fellow partisans, particularly in an era of political polarization, can overcome a divisive nomination, especially one that focuses as much on personal as on policy differences. Other factors, such as the electoral environment, the quality of the candidates, and situational factors such as the recessions of 1992 and 2008, seem to have a much greater impact on the general election than does the residue from the nomination process.[25]

WINNERS AND LOSERS

Rules changes are never neutral. They usually benefit one group at the expense of another. Similarly, they tend to help certain candidates and hurt others. That is why candidates have tried to shape the rules and why the rules themselves have been changed so frequently. Candidate organizations and interest groups have put continuous pressure on state and national parties to modify the calendar, eligibility rules, and vote allocation to increase their own influence in the selection process.

Clearly, the prohibition of discrimination, the requirement for affirmative action, and the rule requiring an equal number of men and women in state delegations have improved the representation of women and minorities for the Democrats. These requirements have also forced candidates seeking their party's nomination to submit balanced slates of delegates pledged to them in the caucuses and primaries.

The openness of the process and the greater participation by the party's rank and file have encouraged those who have not been party regulars to become involved and have created opportunities for outsiders to seek their party's nomination. Businessmen Steve Forbes (1996 and 2000) and Herman Cain (2012), ministers Jesse Jackson (1984) and Pat Robertson (1988), columnist Pat Buchanan (1992, 1996, and 2000), and former senators Paul Tsongas (1992), Bill Bradley (2000), and Rick Santorum (2012), and to some extent even Governors Michael Dukakis (1988), Bill Clinton (1992), and Howard Dean (2004), and three-year senator Barack Obama (2008) have literally come out of political nowhere to win their party's nomination. On the other hand, the more the process concentrates the number of primaries at the beginning of the delegate selection process, the more those who have access to the largest amounts of money, the most political endorsements, and the organizational support from governors and other party and interest group leaders are likely to benefit.

All of this has affected the candidates' quests for the nomination and their ability to govern if elected. It has extended campaigning and made it more arduous and more expensive, and it has made governing more difficult. It has created incentives for candidates to promise more than they can deliver. Thus, the quest for the nomination and what it takes to win may ultimately weaken a newly elected president by hyping performance expectations and then generating discontent when these expectations are not met. Ronald Reagan, Bill Clinton, and Barack Obama each faced this problem in the first years of their presidencies.

SUMMARY

The delegate selection process has changed dramatically over the past four decades. Originally dominated by state party leaders, it has become more open to the party's rank and file as a consequence of the reforms initiated by the Democratic Party. These reforms, designed to broaden the base of public participation, improve the representation of the party's rank and file, and give its partisan electorate more influence over the selection of the party's nominees, have affected the Republicans as well, even though the GOP does not mandate as many national guidelines on its state parties as the Democrats do. Supreme Court decisions have given the parties the authority to dictate rules for their nominating conventions; increasingly, public pressure to reflect popular sentiment and improve representation has led to a greater number of primaries and more delegates selected in them.

Turnout has increased although the proportion of the partisan electorate that participates varies from one nomination to another. The date of the contest, the level of intraparty competition, the amount of money spent, and other candidate-related factors help explain these variations. But the democratic bottom line is that even in highly contested nominations many fewer people follow the nomination contests closely and vote in them than in the general election. The lower the turnout, the more influential party activists tend to be.

WHERE ON THE WEB?

- **The Center for Voting and Democracy**
  www.fairvote.org
  An organization devoted to promoting a more democratic electoral process and publicizing plans to improve it.

- **Democratic National Committee**
  www.democrats.org
  Information on Democratic Party history, rules, convention, and campaigns with links to Democratic youth and state party affiliates.

- **Green Party**
  www.gp.org
  Information on Green Party candidates and platform, press releases, and state party affiliates.

- **The Green Papers**
  www.thegreenpapers.com/P16
  A web site that provides detailed information on the nomination processes and the general election. Contains reports on the changes the parties have approved for 2016.

- **Republican National Committee**
  www.rnc.org
  Information on Republican Party history, rules, convention, and campaigns with links to Republican youth and state party affiliates.

- **Wikipedia**
  en.wikipedia.org/wiki/United_States_presidential_primary
  An online encyclopedia.

EXERCISES

1. Both national parties have been trying to impose a nomination calendar that is less front-loaded. Why have they been unable to do so? What are the incentives for states to schedule their nominations early? Do these incentives undermine a democratic nomination process? Explain. What changes would you suggest to make the nomination process more democratic and/or more likely to result in the selection of a stronger, more popular nominee?

2. Devise what you consider fair and equitable rules for the major parties for the selection of their presidential nominees. How could the national parties encourage states to abide by these fair and equitable rules?

SELECTED READINGS

Altschuler, Bruce E. "Selecting Presidential Nominees by National Primary: An Idea Whose Time Has Come?" *The Forum*, 5 (4): Article 5 (2008). www.bepress.com /forum/vol/iss4/art5

Atkeson, Lonna Rae. "Divisive Primaries and General Election Outcomes: Another Look at Presidential Campaigns." *American Journal of Political Science*, 42 (1998): 257–261.

Bartels, Larry M. *Presidential Primaries and the Dynamics of Public Choice*. Princeton, NJ: Princeton University Press, 1988.

Cohen, Marty, David Karol, Hans Noel, and John Zaller. *The Party Decides: Presidential Nominations Before and After Reform*. Chicago: University of Chicago Press, 2008.

Donovan, Todd and Rob Hunsaker, "Effects of Early Elections in the US Presidential Nomination Contests," *PS: Political Science and Politics* 42 (Jan. 2009): 45–54.

Geer, John G. *Nominating Presidents: An Evaluation of Voters and Primaries*. New York: Greenwood, 1989.

Kamarck, Elaine C. *Primary Politics: How Presidential Candidates Have Shaped the Modern Nomination System*. Washington, DC: Brookings Institution, 2009.

Kaufman, Karen M., James G. Gimpel, and Adam H. Hoffman. "A Promise Fulfilled? Open Primaries and Representation," *Journal of Politics*, 65 (2003): 457–476.

Mayer, William G., and Andrew E. Busch. *The Front-Loading Problem in Presidential Nominations*. Washington, DC: Brookings Institution, 2004.

———. "Reforming the Reforms Revisited," in *Reforming the Presidential Nomination Process*, Steven S. Smith and Melanie J. Springer, eds. Washington, DC: Brookings Institution, 2009.

Norrander, Barbara and Jay Wendland. "The Primary End Game and General Election Outcomes: Are They Connected?" *The Forum*, 10 (4), (2012): 119–126.

———. *The Imperfect Primary*. New York: Routledge, 2010.

Polsby, Nelson W. *The Consequences of Party Reform*. New York: Oxford University Press, 1983.

Redlawsk, David P., Caroline Tolbert, and Todd Donovan. *Why Iowa? How Caucuses and Sequential Elections Improve the Presidential Nomination Process* (Chicago, IL: University of Chicago Press, 2011).

Shafer, Byron E. and Amber Wichowsky. "The Nomination and the Election: Cleaning Away the Underbrush," *The Forum*, 6 (4), 2008: Article 3.

Tolbert, Caroline, and Peverill Squire, eds. "Reforming the Presidential Nomination Process." *PS: Political Science and Politics*, 42 (Jan. 2009): 27–79.

Wayne, Stephen J. *Is This Any Way to Run a Democratic Election?* 5th ed.
Los Angeles: Sage/CQ Press, 2014.

———. "When Democracy Works: The 2008 Presidential Nominations," in *Winning the Presidency*, William J. Crotty, ed. Boulder, CO: Paradigm Publishers, 2009, pp. 48–69.

NOTES

1. McCarthy's name was on the ballot, but the president's name was not. The regular Democratic organization in New Hampshire had to conduct a campaign to have Democrats write in Johnson's name.
2. The groups that were initially identified were Native Americans, African Americans, and youth. Subsequently, the list of affected groups has been altered by the addition of Hispanics, Asian/Pacific Americans, and women, and by the deletion of youth. In 1992, the party also added those with physical disabilities to the list of designated groups.
3. Iowa and New Hampshire both have laws that require their contests to be, respectively, the first caucus and primary. They obviously gain advantages by doing so. The candidates come and visit with voters often. The news media also arrive in force to cover the beginnings of the next campaign. There is an economic gain as well. The early contests generate millions of dollars in revenue from the campaigns, the volunteers and staff that run them and from media coverage and advertising.
4. The Democratic Party commission recommended that the calendar be divided into four stages. The states that held their nomination contests during the first stage, the two-week period beginning with the first Tuesday in March, would receive additional delegates equal to 15 percent of their total number of pledged delegates; if they held their election during stage two, the three-week period beginning the third Tuesday in March, they would receive an additional 20 percent; if their selection date was in the third stage, the three-week period that begins the second Tuesday in April, they would be allocated an additional 30 percent; if they held it after that and before the end of the Democratic nomination process, the second Tuesday in June, they would be entitled to an additional 40 percent.
5. Still concerned about the representativeness of the caucus process, the Democratic Change Commission recommended that caucus states adopt a "Best Practices" program, which would help them plan, organize, and staff their caucuses in such a manner that they would "maximize the opportunity for full participation for all Democratic voters," a recommendation that has been adopted by the Democratic Party. The vagueness of the rule, however, still gives caucus states considerable discretion in designing and conducting their caucuses.
6. Jimmy Carter's difficulties with the Democratic Congress during his presidency were also cited as evidence of the need for closer cooperation between congressional party leaders and their presidential standard-bearer. These PLEOs were designed to facilitate such cooperation.
7. Additionally, the party also provided for the selection of pledged add-on delegates equal to 15 percent of the state's base delegation in order to give representation to a larger number of state party leaders.
8. Under the new rules, states with 30 or more delegates would be reduced to just 12 while states with less than 30 would be reduced to 9.

9. In 1988, George H. W. Bush won 59 percent of the popular vote in states holding winner-take-all primaries but 97 percent of the delegates from these states; in 2008, John McCain received 38 percent of the Republican vote in winner-take-all primaries on or before February 5, but 81 percent of the delegates.

10. The threshold cannot exceed 20 percent.

11. In December 1986, the Supreme Court, in the case of *Tashjian v. Republican Party of Connecticut*, 479 U.S. 208 (1986), voided a Connecticut law that prohibited open primaries. Republicans, in the minority at the time in Connecticut, had favored such a primary as a means of attracting independent voters. Unable to get the Democratic-controlled legislature to change the law, the state Republican Party went to court, arguing that the statute violated its First Amendment rights of freedom of association. In a 5-to-4 ruling, the Supreme Court agreed and struck down the legislation.

12. The formula Republicans use to determine the size of each state delegation is complex. It consists of three criteria: statehood (six delegates), House districts (three per district), and support for Republican candidates elected within the previous four years (one for a Republican governor, one for each Republican senator, one if the Republicans won at least half of the congressional districts in one of the past two congressional elections, and a bonus of four and one-half delegates plus 60 percent of the electoral vote if the state voted for the Republican presidential candidate in the previous election).

13. Under the plan used since 1968 and modified in 1976, the Democrats have allotted 50 percent of each state delegation on the basis of the state's electoral vote and 50 percent on the basis of its average Democratic vote in the past three presidential elections. The rule for apportionment was challenged in 1971 on the grounds that it did not conform to the "one-person, one-vote" principle, but a court of appeals asserted that it did not violate the equal protection clause of the Fourteenth Amendment.

14. Curtis Gans, "2004 Primary Turnout Low." www.american.edu/ccps/files/Files /csae030904.pdf; Linda L. Fowler, Constantine J. Spiliotes, and Lynn VaVreck, "The Role of Issue Advocacy Groups in the New Hampshire Primary," in David B. Magleby, ed., *Getting Inside the Outside Campaign* (Provo, UT: Brigham Young University, 2000), p. 31.

15. Michael McDonald, "Presidential Turnout Rates, 1948–2008." www.electproject .org/2008p

16. Michael M. McDonald, "2012 Presidential Nomination Contest Turnout Rates." www.electproject.org/2012p

17. Ibid.

18. Ibid.

19. Walter J. Stone, Alan I. Abramowitz, and Ronald L. Rapoport, "How Representative Are the Iowa Caucuses?" in Peverill Squire, ed., *The Iowa Caucus and the Presidential Nomination Process* (Boulder, CO: Westview Press, 1989), p. 44.

20. Jon Cohen and Jennifer Agiesta, "Black Vote Was Vital, Not the Whole Story," *The Washington Post* (Jan. 27, 2008). www.washingtonpost.com/wp-dyn/content /article/2008/01/26/AR2008012602741.html; "The Entrance Polls: Why Clinton Won Nevada," *Politico* (Jan. 8, 2008). www.politico.com/news/stories/0108/7994.

21. Seth Motel and Eileen Patten, "Latinos in the 2012 Election: Nevada," Pew Hispanic Center. http://www.pewhispanic.org/2012/10/01/latinos-in-the-2012-election-nevada/

22. Todd Donovan, David Redlawski, and Caroline Tolbert, "The 2012 Iowa Republican Caucus and Its Effects on the Presidential Nomination Contest," *Presidential Studies Quarterly*, 44 (September 2014): 447–466; David P. Redlawski, Caroline Tolbert, and Todd Donovan, *Why Iowa? How Caucuses and Sequential Elections Improve the Presidential Nomination Process* (Chicago: University of Chicago Press, 2011).
23. Marty Cohen, David Carol, Hans Noel, and John Zaller, *The Party Decides: Presidential Nominations Before and After Reform* (Chicago: University of Chicago Press, 2008), p. 232.
24. James I. Lengle, "Divisive Presidential Primaries and the Party Electoral Prospects, 1932–1976," *American Politics Quarterly*, 8 (1980), pp. 261–277; James I. Lengle, Diana Owen, and Molly Sonner, "Divisive Nomination Campaigns and Democratic Party Electoral Prospects," *Journal of Politics*, 57 (1995), pp. 370–383.
25. Barbara Norrander and Jay Wendland, "The Primary End Game and General Election Outcomes: Are They Connected?" *The Forum*, 10 (4), 2012, pp. 119–126; Lonna Rae Atkeson, "Divisive Primaries and General Election Outcomes: Another Look at Presidential Campaigns," *American Journal of Political Science*, 42 (Jan. 1998), pp. 256–271.

5 CHAPTER | CAMPAIGNING FOR THE NOMINATION

INTRODUCTION

Rules changes, finance laws, and press coverage have affected the strategies and tactics of the candidates. Today, entering primaries is essential for everyone, even an incumbent who may be challenged by a fellow partisan. No longer can a front-runner safely sit on the sidelines and wait for the call. The winds of a draft may be hard to resist but, more often than not, it is the candidates and their backers who are manning the bellows.

In the past, candidates carefully chose the primaries they entered and concentrated their efforts where they thought they would run best. Today, they have less discretion, particularly at the beginning of the process, when press coverage elevates the importance of the early contests. Planning for a nomination run starts years in advance. Candidates usually establish exploratory committees following the midterm election. These committees help them test the waters. The money they raise during the preelection stage of the nomination process helps them pay for travel, staff, fund-raising, and other expenses such as designing a web site, building a donor base, hiring campaign consultants, and appealing to party and interest group leaders for endorsements and organizational support.

BASIC STRATEGIC GUIDELINES

Every nomination campaign has to make a number of strategic decisions: when to begin the quest for the nomination and what type of organization to create; how to raise the necessary funds and from which individuals and groups to do so; how, where, and on what activities to spend resources; which issues to stress, messages to emphasize, and images to project; how to design a communication strategy that attracts sufficient and favorable news media coverage, supplements it with effective advertising, and also has the capacity to reach voters directly; what groups to target, appeals to make, and how to personalize them and maximize their impact; how to criticize one's nomination opponents yet be in a position to gain their support after becoming the *de facto* nominee; and finally, how to position the campaign in the months after effectively winning the nomination but before the national nominating conventions are held.

PLAN FAR AHEAD

Creating an organization, devising a strategy, and raising the amount of money necessary to conduct a broad-based campaign all takes time. These needs have prompted potential aspirants for their party's nomination to set up exploratory committees, leadership and candidate-oriented Super PACs, and other organizations in the early months of the election cycle, and sometimes even before it. George McGovern started running for the 1972 Democratic nomination in January 1971; similarly, long-shot Jimmy Carter began his quest in 1974, almost two years before the 1976 Democratic convention. By the end of 2006, eleven Democratic and Republican candidates had either officially declared their candidacy or set up exploratory committees for their party's 2008 nomination. According to Howard Wolfson, Hillary Clinton's 2008 communication director, "You have to move early because the process starts early, and if you are not announcing in the early time, you are going to lose out."[1]

The race for the 2012 Republican nomination began a little more slowly than in previous nominations. Newt Gingrich was the first to declare his candidacy, in May 2001, and Rick Perry the last, in August of that year. The pace picked up for the 2016 nominations with Republican Jeb Bush and Democrat Jim Webb the first to set up their exploratory committees in 2014, more than a year before the first caucus and primary would be held. Other Republicans quickly followed suit. By mid-February 2015, the race for the nomination was clearly underway.

Even incumbent presidents plan for their renomination well in advance of the election year. President Clinton began his reelection bid in the winter of 1994, following his party's defeat in the midterm elections. Clinton never formally announced his candidacy in order to convey the impression that his actions and decisions during this period were motivated solely by the demands of the presidency, not by his desire to run for another term. President George W. Bush, anxious to avoid his father's belated and unsuccessful quest for reelection, began planning his 2004 campaign from almost the moment he was declared the winner of the 2000 election.[2] Barack Obama started raising money and positioning himself for reelection in the aftermath of his party's defeat in the 2010 midterm election. His principal political aides resigned from their White House staff positions at the end of 2010 to return to Chicago to work on his reelection campaign.

CONCENTRATE EFFORTS IN THE EARLY CONTESTS

Doing well in the initial caucuses and primaries, raising money, gaining endorsements and public recognition, organizing the campaign, and staffing it with political professionals are the principal tasks most candidates face. The early contests are particularly important for lesser-known aspirants, less for the number of delegates they can win than for the amount of publicity they can gain, the supporters they can mobilize, and the momentum they can build. That momentum in turn generates money and political endorsements from party and interest group leaders.

For most candidates, visiting Iowa and New Hampshire frequently is essential. Republican candidates for their party's 2012 nomination made 243 visits to Iowa and stayed 507 days; they made 217 trips to New Hampshire and stayed 452 days before the first Republican primary.[3]

Personal contacts are very important in this period because they inform and motivate donors, staff, and volunteers. The small states provide "living-room" opportunities that are lacking in large state mass media campaigns. Retail politics also allows candidates with small organizations and limited finances to "camp out" and build their campaign from the ground up. Rick Santorum lived in Iowa for three months prior to that state's January 2012 caucus. Traveling to small towns in his pickup truck, accompanied by one or two aides, Santorum gradually gained media attention and public recognition, particularly among social conservatives. On the night of the caucus, news reports indicated that he tied Romney in the vote although later recounts showed him a little ahead.

Winning Iowa, the nation's first caucus, is important for several reasons. A victory can elevate the status of a lesser-known candidate overnight as it did for Jimmy Carter in 1976, George H. W. Bush in 1980, Mike Huckabee and Barack Obama in 2008, and, to a limited extent, Rick Santorum in 2012. Even coming in second can be a boost, especially if a second place finish is unexpected as it was for Gary Hart in 1984. Although Hart lost, he received a surprising 16.5 percent of the Democratic caucus vote, thereby giving him more favorable press than he would have otherwise received.[4]

A loss in Iowa, however, can be fatal for a non-front-runner. It was for Democrats Bill Richardson, Joe Biden, and Chris Dodd in 2008 and Republican Michele Bachman in 2012. Keith Nahigian, Michele Bachman's campaign manager, noted dryly, ". . . we needed to shrink the stage. We needed to get rid of people [the other lesser known Republican candidates] as quickly as possible."[5] Bachman was herself a victim of that shrinkage, dropping out after her poor showing in Iowa.

Non-front-runners that win in Iowa still face an uphill battle. Not only do expectations of their future performance increase, making a subsequent defeat more newsworthy, but their press coverage also tends to become more critical after an initial victory. The press takes them more seriously. Gaining momentum after doing well in Iowa has also become more difficult because of the compressed nomination calendar, leaving little time to take advantage of an Iowa win by raising more money, expanding an organization, and moving its operations to other states about to hold their caucuses and primaries.

A loss in Iowa, however, is not necessarily fatal for a front-runner, as Republicans Ronald Reagan (1980), George H. W. Bush (1988), and Robert Dole (1996) and Democrat Hillary Clinton (2008) found out by winning the New Hampshire primary after their Iowa defeats.

After Iowa, attention turns to New Hampshire, the first state to hold a primary in which the state's entire electorate can participate.[6] Candidates who do surprisingly well in this primary have benefited enormously. Eugene McCarthy (1968), George McGovern (1972), Jimmy Carter (1976), Gary Hart (1984), Bill Clinton (1992), Pat Buchanan (1996), John McCain (2000 and 2008), and Mitt Romney (2012) all gained visibility, credibility, and confidence from their New Hampshire performances, although none had a majority of the vote. Bill Clinton actually came in second with 25 percent of the vote in 1992, 8 percent less than former Massachusetts senator Paul Tsongas. Clinton's relatively strong showing, however, in the light of allegations of marital infidelity and draft dodging made his performance impressive in the eyes of the news media, more so than Tsongas's expected win in a neighboring state.

Similarly, John McCain's impressive victory in 2000 over front-runner George W. Bush (by 18 percent) elevated him overnight from just another candidate to a serious contender. His victory in 2008, though smaller, revived his campaign for which the press had already written a premature obituary. Hillary Clinton's win in New Hampshire in 2008 also saved her sagging campaign, energizing her supporters and generating badly needed contributions. Romney's New Hampshire victory in 2012 reinforced his front-runner status and boosted his large resource base.

Like Iowa, New Hampshire also receives extensive media attention. Together, these two states and the other first month caucuses and primaries usually receive disproportionate news coverage. In 2012, 42 percent of the January "newshole" was filled with campaign stories; in February, it was 25 percent, and in March, 19 percent according to a report by the Pew Research Center's Project for Excellence in Journalism.[7]

RAISE AND SPEND BIG BUCKS EARLY

Having a solid resource base at the outset of the nomination process provides a significant strategic advantage. It allows a presidential campaign to plan ahead, to decide where and how many field organizations to establish and how much media advertising to buy. It is no coincidence that the candidates who raise and spend the most money during the nomination period tend to win. The exception was Romney in 2008 but not 2012.

The impact of early money is particularly significant for candidates who do not begin with a national reputation, candidates such as Michael Dukakis in 1988, Bill Clinton in 1992, Howard Dean and John Edwards in 2004, and

Mitt Romney and Barack Obama in 2008. The ability to raise relatively large amounts during the year before the caucuses and primaries gives a candidate an edge in gaining media recognition, building organizational support, raising more money later on, and even discouraging potential rivals from entering the race.

In fact, the amount of money donated to a candidate's war chest and Super PACs supporting that candidate is frequently viewed by the press as a harbinger of their future success or failure. Howard Dean, a former Vermont governor, is a good example. He raised more money than did any of his Democratic rivals in 2003, almost $40 million, much of it from small, online donations. The press took notice. He began to rise in the polls. By November prior to the election year, he was the acknowledged Democratic front-runner.

The ability to raise substantial amounts contributes to getting political endorsements from establishment partisans. Government and party officials and interest group leaders tend to support candidates they perceive as likely winners.

Early money also enhances news media visibility. The press evaluate candidates in part on the basis of how much money they can raise and from how many people they can raise it. Dollars portend votes, the reason why the press calls the year before the election "the invisible primary."

GAIN MEDIA ATTENTION

Candidates cannot win if they are not known. Recognition as a political leader is most important at the beginning of the nomination cycle when the electorate starts to pay attention to electoral politics. Since lesser-known aspirants are not as likely to have large war chests, unless they are independently wealthy, substantial sums left over from previous campaigns, or have wealthy patrons willing to donate millions to their Super PACs, they need free media to draw attention to the seriousness and potential viability of their campaign. Their problem is that coverage and public recognition go hand in hand. Better-known candidates get more coverage precisely because they are better known and thus considered more likely to do well. It is not news when a long shot loses; it is news when a front-runner does. On the other hand, when a long shot does well in raising money, gaining endorsements, drawing crowds, winning straw votes, and especially picking up convention delegates, the press follows the story of the "conquering hero."

What can non-front-runners do to gain more coverage? They can stage events, release a stream of seemingly endless faxes, emails, twitters, and videos to local media and place them on popular Internet sites, such as YouTube, leak unfavorable information about their opponents, and solicit invitations to appear on talk/entertainment programs on radio and television,[8] and participate in debates if invited to do so. During the 2007–2008 nomination campaign, there were twenty-one debates among the Democratic contenders and sixteen among the Republicans; in 2012, the Republicans held 20 debates over the course of nine months. These debates attracted considerable media attention as live encounters among the candidates.

In general, there has been a decline in the amount of time given to election news on the "broadcast" networks and an even larger decline in stories about the candidates on their evening news shows.[9] On the other hand, the 24/7 cable news channels have increased their coverage, as have the web sites of the major news networks and other online sites such as YouTube and Twitter. Candidates gear their campaign to these sites.

Advertising remains one of the most effective ways to reach and inform potential voters. Studies have shown that people tend to retain more information from repetitive candidate commercials than they do from viewing a single news story,[10] a reason why campaigns spend much of their revenues on the design, airing, and targeting of political commercials. Table 5.1 lists the number of ads shown by candidates and their candidate-oriented Super PACs during the competitive phase of the 2011–2012 nominations; Table 5.2 indicates the amount of money spent on these ads by the four principal Republican candidates and their Super PACs from November 1, 2011, to April 15, 2012.

TABLE 5.1 | THE AMOUNT OF CAMPAIGN ADVERTISING (JANUARY 2011–APRIL 22, 2012)

Candidate	Number of Ads	
	Campaign	Super PAC
Jon Huntsman	68	811
Newt Gingrich	6,373	11,558
Rick Santorum	6,330	11,471
Mitt Romney	30,135	49,565
Rick Perry	11,979	6,465
Barack Obama	10,570	2,447
Ron Paul	7,860	755
Total	73,315	83,072

Source: Erika Fowler, "Presidential Ads 70 Percent Negative in 2012, Up from 9 Percent in 2008," Wesleyan Media Project, May 2, 2012. www.mediaproject.wesleyan.edu/2012/05/02/jump-in-negativity

TABLE 5.2 | ADVERTISING EXPENDITURES FOR THE 2011–2012 NOMINATION CYCLE (IN MILLIONS)

Candidate	Expenditure	
	Campaign	Super PAC
Newt Gingrich	$1.9	$5.8
Ron Paul	3.0	0.2
Mitt Romney	14.5	30.7
Rick Santorum	1.7	4.5
Total	21.1	41.2

Source: "Campaign 2012: Mad Money: Campaign Ads," Washington Post, April 24, 2012 (CMAG/Kantar Media). www.washingtonpost.com/wp-srv/special/politics/track-presidential-campaign-ads-2012/?tid=rr_mod

Develop an Organization

The major task of any organization is to mobilize voters and build electoral coalitions among core partisan groups.[11] Gaining media coverage is necessary but not sufficient. Having an organization in the field is deemed especially important in caucus states in order to get supporters and sympathizers to the precinct meetings, which are less well known than the voting places at which people cast their primary and general election ballots.

The increasing use of the Internet to identify, inform, and mobilize voters must still be buttressed by an on-the-ground organization that includes field offices, paid staff, and hundreds of volunteers. Face-to-face contacts are still considered to be the most effective way to turn out the vote.

Super PACs, which raised and spent extensive amounts in 2012, did not mount extensive field operations although candidate organizations and nonparty groups, such as labor unions, the Chamber of Commerce, and active ideological groups, did so. All of these on-the-ground activities require recruitment, training sessions, and coordinated field operations.

Monitor Public Opinion

With intentions clear, money in hand, events planned and scheduled, and an organization in place, it is necessary to monitor public sentiment and try to manipulate it to political advantage. To achieve these goals, polls and focus groups are used.

Republican Thomas E. Dewey was the first candidate to have private polling data available to him when he tried unsuccessfully to obtain the Republican nomination in 1940. John F. Kennedy was the first Democrat to engage a pollster in his quest for the nomination. Preconvention surveys conducted for Kennedy in 1960 indicated that Hubert Humphrey, Kennedy's principal rival, was potentially vulnerable in West Virginia and Wisconsin. On the basis of this information, Kennedy decided to concentrate time, effort, and money in these predominantly Protestant states. Victories in both helped demonstrate his broad appeal, thereby improving his chances for the nomination.

Today, all major presidential candidates commission their own polls. Proprietary surveys provide critical information about the perceptions, attitudes, and opinions of voters as well as the kinds of appeals to which they are likely to be most receptive. Focus groups engage people in conversation and have become an increasingly valuable tool for speechwriters and media consultants. Almost all campaign advertising is pretested by such groups to gauge likely reactions to it. Adjustments, if necessary, are made before the ad is aired; a negative response by the focus group may kill the ad entirely.[12] Experiments and analytics have also become an important component of campaign research and messaging.

Although polls and focus groups affect strategy, tactics, and fund-raising, their impact on the general public is less direct. Despite the fears expressed by politicians, there are few empirical data to suggest that poll results, spotlighted in the news, generate a "bandwagon effect" among the general public; polls are more likely to affect the attentive public. Standing in the polls improves a candidate's ability to attract contributors and volunteers. It also influences the amount and tone of news media coverage.[13]

DESIGN AND TARGET A DISTINCTIVE IMAGE AND MESSAGE

The information obtained from polls, focus groups, and other analyses is used to create and sharpen leadership images and campaign appeals and target them to sympathetic audiences. Candidates first must establish their credentials, then articulate general themes, and finally discuss specific policy positions. For lesser-known candidates, the initial emphasis must be on recognition and qualifications for the presidency.

Designing a distinctive leadership image and policy appeal that falls within the mainstream of partisan views is difficult, especially when there are a lot of candidates competing for the nomination. In the 2008 Democratic race, Obama emphasized change, Clinton experience, and Edwards populism. John McCain began his quest for the 2008 Republican nomination with a reputation for being an independent thinker, not necessarily an advantage in a party with a strong ideological base. In 2012, Mitt Romney stressed his consistency with traditional Republican values and policy positions to counter the impression he was really a Massachusetts moderate. Ron Paul, who advocated a libertarian policy agenda in both 2008 and 2012, distinguished himself from the other Republicans by proposing a less interventionist foreign policy, a stance that raised questions among those who had traditionally backed the party's more assertive national security posture.

The policy debate and image projections attract the attention of those portions of the electorate that participate in the nomination process. The Annenberg Public Policy Center at the University of Pennsylvania has found that people gain greater awareness and knowledge of the candidates and their positions as the nomination process advances, particularly in states in which candidates actively campaign.[14] But the Annenberg survey also noted that there continues to be significant knowledge gaps on the issues among the general public.[15]

Annenberg researchers have also examined the impact of political endorsements and campaign attacks on voters. They concluded that endorsements and attacks can inform voters and, in some cases, do influence voting, but most people are not aware of endorsements, and when they are, deny that they affect the way they vote.[16] Campaign communications that reinforce and are reinforced by news stories and commentaries tend to have the greatest impact.

MAKE EFFECTIVE USE OF COMMUNICATION TECHNOLOGIES

One of the distinctive aspects of nomination campaigns since the beginning of the 1990s has been the propensity of candidates to circumvent the national news for less expensive local media and online social networking. Candidates now try to reach voters directly rather than going through the news media to do so. Keith Madden, a senior adviser to Romney in 2012, put it this way:

> Instead of going to the editorial page and saying give me 750 words in the *New York Times*, you could create your own opinion editorial, put it out to your grassroots supporters, put it up on a campaign blog, ship it to a list of a million people, and have that information processed that way.[17]

The potential of cyberspace is enormous. Communication can be almost instantaneous, continuous, and cheap. By accessing Facebook, YouTube, Twitter, and other sites, campaigns have expanded their reach, reinforced their messaging, and collected personal data to design and target appeals to specific demographic groups. These data also facilitate the solicitation of contributions and the mobilization of volunteers to staff events and turnout voters.

Campaigning on the Internet is not without its problems, however. Squatters have registered web addresses of potential candidates, long before they declare their candidacy, and then demand large sums of money to give them up. Parody sites and linkages have mushroomed. Unsubstantiated rumors circulate widely and rapidly. Security has also become a problem as web sites have become targets of political opponents and unfriendly hackers.

Nonetheless and on balance, the Internet offers more advantages than disadvantages for presidential campaigning. It has become a vehicle for reaching the younger generation, whose online sophistication generally exceeds their political knowledge and activity. It is a way to convert passive observers into more active participants and a means by which candidates can communicate their narratives without media interference. Speeches and rallies can be carried live or made readily available to those who access the site; ads can be viewed in their entirety; and reactions can be solicited and suggestions encouraged. Candidates can also use their sites to maintain a campaign archive for the news media as well as a screen on which to alert the press to new and potentially newsworthy information and events.[18]

COORDINATING STRATEGY WITH CANDIDACY STATUS

Timing, finance, organization, and communication affect the quest for delegates. They help shape the candidates' strategies and tactics for the nomination. Generally speaking, there have been two successful strategic approaches, one for front-runners and another for lesser-known challengers.

CAMPAIGNING AS FRONT-RUNNER

Ronald Reagan's preconvention campaign in 1980 is a good example of a front-runner approach. Reagan raised and spent much of his money in the early primaries and caucuses. His tightly run, top-down campaign built in-depth organizations in key states, obtained the support of many party leaders, and benefited from a large staff of professionals and volunteers. George W. Bush and Al Gore followed similar strategies in 2000 as did Hillary Clinton in 2008 (although, in her case, unsuccessfully), and Mitt Romney in 2012.

Front-runners begin with greater reputations, more resources, and better known national credentials. What they need to do is stay in the lead. The strategy is straightforward—take advantage of their resources: recognition as the potential nominee, the political influence that recognition conveys, a larger war chest, more staff, endorsements, press coverage, volunteers, and the ability to wage a multistate campaign.

A front-runner's advantages are most potent at the beginning of the nomination process when the perceived gap with the other candidates is widest. The front-loading of the primaries provides an additional benefit because it makes it more difficult for lesser-known competitors to parlay an early, unexpected victory into quick other wins. Proportional voting requirements in party primaries, however, make an early knockout less likely than in the past. As Matt Rhodes, Mitt Romney's 2012 campaign manager stated, ". . . we wanted to run a lean campaign, because we knew that the calendar, the way it was, with allocated delegates, it was going to be a long process. And we never expected to win this early, never."[19]

As the nomination campaign progresses, most front-runners have to combat the inevitable "anyone but them" campaign that will be waged by their opponents and the news media's propensity to extend the competition by increasing critical coverage of the front-runner.

CAMPAIGNING AS A NON-FRONT-RUNNER

Candidates that are less well known, staffed, and funded have fewer options. They have to adopt an "exceeding-expectations" strategy. Jimmy Carter is a good example. When he began his quest for the Democratic presidential nomination in 1974, few people had heard of him. Hamilton Jordan, Carter's campaign manager, designed a basic game plan to achieve surprising and newsworthy victories:

> The prospect of a crowded field coupled with the new proportional representation rule does not permit much flexibility in the early primaries. No serious candidate will have the luxury of picking or choosing among the early primaries. To pursue such a strategy would cost that candidate delegate votes and increase the possibility of being lost in the crowd. I think that we have to assume that everybody will be running in the first five or six primaries.
>
> A crowded field enhances the possibility of several inconclusive primaries with four or five candidates separated by only a few percentage points. Such a muddled picture will not continue for long as the press will begin to make "winners" of some and "losers" of others. The intense press coverage, which naturally focuses on the early primaries, plus the decent time intervals, which separate the March and mid-April primaries [in 1976], dictate a serious effort in all of the first five primaries. Our "public" strategy would probably be that Florida was the first and real test of the Carter campaign and that New Hampshire would just be a warm-up. In fact, a strong, surprise showing in New Hampshire should be our goal which would have tremendous impact on successive primaries.[20]

Jordan's plan worked. Dubbed the person to beat after his wins in the Iowa caucus and New Hampshire primary, Carter, with his defeat of George Wallace in Florida, overcame a disappointing fourth place in Massachusetts a week earlier and became the acknowledged front-runner. The Carter effort in 1976 became the model for George H. W. Bush in 1980, Gary Hart in 1984, John McCain in 2000, and most of the Democratic non-front-runners in 2004 and 2008.

Barack Obama faced a similar hurdle in 2008. Although he received a substantial amount of contributions, he needed a victory to demonstrate his viability as a potential nominee. As a minority candidate, he also had to show he could win in states with relatively small minority populations. His victory in Iowa demonstrated that he could. Although he lost the popular vote in New Hampshire, he received half the state's convention delegates and then secured a large electoral victory in the South Carolina primary. These early contests changed the dynamics of the 2008 Democratic nomination; they raised questions about Hillary Clinton's inevitability as the party's standard-bearer, helped solidify Obama's support among African American women, and generated a new round of contributions. He had made the nomination into a two-person contest.

Most non-front-runners are not as successful as Carter and Obama. It is hard to win running uphill. The number of primaries; their concentration at the beginning of the calendar; the difficulty of building, training, and sustaining volunteers; and the disparities in financial resources, especially during the media-heavy phase of the process, make it more difficult for non-front-runners to win today.

USING THE CAMPAIGN AS A PULPIT

If using the public podium is the primary goal and winning the nomination not a realistic possibility, then non-front-runners can last longer and achieve more limited objectives, such as promoting their distinctive ideological views or policy positions or gaining recognition for a future run.

Pulpit candidates cannot afford large staffs, high-priced consultants, or much, if any, paid media. They depend on volunteers, news coverage, and special events (especially debates) if they are invited to participate. In 2004, former Illinois senator Carol Moseley-Braun ran for the Democratic nomination because she did not want her party to take its large female constituency for granted. Believing it important that that there be a woman candidate, Moseley-Braun campaigned on the theme of gender equality in positions of elected leadership. Her biggest applause line was "Take the men-only sign off the White House door." But she could not afford to campaign for long. Unable to raise sufficient funds, even among women, she was forced to drop out before the first contest was held.

Rev. Al Sharpton had greater name recognition than Moseley-Braun when he ran in 2004. He had been at the forefront of various social protests, giving voice to many of the concerns of those at the lower end of the socioeconomic scale. A critic of the war in Iraq and the Bush administration's pro-business economic and social policies, he presented the "other" side, often with great wit, during the debates among the Democratic candidates. Although his campaign helped energize the African American community and bring attention to racial and social issues, he was unable to expand his base of support or his perception that he could not win the party's nomination or the general election.

Dennis Kucinich, a liberal member of Congress and former mayor of Cleveland, ran twice in 2004 and again in 2008. An outspoken critic of President George W. Bush and the war in Iraq, he too lacked money, organization, and visibility. He stayed in the 2004 race until the end but had little effect on its outcome; in 2008, he was forced to drop out early after his congressional seat was challenged by a primary opponent.

Initially, Congressman Ron Paul did not want to run for president. He did not like government and couldn't imagine himself as head of it. Persuaded by aides who wanted to promote a libertarian policy agenda, Paul entered the 2008 Republican nomination process. His goal was to attract Republicans dissatisfied with the Bush administration and libertarians who had made few inroads into that party's nomination process. Although he raised enough money and gained enough support to keep his candidacy alive, he was unable to attract mainstream Republican voters. Similarly in 2012, he remained visible but not competitive for the nomination.[21] His son, Sen. Rand Paul (Rep, Kentucky), moderated some of his father's previous policy positions to make himself more appealing to a broader cross-section of the Republican base as he contemplated running in 2016.

| BOX 5.1 | SUCCESSES AND FAILURES OF FRONT-RUNNER STRATEGIES |

SUCCESS

Democrat John Kerry (2004)
John Kerry had been the early favorite for his party's nomination. A wealthy man, he also had considerable access to outside, private funds. A strong campaigner, he had been elected to the Senate for three terms. Kerry had contemplated running for president for several years; formed his exploratory committee at the end of 2002; hired a well-known, Democratic political consulting firm; and began raising money in the year before the primaries and caucuses. Confident of victory, he hedged on his policy positions, ignored his Democratic opponents, and seemed distant and aloof.

Being the front-runner had also raised expectations about Kerry's position in the polls, his fund-raising totals, and his capacity to energize Democrats, expectations that he was initially unable to realize. Once Governor Howard Dean (VT) began to capture the attention, build a large war chest, and generate an enthusiastic group of supporters, Kerry's star began to fall. His campaign floundered in late 2003. Radical changes were needed if he was to survive.

Kerry fired his campaign manager, shortened his speeches, and interacted more with his audience. He mortgaged his house in Massachusetts for $6.4 million and lent the money to his campaign so that it could stay on the air in Iowa and New

continued

| BOX 5.1 | SUCCESSES AND FAILURES OF FRONT-RUNNER STRATEGIES *continued* |

Hampshire. And then he got unexpected outside help. Jim Rassman, a navy veteran who had served with Kerry in Vietnam, showed up at one of the candidate's rallies in Iowa and testified that Lt. Kerry had saved his life. He said, "I'm not a politician . . . I'm a registered Republican . . . I owe this man my life . . . He's going to get my vote."[22] It was an emotional moment; Kerry embraced him; their reunion brought positive attention to Kerry's military service and solidified his relationship with the veterans who began backing his campaign in Iowa. More importantly, the episode added a human dimension that had been missing up to that point.

During the next six weeks, public opinion shifted toward Kerry. He won the Iowa caucus and New Hampshire primary, regaining his front-runner status. Most Democrats believed him to be their strongest candidate with the best chance of defeating President George W. Bush. After a slow, staged start, Kerry regained his position at the front of the pack, gained momentum, and went on easily to win the Democratic nomination.

Republican John McCain (2008)

In 2000, John McCain had challenged George W. Bush and other Republicans for that party's nomination and lost. He had begun his campaign too late, raised insufficient funds, received few endorsements from Republican leaders, and was unable to generate a genuine grassroots movement in states in which only Republicans could participate. His reputation for independence, so appealing to the general public, worried partisans; his emphasis on national security issues raised questions about his priorities, particularly among social conservatives. Clearly, McCain need to refashion his conservative image and strengthen his appeal among Republican leaders if he was going to run again. And he did.

As the 2007–2008 campaign got underway, McCain stayed in the public eye, touted his experience, and proclaimed his loyalty to basic conservative principles. Well known and respected by Republicans, he began as the party's front-runner. He also adjusted his campaign strategy accordingly, from renegade in 2000 to that of the leading candidate in 2008. As his campaign manager, Rick Davis, described it:

> The campaign at the get-go was, to some degree, a reaction to the campaign in 2000. We ran a totally different campaign in 2000 and it lost. . . . The win quotient was probably the strongest motivator for our design and strategy. Therefore, we looked at the Bush successes in both 2000 and 2004. We believed bigger was better.[23]

Unfortunately for McCain, Republican losses in the 2006 midterm elections and a slowing economy marred his fund-raising and party mobilization efforts. Moreover, his history of independence, his support of immigration reform, and his deemphasis of social issues also continued to generate concerns about his beliefs. The financial and political support he anticipated from Republicans did not materialize.

By the summer of 2007, the press was reporting that McCain's campaign was suffering from internal divisions, insufficient revenue, and an incoherent strategic plan. Top aides were let go; the candidate had to borrow $4 million in November just to keep his campaign afloat. He used anticipated government matching funds as collateral. He had obviously failed as a celebrity candidate. As a consequence, he was forced to change his strategy, adopting one that was more consistent with his personal character and political style.

BOX 5.1	SUCCESSES AND FAILURES OF FRONT-RUNNER STRATEGIES *continued*

McCain decided to skip the Iowa caucus, a state with a large number of socially conservative Republicans . That decision proved wise as two of the other major candidates, Massachusetts governor, Mitt Romney, and former New York City mayor, Rudolph Giuliani, were defeated by former Arkansas governor Mike Huckabee. Their status as viable nominees declined, but McCain's was relatively unaffected. In the next nomination contest, the New Hampshire primary, McCain received 37.1 percent of the vote, substantially less than he got in 2000 but more than any of his opponents. Romney again came in second.

McCain lost the next primary to Romney in Michigan, a state in which Romney's father had served as governor, but when the campaign shifted to South Carolina, McCain who had secured the support of state party leaders won the popular vote and nineteen of the state's twenty-four convention delegates.

Florida, the next big Republican primary, a do-or-die state for Giuliani who had done poorly thus far, provided the opportunity for McCain to break out from the pack. He had received an infusion of contributions following his wins in New Hampshire and South Carolina and used that money to mount a large media effort in the final 10 days before the Florida vote. Even though he was only a plurality winner with 36 percent, he won all the convention delegates because Florida was a winner-take-all state. McCain had momentum going into the 21 Super Tuesday caucuses and primaries.[24] His star was rising.

McCain won all the big states on Super Tuesday, California, Illinois, Missouri, New Jersey, and New York, states that allocated most of their delegates to the popular-vote winner. Thus, he added a large number of delegates to the lead he already had built. By the beginning of the next month, he had a majority of the convention delegates. The race was over.

Republican Mitt Romney (2012)

In 2008, Mitt Romney had floundered despite spending the most money. However, he gained national recognition. In the years that followed, he mended his ties with party leaders, received substantial contributions from partisans, and became the candidate to beat as the 2011–2012 election cycle got underway.

Romney's strategy, much like other front-runners, was to play it safe and campaign as if he were the nominee. He purposely maintained a low public profile. His campaign staged fewer media events and aired fewer commercials than it had four years earlier. Aides limited press access to him; they structured the interviews he had with reporters and kept him to script. He was cautioned not to ad lib.

Romney made only 11 visits to Iowa prior to its caucus.[25] Matt Rhoades, Romney's 2012 manager, commented: ". . . we didn't want to chase shiny objects, things like straw polls, topics we didn't want to talk about . . . the plan in the primary was to focus the campaign on the president's record on jobs and the economy."[26] Only after polls revealed him running into electoral difficulty when Governor Rick Perry (Texas) entered the race in summer of 2011, did Romney redirect his attention to his partisan opponents and unleashed a negative advertising campaign against them. By doing so, he took some of the heat off his own personal and policy vulnerabilities, particularly his support for Massachusetts health care as governor, and his decisions as head of Bain Capital.

continued

BOX 5.1	SUCCESSES AND FAILURES OF FRONT-RUNNER STRATEGIES *continued*

The strategic approach was successful. After tying Santorum in Iowa, winning in New Hampshire, and losing to Gingrich in South Carolina, Romney won primaries in Florida, Arizona, and Michigan, extending his delegate lead. His organizational and financial resources were greater than those of his opponents combined. Unable to close the delegate gap or the perception that Romney was the most electable of the Republican candidates, each of his challengers dropped out of the race, one by one. The last to do so, Rick Santorum, ended his candidacy on April 10, 2012. The Republican front-runner had won again, using his superior resources, reputation, and perceived electability to gain the GOP nomination.

FAILURE

Democrat Hillary Clinton (2008)
Hillary Rodham Clinton began her quest for the 2008 Democratic nomination with a carefully calculated and scripted campaign that focused on the large states with the strongest Democratic base. She relied on many of the advisers and fundraisers who had worked in her husband's presidential campaigns. Seeking to maximize her front-runner's advantage, she raised a lot of money quickly, transferred $10 million in unspent funds from her 2006 Senate campaign, and gained the endorsements of many well-known Democrats. She led Barack Obama, her principal nomination opponent in the 2007 prenomination polls, by about 25 percent and seemed well on her way to her party's nomination.

Clinton's strategic goal was to use her financial resources to score an early knockout. Victories in the initial contests would reinforce the "inevitability" theme of her nomination. She directed her appeal to rank-and-file Democrats, especially to women, minorities, and blue collar workers. Her plan was to campaign as a centrist. She refused to apologize for her 2002 Senate vote to give President Bush the authority to use force in Iraq, which she claimed was the correct decision based on the information available to members of Congress at that time. She also supported a congressional resolution that categorized the Iranian Revolutionary Guard as a terrorist organization. Her Democratic opponents hammered her on these votes; they pointed to her high negatives among Republicans and Independents as an indication that she could not win a general election. These negative perceptions discouraged her campaign from confronting and criticizing her principal Democratic challenger, Barack Obama, despite the advice from her pollster, Mark Penn, that she do so by embracing her American values and criticizing Obama's "lack of American roots." In a memo to the candidate, Penn wrote:

> Every speech should contain the line you were born in the middle of America to the middle class in the middle of the last century. And talk about the . . . deeply American values you grew up with, learned as a child and that drive you today. Values of fairness, compassion, responsibility, giving back.[27]

Clinton did not spend as much time in Iowa as did her nomination opponents. Nor did she have a large and active on-the-ground operation in that state. She came in third in the caucus vote, a very disappointing result for the "inevitable" nominee.

| BOX 5.1 | SUCCESSES AND FAILURES OF FRONT-RUNNER STRATEGIES *continued* |

After her loss in Iowa, Clinton became more aggressive and less staged. She needed to reconnect to her Democratic base. An incident in New Hampshire in which she showed emotion from the pressures of the campaign helped reveal a personal dimension that had been lacking previously. When asked how she was doing after Iowa, she seemed to choke up as she explained how important the election was to the country. Her show of emotion resonated particularly well with women voters who shifted their support to her in the final days before the New Hampshire primary. Clinton won 39 percent of the popular vote compared to Obama's 36 percent in New Hampshire, but they split the state's convention delegates.

Although Clinton's popular vote victory gave her a much needed boost, it also drained her war chest. Her campaign had gone through $100 million from the announcement of her candidacy through the first primary. As one of her senior advisers, Harold Ickes, told her and others on the staff, "the cupboard is bare." Unable to match Obama's fund-raising in the early months of 2008, Clinton had to lend her campaign $5 million just to stay in the running.

Lack of money and organization forced Clinton to focus her efforts on the larger states on Super Tuesday when 15 primaries and 7 caucuses were held. Although she won the popular vote in most of the big states, she did not win the largest number of delegates from these states because of her campaign's failure to concentrate on the delegate-rich districts in cities that had high concentrations of African Americans. Clinton did not compete with Obama in most of the caucus states and lost all of them but one, Colorado. When the results of that delegate selection process on Super Tuesday were tallied, Clinton trailed Obama by about fifty pledged delegates. In a nomination process based on proportional voting, she found herself at an increasing disadvantage.

February proved to be her worst month. She lost the five caucuses and five primaries in that month, swelling Obama's pledged delegate lead to around 150. She also fell further behind in the money race and was forced to lend her campaign more money.

Internal rivalries among her advisers began to unravel her organization. She fired her manager. Her campaign was clearly on the ropes. Just to catch up, Clinton had to win the remaining large states, Texas, Ohio, Indiana, and Pennsylvania, by a sizable percentage of the popular vote if she was to narrow Obama's delegate lead. She won three of them but not by enough to close the pledged delegate gap.

The only other option was to turn to the unpledged superdelegates, many of whom had initially endorsed her or were sympathetic to her candidacy. The support of these delegates, however, was difficult to sustain. Superdelegates are politicians who are sensitive to public opinion; most of them believed that they had to support the democratic process in their own states, that is, vote as their state voted.

The front-runner had lost; she had been overtaken by a more skillful campaign waged by a more charismatic candidate with a more popular message and a more energetic base of supporters.

BOX 5.2 | FAILURES AND SUCCESSES OF NON-FRONT-RUNNER STRATEGIES

FAILURE

Democrat Howard Dean (2004)

For political pundits, campaign operatives, and the news media, the big news of the 2003–2004 Democratic nomination process was the rise and fall of Howard Dean. When Dean announced his presidential ambitions in the fall of 2001, few took him seriously. How could a political unknown from a small, rural state (Vermont) have a realistic chance of winning the Democratic Party's presidential nomination? It was not 1976, when a poisonous political climate in Washington (the Watergate scandal and President Gerald Ford's pardon of Richard Nixon) and an extended Democratic primary process allowed Georgia governor Jimmy Carter to parlay early and surprising victories into a nomination victory.

Nor did Dean fit the mode of successful Democratic presidential candidates. He did not come from a southern state as Carter and Clinton had. He was not associated with the moderate wing of his party as both of them were. In fact, his support of a bill to grant civil unions to same-sex adults was seen as a major liability in 2004. Nor did he have a lot of wealthy backers, a national political organization, or even much public recognition. How, then, did he become the Democratic front-runner, and why did his campaign collapse so quickly?

Dean's rise to prominence was a result of his innovative campaign appeal and an Internet-based communications.[28] Recalling the idealism of the 1960s, Dean talked about empowering people who felt alienated by the policies and practices of the George W. Bush administration; he had categorically opposed the war in Iraq in contrast to most of the other Democratic candidates, most of whom had been senators and voted in favor of a resolution allowing the president to use military force.

Dean used the Internet to solicit funds, involve those who accessed his web site in the activities of his campaign, and provide them with information to convince others to join the cause. Live and recorded speeches, advertisements, and even responses to criticisms were accessible on his web site. He raised more money than any of the other Democratic candidates in the year prior to the election, and he did so from small donors. His broad-based financial support suggested that he was tapping into a large segment of the Democratic base and possibly beyond it, reaching and energizing young people. That political perception gave credence to his candidacy.

Dean's rhetoric, fund-raising, and Internet operations were newsworthy. They attracted the attention of the reporters who evaluate the candidates in the year before the election on the basis of the money they raise, the recognition they gain, the distinctiveness of their campaign, and their standing in the polls. Dean scored well in all these categories. He became the front-runner in the fall of 2003. Former vice president and presidential candidate Al Gore endorsed him as did several labor unions in December 2003. These endorsements from political insiders, however, raised questions about Dean's status as an outsider, anti-establishment fighter.

Being number one in the polls also meant being the number one target. Dean did not fare well under the microscope of news media and attacks by his political opponents. His words and actions during the period in which he was the governor of Vermont were used against him. As governor, he had once called Medicare "a bureaucratic disaster," disparaged the Iowa caucus as "controlled by special interests," and asserted after the capture of Saddam Hussein, "America was no safer than before the Iraqi dictator was apprehended," a claim that most Americans disputed.

| BOX 5.2 | FAILURES AND SUCCESSES OF NON-FRONT-RUNNER STRATEGIES |

Dean's campaign comments were highlighted as evidence that he lacked the temperament, thoughtfulness, and truthfulness to be president. He was rebuked for implying that his brother (who had been missing and believed dead since he traveled to Southeast Asia in 1974) had served in the military when he had not done so, rebuked for stating that U.S. policy in the Middle East was unbalanced and unfair, and rebuked for the comment "I still want to be the candidate for guys with Confederate flags in their pickup trucks," a comment that some interpreted as racist. Dean's opponents asked: Was he ready for prime time? Could he be elected if he were the Democratic nominee?

Dean's temperament, particularly the anger and emotion he displayed, also raised questions about his mental balance and emotional stability. His "screaming" speech to supporters after his disappointing finish in the Iowa caucus was played and replayed by the news media and became the target of late-night comics. Had he snapped under the pressure? Would he do so in the White House?

The Dean campaign also suffered from internal staff strife and turnover.[29] He had squandered his financial lead by advertising before most Democrats were tuned to the contest, expanded his staff too quickly, and decentralized his campaign's decision-making structure too much. Nor did his web supporters congeal into an effective grass-roots force. After losing in Iowa and New Hampshire, he had difficulty raising enough money to continue his campaign in the Michigan and Wisconsin, primaries that sealed his fate. He dropped out in mid-February, and a month later endorsed Kerry.

SUCCESS

Democrat Barack Obama (2008)

The people who ran the Obama 2008 campaign learned from Dean's mistakes. Preliminary planning for Obama's presidential campaign began in 2006, right after the midterm elections. David Axelrod and David Plouffe, the political consultants who had managed his 2004 Senate campaign, met with him in November 2006 to explore the possibilities of a presidential run in 2008. Obama indicated that he was interested but still undecided. Clinton's large lead in the polls and the effect of a presidential campaign on his family were major concerns. It was not until January 2007 that he decided to toss his hat into the ring.

Intense planning began after he made his decision to run. David Plouffe, his campaign manager, and David Axelrod, chief strategist, wanted the organization to be lean and highly focused on critical needs: hiring key personnel, raising money, mobilizing a base of supporters, and scheduling and advancing campaign events. Special units were established to handle relations with Democratic Party leaders and elected officials, volunteers, communications technology, and strategic operations.[30]

Winning the Iowa caucus was the campaign's initial goal. Iowa was important for three reasons: to demonstrate that Obama, an African American, could win in a predominantly white state; to show that Hillary Clinton's nomination was not inevitable; and to prove that an army of volunteers could be identified, organized, and mobilized from the Internet. Since Clinton had the endorsements of many prominent state and national party leaders, labor union officials, and the sympathy of much of the Democrats' rank-and-file voters, Plouffe concluded that the only way

continued

BOX 5.2	FAILURES AND SUCCESSES OF NON-FRONT-RUNNER STRATEGIES

Obama could win in Iowa and other states was to enlarge the Democratic electorate by attracting new voters and appealing to independent-leaning Democrats.

With the caucus a year away, the campaign literally set up shop in Iowa along with most of the other Democratic candidates, except for Clinton.[31] During his visits to that state, Obama held up to six events a day. His campaign flooded the state with volunteers who went to every high school, college, and university to inform students about Obama, recruit in-state volunteers, and generate excitement about his candidacy. Major events, geared to attracting a popular base, were also a source of data on the attendees. Their e-mail addresses, cell phone numbers, and zip codes were collected and stored in the campaign's data bank and used to stay in touch, staff future events, gain more "friends," and register and turn out voters.[32]

Obama loved the crowds and drew energy from them. His stump speeches, which he refined in the early months of the campaign, inspired and motivated many in attendance to work on his behalf. Social networking increased their numbers.

To convert the volunteers into a viable grassroots organization, the Obama camp set up three- to four-day training sessions at which volunteers, many of whom had never worked in a political campaign, were given instruction on how to identify potential supporters, mobilize them, and persuade them to vote for Obama. The payoff was evident at caucus night in Iowa when almost twice as many people turned out in 2008 than in the party's previous presidential caucus in that state. Obama won 37.6 percent of the vote compared to Edwards's 29.7 percent and Clinton's 29.5 percent.

Although his strategy was producing a growing coalition, his candidacy had not yet commanded national attention until his surprising victory in Iowa. Obama surged ahead of Clinton after the Iowa vote. He also drew even with her in fundraising. In fact, Obama had a financial advantage going into election year, a larger base of small donors from whom he could solicit additional contributions. A larger proportion of Clinton's donors had already given the maximum amount. After his victory in Iowa, Obama's revenues shot up; he received $90.5 million in January and February of 2008, almost equal to the amount he raised the previous year, and almost double the amount Clinton got during the same period. His campaign was also more frugal in spending.[33]

The victory in Iowa raised expectations for Obama, but the New Hampshire primary, scheduled five days later, presented additional problems for the grassroots component of his campaign.[34] Clinton had a stronger ground operation in New Hampshire, one that included the support of most state party leaders, labor unions, and Emily's List, an organization devoted to the election of women candidates. Moreover, Obama was competing against McCain for the votes of Independents.[35]

Clinton beat Obama by 3 percent of the popular vote in New Hampshire, but they divided the delegates evenly, moderating the significance of her win. Following New Hampshire, the Democratic contest turned to the Nevada caucus, in which Clinton won the popular vote by 6 percent, but the delegates were again divided with Obama eventually getting a majority. South Carolina, the last primary before Super Tuesday when Clinton was expected to do well, was critical for Obama who needed a victory to regain momentum he lost after Iowa. He got it, receiving 55 percent of the popular vote and twenty-five of the state's forty-five delegates.

BOX 5.2	FAILURES AND SUCCESSES OF NON-FRONT-RUNNER STRATEGIES

Obama used his financial advantage to advertise extensively in the large states that held their primaries on Super Tuesday in early February; he also competed in all of the smaller caucus states whereas Clinton contested only one of them. Obama's strategy proved successful. Although Clinton won the large states and Obama the smaller ones, he received a total of fifteen more delegates than she did. He had survived Super Tuesday and was in position to extend his delegate lead during the rest of the month. By the beginning of March, he held a 150 pledged delegate lead.

At this point, the press's campaign narrative began to change from its emphasis on popular vote to one that emphasized pledged delegates. David Plouffe had convinced the *New York Times* to count delegates in caucus states on the basis of the vote in the first stage of the caucus process even though the actual delegates would not be chosen until state conventions later in the spring. Plouffe pointed out to Adam Nagourney, the *Times* chief political correspondent, that the initial caucus vote almost always reflected the final allocation of delegates chosen at state conventions.[36]

Even though Clinton won the Ohio, Texas, and Rhode Island primaries on March 4, she was able to reduce Obama's lead by only 6 delegates. At this point, the 852 unpledged superdelegates, 19 percent of the Democratic convention, were the only significant hurdle that stood in the way of his nomination. As Obama built a lead among the pledged delegates, his campaign launched a public relations effort to convince these "supers" to support him despite the initial orientation of many of them toward Clinton. In his book *The Audacity to Win*, Plouffe wrote, "We assumed that if we did well at the polls, the supers would follow, and if we stumbled early, it wouldn't matter."[37] And he was right. The superdelegates began to fall into the Obama camp, reflecting the choice of voters in their states.

Although the Democratic contest continued until all the primaries and caucuses had concluded, Obama never relinquished his delegate lead. His campaign had designed and executed a successful, delegate-oriented strategy. The use of the Internet as a communication tool contributed to his success and became the model for future elections.

SUMMARY

In running for their party's nomination, candidates have to make a number of important strategic decisions. These include when to begin, how to organize, where to concentrate their early efforts, how to raise money and on what to spend it, how to gain the necessary news media coverage, monitor public opinion, and design and target a distinctive appeal and simultaneously create an authentic leadership image. Making effective use of modern communication technologies is essential to campaign success.

Decisions on mobilizing and allocating sufficient resources to build and maintain delegate support depend on the particular status and circumstances of individual candidates, the environment in which the nomination occurs, and the time frame needed to implement a strategic plan. The new technologies of the late twentieth and early twenty-first centuries figure prominently in this effort. They have extended the reach but shortened the candidate's reaction time. Public opinion polls and focus groups are now used to design, test, and track political advertising; targeted appeals are calibrated to arouse particular emotions in selective political communities; and interactive campaigning online is now standard fare. The use of these technologies requires expertise and financial resources—another reason for having a large war chest early in the campaign. In general, there have been two successful prototypes for winning the nomination: "the out-front, big-bucks, challenge-me-if-you-dare approach" of the leading candidates and "the come-from-the-pack approach" of the non-front-runners.

Front-runners have to maintain their position as likely nominees. That position brings recognition, money, and political endorsements. These resources, in turn, provide flexibility and allow candidates to wage multistate campaigns, but also have higher expectations to meet to maintain their leading-candidate status. The concentration of caucuses and primaries at the beginning of the nomination calendar and usually, the requirement for proportional voting, adds to the front-runners' advantage.

In contrast, non-front-runners need stepping stones to the nomination. Their initial goal must be to establish their viability as candidates. At the outset, the key is recognition. Over the long haul, it is momentum. Recognition is bestowed by the news media on those who do well in the early caucuses and primaries; momentum is achieved by winning a series of prenomination contests. Together, recognition and momentum compensate for what the non-front-runners lack in reputation and popular appeal. That is why non-front-runners must concentrate their time, efforts, and resources on the first few caucuses and primaries. They have no choice: winning will enhance their status; losing will confirm their secondary position. It is an uphill struggle that few non-front-runners have successfully overcome, Carter and Obama being the principal exceptions.

In the end, the ability to generate a popular appeal among the party's electoral base is likely to be decisive. Only one person in each party can amass a majority of the delegates, and that is the individual who can build a broad-based coalition. Although specific groups may be targeted, if the overall constituency is too narrow, the nomination cannot be won. That is why most candidates tend to broaden and moderate their appeal over the course of the nomination process.

WHERE ON THE WEB?

The Nomination Campaign
www.P2016.org
> A web site that provides pertinent and up-to-date information on the current or next campaign with links to other sources.

www.4President.org
> Contains information on candidates, their web sites, and commercials. Also maintains a blog on the campaign and election.

www.gallup.com
> Check this site for up-to-date polling data and analyses.

www.nationaljournal.com
> There are many news sources for following the presidential primaries and caucuses; the *National Journal*'s site is one of the best.

www.nytimes.com
> *The New York Times* prides itself on being a paper of record. You will find much information on the policy positions and speeches of the candidates in this newspaper and on its website as well as the latest delegate count and prenomination polls.

www.politico.com
> A daily news site that focuses on national and state politics and government.

www.pollingreport.com
> Summarizes public polls on the election.

www.realclearpolitics.com
> Another web site that focuses on politics and government.

EXERCISES

1. Check the official and unofficial web sites of the candidates. Use the information from these web sites to compare and contrast their positions on the most controversial issues in the campaign. Then compare the personal images that they have tried to project. On the basis of these comparisons, whom do you think has positioned themselves best for their party's nomination and why?

2. Follow the news of the nomination campaign from different news media sources: a major news organization, local television station, and print or online magazine. How does their coverage differ? From which source did you learn the most about their campaign strategy? From which did you learn the most about the candidates themselves?

3. Analyze the nomination campaign on the basis of the candidates' basic strategic approaches, policy appeals, and personal images. Use Internet sources from the candidates, the news media, and public interest web sites to obtain the information you need for your analysis.

SELECTED READINGS

Aldrich, John. "The Invisible Primary and Its Effects on Democratic Choice," *PS: Political Science and Politics*, 42 (Jan. 2009): 33–38.

Burden, Barry. "The Nominations: Ideology, Timing, and Organization," in *The Elections of 2012*, Michael Nelson, ed. Washington, DC: Sage/CQ Press, 2014, pp. 21–46.

Burton, Michael John. "The Republican Primary Season: Strategic Positioning in the GOP Field," in *Campaigning for President 2012*, Dennis W. Johnson, ed. New York: Routledge, 2012, pp. 43–56.

Doherty, Brendan J. *The Rise of the President's Permanent Campaign.* Lawrence, KS: University of Kansas Press, 2012.

Green, Joshua. "The Front-Runner's Fall," *The Atlantic*, Sept. 2008. www.theatlantic
.com/magazine/print/2008/09/the-front-runner-8217-s-fall/6944

Halperin, Mark, and John Heilemann. *Double Down: Game Change 2012*. New
York: Penguin Press, 2013.

Jamieson, Kathleen Hall, ed. *Electing the President, 2012: The Insider's View*.
Philadelphia: University of Pennsylvania Press, 2013.

Kennedy Institute of Politics. *Campaign for President: The Managers Look at 2012*.
Landam, MD: Rowman & Littlefield, 2013.

Magleby, David B. *Getting Inside the Outside Campaign*. Provo, UT: Brigham Young
University, 2000.

Mayer, William G., and Jonathan Bernstein, eds. *The Making of the Presidential
Candidates 2012*. Lanham, MD: Rowman and Littlefield, 2012.

Norrander, Barbara. "Democratic Marathon, Republican Sprint: The 2008 Presidential Nominations," in *The American Elections of 2008*, Janet M. Box-
Steffensmeier and Steven E. Schier, eds. Lanham, MD: Rowman & Littlefield,
2009, pp. 33–53.

Plouffe, David. *The Audacity to Win*. New York: Viking, 2009.

Sides, John, and Lynn Vaverck. *The Gamble: Choice and Chance in 2012 Presidential
Election*. Princeton, NJ: Princeton University Press, 2013.

Simien, Evelyn M. "Clinton and Obama: The Impact of Race and Sex on the 2008
Democratic Presidential Primaries," in *Winning the Presidency*, William J. Crotty,
ed. Boulder, CO: Paradigm Publishers, 2009, pp. 123–134.

NOTES

1. Howard Wolson, *Campaign for President: The Managers Look at 2008*.
   (Lanham, MD: Rowman & Littlefield, 2009), p. 45.
2. In his first three years in office, Bush took 40 percent of his domestic trips from
   the White House to states he won or lost by 6 percent of the vote or less. Kathryn
   Dunn Tenpass and Anthony Corrado, "Permanent Campaign Brushes Aside
   Tradition," *Arizona Daily Star* (March 30, 2004). www.brookings.edu
        See also Brendan J. Doherty, *The Rise of the President's Permanent
   Campaign* (Lawrence, KS: University of Kansas Press, 2012).
3. "Iowa and New Hampshire," Democracy in Action. www.p2012.org/chrnnewh
   /newhvisits12.htm
4. John Edwards did not benefit nearly as much from his second-place finishes in
   Iowa in 2004 or 2008. Kerry's victory in 2004 launched his candidacy while
   Howard Dean's poor showing and his antics on election night after that caucus
   doomed his. Trying to encourage his disappointed workers and supporters, Dean
   gave a passionate speech ending with a yell that looked to television viewers as
   if he had lost control of himself. Kerry's victory and Dean's scream were newsworthy; they dominated the headlines. Edwards's relatively strong performance
   did not.
        News media coverage had a similar effect in 2008. Even though Edwards
   came in second ahead of Hillary Clinton in Iowa, Obama's win and Clinton's
   defeat were the big stories, not Edwards's second place. Moreover, the fact that
   Edwards was known to Iowa voters campaigned vigorously in that state and still
   did not win the caucus vote contributed to his political obituary.
5. Keith Nahigian, *Campaign for President: The Managers Look at 2012* (Lanham,
   MD: Rowman and Littlefield, 2013), p. 27.

6. New Hampshire brags that its primary has been the first in the nation since 1920. "First in the Nation," in *The New Hampshire Primary: What It Means to the State and the Nation* (published by the State of New Hampshire, 2000), p. 26.
7. "This Time Around Less News from the Campaign," Pew Research Center's Project for Excellence in Journalism, May 17, 2012. www.journalism.org/number /time-around-less-news-campaign-front/
8. Pat Buchanan's 1996 campaign manager described a typical media day for his candidacy in Iowa:

> Gregg [Mueller, the press secretary] and Pat would get up at about five in the morning, get some coffee, get in the minivan, and go from one TV station to the other, in the local market, wherever they had morning shows, and they would do a live segment on every morning television show.
>
> Then they'd come back to the hotel, read through the newspapers and at 10 A.M., we'd go out and do our theme event for the day—drive whatever our message was, get out a press release, which we faxed out everywhere and let that, hopefully, resonate into the newspapers.
>
> At noon, we'd go back to the television stations, if they would have us, or else we'd drive into a new market . . . all the time that they would be driving the van, Greg would have Pat on the cell phone doing radio interviews. . . . Buchanan would literally go from one station to the other to the other, go back to the hotel, maybe take a nap in the afternoon, then you go out at 5 P.M. and you do the evening TV stations. If you literally saturated the local TV market, you try to get to the next one. You try to maximize the amount of time you could get on TV in a state while you were there.

Terrence Jeffrey, *Campaign for President: The Managers Look at '96* (Hollis, NH: Hollis Publishing Company, 1997), pp. 7–8.
9. "Election Watch '08: The Road to the Conventions," *Media Monitor,* 22 (Summer 2008). www.cmpa.com.
10. Thomas E. Patterson and Robert D. McClure, *The Unseeing Eye* (New York: Putnam, 1976), p. 58.
11. Dante J. Scala notes that the Democratic candidates who have been most successful in New Hampshire are those whose campaigns built such partisan coalitions. Dante J. Scala, "Rereading the Tea Leaves: New Hampshire as a Barometer of Presidential Primary Success," *PS: Political Science and Politics,* 36 (April 2003), pp. 187–192. John Kerry and Hillary Clinton also emphasized their partisan base in New Hampshire.
12. Dick Morris, the political strategist behind Clinton's 1996 reelection campaign, described the process by which media advertising was designed:

> We prepared several different rough versions of the ads, called animatics, which [pollster] Mark Penn would arrange to test at fifteen shopping malls around the nation. After the Republicans began to attack us in their own ads, Penn tested the opposition ad and our reply at the same time to measure their relative impact. Penn's staffers would set themselves up in a mall and invite shoppers one by one to fill out a short questionnaire about Clinton, Dole, and their own political views. Then they would show the voters the ad we wanted to test. Afterward the shopper would fill in the same questionnaire and Penn would measure any changes in opinion.
>
> Based on the mall tests, we decided which ad to run and whether to combine it with elements from ads that did not do as well. We worked for hours to make the ad fit thirty seconds. Then we'd send the script to Doug Sosnik, the White House political director, who gave it to the president for his OK.

Dick Morris, *Behind the Oval Office* (New York: Random House, 1997), pp. 146–147.

13. Ernest B. McGowen and Daniel J. Palaqzzolo, "Momentum and Media in the 2012 Republican Presidential Nomination," *Presidential Studies Quarterly*, 44 (Sept. 2014), pp. 431–446.

14. "About One Third of Super-Tuesday Democratic Voters Say They Know Enough to Make an Informed Choice." Annenberg Public Policy Center of the University of Pennsylvania (February 27, 2004). www.annenbergpublicpolicycenter.org /naes/2004_03_knowledge-dem-candidates-supertuesday_02–27_pr

15. "Public Has a Lot to Learn about the 2012 Presidential Race but Those Who Seek Out Fact Checking on the Internet Know More," Flackcheck.org (September 26, 2008). http://www.flackcheck.org/press/the-public-still-has-a-lot-to-learn-about-the-2012-presidential-race-but-those-who-seek-out-fact-checking-on-the-internet-know-more

16. "Endorsements Don't Sway the Public—With a Few Exceptions," Annenberg Public Policy Center (March 5, 2008). www.annenbergpublicpolicycenter.org.

17. Keith Madden, *Electing the President 2012: The Insiders' View*, Kathleen Hall Jamieson, ed. (Philadelphia: University of Pennsylvania Press, 2013), p. 57.

18. According to a survey conducted by the Pew Research Center for the People and the Press, 11 percent of the population reported the Internet as their primary source of news about the 2000 election campaign, 21 percent about the 2004 campaign, 40 percent for the 2008 election, and 47 percent in 2012. "Low Marks for the 2012 Election, Pew Research Center for the People and the Press (Nov.15, 2012). http://www.people-press.org/2012/11/15/section-4 -news-sources-election-night-and-views-of-press-coverage/

19. Matt Rhodes, *Campaign for President: The Managers Look at 2012* (Landham, MD: Rowman and Littlefield, 2012), p. 35.

20. Hamilton Jordan, "Memorandum to Jimmy Carter, August 4, 1974," in Martin Schram, *Running for President 1976* (New York: Stein & Day, 1977), pp. 379–380.

21. According to Paul's 2008 campaign manager, Lew Moore, "At some point it [the campaign] caught on fire on the Internet and we were able to start raising money. We were able to start building an organization through Meetup. Before the end of the campaign, we had seventy-five thousand people in Meetup groups and we raised thirty-five million dollars." Lew Moore, *Campaign for President: The Managers Look at 2008*, p. 22.

22. Patrick Devlin, "Contrasts in Presidential Primary Campaign Commercials of 2004," Paper presented at Georgetown University, November 2004, p. 26.

23. Rick Davis, *Campaign for President: The Managers Look at 2008*, pp. 5–6.

24. Giuliani's withdrawal and his quick endorsement of McCain along with the endorsement of California governor Arnold Schwarzenegger added to that momentum.

25. In 2007, four years earlier, he had made 43 visits and stayed 77 days. "P2008: Race for the White House," Democracy in Action. http://www.gwu.edu/~action /P2008.html

26. Matt Rhodes, *Campaign for President: The Managers Look at 2012*, p 36.

27. Joshua Green, "The Front-Runner's Fall," *The Atlantic*, (Sept. 2008). www .theatlantic.com/magazine/print/2008/09/the-front-runner-8217-s-fall/6944

28. The Dean campaign maintained an ongoing conversation with people who frequented his web site. The campaign requested comments and suggestions from those who accessed the site and posted them on the blog, which became an ongoing political forum. Campaign officials, including manager Joe Trippi, spent hours communicating with people who had asked questions and made recommendations. By the end of 2003, the names of 500,000 subscribers were in the campaign's data bank, ready to be mobilized for the caucus and primary campaigns.
29. Dan Balz and Jonathan Finer, "Dean Staff Shake-Up Long Coming," *Washington Post* (January 30, 2004), p. A18. http://www.washingtonpost.com/wp-dyn/articles/A61580-2004Jan29.html?nav=hptop_ts
30. David Plouffe, *The Audacity to Win* (New York: Viking, 2009), p. 30.
31. Obama visited Iowa forty-four times and stayed there a total of eighty-nine days. "Democracy in America: Race for the White House, 2008." www.gwu.edu/~action/2008/ia08/iavisits08d.html
32. Plouffe, *Audacity*, p. 48.
33. Ibid., pp. 35–36.
34. Although Obama had visited New Hampshire often, his grassroots operation was smaller than in Iowa. Democracy in Action. www.gwu.edu/~action/2008/nh08/nhvisits08d.html
35. David Plouffe writes that the Obama campaign received numerous reports of Independents telling them, "Your guy is going to win. I think McCain is the best Republican, it will give us a good choice. But don't worry, I'm voting Obama in November." Plouffe, *Audacity*, p. 153.
36. Ibid, pp. 183–184.
37. Ibid., p. 183.

6 CHAPTER | THE POST-PRIMARY CAMPAIGN

INTRODUCTION

Caucuses and primaries start early in the year, and recent nominating conventions occur in mid to late summer, leaving a period of four to five months from the time a nominee has been effectively determined to the time that nominee is officially "crowned" as the party's standard-bearer. This interregnum is a very important recovery, reconsolidation period for the candidate who has won a highly competitive nomination as well as for the party in which that nomination contest has occurred.

The successful nominees need to repair any damage that the process inflicted on their electoral coalition, policy stands, and leadership imagery. They also need to replenish their war chests, restructure and expand their organization, stay in the news, shift their criticisms to their partisan opponent, design a broader-based appeal, and tell a winning campaign narrative—a lot to be done in a short period of time.

After a divisive nomination, the party also has to reunify and reenergize its base, raise money for its election committees, and promote all its candidates for the general election.

The spring of the election year is also a critical period for incumbents running for reelection as well *even if they were not challenged for renomination*. During this period, they need to remain in their presidential mode in public while strengthening their organizational, financial, and political base behind-the-scenes. This time frame, approximately a year and three or four months, depending when their partisan opponent is determined, enables them to extend their incumbency advantage in the general election.

THE NONCOMPETITIVE PRECONVENTION PHASE
HEALING PARTISAN DISCORD

It is necessary for the winning candidate to consolidate the party, appealing to partisans who supported other candidates. The sooner such an effort is undertaken the better, since the news media will continue to highlight rifts within the party as potential problems for the campaign. Egos must be soothed, losing candidates invited to participate in the convention, and the electoral base has to be extended.

Both candidates in 2008 faced unification issues with their partisan core. McCain's maverick appeal did not sit well with Republican activists who desired a candidate who advocated and prioritized their values and beliefs. Although McCain said he was a Reagan conservative, his emphasis on his own independence and the need for policy change did not sit well with social conservatives. His choice of Sarah Palin as his running mate did, however. Her nomination as vice presidential candidate energized the Republican base, so much so that McCain began to appear at *her* rallies.

Although Obama did not face the financial constraints that confront most winners after a divisive nomination in 2008, he did have to gain the support of Clinton voters, particularly women and organized labor, and do so in a much shorter period of time, only 10 weeks from the end of the Democratic primaries in June to the beginning of its convention at the end of August. To accomplish this goal, Obama met secretly with Clinton, two days after the last primaries were held, to begin the healing process. To encourage Clinton's volunteers and donors to work for him in the general election, he promised her and her husband a major role at the Democratic convention and agreed to help pay off some of her campaign debt. The Clintons' convention prime-time speeches and subsequent campaigning for Obama ended the bitterness and brought her supporters quickly into the Democratic fold.

In 2012, Romney had little difficulty coalescing the Republican base. The strength of partisan loyalties, the negative across-the-board evaluation of President Obama by Republicans, and Romney's selection of economic conservative Paul Ryan as his running mate contributed to the strong backing he received from fellow Republicans, even those that did not support him initially in the caucuses and primaries. He was generally well liked, adequately conservative, and perceived as the most electable of all the GOP candidates.[1]

REPOSITIONING AND REPRIORITIZING THE ISSUES

In addition to unifying the party, the winners of the nomination process also have to reposition themselves and usually reshape and reprioritize their campaign narrative. After moving toward their party's ideological core during the contested phase of the nomination and emphasizing the issues most important to partisan activists, they usually have to soften and broaden their appeals, moving toward the political center, repositioning issue stands for the general election, and restructuring their campaign narrative.

Repositioning and reprioritizing can be tricky business, however, since the news media and opposition party are sure to point out the policy inconsistencies, strident rhetoric, and the most controversial stands candidates have taken and reiterated throughout the contested stage of the nominations, raising, questions about the candidates' credibility and dependability to follow through on their campaign promises if elected.

George W. Bush adopted the move-to-the-middle strategy in 2000. Forced to appeal to the conservative Republicans to win the GOP nomination in 2000, Bush then accentuated the positive, stressed his compassion, and focused on issues such as education, housing, Medicare, and Social Security—issues that had special appeal to Democrats, and especially to women voters. By taking moderate stands on social issues, Bush was following the same strategy that Clinton used in 1995–1996 when he emphasized the Republican ideological policy agenda but took more centrist positions than did their congressional leadership.[2]

In 2004, however, Bush campaigned for president as if he were running for the Republican nomination. His conservative orientation was consistent with the policies of his administration, although he did place greater emphasis on domestic issues in the 2004 campaign than he was able to do as president after the terrorist attacks of September 11, 2001.

Bush's conservative policy emphasis in 2004 was a response to the highly polarized political climate in the United States. In that election and the ones that followed, Republican strategists have operated on the basis of three assumptions: that the country is evenly divided between Republicans and Democrats; that most partisans have already made up their minds for whom to vote; and that the proportion of independent or swing voters has shrunk to a very small percentage of the population. Bush's advisers believed that they stood a better chance of winning by motivating their base than persuading the relatively few undecided voters to support him.[3]

In 2008, with public dissatisfaction rising, the issue was change and the presidential leadership needed to achieve it. McCain stressed his independence and experience; he also pointed to his family values and voiced support for continuing the Bush tax cuts, which he had opposed as a senator. In contrast, Obama drew a sharp distinction between the economic policies of the Bush administration and his policies, which he said would bring greater benefit to the middle class.

In 2012, the Obama campaign had a choice: paint Romney as a flip-flopper, given the moderate policies he pursued as governor of Massachusetts, including the support of a state health care program similar to the Affordable Care Act; or describe him as an ideological conservative, given the positions he had articulated to win the Republican nomination. The campaign decided to do both, but in different stages.

During 2011, when the news media's narrative focused on Romney's policy inconsistencies, the Obama campaign took the position that Romney lacked core beliefs, that he would say and do anything that worked to his political advantage. Later on, Obama and his surrogates emphasized the conservative policy stands Romney was forced to take to win the Republican nomination. According to political strategist, David Axelrod, the campaign's goal was to extend the Republican primary process, get Romney's more conservative challengers to question his beliefs and the intensity with which he held them, and then emphasize the difference between the president's issues stands and the governor's in the general election.[4]

The task for Romney after winning a majority of the delegates in early April 2012 was to turn the focus toward Obama and his economic and social policies. With the country still mired in the residue of the great recession, with high unemployment, tight credit, decreased real estate values, and general economic pessimism, the Romney campaign presented the election as a referendum on the president and the failure of his policies to turn the economy around. The Republican narrative emphasized its candidate's successful business career as evidence that he had the vision, experience, and knowledge to improve economic conditions.[5]

REPAIRING LEADERSHIP IMAGES

In a competitive nomination, the more negative the campaign, the more likely that the eventual nominee's personal image will have been tarnished, policy positions questioned, and divisions within the party widened. Each of these election-oriented problems requires attention and a private and public campaign to overcome them.

Candidates may have to reintroduce themselves to the voters to regain the electorate's attention and to remove or at least reduce the negative stereotypes by which their partisan opponents, other party candidates, and the news media and late-night comics characterized them. Biographical ads, public testimonials, and convention speeches given by distinguished public officials and party leaders can help alter a less-than-flattering public image.

Bill Clinton faced this problem after winning the Democratic nomination in 1992. Savaged first by press allegations of womanizing, draft dodging, and smoking marijuana, and later by criticism of his centrist policy positions by his opponent, former California governor Jerry Brown, Clinton needed to reconstruct his presidential image. To do so, his campaign designed a series of commercials that detailed the hardships and struggles that this poor boy from Arkansas encountered growing up and ultimately surmounted in his rise to political prominence. The ads, combined with talk-show appearances in which the candidate reminisced about his upbringing, gradually clouded aspects of Clinton's self-serving personal behavior that marred his leadership image.

Al Gore and George W. Bush faced a different type of problem in the spring of 2000. They needed to establish their own presidential credentials by moving out of a president's shadow, in Bush's case, his father's and in Gore's, Bill Clinton's. The primaries had not enabled them to do so fully, in part because they won easily and early. To gain stature, Bush needed to highlight his tenure as a popular, twice-elected, governor of Texas. Gore had two options; either stand on his own or be credited with some of the economic successes of the Clinton administration. He chose the former, asserting his independence, distancing himself from the president, and thereby making it harder for him to claim credit for the administration's accomplishments.

McCain had no alternative but to stress his independence in 2008, given the unpopularity of the Republican incumbent, George W. Bush. The plan, according to campaign manager, Rick Davis, was for McCain to visit the White House and Republican National Committee the day after he had won a majority of the delegates and not go near it again.[6] The financial crisis in September, however, forced McCain to return to Washington to participate in the emergency meetings with the president and members of Congress. Nor could he escape his partisan label, age, or tie to the Republican political establishment.

Obama faced a different challenge in 2008, demonstrating that his lack of experience was not a liability but an asset, that he had the knowledge, judgment, and stature to be a successful president. He displayed his knowledge in detailed policy discussions with the press, hundreds of one-on-one interviews, and candidate debates as well as in a book he had written, *The Audacity of Hope*,[7] published prior to his presidential campaign. He also took the ritual trip abroad to raise his international stature.

His eight-day itinerary took him to Britain, France, Germany, Israel, and Iraq with a huge media entourage. All three anchors of the broadcast evening news traveled with Obama and reported from the countries he was visiting. Large crowds attended his public events. The attention Obama received from his trip abroad was substantially greater than that which McCain received from his international travels and literally left McCain in the dark and out of the news. To counter their predicament, McCain's media consultants designed and aired a clever political commercial that compared the Democratic candidate's notoriety to that of singer Britney Spears and socialite Paris Hilton; the intent was to paint the Democratic candidate as a celebrity but at the same time question his leadership credentials.[8]

GAINING PRESIDENTIAL STATURE

The image problems that challengers face are magnified when running against incumbent. Less well known to the country, less experienced in higher office, and with fewer major accomplishments associated with their public career, challengers have to present and enhance their leadership credentials at the same time they are raising money, unifying their party, refocusing their criticism, and restructuring their campaign. Nor do they have as loud a pulpit to do so until their party's convention and the presidential debates. It is a tough job that takes time.

Few candidates emerge from contested nominations with a sizable war chest. Lack of money is a major strategic disadvantage during this period. Matt Rhoades, Romney's manager, described his candidate's predicament in 2012:

> . . . we had spent $87 million to secure the nomination, become the presumptive nominee. And we were not going to take matching funds so that we could be more competitive down the stretch. So that meant that were being outspent over the summer, and we always understood that that was going to be one of the bigger challenges that we had, even to the point where we did take out a loan at the end of the primary process going into the convention.[9]

Diminished funds for the prospective nominee require that candidates depend on their party's national committee and interest groups, especially Super PACs, for criticizing the incumbent and defining and defending themselves. But the party has other candidates to worry about as well. The groups with the money, those that can accept unlimited contributions, the Super PACs, 501c, and 527s, are prohibited by law from coordinating their campaigns with candidate committees. Not knowing what the appeal their candidate wishes to articulate and when they want to make it, Super PACs tend to concentrate their spending on advertising that criticizes the opponent.

The 2004 and 2012 interregnum period between the primaries and the convention illustrate the challenger's dilemma. After John Kerry had effectively secured the Democratic nomination in March of 2004, the first objective of Bush and the Republicans' reelection advertising was to reduce his stature. Almost immediately, the Bush campaign aired negative Kerry commercials that presented the Massachusetts senator as a flip-flopper who regularly voted on both sides of controversial issues. The Kerry campaign needed time to reorganize itself, raise money, and tailor a biographical portrait of its candidate, so it chose not to reply to the various allegations that Republicans were directing at him. By not directly confronting the flip-flopper accusation, however, Kerry inadvertently let the charges stick. His personal negatives increased; his standing in the polls declined; and he lost much of the luster that he had gained by winning the Democratic nomination.

The same thing happened to Romney in 2012. The Obama campaign front-loaded its advertising in order to frame the election as quickly as possible to its advantage. David Axelrod, the campaign's senior political strategist, reflected on the strategy:

> My reading of history was that there was no ad that ran after the convention that ever in the modern era won a presidential race; paid media becomes largely irrelevant in the general election after the conventions because the debates take over for better or worse. We did that [frontloaded] in part because we thought the combined forces of the super PACs and your [Republican] spending were going to be great, but also because we knew that we had to define the race before the conventions.[10]

In short, the interregnum period that extends from the time one candidate wins a majority of the delegates to the start of the party's national convention provides unopposed incumbents with considerable advantages. Since a large proportion of voters decide how they will vote by the end of the nominating conventions, and since both candidates and most nonparty groups will be campaigning full blast after those conventions, the incumbent starts out ahead, and it is difficult for the challenger, barring unforeseen episodes, revelations, or events, to catch up.

PRELUDE TO THE CONVENTIONS

Considerable planning and much hype go into the convention buildup. Media attention turns to the vice presidential selection, usually the only unknown left before the big show. That choice is the presidential standard-bearer's. The last time that a convention actually selected the vice presidential nominee rather than ratified the person whom the winning presidential candidate designated was in 1956 when Adlai Stevenson, the Democratic candidate, professed no choice between Senators John F. Kennedy and Estes Kefauver, both of whom were vying for the vice presidential nomination. The convention chose Kefauver.

Picking the Vice Presidential Nominees

The selection of the vice presidential nominee is one of the most important decisions that the prospective nominee must make. It is a character judgment that reflects directly on the presidential nominee. Picking an experienced, well-respected person who might have been or perhaps could become a candidate for the presidency sometime in the future usually suggests a willingness to delegate power as well as share some decisional responsibility. Another factor is the political benefit that the vice presidential nominee brings to the ticket. In the past, the vice presidential nominee has been selected in part to provide geographic or ideological balance. Occasionally, demographic variables, such as gender and age, have also been factors.

Bill Clinton broke with tradition in 1992 when he chose a fellow southerner and moderate, Al Gore, to reinforce the New Democrat image that Clinton wanted to project to the American people. George W. Bush's selection of Dick Cheney—a former White House chief of staff, representative from Wyoming, member of the Republican House leadership, and defense secretary in his father's administration—brought experience, particularly in national security affairs, expertise that Bush initially lacked as a state governor. The choice of a governing mate more than a running mate also broke with tradition and suggested an enhanced vice presidency in a Bush administration.

There had been speculation and even a campaign launched by Hillary Clinton's supporters to urge Obama to choose her for the number-two spot in 2008. Such a choice would have quickly unified the party, but it would also have put a person who had been highly critical of Obama on the same ticket, and if successful, another Clinton and potential presidential rival in

the White House. Obama did not want to encourage the kind of press coverage that focused on internal rivalry between the president and vice president
during the last two years of Bill Clinton's administration, nor did he want the
former president in or near the White House.[11] Instead, he chose Joe Biden.
As chair of the Senate Foreign Relations committee, Biden had the experience
that Obama lacked in foreign affairs. He was also popular with rank-and-file
Democrats, many of whom had supported Hillary Clinton.[12]

McCain chose Sarah Palin as his running mate in 2008 because he needed
a "game changer," according to Nicolle Wallace, a senior adviser to his campaign.[13] He also wanted to appeal to women, both disaffected Clinton supporters as well as others who seemed more sympathetic to the Democratic Party.
With her reputation as a reform governor, Palin would complement McCain's
record of independence and his opposition to special interest politics.

Romney began his search for a vice presidential candidate in April 2012
after he had secured the Republican nomination. Tasking senior adviser, Beth
Myers, with compiling a list of candidates, Romney established three criteria:
qualified to be president from day one, compatible ideologically and personally with him, and with a past that was unlikely to detract attention from the
themes and messages of his campaign. Before making his selection, Romney
made a point of campaigning with each of his potential vice presidential running mates; he and his staff reviewed their appearances on news shows and
in interviews, evaluating their partisan and public support and how their
staffs interacted with people in the main campaign organization. Paul Ryan's
relative youth, economic conservatism, knowledge of budgetary matters, and
his Midwest background, particularly coming from a battleground state,
Wisconsin, were seen as pluses.

Because so much media attention is directed toward the vice presidential
selection, nominees and their advisers try to keep their decisions secret for as
long as they can.[14] The preoccupation with surprise, however, has often precluded adequate screening of the candidates for fear that the news media will
find out the identity of the prospective choice before the presidential candidate
announces it. The worst-case scenario of this charade occurred in 1972 when
George McGovern selected Thomas Eagleton, a senator from Missouri, as his
running mate. Although McGovern had spoken with the Democratic governor of
the state, the senator himself, and the Missouri press, he had not been informed
of Eagleton's hospitalization for depression and the shock treatments he received
for it at the Mayo Clinic.[15] When this information was revealed by the news
media, McGovern was caught in a dilemma—he could admit he made a mistake
and drop Eagleton from the ticket, looking weak and perhaps mean-spirited in
the process, or he could indicate that it wasn't a mistake and stick with him.
Initially, McGovern chose the latter strategy. However, when medical authorities suggested that the malady was serious and too risky for a person who might
become president, McGovern was forced to drop him and select another person.

George H. W. Bush faced a similar dilemma in 1988. Although he had chosen Indiana senator Dan Quayle, in part because he wanted a person who could
appeal to the next generation of voters, Bush was unaware of Quayle's mediocre

record as a student or his family's help in getting him an appointment in the Indiana National Guard, which lessened the possibility of active-duty service during the Vietnam War. Bush, who had been accused of being a "wimp," felt he could not back off when the going got tough. He stayed with Quayle.

In the case of Sarah Palin, the problem she encountered after her selection and rousing convention speech was knowledge lapses that negatively reflected on her intellectual abilities. Palin had not been adequately briefed by McCain's policy aides, and showed it in her responses to interviewers' questions. She did not seem to know the Bush doctrine in foreign affairs; she became confused over the bailout of Wall Street investment firms, large banks, and the insurance giant AIG. Pundits questioned her understanding of world affairs while Tina Fey, a comedian, mocked her intelligence on *Saturday Night Live*.

Paul Ryan, who had served over a decade in Congress, was Republican chair of the House Budget Committee, and had proposed an alternative to the president's 2012 budget, did not evidence such difficulties. However, as an advocate for changing Medicare into a voucher program, he did provide Democrats with the opportunity to associate him with a proposal most senior citizens, Obama's least supportive age cohort, opposed.

Overseeing Convention Planning

In addition to the vice presidential selection, the prospective nominee also must oversee the planning for the national nominating convention. One objective of this planning is to avoid any problems, especially factional divisions that carry over from the primaries or are generated by a dispute over policy. A unified convention is viewed as the most successful way to launch a presidential campaign, energize the party, and frame the issues for the forthcoming general election.

Candidates and their handlers go to great lengths to orchestrate public events leading up to the convention. Nothing is left to chance. In 2000, George W. Bush let it be known that he opposed changes to the traditional positions the party took in its platform. He did not want to alienate any group in the Republicans' core constituency. Obama and McCain had similar objectives in 2008. They wanted to minimize internal dissent, a major reason that Hillary Clinton was given a prominent convention role and made the motion to make Obama's nomination unanimous. On the Republican side, McCain's senior aides nixed his desire to pick his close friend and former Democratic vice presidential candidate, Joe Lieberman, as his running mate because they feared that such a choice would have divided the convention, resulted in considerable internal opposition, and could have been defeated.[16] Harmony is the name of the game for contemporary nominating conventions.

NATIONAL NOMINATING CONVENTIONS

National nominating conventions were at one time important decision-making bodies. They were used to decide on the party's nominees, platforms, and rules and procedures, as well as to provide a podium for launching presidential campaigns. They also became an arena for settling internal party disputes, unifying the delegates, and getting ready for the general election campaign. Today, however, they are not nearly as important and certainly not as newsworthy. They are theater, orchestrated for television. Conventions are designed to present a picture of a cohesive and energized party that enthusiastically supports its nominees and its platform and optimistically launches its presidential campaign.

THE POLITICS OF CONVENTIONS PAST

As noted previously, nineteenth- and twentieth-century conventions until the 1970s were brokered by party leaders who exercised considerable influence over the selection and actions of their state delegations. The leaders debated among themselves, formed coalitions, and fought for particular candidates and over credentials, rules, and platform planks. These internal disputes occurred within committees that were charged with credentialing the delegates, establishing the rules by which the convention would be governed, and drafting the platform on which the party would stand in the general election.

Twice in the twentieth century, Republican conventions were the scene of major credential challenges that ultimately determined the nominees. William Howard Taft's victory over Theodore Roosevelt in 1912 and Dwight Eisenhower's victory over Robert Taft in 1952 followed from convention decisions to seat certain delegates and reject others.[17] Rules fights have also been surrogate disputes over the selection of the nominees. Until 1936, the Democrats operated under a rule that required a two-thirds vote for winning the nomination. James K. Polk's selection in 1844 was a consequence of Martin Van Buren's failure to obtain the support of two-thirds of the convention, although Van Buren had a majority. The two-thirds rule in effect permitted a minority of the delegates to veto a person they opposed.

Today most convention rules are accepted without controversy. The most recent rules controversy that potentially could have affected the outcome of a major party nomination occurred in 1980 at the Democratic convention. At issue was a proposed requirement that delegates vote for the candidate to whom they were publicly pledged at the time they were chosen. Trailing Jimmy Carter by about 600 delegates, Ted Kennedy, who had previously supported this requirement, urged an open convention in which delegates could vote their consciences rather than merely exercise their commitments. Naturally, the Carter organization favored the pledged delegate rule and lobbied strenuously and successfully for it. Subsequently, the Democrats modified the rule to allow delegates must reflect in good conscience the sentiments of those who elected them and the candidates to whom they were pledged.[18]

The Democrats had a major policy dispute in 1948 that led to a walkout of delegates from several southern states. At issue was the party's stance of a civil rights plank. When they were unable to get the convention to change its position, several of the southern delegations left the convention and backed the States' Rights candidacy of Strom Thurmond for president. In 1964,

Republican delegates fought over proposed amendments opposing extremism and favoring a stronger position on civil rights, amendments that delegates supporting Barry Goldwater defeated. The 1968 Democratic convention witnessed an emotional four-hour debate on U.S. policy in Vietnam. Although the convention voted to sustain the majority's position, which had the approval of President Johnson, the discussion, carried on television, reinforced the image of a divided party to millions of home viewers.[19]

Before the choice of the nominee was dictated by the results of the caucuses and primaries, the delegates had to make that decision themselves by voting on the convention floor. Sometimes agreeing on a nominee took several votes. In 1924, Democratic delegates cast 103 ballots before they agreed on John W. Davis and Charles W. Bryan as their nominees; in 1932, they took four roll calls before obtaining the two-thirds vote they needed to nominate Franklin Roosevelt. After the two-thirds rule was changed to a simple majority, the Democratic conventions had much less difficulty agreeing on its nominees. In fact, the only other Democratic convention that took more than one ballot was in 1952 when it took three votes to nominate Adlai Stevenson. In 1940, Republican Wendell Willkie was selected on the eighth ballot, breaking a deadlock among Thomas Dewey, Arthur Vandenberg, and Willkie himself. Eight years later, Dewey was nominated on the third ballot.

Since 1980, a first-ballot nomination is preordained by the results of the caucuses and primaries. Few disputes make it to the convention floor because the winning candidate controls a majority of the delegates and wants to project unity within the party.

CONTEMPORARY CONVENTIONS

Modern conventions are made-for-television productions. They are designed and organized by convention planners months before they are scheduled. And there is much to plan and orchestrate. The number of participants in contemporary conventions runs into the thousands. In 2012, the Republicans had 2,286 delegates and the Democrats had 5,554. Democrats reduced their numbers to about 4,500 for 2016 while the Republicans maintained their size of approximately 2,400 delegates.

The demographic composition of the delegates tends to reflect their electoral constituencies. When the candidates for the nomination compose their slates of delegates, they try to balance them so as to achieve broad representation. Democratic rules require an even gender division. Republican rules do not, with the result that a higher proportion of the GOP delegates have been men; a higher proportion of Republican voters are also men. Racial and ethnic minorities that contribute disproportionately to the Democrats' electoral base also have greater representation in their conventions. In 2012, 26 percent of the Democratic delegates were African American compared to 2 percent of the Republican delegates.[20] From an attitudinal perspective, delegates reflect their party's ideological orientation and partisan positions, more so than the average partisan and much more so than the general public.

Although the convention is planned by representatives of the winning candidates, preliminary decisions, such as where to hold it and who should run it, are made by the party's national committee, usually on the recommendation of its chair and appropriate convention committees. An incumbent president normally exercises considerable influence over many of these decisions: the choice of a convention city, the selection of temporary and permanent convention officials, and the designation of the principal speakers.

In choosing a site, many factors are considered: the size, configuration, and condition of the convention hall; transportation to and from it; financial inducements; the geographic area; and the cultural ambiance of the city itself. The site often reflects a strategic political decision, focusing attention on a state the party believes it can win in the general election. Democratic convention sites of Denver, Colorado (2008), Charlotte, North Carolina (2012), and Philadelphia, Pennsylvania (2016) and Republican ones in St. Paul, Minnesota (2008), Tampa, Florida (2012), and Cleveland, Ohio (2016) reflect such a calculus.

Conventions are very costly affairs. In addition to the federal government's grant, which was awarded to the parties through 2012 and money for security, local authorities contribute to nonadministrative costs, construction, and transportation and also provide security. The rest comes from private donations, mostly from large contributors who are given a variety of convention-related perks ranging from deluxe hotel suites, to box seats at the convention, to invitations to meet with the candidates and party leaders, to tickets to the receptions and other events. Major corporations and associations, whose lobbyists are frequently in attendance, also provide money, transportation, food, and entertainment.[21] It is a big party for the delegates, party leaders and elected officials, and the generous donors. The delegates also spend a lot of money, which is a principal reason (along with the publicity) that cities bid to hold the meetings.

The period during which conventions are held and the time at which speeches, roll calls, and reports occur are also important. Parties want to attract as large an audience as possible. Conventions have to be scheduled so as not to compete with other major events, such as the summer Olympics or the traditional Labor Day holiday. Generally speaking, the party that does not control the White House holds its convention first to gain more public attention for its nominees and policy positions. So long as public funding was accepted by major party candidates, that practice turned into a disadvantage because it lengthened the period during which those federal grants could be spent. Today, with both Democratic and Republican standard-bearers relying on private funding, it no longer is.

Conventions have become faster paced and more varied, primarily to keep their viewing audience's attention as long as possible. From the standpoint of the parties' convention planners, the more cogent the message and the more entertaining the proceedings, the more likely the convention will have a positive impact on the voters. Modern-day conventions entertain, inform, and provide opportunities for party leaders to gain media attention; present the policy positions for which the party stands in its platform; and anoint their presidential and vice presidential candidates by formally nominating them. Ritual surrounds each of these functions.

Oratory

Conventions are full of speeches. Some of political oratory has been very powerful, occasionally eloquent, and almost always emotive, designed to "turn on" the delegates and their partisan brethren who are watching. The substance of the oratory is also readily predictable. The speakers trumpet the achievements of their party, eulogizing their leaders and criticizing, often harshly, their opponents. They also reinforce and validate their party's ideological and policy positions.

Most contemporary conventions are highly scripted.[22] Little is left to chance. Distractions are kept to a minimum. Controversial and unpopular party and elected officials are kept out of the public spotlight as much as possible and usually do not get speaking slots during prime viewing hours.[23]

In 2008, the Republicans had to schedule an address by President George W. Bush, whose job approval ratings were under 30 percent. McCain and his fellow Republicans had wanted to distance themselves from the unpopular president. Bush and his wife were scheduled to speak on the first night and then depart for the White House. However, with a severe hurricane threatening and the memories of the government's inadequate response to Katrina still vivid, McCain canceled the public events of the first day, Bush remained in the White House, and his speech was broadcast by satellite the next day.

The Democrats have had the same problem with ex-president Carter. Unpopular during his presidency and controversial thereafter, convention planners have tried to limit Carter's public visibility by scheduling him for short appearances early in the evening before the prime viewing audience tunes in.

Another problem is speakers who do not adhere to the script, who submit one speech to convention reviewers and give another.[24] Pat Buchanan, who had challenged President G. H. W. Bush for the Republican nomination in 1992, did the "bait and switch" at its convention that year. His strident rhetoric and arch conservative political views excited the delegates, drew press attention, and raised controversial positions that the convention planners had wished to avoid. The same thing happened at the 2012 Republican convention when Clint Eastwood, Hollywood movie star and director, surprised Republican leaders by giving an impromptu speech to an empty stool upon which he imaged President Obama was sitting. The talk, given before Mitt Romney's acceptance speech, drew attention from Romney, a negative reaction from the public, and a surge in donations to the Obama campaign.[25]

Themes

Usually each of the four days of the meetings has an overall theme; the speakers are chosen and their speeches written with this theme in mind. The theme for 2012 Republican convention was "We Built It," emphasizing individual initiative and achievement within a free enterprise system. The Democrats, seeking to connect Obama to the dreams and aspirations of the middle class, painted the Republicans as the party of wealth and special interests.

In past conventions, there used to be a keynote address, which occurred early in the convention and was intended to unify the delegates, smoothing over any divisions that may have emerged during the preconvention campaign, and arouse the delegates, partisans, and the general public for the forthcoming election.[26] In 1988, a folksy and humorous address at the 1988 Democratic convention, Ann Richards, then treasurer of Texas, ridiculed George H. W. Bush for being aloof, insensitive, and uncaring. She concluded sarcastically, "He can't help it. He was born with a silver foot in his mouth."[27] Richards's comment so irritated George W. Bush that he resolved to run against her for governor, a race that he won, and later for president. In 2004, it was Barack Obama's well-received keynote address that gave him national recognition and initiated blogs encouraging him to run for the nation's highest elective office. Former president Bill Clinton energized Democratic delegates and partisans in 2012 with his comparison of the achievements of the Obama administration with the failures of the George W. Bush administration. He said:

> "If you want a winner-take-all, you're-on-your-own society, you should support the Republican ticket. But if you want a country of shared opportunities and shared responsibilities, a we're-all-in-this-together society, you should vote for Barack Obama and Joe Biden."[28]

In recent conventions, the vice presidential candidate is nominated and gives an acceptance address on the third night, a practice that both parties followed in 2008, but the Republicans had to modify in 2012 to avoid a conflict with the televising of the first regular season game of the National Football League. The vice presidential candidate's speech recounts the positive images and deeds of the party and its presidential nominee and attacks the opposing presidential candidate.

Democrat Joe Biden stuck to script in both his speeches. In 2008, he criticized the Bush administration's failed policies, tied McCain to those policies, and emphasized the need for policy change, the theme of the Obama campaign. In 2012, he testified to the president's strong personal leadership, his decisiveness in saving General Motors and ordering the attack on Osama bin Laden, and contrasted Obama's empathy with average Americans to Romney's cold, calculating manner. Republican Sarah Palin, a surprise choice in 2008, introduced herself and lampooned Barack Obama, comparing his lack of experience and accomplishments in public office to McCain's heroism, character, and years in the Senate. Paul Ryan, the Republican nominee in 2012, talked about the desirability of personal choice versus the strictures and inefficiencies of government-mandates, using Obamacare as his negative example.

The final night is devoted to the nominees. Preceded by a biographical video, the nominees are introduced by leaders of the party for their accomplishments and extraordinary qualifications; they are projected in larger-than-life terms. To balance that projection, it has become customary for their spouses to testify to their more human qualities: their sincerity, thoughtfulness, honesty, integrity, and empathy, using stories with which average Americans can identify. The finale and highlight is the acceptance speech by the presidential nominee that marks the end of the nomination and the beginning of the general election campaign. (See Box 6.1.)

BOX 6.1	A BRIEF HISTORY OF ACCEPTANCE ADDRESSES

The custom of the presidential standard-bearer giving an acceptance speech began in 1932 with Franklin Roosevelt. Before that time, conventions designated committees to inform the presidential and vice presidential nominees of their selection. Journeying to the candidate's home, the committees would announce the choice in a public ceremony. The nominee, in turn, would accept in a speech stating his positions on the major issues of the day. The last major party candidate to be told of the nomination in this fashion was Republican Wendell Willkie in 1940.

Today, acceptance speeches are both a call to the faithful and an address to the country. They articulate the principal themes for the general election and the priorities the nominee attaches to them. Harry Truman's speech to the Democratic convention in 1948 is frequently cited as one that helped to fire up the party. Truman chided the Republicans for obstructing and ultimately rejecting many of his legislative proposals and then adopting a party platform that called for some of the same social and economic goals. He electrified the Democratic convention by challenging the Republicans to live up to their convention promises and called a special session of Congress to enact those promises. When the Republican-controlled Congress failed to do so, Truman was able to pin on them a "do-nothing" label and make that label the basic theme of his successful presidential campaign.

In 1984, Democratic candidate Walter Mondale made a mammoth political blunder in his acceptance speech. Warning the delegates about the U.S. budget deficit that had increased dramatically during Reagan's first term, Democrat Mondale said that he would do something about it if he were elected president: "Let's tell the truth. Mr. Reagan will raise taxes, and so will I. He won't tell you. I just did." Democratic delegates cheered his candor, directness, and boldness; the public did not. He and his party were saddled with the tax issue throughout the entire campaign.

One of the most notable acceptance speeches was Barack Obama's in 2008. Desiring to highlight their candidate's rhetorical skills and inspirational oratory, the Democrats moved his speech from the convention hall to a football stadium that could accommodate 75,000 people. The speech in which Obama pledged to transform policy and politics received an enthusiastic response, media plaudits, and ignited Democrats in their forthcoming campaign.

In 2012, Obama toned down his transformational rhetoric, admitted that his goals needed more time to be achieved, but stuck with his vision making the American dream possible for all.

> I never said this journey would be easy, and I won't promise that now. Yes, our path is harder, but it leads to a better place. Yes, our road is longer, but we travel it together.
>
> We don't turn back. We leave no one behind. We pull each other up. We draw strength from our victories. And we learn from our mistakes. But we keep our eyes fixed on that distant horizon knowing that providence is with us and that we are surely blessed to be citizens of the greatest nation on earth.[29]

In 2008, the Republicans, fearful that John McCain's acceptance speech would be anticlimactic after the enthusiasm that greeted Sarah Palin the night before, tinkered with the setting in which McCain would address the delegates. They moved him closer to the audience, recreating the town meeting environment in which he was familiar and did well. McCain personalized his remarks, referring to himself as a

| BOX 6.1 | A BRIEF HISTORY OF ACCEPTANCE ADDRESSES *continued* |

maverick, contrasting his policy positions to Obama's, emphasizing his experience in foreign affairs, and ending with the story about his own mistreatment and forced confession as a prisoner of war in Vietnam:

> I was in solitary confinement when my captors offered to release me. I knew why. If I went home, they would use it as propaganda to demoralize my fellow prisoners. Our Code said we could only go home in the order of our capture, and there were men who had been shot down before me. I thought about it . . . But I turned it down. . . . after I turned down their offer, they worked me over harder than they ever had before. For a long time. And they broke me.
>
> When they brought me back to my cell, I was hurt and ashamed, and I didn't know how I could face my fellow prisoners. The good man in the cell next door, my friend, Bob Craner, saved me. Through taps on a wall he told me I had fought as hard as I could. No man can always stand alone. And then he told me to get back up and fight again for our country and for the men I had the honor to serve with. Because every day they fought for me.[30]

Mitt Romney, not a great orator, also had to distinguish himself, present his credentials, and at the same time reiterate the themes articulated at the convention that were to guide his presidential campaign. Highlighting his personal and professional accomplishments, he said:

> I am running for president to help create a better future, a future where everyone who wants a job can find a job, where no senior fears for the security of their retirement, an America where every parent knows that their child will get an education that leads to a good job and a bright horizon, and unlike the president, I have a plan to create 12 million new jobs.[31]

Platform

In addition to the speeches, conventions must approve the party's platform, which is a statement of the party's principal positions and agenda for the fall campaign. Contrary to popular belief, platforms are important even though few people read them in their entirety or know what is in them. They are important because they help shape the agenda for the government if the party is successful and wins control of Congress and the presidency.

Political scientists have found that elected officials of both parties have a relatively good record of redeeming their campaign promises and platform planks. Although party platforms contain high-sounding rhetoric and lofty goals, they also have fairly specific policy pledges. Of these, the majority have been proposed as laws or implemented as executive actions if the party's candidates are successful.[32] Party leaders in government follow through on their platform's promises because they believe in them personally, want to demonstrate their partisan loyalty, and need to maintain the support of their electoral coalition and their own credibility as elected officials.

Incumbents running for reelection will normally control their party's platform committees. In most cases, the successful presidential nominee's delegates will constitute a majority of the committee drafting the platform and thus ensure that the nominee's priorities and policy positions are consistent with the party's.[33]

Democratic and Republican platforms differ from one another in substance, more than style, and now more than in the past. In an examination of the Democratic and Republican platforms between 1944 and 1976, political scientist Gerald Pomper found that most of the differences were evident in the planks incorporated by one party but not by the other.[34] Contemporary platforms have become more detailed, policy specific, and philosophically divergent. A recent study of party platforms from 1944 to 2012 found that the ideological differences began to emerge clearly in the 1980s when the Republicans articulated economic policies significantly different from the Democrats. Positions on social issues also became more distinctive, reflecting the ideological polarization that characterizes the major parties today.[35] Box 6.2 contrasts the 2012 Republican and Democratic Party platforms on several of the most salient contemporary issues of that election year.

| BOX 6.2 | EXCERPTS FROM THE 2012 REPUBLICAN AND DEMOCRATIC PLATFORMS |

REPUBLICANS	DEMOCRATS
Abortion	
We support a human life amendment to the Constitution and endorse legislation to make clear that the Fourteenth Amendment's protections apply to unborn children.	The Democratic Party strongly and unequivocally supports *Roe v. Wade* and a woman's right to make decisions regarding her pregnancy, including a safe and legal abortion, regardless of ability to pay.
Economy/jobs	
The best jobs program is economic growth. . . . Republicans will pursue free market policies that are the surest way to boost employment and create job growth and economic prosperity for all.	We continue to fight for measures that would strengthen the recovery and create jobs now, including keeping teachers and first responders on the job, putting construction workers back to work by investing in our roads, bridges, schools, and water supply, helping families refinance their mortgages that save hundreds of dollars a month, cutting taxes for small businesses that invest and hire, and putting veterans back to work.
Energy/environment	
The most powerful environmental policy is liberty, the central organizing principle of the American Republic and its people. Liberty alone fosters scientific inquiry, technological innovation, entrepreneurship, and information exchange. Liberty must be the core energy behind American's environmental improvement.	We affirm the science of climate change, commit to significantly reducing the pollution that causes climate change, and know we have to meet this challenge by driving smart policies that lead to greater growth in clean energy generation and result in a range of economic and social benefits.

| BOX 6.2 | EXCERPTS FROM THE 2012 REPUBLICAN AND DEMOCRATIC PLATFORMS *continued* |

Gun control

We uphold the right of individuals to keep and bear firearms, a right which antedated the Constitution and was solemnly confirmed by the Second Amendment. We acknowledge, support, and defend the lawabiding citizen's God-given right of self-defense.

We recognize that the individual right to bear arms is an important part of the American tradition, and we will preserve Americans' Second Amendment right to own and use firearms. We believe that the right to own firearms is subject to reasonable regulation.

Immigration

. . .We oppose any form of amnesty for those who, by intentionally violating the law, disadvantages those who have obeyed it. Granting amnesty only rewards and encourages more law breaking.

. . .the country urgently needs comprehensive immigration reform that brings undocumented immigrants out of the shadow and requires them to get right with the law, learn English, and pay taxes in order to get on a path to earn citizenship.

Medicare

While retaining the option of traditional Medicare in competition with private plans, we call for a transition to a premium support model for Medicare, with an income adjusted contribution toward a health plan of the enrollee's choice.

Democrats adamantly oppose any efforts to privatize or voucherize Medicare.

Same-sex marriage

We reaffirm our support for a Constitutional Amendment defining marriage as the union of one man and one woman.

We support marriage equality and support the movement to secure equal treatment under law for same-sex couples.

Taxes

Extend the 2001 and 2003 tax relief packages—commonly known as the Bush tax cuts—pending reform of the tax code, to keep tax rates from rising on income, interest, and capital gains.

Extend key tax relief for working families and those paying for college, while asking the wealthiest and corporations to pay their fair share.

Voting

Democrats know that voter identification laws can disproportionately burden young voters, people of color, low-income families, people with disabilities, and the elderly, and we refuse to allow the use of political pretexts to disenfranchise American citizens.

Source: Adapted from the 2012 Republican and Democratic Party platforms, which are available at the Web site of the American Presidency Project at the University of California at Santa Barbara. www .presidency.ucsb.edu/ws/index.php?pid=101961

NEWS MEDIA COVERAGE OF POLITICAL CONVENTIONS

Political conventions used to be major newsworthy events. Radio began covering national conventions in 1924 and television in 1956. Because conventions in the 1950s were interesting, unpredictable events in which important political decisions were made, they attracted a large audience, one that increased rapidly as the number of households having television sets expanded. During the 1950s and 1960s, about 25 percent of the potential viewers watched the conventions, with the numbers swelling to 50 percent during the most significant part of the meetings.

The sizable audience made conventions important for fledgling television news organizations, which were beginning to rival newspapers for news reporting. Initially, the three major networks provided almost gavel-to-gavel coverage. They focused on the official events, that is, what went on at the podium. Commentary was kept to a minimum. The changes in the delegate selection process that began in the 1970s had a major impact on the amount and type of television coverage as well as the size of the viewing audience. As the decision-making capabilities of conventions declined, their newsworthiness decreased, as did the proportion of households that tuned in and the amount of time spent watching them.

With the exception of the public broadcasting system (PBS), the major broadcast networks (ABC, CBS, and NBC) subsequently reduced their coverage. In 1992, they covered each of the conventions for a total of fifteen hours; in 1996, they reduced that coverage to twelve hours; in 2000, to eight and a half hours; and beginning in 2004 to about one hour per night.

Although coverage on the major broadcast networks has declined, cable news, C-Span, public television, and the web sites of major news organizations have picked up some of the slack. The audience for 2008 was larger than in 2012. According to the Nielsen Company, which monitors the size of the viewing audience, 38.9 million watched John McCain's acceptance speech in 2008 and 38.4 million saw Obama's; the figures were 30.5 million for Romney and 35.7 million for Obama in 2012.[36]

Viewership varies with partisanship. Partisans watch their party's convention more than do Independents and people who identify with other parties. The composition of the viewing audience is also disproportionately older and more educated than the population as a whole.[37]

Since conventions are less newsworthy, reporters who cover them have to search for news. Television cameras constantly scan the floor for dramatic events and human-interest stories. Delegates are pictured talking, eating, sleeping, parading, even watching the convention on television. Interviews with prominent party leaders and elected officials, rank-and-file delegates, and family and friends of the candidate are interspersed with the speeches, convention movies, and the breaks for advertising. To provide a balanced presentation, supporters and opponents are frequently juxtaposed. To maintain the audience's attention, the interviews are kept short, usually focusing on reactions to actual or potential political problems. There are also endless commentaries, prognoses, and forecasts of how the convention is likely to affect the electorate and their voting decisions.

Coverage inside the convention is supplemented by coverage outside the hall. Knowing this, groups come to the convention city to air grievances and to protest. The most violent of these political demonstrations occurred in 1968 in Chicago, the city in which the Democratic Party was meeting. Thousands of people, many of them students, marched through the streets and parks protesting U.S. military involvement in the Vietnam War. Police set up barricades, blocking, beating, and arresting many of the protestors. Claiming that the events were newsworthy, the broadcast networks broke away from their convention coverage to report on these activities and show tapes of the bloody confrontations between police and protestors. Critics charged that the presence of television cameras incited the demonstrators and that coverage was disproportional and distracted from the proceedings. In response, one network, CBS, reported that it had devoted only thirty-two minutes to these "outside" events out of its thirty-eight hours of convention coverage.[38] At subsequent conventions, protests have occurred but have not received as much attention from the mainstream press. Only alternative radio gave them substantial coverage.

The news media's orientation, which highlights conflict, drama, and human interest, obviously clashes with the party leadership's desire to present a united and enthusiastic front to launch the presidential campaigns. The clash between these two conflicting goals has resulted in a classic struggle for control between the news media and convention planners. That the managers have been more successful in orchestrating their meetings to achieve their objectives than the news media is a principal reason for the decline in news coverage and the audience watching it. Both major parties also have convention web sites and blogs to reach a broader cross section of people, mainly partisans that access these sites.

When the conventions are over, however, they are rarely mentioned in the reporting of the campaign, although clips of their highlights, especially from the acceptance speeches of the nominees, reappear in candidate advertising. Nonetheless, the national party conventions still receive a bigger audience than any other election event except for the debates between the major party presidential and vice presidential candidates.

MINOR PARTY CONVENTIONS

Although the major parties get limited coverage on most of the broadcast networks, minor party conventions get almost no coverage, not even on cable news networks. The absence of competition within most of these parties combined with the improbability of their candidates winning the election or even affecting its outcome explain the low visibility given to these events. The one exception was the Reform Party's conventions in 1996 and 2000, which received some attention from the cable news and public affairs networks. The broadcast networks covered these conventions only as items on their news shows. H. Ross Perot, the party's founder and financial backer, had much to do with getting coverage in 1996, whereas the attraction in 2000 was the battle between supporters and opponents of Pat Buchanan, the former Republican who left that party to run as the Reform candidate.

In 1996, the Reform Party held a two-stage convention. At the first stage of the nomination process, Perot and his opponent, former governor Richard D. Lamm of Colorado, were given an opportunity to address the assembled delegates. During the next week, partisans voted by regular mail or e-mail, and the results were announced at the second convention, which also provided an opportunity for the winning candidate, Perot, to announce his vice presidential selection and make his acceptance speech.

In 2000, there was also a mail ballot as well as a convention vote, but it was the organizational battle over Buchanan's candidacy in the months leading up to the convention that attracted media attention. The hardball tactics that Buchanan's supporters employed to oust state party officials who opposed his candidacy created deep divisions within the party and ultimately led to a walkout by delegates hostile to Buchanan. These angry delegates proceeded to hold their own convention, nominate their own candidates, and claim the Reform Party label as their own, while Buchanan's backers nominated him as their Reform Party candidate. The dispute ended up in the courts, which had to decide which of these two sets of candidates should be listed as the Reform nominees for 2000. Similarly, the Federal Election Commission had to determine which of them was entitled to the $12.6 million the party was to receive on the basis of Perot's 1996 vote. The Commission chose Buchanan.[39]

ASSESSING CONTEMPORARY CONVENTIONS' IMPACT ON VIEWERS AND VOTERS

Do national nominating conventions have an impact on the election? Most observers believe that they do. Why else would the major parties devote so much time, money, and effort to these events? Why else would party leaders and academics concerned with civic education bemoan the reduction of convention coverage by the broadcast networks? Why else would the parties conduct focus groups, consult poll data, and even tally hits on their convention web sites, monitor e-mail responses, and twitter continuously? And why else would people watch them when they know the identity of the nominees, have a general sense of the parties' political stands, and probably have heard portions of the successful nominees' campaign speeches during the nomination process? Political scientists also believe that conventions matter. They have hypothesized that there is a relationship between convention unity and electoral success. Convention planners believe this hypothesis as well and do everything they can to promote unity during the meetings.

In the short run, conventions almost always boost the popularity of their nominees and decrease that of their general election opponents. This boost is referred to as the convention "bounce," which tends to average about a 5 to 6 percent gain in the public opinion polls.[40] The only recent nominees who did not get a bounce from their conventions were George McGovern in 1972, John Kerry in 2004, and Mitt Romney in 2012. Table 6.1 indicates

TABLE 6.1 | CONVENTION BOUNCES, 1964–2012

Year	Democratic Candidate	Post-Dem. Convention Bounce	Republican Candidate	Post-Rep. Convention Bounce
2012	Obama	3	Romney	−1
2008	Obama	4	McCain	6
2004	Kerry	−1	G. W. Bush	2
2000	Gore	8	G. W. Bush	8
1996	Clinton	5	Dole	3
1992	Clinton	16	G. H. W. Bush	5
1988	Dukakis	7	G. H. W. Bush	6
1984	Mondale	9	Reagan	4
1980	Carter	10	Reagan	8
1976	Carter	9	Ford	5
1972	McGovern	0	Nixon	7
1968	Humphrey	2	Nixon	5
1964	Johnson	3	Goldwater	5

Historical Convention Bounces, 1964–2012 Gallup Polls, Registered Voters (in percentage points).

Source: Jeffrey M. Jones, "Obama Gets Three-point Convention Bounce," Gallup Poll, September 11, 2012 (Survey of Registered Voters). http://www.gallup.com/poll/157406/obama-gets-three-point-convention -bounce.aspx?versi

the bounces that nominating conventions since 1960 have given their party's nominees. The bounces can be very short-lived, however.

The long-term impact is more difficult to measure. Nonetheless, political scientists have suggested three major effects of conventions on voters: (1) the conventions heighten interest, thereby increasing turnout; (2) they arouse latent feelings, thereby raising partisan awareness; and (3) they color perceptions, thereby affecting personal judgments of the candidates and their stands on issues.[41] Surveys taken before, during, and after conventions attest to increased public interest and information that results from the conventions and the news about them.[42] Convention watchers tend to make their voting decisions earlier in the campaign.[43] Whether they make those decisions because they watch the convention or whether they watch the convention because they are more partisan and politically aware and have made or are making their voting decisions is unclear.

In brief, conventions can have a powerful psychological impact on those who watch them for extended periods of time. They make viewers more inclined to follow the campaign after the convention is over and vote for their party's candidates. Conventions usually energize partisans. They can also have an organizational effect, fostering cooperation among the different and frequently competing groups within the party, encouraging them to submerge their differences and work toward a common goal.[44]

CHARACTERISTICS OF THE NOMINEES

In theory, many are qualified to be nominated for the presidency. The Constitution prescribes only three formal criteria: a minimum age of thirty-five, a fourteen-year residence in the United States, and native-born status. Naturalized citizens are not eligible for the office.

In practice, a number of informal qualifications have limited the pool of potential candidates. Successful nominees have usually been well known and active in politics and have held high government positions. Of all the positions from which to seek the presidential nomination, the presidency is clearly the best. Only five incumbent presidents (three of whom were vice presidents who became president through the normal succession process) have failed in their quest for the nomination.

Over the years, there have been a variety of paths to the White House. When the congressional caucus system was in operation, the position of secretary of state was regarded as a stepping-stone to the nomination if the incumbent chose not to seek another term. When brokered national conventions replaced the congressional caucus, the Senate became the incubator for most successful presidential candidates. After the Civil War, governors emerged as the most likely contenders, particularly for the party that did not control the White House. Governors of large states possess a political base, a prestigious executive position, and leverage by virtue of their control over their delegations. They also are *not* forced to take stands on as many controversial national issues as members of Congress must do during their terms in office and do not get as much critical coverage in the national news media as do Washington-based politicians.[45] Today, the vice presidency is also seen as a stepping-stone to the presidential nomination.

There are other informal criteria, although they have less to do with qualifications for office than with public attitudes about religion, race, ethnicity, and gender. Prior to John F. Kennedy's election in 1960, no Catholic had been elected, although in 1928 the Democrats nominated Governor Alfred E. Smith of New York, a Catholic, who did not win. Prior to Joseph Lieberman's selection as Al Gore's running mate in 2000, no Jewish American had been nominated for that position. The selection of Barack Obama as the Democratic standard-bearer in 2008 marked the first time an African American candidate had been chosen to lead his party. The gender barrier fell for vice presidential nominations in 1984 when the Democrats chose Geraldine Ferraro and in 2008 when the Republicans selected Sarah Palin and will fall for the presidency if Hillary Rodham Clinton is selected as the Democratic nominee in 2016.

Public attitudes are changing. The American people are becoming more open to candidates that mirror the country's diversity, although contemporary surveys do indicate that atheists and homosexuals might still have barriers to overcome to be nominated by major parties as their presidential candidates.[46]

Health is still relevant. After Alabama governor George Wallace was disabled by a would-be assassin's bullet in 1972, even his own supporters began to question his ability to cope with the rigors of the office. As noted previously, Senator Thomas Eagleton was forced to withdraw as the Democratic vice presidential nominee in 1972 when his past psychological illness became public knowledge. Before George W. Bush announced Dick Cheney's selection as his running mate, he had his father, former president George H. W. Bush, inquire about Cheney's medical condition. Cheney had suffered three heart attacks in the 1980s, but his Houston doctors described his health as excellent.[47]

Family ties have also affected nominations and elections, as the father–son relationships of the Adams and the Bushes and the marriage between Bill and Hillary Clinton demonstrate. Only two bachelors have been elected president, James Buchanan and Grover Cleveland.[48] During the 1884 campaign, Cleveland was accused of fathering an illegitimate child and was taunted by his opponents with the jingle, "Ma, Ma, Where's my Pa? Gone to the White House, Ha! Ha! Ha!" Cleveland admitted responsibility for the child, even though he could not be certain he was the father.

Until 1980, no person who was divorced had ever been elected. Andrew Jackson, however, married a divorced woman, or at least a woman he thought was divorced. As it turned out, she had not been granted the final court papers legally dissolving her previous marriage. When this information became public during the 1828 campaign, Jackson's opponents asked rhetorically, "Do we want a whore in the White House?"[49] Jackson and Cleveland both won. That a candidate has been divorced and remarried seems to have little impact or even gain much notoriety today, although being divorced and remarried several times still may.

Adultery is another matter. Senator Edward Kennedy's marital problems and his driving accident on Chappaquiddick Island, off the coast of Massachusetts, in which a young woman riding with the senator was drowned, were serious impediments to his presidential candidacy in 1980. Gary Hart's alleged "womanizing" forced his withdrawal in 1988 and made his reentry into Democratic presidential politics problematic. On the other hand, Bill Clinton was elected despite persistent allegations of sexual improprieties; Herman Cain, however, was pressured to withdraw from the 2012 Republican nomination process after sexual harassment charges during his years as a business executive surfaced.

Nonetheless, Bill Clinton's nomination in 1992, despite the allegations of marital infidelity, marijuana smoking, and draft dodging, and in 1996, despite a pending sexual harassment suit by an Arkansas employee and the ongoing Whitewater investigation, as well as George W. Bush's self-admitted binge drinking as a younger man and Barack Obama's admission that he smoked marijuana and used drugs in his teens, suggest that the electorate is more concerned about contemporary behavior than it is with previous relationships and actions of the distant past.

SUMMARY

With the end of the competitive stage of the caucuses and primaries coming months before the nominating conventions, victorious candidates have to continue campaigning even though their nomination seems to be a certainty. During this interregnum, which can last three to six months depending on when the competitive phase of the nomination is over and the conventions are scheduled, the would-be nominees must consolidate and expand their base, unify their party, and gain the support and endorsements of their political opponents. In addition, if they were in a competitive campaign, they will have to raise money to pay off their debts and frequently help primary opponents pay theirs, continue their campaign, help their party, and build a war chest for the general election. They also have to design their election strategy, developing and testing the themes they plan to emphasize, the policy stands they take, and the personal images they project. Moreover, they have to stay in the news, avoid mistakes, and build their campaign organization. There is little rest for the weary.

As the nomination process now preordains the party's presidential candidate and control of the committees that set the rules, review the credentials, and draft the platform, the national nominating conventions have become more scripted than spontaneous, more glamour than substance, and more entertaining than newsworthy. They have become theater designed to energize the participants, attract viewers, emphasize certain policy goals and positions, create or reinforce leadership images, and launch the presidential campaign.

The parties still see their conventions as important events that provide a favorable environment for beginning their fall campaigns. From the perspective of convention planners, the goals are to generate and illustrate partisan unity and enthusiasm for the nominees, inform and energize the partisans who watch, and provide media exposure for the politicians who attend—exposure that may help them in their reelection campaigns and also will be salve for their egos. From the perspective of the party, the goals are to raise the spirits and hopes of its workers and expand its base of volunteers, both delegates and the partisans at home; obtain even more donations; mobilize the faithful; and educate the public. From the perspective of the nominees, the goals are to demonstrate their broad-based policy appeals and strong leadership images.

The press that covers the convention have different objectives. Not oblivious to their public service function, they still need to maximize their viewing audience by reporting the convention as news, as well as presenting it as the party's public relations spectacular. To do this, they must find and report newsworthy events, especially those that are dramatic, divisive, and unexpected; provide analysis; and engage in endless prognosis about what it all means for the election and for the next government. The commercial broadcast networks seem to be giving up this task, leaving most of the coverage to the public broadcasting system, C-Span, and the cable news networks.

Although contemporary conventions are more theatrics than politics and more rhetoric than action, they continue to attract public attention, although a smaller proportion of the electorate sees or hears them today and for less time than they did two or three decades ago. For those who watch them, inadvertently or deliberately, conventions do increase awareness and shape perceptions of the candidates, parties, and their respective issue positions.

The impact of conventions varies with the attitudes and predispositions of those who watch or read about them. For partisans, conventions reinforce allegiances, making party identifiers more likely to vote and work for their party's nominees. For those less oriented toward a particular party, conventions deepen interest in the campaign and knowledge about the candidates, which enables them to make a more informed voting decision.

The changes in the nominating process have also enlarged the field of candidates. Times have changed; the electorate, reflecting the mores of the society, has become more accepting of candidates who mirror the country's diversity today. More people have a realistic chance of being nominated by their party for president.

WHERE ON THE WEB?

The political parties are obviously a good source of information about their nominating conventions. Here again are the sites for the major parties and the Green and Reform parties.

- **Democratic National Committee**
  www.dnc.org
- **Green Party**
  www.gp.org
- **Reform Party**
  www.reformparty.org
- **Republican National Committee**
  www.rnc.org

EXERCISES

1. Compare the most recent Democratic and Republican conventions on the basis of their schedules, the tenor of their televised speeches, and their video presentations. Which did you find more interesting and why?

2. Compare the acceptance speeches of the major party candidates for the presidential and vice presidential nominations. On the basis of your comparison, indicate to what extent these speeches previewed the principal appeals of the candidates in the general election. Compare these appeals to those of the minor party candidates.

3. To what extent do the major party platforms today reflect the increasing ideological content of contemporary politics? Are there any major areas in which the major parties take similar stands and/or use similar rhetoric today? You can access previous national conventions at the web site of the American Presidency Project (www.presidency.ucsb.edu).

4. Contrast the major party platforms with those of two minor parties, one on the left of the political spectrum and one on the right. Would you categorize the major parties as more centrist than the minor ones? Are the Democratic and Republican platforms still within the mainstream of American public opinion?

5. Looking back toward the previous presidential campaign, indicate which parts of the winning party's platform and promises of the winning candidate were enacted into law and which planks and promises were not. (You can get help on this exercise by going to Politifact.com (http://www.politifact.com/). Were there any promises or platform planks that the winners ignored?

6. Examine the inauguration address of the newly elected president and any other major addresses made within the first 100 days in office to see which of the party's platform positions are highlighted and which are not. On the basis of your analysis, do you think that platforms are important agenda-setters for the new administration?

Selected Readings

Adler, Wendy Zeligson. "The Conventions on Prime Time," in *The Homestretch: New Politics*, Martha FitzSimon and Edward C. Pease, eds. New York: The Freedom Forum Media Studies Center, 1992, pp. 55–57.

Brown, Gwen. "Change in Communication Demands of Spouses in the 2012 Nomination Conventions," in *The 2012 Presidential Campaign: A Communication Perspective*, Robert E. Denton, Jr., ed. Lanham, MD: Rowman & Littlefield, 2014, pp. 23–44.

Holloway, Rachel L. "The 2012 Presidential Nominating Conventions and the American Dream: Narrative Unity and Political Division," in *The 2012 Presidential Campaign: A Communication Perspective*, Robert E. Denton, Jr., ed. Lanham, MD: Rowman & Littlefield, 2014, pp. 1–22.

Jordan, Soren, Clayton McLaughlin Webb, and B. Dan Wood. "The President, Polarization and the Party Platforms, 1944–2012," *The Forum*, 13 (1), April 2014.

Maisel, L. Sandy. "The Platform-Writing Process." *Political Science Quarterly*, 108 (Winter 1993–1994): 671–698.

New York Times. "At the National Conventions, the Words They Used," September 6, 2012. www.nytimes.com/interactive/2012/09/06/us/politics/convention-word-counts.html

Panagopoulos, Costas, ed. *Rewiring Politics: Presidential Nominating Conventions in the Media Age*. Baton Rouge, LA: Louisiana State University Press, 2007.

Pavlik, John V. "Insider's Guide to Coverage of the Conventions and the Fall Campaign," in *The Homestretch: New Politics*, Martha FitzSimon and Edward C. Pease, eds. New York: The Freedom Forum Media Studies Center, 1992, pp. 40–54.

Shafer, Byron E. *Bifurcated Politics: Evolution and Reform in the National Party Convention*. Cambridge, MA: Harvard University Press, 1988.

Simas, Elizabeth and Kevin Evans, "Linking Party Platforms to Perceptions of presidential Candidates' Policy Positions, 1972–2000." *Political Research Quarterly*, 64 (4), 2011: 831–839.

Smith, Larry David, and Dan Nimmo. *Cordial Concurrence: Orchestrating National Party Conventions in the Telepolitical Age*. New York: Praeger, 1991.

NOTES

1. In their analysis of the 2012 electorate, political scientists John Sides and Lynn Vavreck argue that voters' perceptions of candidate electability were more highly correlated with their voting preferences than was their ideological proximity to the candidates. In other words, Republican primary voters were more concerned with who was most likely to beat Obama than whose beliefs were closest to their own. John Sides and Lynn Vavreck, *The Gamble: Choice and Chance in the 2012 Presidential Election* (Princeton, NJ: Princeton University Press, 2013), p. 91.
2. Alison Mitchell, "Bush Strategy Recalls Clinton on the Trail in '96." *The New York Times* (April 18, 2000), p. A18.
3. Matthew Dowd, *Campaign for President: The Managers Look at 2004* (Lanham, MD: Rowman and Littlefield, 2005), p. 100.
4. Axelrod added: ". . . in the long run, flip-flopper was not a very good argument for us in the general election context because we didn't want to give people an out to say, Well yeah, his ideas seem kind of nutty, but he doesn't really mean them." David Axelrod, *Campaign for President: The Managers Look at 2012* (Landam, MD: Rowman and Littlefield, 2013), p. 112.
5. Stuart Stevens, *Electing the President 2012: The Insiders' View*, Kathleen Hall Jamieson, ed. (Philadelphia, PA: University of Pennsylvania Press, 2013), pp. 28–29.
6. Rick Davis, *Campaign for President: The Managers Look at 2008* (Lanham, MD: Rowman & Littlefield, 2009), p. 88.
7. Barack Obama, *The Audacity of Hope* (New York: Crown/Three Rivers Press, 2006).
8. The narrator in the ad said about Obama:

   > "He's the biggest celebrity in the world.
   > But, is he ready to lead?
   > With gas prices soaring, Barack Obama says no to offshore drilling.
   > And, says he'll raise taxes on electricity.
   > Higher taxes, more foreign oil, that's the real Obama.
   > Britney Spears, Paris Hilton . . . Barack Obama?"

   The press enhanced the impact of the ad by reporting it as a news item. "Celebrity" had the effect of diminishing some of the bounce Obama received from the trip; it even caused his campaign to limit the number of big rally events planned before the 2008 Democratic convention.
9. Matt Rhoades, *Campaign for President: The Managers Look at 2012*, p. 95.
10. David Axelrod, *Electing the President 2012: The Insiders' View*, pp. 38–39.
11. In 2011 with the economy in doldrums and the president's reelection uncertain, Obama's political advisers toyed with the idea of replacing Joe Biden on the 2012 ticket with Hillary Clinton. Polling results and focus group discussions, however, indicated little benefit from such a switch and the suggestion was quickly dropped. Jonathan Martin, "Book Details Obama Aides' Talks about Replacing Biden on 2012 Ticket," *New York Times*, October 31, 2013. http://www.nytimes.com/2013/11/01/us/politics/book-details-consideration-of-replacing-biden-on-2012-ticket.html?_r=0
12. David Plouffe, *Campaign for President: The Managers Look at 2008*, p. 155.
13. Nicole Wallace, *Electing the President 2008: The Insiders' View* (Philadelphia, PA: University of Pennsylvania Press, 2009), p. 27.

14. Rick Davis, McCain's campaign manager, explains the need for secrecy: "The trick for us was to be able to do it in some degree of secrecy, in order for it not to spill out and then get tangled up in the Democratic convention—because you are not going to compete with Barack Obama on a Thursday night with a hundred thousand people in a stadium." Rick Davis, *Campaign for President: The Managers Look at 2008*, p. 9.

　　Palin was flown out of Alaska by private plane in the middle of the night to meet with McCain, his wife, and a few top aides in Arizona and then flown to a "very dingy hotel in Youngstown, Ohio." Nicole Wallace, a senior adviser to McCain, added: "Our joke was they will never suspect we're here. The campaign staff would never stay in a place like this." Nicole Wallace, *Electing the President 2008: The Insiders' View*, p. 14.

15. George McGovern, conversation with author.

16. Steve Schmidt in *Electing the President 2008: The Insiders' View*, p. 30.

17. In both cases, grassroots challenges to old-line party leaders generated competing delegate claims. The convention in 1912 rejected these challengers and seated the regular party delegates, producing a walkout by Roosevelt's supporters and giving the nomination to Taft. Forty years later, the delegates denied the nomination to Taft's son by recognizing the credentials of delegates pledged to Eisenhower and rejecting those supporting Senator Taft. There was no delegate walkout in 1952.

18. During the 1976 Republican convention, the Reagan organization proposed a rules change that would have required Gerald Ford to name his choice for vice president before the convention's vote for president, as his opponent, Ronald Reagan, had done. Ford's supporters strongly opposed and subsequently beat this amendment. As a consequence, there was no way for Reagan to shake the remaining delegates loose from Ford's coalition.

19. There was a minor policy controversy in 2012 at the Democratic convention when a former governor of Ohio introduced an amendment to the proposed platform that reinserted references to God, God-given rights, and referred to Jerusalem as the capital of Israel. After three unclear voice votes, the chair of the meetings ruled that the amendments were enacted.
Matea Gold and Michael Memoli, "Democrats Put God, Jerusalem Back in Platform over Objections," *Los Angeles Times*, September 5, 2012. http://articles.latimes.com/2012/sep/05/news/la-pn-dnc-platform-god-jerusalem-20120905

20. David Bositis, "Blacks and the 2012 Republican Convention," Joint Center for Political Studies, August 2012. www.jointcenter.org/blacks-and-the-2012-republican-national-convention; "Blacks and the 2012 Democratic Convention," Joint Center for Political Studies, September 2012. www.jointcenter.org/blacks-and-the-2012-democratic-national-convention

21. The Democrats did not accept corporate financial contributions for their 2012 meeting.

22. Despite the planning, occasional unexpected events occur, which are usually highlighted by the news media. In 1956 after Vice President Richard Nixon was to be unanimously renominated by the Republicans, a delegate from Nebraska grabbed the microphone during the roll call of states and said he had a nomination to make. "Who?" said Joseph Martin, chair of the convention, surprised at this deviation from the script. "Joe Smith," the delegate replied. Martin did not permit the name of Joe Smith to be placed in nomination, although the Democrats were later to contend that any Joe Smith would have been better than Nixon.

23. For an excellent discussion of how these themes fit into each party's ideological narrative see Rachel L. Holloway, "The 2012 Presidential-Nominating Conventions and the American Dream: Narrative Unity and Political Division," in Robert E. Denton, Jr., ed., *The 2012 Presidential Campaign: A Communication Perspective* (Lanham, MD: Rowman and Littlefield, 2014), pp. 1–22.

24. Some speakers bridled at the scripting. When Ron Paul was given an opportunity to address the 2012 Republican convention, told he had to endorse the nominee, and have his remarks approved by the Romney's communications team, he refused, saying, "It wouldn't be my speech. That would undo everything I've done in the last 30 years. I don't fully endorse him for president."
Teddy Goff and David Axelrod, *Campaign for President: The Managers Look at 2012*, p. 126.

25. Mike Allen and Jim Vandehei, "Inside the Campaign: How Mitt Romney Stumbled," *Politico* (Sept. 16, 2012). politico.com/news/stories/0912/81280.htm/

26. The keynoter for the party that did not control the White House usually sounded a litany of failures and suggested that the country needed new leadership. Naturally, the keynoter for the party in office reversed the blame and praise. Noting the accomplishments of the administration and its unfinished business, the speaker urged a continuation of the party's effective leadership and policy successes.

27. Ann Richards, "Address to the Democratic Convention in Atlanta, Georgia, on July 19, 1988," as quoted in *Congressional Quarterly*, 46 (July 23, 1988): p. 2024.

28. Bill Clinton, Address to the Democratic National Convention, Charlotte, North Carolina, September 6, 2012. www.youtube.com/watch?v=i5knEXDsrL4

29. Barack Obama, "Excerpts from Acceptance Address at the Democratic National Convention, Charlotte, North Carolina, Colorado, September 6, 2012." https://www.youtube.com/watch?v=udWrkd6OAzE

30. John McCain, "Acceptance Address at the Republican National Convention, Minneapolis, MN, September 4, 2008." www.presidency.ucsb.edu/ws/index/.php?pid=78576

31. Mitt Romney, "Acceptance Address at the Republican National Convention, Tampa, Florida, August 30, 2012." http://www.npr.org/2012/08/30/160357612/transcript-mitt-romneys-acceptance-speech

32. Gerald M. Pomper, "Control and Influence in American Politics," *American Behavioral Scientist,* 13 (Nov./Dec. 1969): pp. 223–228; Gerald M. Pomper with Susan S. Lederman, *Elections in America* (New York: Longman, 1980), p. 161; Jeff Fishel, *Promises and Performance* (Washington, DC: CQ Press, 1994), pp. 38, 42–43.

33. Stephen A. Borrelli, "Finding the Third Way: Bill Clinton, the DLC, and the Democratic Platform of 1992," *Journal of Policy History*, 13 (4), 2001: 429–462.

34. Pomper, "Control and Influence," p. 161.

35. Soren Jordan, Clayton McLaughlin Webb, and B. Dan Wood, "The President, Polarization and the Party Platforms, 1944–2012," *The Forum*, 12 (April 1, 2014).

36. "Final Night of Republican National Convention Draws 30.3 Million Viewers," Nielsen Company, Newswire, August 31, 2012. http://www.nielsen.com/us/en/newswire/2012/final-night-of-republican-national-convention-draws-30-million-viewers.html
    "Closing Night of Democratic National Convention Draws 35.7 Million Viewers," Nielsen Company, Newswire, September 7, 2012. http://www.nielsen.com/us/en/newswire/2012/closing-night-of-democratic-national-convention-draws-35-7-million-viewers.html

37. Ibid.
38. "Republicans Orchestrate a Three-Night TV Special," *Broadcasting* (August 28, 1972), p. 12.
39. The other minor party that received some national coverage in 2000 was the Green Party, which nominated consumer advocate and anti-corporate crusader Ralph Nader. Holding its convention in June before those of the Republicans and Democrats, the Green Party gained coverage by virtue of Nader's reputation as an outspoken critic of corporate America and special interest politics as well as the results of early polls that indicated his candidacy could make a difference in the outcome of the Bush–Gore contest. In other words, Nader provided the party with visibility, and the party gave him a pulpit from which to articulate his beliefs. Nader did not receive the Green Party nomination four years later. He ran as an Independent then and in 2008.
40. Robert S. Erickson and Christopher Wiezien, *The Timeline of Presidential Campaigns* (Chicago: University of Chicago Press, 2012).
41. Thomas E. Patterson, *The Mass Media Election* (New York: Praeger, 1980), pp. 72–74.
42. "Conventions Still Draw Sizable Audience, Boost Campaign Interest," Pew Research Center for the People and the Press, August 22, 2012. http://www.people-press.org/2012/08/22/conventions-still-draw-sizable-audience-boost-campaign-interest/
43. Patterson, *Mass Media Election*, p. 103.
44. The ticket that is ahead at the end of the nominating conventions usually wins the presidential election. Public opinion just doesn't change all that much after then.
45. The House of Representatives has not been a primary source of nominees. Only one sitting member of the House, James A. Garfield, has ever been elected president, and he was chosen on the thirty-fifth ballot. In recent nominations, there have been House candidates, but they have not done well. Most lack national visibility, even those who have been in office for many years.
46. Gallup polls taken during the 2007–2008 election cycle raise questions about whether candidates who are Hispanic or Asian or a candidate who is a Mormon could be elected. See Jeffrey M. Jones, "U.S. Ready for a Female President," October 3, 2006. www.gallup.com/content/?ci=24832&pg=1; Jeffrey M. Jones, "Atheists, Muslims See Most Bias as Presidential Candidates," Gallup Poll, June 21, 2012. http://www.gallup.com/poll/155285/Atheists-Muslims-Bias-Presidential-Candidates.aspx
47. Republican John McCain had been treated for skin cancer on at least two occasions, but neither that treatment nor his age of 72 seemed to be factors that affected voting behavior in 2008. Contemporary presidential and vice presidential candidates are expected to release detailed medical reports to demonstrate that they are in good health and capable of performing the duties of president and vice president.
48. Historian Thomas A. Bailey reports that James Buchanan was once greeted by a banner carried by a group of women that read, "Opposition to Old Bachelors," *Presidential Greatness* (New York: Appleton-Century Crofts, 1966), p. 74.
49. Ibid.

THE GENERAL
ELECTION CAMPAIGN

PART **III**

Stephen J. Wayne

7 CHAPTER | STRATEGY, TACTICS, AND OPERATIONS

INTRODUCTION

Elections have been held in the United States since 1789; campaigning by parties for their nominees began soon thereafter. It was not until the end of the nineteenth century, however, that presidential candidates actively ran in the campaigns. Personal solicitation was viewed as demeaning and unbecoming of the dignity and stature of the presidency.

Election paraphernalia, distributed by the parties, first appeared in the 1820s; by 1828, there was extensive public debate about the candidates. Andrew Jackson and, to a lesser extent, John Quincy Adams generated considerable commentary and controversy. Jackson's supporters lauded him as a hero, a man of the people, "a new or second Washington"; his critics referred to him as "King Andrew the first," alleging that he was immoral, tyrannical, and brutal.[1] Adams was also subjected to personal attack. Much of this heated rhetoric appeared in the highly partisan press of the times.

The use of the campaign to reach, entertain, inform, and mobilize the general electorate began on a large scale in 1840. Festivals, parades, slogans, jingles, and testimonials were employed to energize voters. The campaign of 1840 is best remembered for the slogan "Tippecanoe and Tyler too"—promoting

Whig candidates General William Henry Harrison, hero of the battle of Tippecanoe in the War of 1812, and John Tyler—and for its great jingles:

WHAT HAS CAUSED THIS GREAT COMMOTION?

(SUNG TO THE TUNE OF "LITTLE PIG'S TAIL")

What has caused this great commotion, motion, motion,
Our country through?
It is the ball a rolling on, on.
Chorus
For Tippecanoe and Tyler too—Tippecanoe and Tyler too,
And with them we'll beat little Van, Van, Van, [Martin Van Buren]
Van is a used up man, And with them we'll beat little Van.[2]

The successful Whig campaign made it a prototype for subsequent presidential contests.

THE EVOLUTION OF PRESIDENTIAL CAMPAIGNS

The election of 1840 was also the first in which a party nominee actually campaigned for himself. General William Henry Harrison made twenty-three speeches in his home state of Ohio.[3] He did not set a precedent that was quickly followed, however. It was twenty years before another presidential candidate took to the stump and then under the extraordinary conditions of the onset of the Civil War and the breakup of the Democratic Party.

Senator Stephen A. Douglas, Democratic candidate for president, spoke out on the slavery issue to try to heal the split that it had engendered within his party. In doing so, however, he denied his own personal ambitions. "I did not come here to solicit your votes," he told a Raleigh, North Carolina, audience. "I have nothing to say for myself or my claims personally. I am one of those who think it would not be a favor to me to be made President at this time."[4]

Abraham Lincoln, Douglas's Republican opponent, refused to reply, even though he had debated Douglas two years earlier in their contest for the Senate seat from Illinois, a contest Douglas won. Lincoln, who almost dropped out of public view when the campaign was underway, felt that it was not even proper for him to vote for himself.[5] He cut his own name from the Republican ballot before he cast it for others in the election.[6] For their part, the Republicans mounted a massive campaign on Lincoln's behalf. They held what were called "Wide Awake" celebrations in which large numbers of people were brought together. An account of one of these celebrations reported:

> The Wide-Awake torch-light procession is undoubtedly the largest and most imposing thing of the kind ever witnessed in Chicago. Unprejudiced spectators estimate the number at 10,000. Throughout the whole length of the procession were scattered portraits of Abraham Lincoln. Banners and transparencies bearing Republican mottoes, and pictures of rail splitters, were also plentifully distributed. Forty-three bands of music were also in the procession.[7]

From Porch to Train

Presidential candidates remained on the sidelines until the 1880s. Republican James Garfield broke the tradition by receiving visitors at his Ohio home. Four years later in 1884, Republican James Blaine made hundreds of campaign speeches in an unsuccessful effort to deny public accusations that he profited from a fraudulent railroad deal. Benjamin Harrison, the Republican candidate in 1888, resumed the practice of seeing people at his home, a practice that has been referred to as front-porch campaigning. Historian Keith Melder writes that Harrison met with 110 delegations consisting of almost 200,000 people in the course of the campaign.[8] William McKinley received even more visitors at his front-porch campaign in 1896. He spoke to approximately 750,000 people who were recruited and in some cases transported to his Canton, Ohio, home by the Republican Party.[9]

McKinley's opponent in that election, William Jennings Bryan, actually traveled around the country making speeches at Democratic political rallies. By his own account, he logged more than 18,000 miles and made more than 600 speeches, and, according to press estimates, he spoke to almost 5 million people, nearly collapsing from exhaustion at the end of the campaign.[10]

In 1900, Republican vice presidential candidate Theodore Roosevelt took on Bryan, "making 673 speeches, visiting 567 towns in 24 states, and traveling 21,209 miles."[11] Twelve years later, ex-president Theodore Roosevelt once again took to the hustings, only this time he was trying to defeat a fellow Republican president, William Howard Taft, for his party's nomination. Roosevelt won nine primaries, including one in Ohio, Taft's home state, but was denied the nomination by party leaders. He then launched an independent candidacy in the general election, campaigning on the Progressive, or "Bull Moose," ticket. His Democratic opponent, Woodrow Wilson, was also an active campaigner. The Roosevelt and Wilson efforts ended the era of passive presidential campaigning. The last front-porch presidential campaign was waged by Warren G. Harding in 1920.

From Rally to Radio and Television

Harding's campaign was distinguished in another way: He was the first to use radio to speak directly to voters. This new electronic medium and television, which followed it, radically changed presidential campaigns. Initially, candidates were slow to adjust their campaign styles to these new techniques.[12] It was not until the candidacy of Franklin Delano Roosevelt in 1932 that radio was employed skillfully in political campaigns. Roosevelt also pioneered the "whistle-stop" campaign train, which stopped at railroad stations along the route to allow the candidate to address the crowds that came to see and hear him. In 1932, Roosevelt, who personally took a train to Chicago to accept his nomination, visited thirty-six states, traveling some 13,000 miles. His extensive travels, undertaken in part to dispel a whispering campaign about his health—he had polio as a young man, which left him unable to walk or even stand up unaided—forced President Herbert Hoover onto the campaign trail to defend his presidency and seek reelection.[13]

Instead of giving the small number of speeches he had originally planned, Hoover traveled more than 10,000 miles across much of the country. He was the first incumbent president to campaign actively for reelection. Thereafter, with the exception of Franklin Roosevelt during World War II, personal campaigning became standard for incumbents and nonincumbents alike.

Harry Truman took campaigning by an incumbent a step further. Perceived as the underdog in the 1948 election, Truman whistle-stopped the length and breadth of the United States, traveling 32,000 miles and averaging ten speeches a day. In eight weeks, he spoke to an estimated 6 million people.[14] While Truman was rousing the faithful with his down-home comments and hard-hitting criticisms of the Republican-controlled Congress, his opponent, Thomas E. Dewey, was promising new leadership but providing few particulars. His sonorous speeches contrasted sharply and unfavorably with Truman's straightforward remarks.

The end of this era of presidential campaigning occurred in 1948. Within the next four years, television came into its own as a communications medium. The number of television viewers grew from less than half a million in 1948 to approximately 19 million in 1952, a figure that was deemed sufficient in the minds of campaign planners to launch a major television effort. The Eisenhower presidential organization budgeted almost $2 million for television, and the Democrats promised to use both radio and television "in an exciting, dramatic way" in that election.[15]

The potential of television was evident from the outset. Republican vice presidential candidate Richard Nixon took to the airwaves in 1952 to reply to accusations that he had appropriated campaign funds for his personal use and had received money and other gifts from wealthy supporters, including a black-and-white cocker spaniel named Checkers. Nixon denied the charges but said that under no circumstances would he and his family give up the dog, which his children dearly loved. A huge outpouring of public sympathy for Nixon followed his television address, effectively ending the issue, keeping him on the ticket, and demonstrating the impact television could have on a political career and a presidential candidate. Ironically, it was the televised Senate hearings into the practices of Nixon's 1972 reelection committee that informed the public of the dirty tricks in which his campaign had engaged and the taping system in the White House that revealed the president's culpability in the Watergate cover-up.

Television made mass appeals easier, but it also created new obstacles for the candidates. Physical appearance became more important as did oratorical skills. Instead of just rousing a crowd, presidential aspirants had to convey a personal message and a compelling image to television viewers. Television had other effects as well. It eventually supplemented the party as the principal link between its nominees and the voters. It decreased the incentive for holding so many public events since more people could be reached through this mass communications medium than at a rally, parade, or speech. But it also increased the need to participate in personal interviews, appear on news, talk, and eventually, entertainment shows, and hire campaign staff skilled in visual communications. The candidates became show-biz celebrities.

Campaign activities and events had to be carefully orchestrated and scripted, keeping in mind how they would appear on the screen and what images they would convey to voters. Off-handed comments and quips were discouraged because they invariably got candidates into trouble and diverted attention from the narrative of their campaign.

From Art to Science

The people who organized and ran the campaigns were also affected. Public relations experts were called on to apply mass-marketing techniques. Pollsters and media consultants supplemented and to some extent replaced old-style politicians in designing and executing campaign strategies. Even the candidates seemed a little different. With the possible exception of Lyndon Johnson and Gerald Ford, both of whom succeeded to the presidency through the death or resignation of their predecessors, incumbents and challengers alike reflected the grooming and schooling of the age of mass communications. And where they did not, as in the cases of Walter Mondale, Michael Dukakis, and Robert Dole, they fared poorly.

The age of television campaigning is obviously not over, but the revolution in the new media from cable to Internet streaming to interactive web sites, communications technology from search engines to apps to social networking, and the collection, integration, and programming of large data sets of personal information has provided political campaign organizations with the means to discern and disaggregate public opinion, target and communicate messages to specific groups, and energize and turn out voters identified as likely supporters.

This chapter and the one that follows discuss these aspects of modern presidential campaigns. We begin by discussing the broad strategic components: basic appeals, leadership imagery, and Electoral College coalition building. We illustrate that discussion with a box outlining the major party candidates' strategies in the 2004, 2008, and 2012 presidential elections. We then turn to more specific tactical decisions: the staging, timing, and "war room" reactions to unexpected events, verbal miscues, and embarrassing situations that occur from time to time. Finally, we examine the complexities of organization and operations at the headquarters and in the field, ending with a box that focuses on the new technologies incorporated in Obama's 2012 presidential campaign.

STRATEGIC OBJECTIVES

As we noted in Chapter 5, strategies are game plans, blueprints, and calculated efforts to convince the electorate to vote for a particular candidate. They include a basic appeal as well as a plan for implementing it.

Certain decisions cannot be avoided when developing an electoral strategy. These decisions stem from the rules of the system, the costs of the campaign, the character of the electorate, and the environment in which the election occurs. Each decision involves identifying objectives, allocating resources, and monitoring and adjusting that allocation over the course of the election. That is what a strategy is all about: It is a plan for developing and deploying campaign resources, targeting them to specific areas and groups, tracking their impact, and mobilizing the vote.

Most strategies are designed well before the race begins; a few are finalized after the nominations have been determined and then may have to be readjusted during the election, particularly if a campaign perceives itself as losing. Long-term planning frequently starts two years ahead of the election for challengers; incumbents begin to consider reelection from the moment that they take office. Raising money, hiring staff, and soliciting volunteers usually begin early in the year before the election.

DESIGNING A BASIC APPEAL

The first step in constructing a campaign strategy is fashioning a basic appeal. This appeal has two principal components: partisan imagery and policy beliefs often disaggregated into specific issue positions and priorities. The objective is to frame the electoral choice in as advantageous a manner as possible to as many people as possible as soon as possible.

Partisan Images
All things being equal, the candidates of the dominant party have an advantage that they try to maximize by emphasizing their partisan affiliation, lauding their partisan heroes, and making a blatant partisan appeal. When the Democrats were the majority, their candidates traditionally clothed themselves in the garb of their party. During the period when the Republicans were in the minority, they did not. Eisenhower, Nixon, and Ford downplayed partisanship, pointing instead to their personal qualifications and policy preferences. As the partisan gap narrowed, Republican candidates became more willing to point to their partisan affiliation. Today, they utilize that affiliation to identify themselves, their most intense supporters, and others whose values and beliefs would lead them in the same partisan direction.

Since 2000, the major parties have been at or near parity with one another. In 2000, both major party candidates moved toward the political center after they had won their party's nomination in order to appeal to independent voters and weak party identifiers. Since 2004, they have not. Rather they have tried to maximize their electoral base on the belief that voters have a partisan orientation even if they do not personally identify themselves as Republican or Democrats.

Regardless of how much emphasis is placed on partisanship, the popular images of the party still evoke strong feelings. Those feelings have both policy and personal dimensions. For the Democrats, common economic interests have been the most compelling cue for most of their supporters. Perceived as the party that got the country out of the Great Depression and Great Recession, the party of the middle class, broad-based and composed of labor and minority groups, Democratic candidates tend to stress "bread-and-butter" issues: jobs, wages, education, and other benefits for the working and middle classes. The Democrats contrast their concern for the plight of average Americans with the Republicans' ties to the wealthy, especially to big corporations, banks, and investment capitalists.

An issue appeal to voters in the middle and the lower parts of the economic and social strata gives Democratic candidates an empathy advantage. They are seen as more understanding and sympathetic to the problems that average people face in their daily lives.[16]

The downside to this perception, however, is the Republican contention that Democratic policies discourage individual initiative, impede the private sector, and create dependency on government. Since the days of the New Deal, the GOP has typecast Democratic presidential candidates as liberal, "tax and spend," big government advocates, often using the word "socialist" to describe their programs and political orientations.

Bill Clinton sought to reassert his party's middle-class appeal in his two presidential campaigns. Calling himself a "New Democrat," Clinton took pains to distinguish his own moderate views from those of his more liberal Democratic predecessors and conservative ideology of his Republican opponents. He presented himself as a change-oriented candidate in 1992 and as a builder of progress in 1996. In contrast, Al Gore and John Kerry took more populist stands, emphasizing their desire to help working families and average Americans. Obama also targeted those in the middle class in both his 2008 and 2012 elections, pointing to the plight most Americans face in maintaining, much less improving, their standard of living and their opportunities for economic advancement.

Whereas economic issues have tended to unite the Democrats, social issues have been more divisive. Since the 1970s, Republican presidential candidates have taken advantage of these divisions by focusing on those matters on which the Democrats' electoral constituency has been divided, issues such as school vouchers, welfare programs, free trade, affirmative action, abortion, and, until recently, same-sex marriage. In doing so, the Republicans appealed to the fears and frustrations of older, conservative, and predominantly white voters. The party reiterated its support for the traditional American values of individualism, family, and community. Changes in the demography of the electorate, its more multiracial and ethnic character, however, have undermined the potency of this appeal in national elections at the presidential level.

When foreign policy, national security, and, more recently, homeland security issues are salient, Republican candidates have traditionally done better. They have been viewed as stronger and more assertive leaders than their Democratic opponents. In 1952, Eisenhower campaigned on the theme "Communism, Corruption, and Korea," projecting himself as the candidate most qualified to end the war. Nixon took a similar tack in 1968, linking

Humphrey to the Johnson administration and the war in Vietnam. Four years later, Nixon varied his message, painting George McGovern as the "peace at any price" candidate and himself as the experienced leader who could achieve peace with honor. Gerald Ford was not nearly as successful in conveying his abilities in foreign affairs but compensated for his shortcomings by relying on Dr. Henry Kissinger, his secretary of state and principal foreign policy spokesman. Ronald Reagan, despite his own lack of experience in foreign affairs, pointed to the Soviet invasion of Afghanistan and to the Iranian hostage crisis to criticize Carter's foreign policy leadership. George H. W. Bush cited his experience in foreign affairs and his personal acquaintance with many world leaders in 1988, although his emphasis on foreign policy became a liability four years later with the Cold War over, the Persian Gulf War concluded, and the public preoccupied with a recessed domestic economy.

Lacking his father's expertise in foreign affairs, George W. Bush did not stress foreign policy in his 2000 campaign, but did point to the war on terrorism, which he declared after the 9/11 attacks. Foreign policy issues took a back seat to economic concerns in 2008 and 2012, thereby reducing the advantage that John McCain's experience in national security affairs might have afforded him had those issues been more salient. As a former governor and business executive, Mitt Romney had to demonstrate competence in foreign affairs but kept his focus on the economy.

The general perception that the Democrats are weaker in foreign and military affairs has prompted some of their recent standard-bearers to talk even tougher than their Republican opponents on national security issues. In his 1976 campaign, Carter vowed that an Arab oil embargo would be seen by his administration as an economic declaration of war. In 1984, Walter Mondale supported the buildup of U.S. defenses, including Reagan's strategic defense initiative. In 1988, Dukakis spoke about the need for the United States to be more competitive within the international economic arena, as did Clinton in 1992. Gore and Kerry emphasized the foreign policy expertise they gained in the Senate, their military service in Vietnam, and their support for a strong American presence around the world. With the nation mired in two unpopular wars, Obama emphasized the value of diplomacy and multistate coalitions in resolving international conflicts that threatened U.S. interests and security.

Salient Issues
The electoral environment affects the priorities and substance of a candidate's policy appeal. In 1992, the electorate was concerned about the economy, particularly the loss of American jobs at home and the growing federal government's budget deficit. In 1996, with the economy strengthened, unemployment low, inflation in check, and a strong stock market, the electorate in general expressed satisfaction with the country's economic condition, a situation that favored the incumbent. The salient issues in 2000 were how to improve education, provide tax relief, and put Social Security and Medicare on a firmer financial foundation; in 2004, the war in Iraq was a primary concern, along with continuing budget deficits, unequal economic growth, the shift of

manufacturing jobs overseas, and social issues such as same-sex marriage. In 2008, the most important issue was the deep and broad economic recession, while four years later it was the nation's slow economic recovery and persistently high unemployment.

In general, economic problems tend to be the most recurrent themes in American elections. Ronald Reagan drove this home in 1980 with the question he posed at the end of his debate with President Jimmy Carter, a question he directed at the American people: "Are you better off now than you were four years ago?" Similarly, James Carville, Clinton's chief strategist in the 1992 campaign, kept a sign over his desk that read, "It's the economy, stupid." He did not want anyone in the Clinton organization to forget that the poor economy was the campaign's primary selling point. In 2008 and again in 2012, perceptions of the economy, its future, and the direction in which the country was heading drove the election and influenced the outcome.[17]

A strong economy helps the party in power but not to the extent that a weak one can hurt it. Job losses, inflation increases, flat or falling incomes, and stock market skids motivate voting against the party and president on whose watch these problems occurred.

CREATING A LEADERSHIP IMAGE

Regardless of the partisan imagery and thematic emphases, candidates for the presidency must stress their own qualifications for the job and cast doubt on those of their opponents'. They must appear presidential, demonstrating those personal attributes and leadership qualities the voters consider essential and those that the current president is perceived to lack. In the words of David Axelrod, Obama's senior consultant in his two presidential campaigns:

> With very few exceptions, the history of presidential politics shows that public opinion and attitudes about who should next occupy the oval office are largely shaped by perceptions of the retiring incumbent. And rarely do the voters ask for a replica. Instead they generally choose a remedy, selecting a candidate who will address the deficiencies of the outgoing President.[18]

When incumbents are running for reelection, their experience in office usually works to their political advantage. They are seen as more knowledgeable than their opponents, as leaders who have stood the tests of time. Stability and predictability satisfy the public's psychological needs unless conditions are deemed unsatisfactory; the certainty of four more years with a known quantity is likely to be more appealing than the uncertainty of the next four years with an unknown one, provided the incumbent's job performance has been perceived as generally acceptable.

Accentuating the Positive
A positive public image, of course, cannot be taken for granted. It has to be created, or at least polished. Contemporary presidents are expected to be

strong, assertive, and dominant, although if their policies are not successful, they may be criticized for the way in which they exercised power. During times of crisis or periods of social anxiety, these leadership attributes are considered absolutely essential. The strength that Franklin Roosevelt was able to convey by virtue of his successful bout with polio, Dwight Eisenhower by his military command in World War II, and Ronald Reagan by his tough talk, clear-cut solutions, and optimistic vision contrasted sharply with the perceptions of Adlai Stevenson in 1956, George McGovern in 1972, Jimmy Carter in 1980, and Walter Mondale in 1984 as weak and indecisive.

For challengers, the task of seeming to be powerful, confident, and independent (of being one's own person) can best be imparted by a no-nonsense approach, a conviction that success is attainable, and clear, coherent, and consistent political beliefs that can be converted into specific policy positions. John Kennedy's rhetorical emphasis on activity in 1960 and Richard Nixon's tough talk in 1968 about the turmoil and divisiveness in the country helped generate the impression of a take-charge personality. Kennedy and Nixon were seen as leaders who knew what had to be done and would do it. Ronald Reagan's simple but direct language, his strong, consistent anti-communist beliefs, and the confidence with which he presented his views contrasted sharply with Jimmy Carter's inaction during the Iranian hostage crisis, his penchant for self-criticism, his demands for public sacrifice, and his bland, emotionless rhetoric.

In addition to seeming tough enough to be president, it is also important to exhibit sufficient knowledge and skills for the job. One of the reasons that the Obama campaign wanted the first presidential debate in 2008 to be on foreign policy was to demonstrate that its candidate was as knowledgeable and thoughtful as his older and more seasoned Republican opponent, John McCain.[19] Experience can also become an issue for candidates who have not held national office. State governors, particularly those from small states, need to prove that they can handle a job as difficult, complex, and pressured as the presidency. Obama's limited experience in national office was criticized by his nomination and general election opponents. However, the choice of a first-term governor of Alaska, Sarah Palin, as the Republican vice presidential nominee by McCain undermined his argument about the importance of experience for the presidency since she lacked that experience. It also brought attention to his McCain's health and age (72).

What many candidates without national experience do is run against Washington, pointing out that they are not part of the problem so they are better able to fix it. Obviously, such a strategy works only if the public has a lot of grievances against those in power. This was the message Jimmy Carter presented after Watergate and Obama emphasized during the Great Recession when much of the discontent was directed toward President George W. Bush.

Empathy is also an important attribute. People want a president who can respond to their emotional needs, one who understands what and how they feel. Roosevelt and Eisenhower radiated warmth. Carter, Clinton, and George W. Bush were particularly effective in generating the impression that they cared, whereas McGovern, Nixon, Dukakis, and Dole appeared cold, distant, and impersonal. Obama was also criticized for seeming distant and unemotional in 2008; Republicans accused him of being elitist. In response to that criticism, Obama recounted his growing up as a child of a single mom, an absent father, and living with his grandparents in very modest economic circumstances. He also used his story to convey his understanding of the problems ordinary people face and to provide hope that Americans of all walks of life could achieve their dreams and aspirations. In 2012, the Obama campaign took the tact his opponents took four years earlier, portraying Romney as insensitive and out of touch with the problems of the middle class.

Candor, integrity, and trust emerge periodically as important attributes in presidential image building. Most of the time these traits are taken for granted. Occasionally, however, a crisis of confidence, such as Watergate or the Clinton impeachment, dictates that political skills be downplayed and these personal qualities stressed. Such crises preceded the elections of 1952, 1976, 2000, and 2008. In the first two of these elections, Dwight Eisenhower, a war hero, and Jimmy Carter, who promised never to tell a lie, both benefited from the perception that they were honest, decent men not connected with the "mess" in Washington. George W. Bush made much of the scandalous behavior in the Clinton administration during his nomination campaign but much less during the general election campaign. However, he often repeated the line that brought him the most accolades from Republican audiences: "When I put my hand on the Bible, I will swear to not only uphold the laws of our land, I will swear to uphold the honor and dignity of the office to which I have been elected, so help me God."[20]

In 2008, the issue was not integrity but judgment. The war in Iraq and the economic meltdown raised questions about President George W. Bush's decision making, whether he had rushed to judgment in Iraq, was overly influenced by a "groupthink" mentality of his national security advisers, and understood the complexities of international and domestic economic problems. The 2012 election was about policy direction: which set of beliefs, those of the Republicans or those of the Democrats, would produce the economic upturn that the public desired.

Character is important in elections when issues involving personal behavior preoccupy the administration in power. Character also tends to be more important when less is known about the candidates—at the beginning of their presidential quest. It is less important for incumbents running for reelection because the electorate has had time to judge their values and attributes in the presidency.

Highlighting the Negative

Naturally, candidates can be expected to raise questions about their opponents. These questions assume particular importance if the public's initial impression of the candidates is fuzzy, as it may be with outsiders who win their party's nomination. When Republican polls and focus groups commissioned by the George H. W. Bush campaign in 1988 revealed Dukakis's imprecise public image, Bush campaign advisers devised a strategy to discredit him. The strategy was based on the premise that the higher the negatives of a candidate, the less likely that candidate would be to win.[21]

The emphasis on negativity has continued in each subsequent election. In 1992 and 1996, Republicans criticized Clinton's moral character, integrity, and truthfulness. The Clinton campaign responded quickly to these charges unlike Dukakis four years earlier who did not want to dignify them with a reply. Not only did Clinton want to deflect the criticism, but he wanted to refocus the press on the principal theme of his campaign, the economy.

It was more of the same in 2000. Republicans questioned Gore's credibility, particularly his tendency to exaggerate his own importance and embellish stories about himself; Democrats criticized Bush's lack of knowledge, rush to judgment, and his overall competence to be president. In 2004, the Bush campaign described Kerry as indecisive, inconsistent, and sometimes incoherent—a flip-flopper. Kerry, who wanted to wage an upbeat, more positive campaign, focused his criticism on the president's economic and national security policies.

The policies of the Bush administration were again the target of criticism in 2008 even though the president was ineligible to run for reelection. Obama tied his Republican opponent to the failed policies of the incumbent while McCain pointed to Obama's lack of experience and accomplishments in a not-so-subtle contrast to his own distinguished record of public service in the military and in the Congress.[22]

Negativity increased in 2012, fueled by the avalanche of negative ads by Super PACs and other groups including the parties and the presidential candidates' campaigns. Obama was described by his opponents as a big government, liberal who had increased the deficit without improving the economy; Democrats described Romney as the candidate of the wealthy, uncaring and insensitive to the problems most Americans confront in their daily lives.

In summary, candidates try to project images of themselves that are consistent with public expectations of the office and its occupant and project images of their opponents that are inconsistent with those expectations. Traits such as inner strength, decisiveness, competence, and experience are considered essential for the presidency, as are empathy, sincerity, credibility, and integrity. Which traits are considered most important vary to some extent with the assessment of the strengths and weaknesses of the incumbent and the nature of the times. Challengers try to exploit an incumbent's vulnerabilities by emphasizing the very skills and qualities that the incumbent president is perceived to lack.

DEALING WITH INCUMBENCY

Claiming a leadership image requires a different script for an incumbent than for a challenger. As noted previously, incumbents usually have an advantage. Between 1900 and 1972, thirteen incumbents sought reelection and eleven won; the two who lost, Taft in 1912 and Hoover in 1932, faced highly unusual circumstances. In Taft's case, he was challenged by the independent candidacy of former Republican president Theodore Roosevelt. Together, Taft and Roosevelt split the Republican vote, enabling Democrat Woodrow Wilson to win with only 42 percent of the total vote. Hoover ran during the Great Depression, for which he received much of the blame. (Box 7.1 summarizes the advantages and disadvantages of incumbency in running for reelection.)

BOX 7.1 | An Incumbency Balance Sheet

Incumbency can be a double-edged sword, strengthening or weakening a claim to leadership. Incumbents ritually point to their accomplishments, noting the work that remains and sounding a "stay-the-course" theme; challengers argue that it is time for a change and that they can do better.

Advantages of Incumbency

Being president is thought to help an incumbent in the quest for reelection more often than not. The advantages stem from the visibility of the office, the esteem it engenders, and the influence it provides.

The public's familiarity and comfort with incumbents permit presidents running for reelection to highlight their opponent's lack of experience, limited leadership qualities, and few public policy accomplishments and contrast these deficiencies with their own experience and record in office. Carter used a variation of this tactic in 1980, but to no avail when he described the arduous job of the president and then compared his energy, knowledge, and intelligence with his thirteen-year older political opponent, Ronald Reagan. Clinton and Obama campaigned as candidates for the future, pointing to their opponents' failed policies. George W. Bush and his father both ran for reelection on their national security records. For George H. W. Bush, that record was not sufficient because of the economic recession in 1992; for George W. Bush in 2004, it was. Public grievances must be sufficiently intense and broad-based to oust an incumbent.

The ability of presidents to make news, to affect events, and to dispense the "spoils" of government can also work to their advantage. Presidents are in the limelight and can maneuver to remain there. Having a "bully pulpit" gives them an agenda-setting advantage. All recent presidents campaigning for reelection have utilized the status, perquisites, and ceremonial aspects of their office to enhance their personal image in seemingly nonpolitical roles. Obama was helped by Hurricane Sandy, which occurred a week before the 2012 election; the huge storm and the damage and distress it created enabled him to act presidential by showing empathy and promising to help.

Presidents have another trump card. Presumably, their actions can influence events. They try to gear economic recoveries to election years. They also use their discretionary authority to distribute government resources such as grants, contracts, and emergency aid, being careful not to seem overtly partisan when doing so. The incumbency advantages extend to vice presidents seeking their party's presidential nomination but not nearly as much to their general election campaign. Of the four most recent vice presidents who tried to succeed to the presidency directly from the vice presidency—Nixon (1960), Humphrey (1968), George H. W. Bush (1988), and Al Gore (2000)—only Bush was successful.

The difficulty that incumbent vice presidents face is that they cannot demonstrate leadership from a position of followership. To establish their leadership credentials, vice presidents need to get out of their president's shadow; they have to separate themselves. If they do so, however, it becomes that much more difficult for them to claim and share the administration's successes. George H. W. Bush dealt with this problem by stating that he would pursue Reagan's agenda but do so in a kinder and gentler way. Al Gore, on the other hand, articulated a populist appeal in contrast to the Clinton administration's more moderate, mainstream approach.[23]

| BOX 7.1 | AN INCUMBENCY BALANCE SHEET *continued* |

Disadvantages of Incumbency

The challenges that contemporary presidents face, the persistent media criticism they engender, and the anti-Washington, anti-politician mood of the electorate since the late 1960s can offset the incumbency advantage when the economy is weak.

In their campaigns for office, presidential candidates hype themselves, make promises, and create expectations. Once in office, they find these expectations difficult to meet in a constitutional system that divides authority, in a political system that decentralizes power, and in a representative democracy in which public opinion is fluid, ambiguous, and often inconsistent—hence their promise versus performance gap.

Persistent media criticism contributes to these difficulties. With radio and television talk-show hosts railing against them, their policies, and their actions in office, with television and newspaper investigative reporters heightening awareness of policy problems and inadequate governmental responses to them, and with network news coverage generally more critical of incumbents, particularly during presidential campaigns,[24] presidents often find it hard to maintain a positive leadership image, although Reagan was able to do so and Clinton gained high job approval ratings during his last five years in office. George W. Bush and Barack Obama's images were mixed with their job approval ratings hovering between 53 and 55 percent during much of their reelection campaigns and skewed heavily along partisan lines.[25]

Since 1932, only three other incumbents have lost. Adverse political and economic factors help explain their defeats. The worst political scandal in the nation's history and the worst economic recession in forty years hurt Gerald Ford's chances, as did his pardon of Richard Nixon. A weak economy and a loss of confidence in the president's leadership abilities contributed to Jimmy Carter's defeat in 1980 and to George H. W. Bush's in 1992. Bill Clinton, George W. Bush, and Barack Obama, the last three incumbents to run for reelection, won.

Incumbents are helped or hurt by their perceived performance in office. Having a good record contributes to a president's reelection potential just as a poor record detracts from it. Bad times almost always hurt an incumbent. A crisis, however, helps, at least in the short run. Rightly or wrongly, the public places more responsibility for domestic economic conditions, internal social relations, and foreign policy on the president than anyone else in government; that a president may actually exercise little control over some of these external factors seems less relevant to the electorate than do negative conditions they perceive, the desire that they be improved, and the expectation that the administration in power should have done something about them.

Attributes such as personal favorability appear to be less important. Both Carter and George H. W. Bush had favorable personal ratings, yet both were defeated in their reelection attempts. Clinton's favorability evaluation was much less positive, yet he was easily reelected in 1996. However, his highly negative ratings in 2000 may have hurt Gore, or so Gore feared when he designed a strategy to separate himself from Clinton.

BUILDING A WINNING GEOGRAPHIC COALITION

In addition to designing a general appeal and addressing leadership and related incumbency issues, assembling a winning geographic coalition is also a critical strategic component of every presidential campaign. Since the election is decided in the Electoral College, the primary objective must always be to win a majority of the college, not necessarily a majority of the popular vote.

Electoral College strategies almost always require candidates to campaign in the most competitive states, giving priority to those with the most electoral votes. These states are the most important in an Electoral College system because of the winner-take-all method by which the votes are allocated in all but two states, Maine and Nebraska.

One criterion for assessing the level of competition, at least at the beginning of the election cycle, is the state vote in the previous presidential election. If the popular vote had been within the range of 1 to 5 percent, the state is considered competitive; if not, it would probably not be unless a large influx or exodus of residents to or from that state occurred after the election. The movement of Hispanic immigrants into the Southwest, Colorado, and southern California is a case in point. States that had long-established Republican voting patterns, such as Arizona and Colorado, have become much more competitive as a consequence of immigration from south of the border, while California, which had been competitive, is now tilting Democratic at the presidential level because of the growth of its Hispanic population. In contrast, Louisiana, which had a long tradition of supporting Democratic presidential candidates, has become more Republican, particularly after the departure of thousands of African Americans in the aftermath of Hurricane Katrina in 2005.

Another strategic factor that can influence resource allocation is the existence of a third-party or independent candidate such as H. Ross Perot in the 1992 and 1996 and Ralph Nader in 2000 and 2004. Nader's vote in Florida substantially exceeded the margin of Bush's 2000 victory in that state, yet the Gore campaign prematurely decreased its advertising in Florida, unaware that the Nader vote could be the difference between victory and defeat. The Kerry campaign, determined not to make the same mistake four years later, worked hard at limiting Nader's ballot access and his popular vote in competitive states. There have been no major third-party or independent campaigns since then, although New York City mayor, Michael Blumenthal, considered such a run in 2012 but concluded that partisan orientation of the country and its Electoral College voting system made the hurdles too high, even for a billionaire willing to spend his own money.

In building their Electoral College coalitions, candidates start with their base—areas that have been traditionally favorable to their party's nominees. Following the Civil War, the Democrats could depend on the "Solid South," while Republicans were stronger in the Northeast. Beginning in the 1960s, these areas began to shift their partisan allegiances. By the mid-1990s, the South had become solidly Republican while the Northeast was becoming more Democratic. With the Rocky Mountain region strongly Republican and the mid-Atlantic and Pacific Coast states leaning Democratic, the focus of recent campaigns has been on a relatively small number of competitive states, about twenty at the beginning of the campaign and less than ten by the end.

The enlargement of the Democratic electorate by the Obama campaigns has enhanced the Democrats' opportunities in the Electoral College. In both 2008 and 2012, the Democrats assumed that its candidate could win the states Kerry carried in 2004 plus Iowa, a state in which Obama achieved his first caucus victory, and New Mexico, a state with an increasing Hispanic population.[26] In both of his campaigns, Obama won two additional southwestern states, Colorado and Nevada, and two southern ones, Florida and Virginia, plus most of the traditional battleground states of the Midwest.[27]

The Democratic strategy has narrowed the Republicans' Electoral College map. Winner-take-all voting in most of the states gives advantage to the candidate that carries the most populous ones. Of the seven largest states, only Texas has consistently voted Republican since 1968 while California, Illinois, New York, and Pennsylvania have consistently voted Democratic. Ohio and Florida remain highly competitive.

| BOX 7.2 | PRESIDENTIAL CAMPAIGN STRATEGIES, 2004–2012 |

The 2004 Election
George W. Bush: A New Strategy for Staying in Place
The components of Bush's 2004 election strategy were derived from the political environment in which the country found itself at the beginning of the twenty-first century, the character strengths George W. Bush demonstrated as president following the terrorist attacks on September 11, 2001, John Kerry's perceived policy inconsistencies, and the advantages incumbents have in seeking reelection when national security issues are dominant.

The principal goal of Bush's reelection strategy, to expand the Republican electorate, was based on the assumption that most voters had already made up their minds and were strongly inclined to cast ballots in accordance with their partisan loyalties. There simply were not that many undecided voters in 2004. This election strategy grew out of the failure of Bush's 2000 election campaign to win a popular vote victory. Republican planners chided themselves for not maximizing their base vote in that election. They were determined not to repeat this error.

Efforts to improve partisan turnout began immediately after the 2000 presidential campaign. Fifty million dollars were spent in 2002 alone, developing and testing "victory-type" programs.[28] Convinced that the old-style turnout efforts were no longer sufficient, Republican political strategists decided on a multifaceted approach to identify and contact people with Republican leanings.

The plan required well-trained and committed partisans who could be counted on to initiate and maintain personal contacts with potential GOP supporters. In the past, both parties had turned to paid organizers, party professionals, labor unions, nonparty groups, and even profit-making firms to do so. The Republican plan deviated from past grassroots efforts by depending primarily on community-based volunteers.

continued

| BOX 7.2 | PRESIDENTIAL CAMPAIGN STRATEGIES, 2004–2012 *continued* |

The strategy depended on people's positive feelings toward the president. In 2004, those feelings were evident although they weakened considerably in subsequent years. Democrats also felt strongly and, for the most part, negatively about Bush and his policies in 2004, but many of them did not feel as strongly and positively about Kerry. In other words, Republicans displayed greater intensity toward Bush than Democrats did toward Kerry.

Another important component of the Republican ground campaign in 2004 was its focus on the social issues. Eleven state ballot initiatives against same-sex marriage, the president's repeated reference to a constitutional amendment defining marriage as a union between man and woman, and his frequently stated beliefs about God and the sanctity of human life all contributed to the success of the Republican's get-out-the-vote strategy.

A second strategic thrust of Bush's reelection campaign was to emphasize his leadership during crises. Even if people disagreed with his policies, they acknowledged his attributes of strength, conviction, determination, and purpose after the terrorist attacks of 9/11. Bush had passed the leadership test; Kerry had not taken it—that was the difference.[29] Being the incumbent helped the president use his bully pulpit to frame the campaign debate.

John Kerry: "Anything You Can Do, I Can Do Better"
With the electorate divided along partisan lines and Kerry's leadership qualities disputed, the Democratic challenger did not have an obvious or easy road to the White House. In fact, he began with several disadvantages. One was the five-week period following the Democratic convention and before the Republicans one, a period during which the Democratic candidate did not want to spend his limited federal funds. So he did not respond to allegations by the Swift Boat Veterans for Truth that criticized his war record and antiwar activities after he left the military.

A second problem for Kerry concerned the president's personal favorability ratings that precluded a campaign to demonize him. Kerry went after Bush's policies with some success among Democrats but not among Republicans. Nor was the proportion of undecided Independents large enough or angry enough for Kerry to gain a decisive edge.

Advocating leadership change in times of crisis is difficult for challengers unless they can demonstrate that the incumbent's policies or actions were responsible for the crisis and that the challenger had superior leadership qualities to deal with it. The Kerry campaign did not try to tag Bush with the responsibility for 9/11, only with a failed policy in Iraq. In the end, that was not sufficient to convince voters that the Democratic challenger could provide stronger, more dependable, more coherent leadership in the war on terrorism than the president.

The 2008 Election
Barack Obama: Empowering the People for Change
Every campaign tries to maximize its strengths. For Obama, the advantages were its financial resources, grassroots operation, and the high level of public dissatisfaction. Obama's Internet campaign had raised record amounts of money during the nomination and his volunteers had enlarged the Democratic electorate by their registration and get-out-the-vote activities. The plan was to do the same in the general election.

BOX 7.2

PRESIDENTIAL CAMPAIGN STRATEGIES, 2004–2012 *continued*

Obama's campaign message in 2008 was political and policy change. He appealed for unity in a country deeply divided by partisanship and ideology and gave hope and conveyed optimism to a public increasingly nervous about the depressed and deteriorating economy.

The emotion Obama generated provided his campaign with several strategic opportunities that his opponent lacked—a large war chest capable of expanding even further, virtual and actual on-the-ground operations, and as we have noted, an ability to alter the traditional red–blue coloration of the Electoral College map. "Our goal was to force them to defend Bush states," wrote David Plouffe in his book *The Audacity to Win.* "We saw little to no evidence that they could add to the Bush Electoral College margin."[30]

The rejection of federal funds was critical to Obama's success. Not only did it give him a significant resource advantage, but it enabled his campaign to control their own advertising and field operations, without depending on the Democratic National Committee and nonparty groups to help them do so.

Initially, the message was about the need for change and who could best achieve it. Over time, the narrative turned increasingly to the economy and the candidate and the party best able to fix it. After the mid-September financial meltdown, when McCain said, "The fundamentals of our economy are strong," the Obama campaign pointed to McCain's ill-chosen words and his erratic behavior.[31]

The gambit was successful. A disciplined campaign, financial advantages, a more appealing message, and a stronger field organization contributed to Obama's victory. There was little that McCain could say or do to improve the economy or shift the blame from Republican George W. Bush.

John McCain: An Experienced Maverick

Although John McCain wrapped up the Republican nomination in early March, he was not able to generate much enthusiasm for his candidacy. His choice of Sarah Palin was intended to be a game changer; it helped solidify his Republican base[32] but also gave the press and his Democratic rival a target of opportunity. The initial enthusiasm for Palin's selection contributed to a first-time lead in the national public opinion polls for McCain following the Republican convention.

The choice of Palin also affected press coverage. The news media shifted the spotlight to Palin and the excitement she generated among Republicans. But with greater coverage also came greater scrutiny. In one-to-one interviews with broadcast journalists, Palin did not do nearly as well as she had done reading prepared speeches and interacting with Republican partisans. She did not seem to know the Bush Doctrine in foreign policy nor did she have a keen understanding of the complexities of other international or domestic policy issues. Her lack of knowledge raised questions about her competence and suitability as vice president, much less president. Late-night comedians had a field day.

Since McCain began the general election with a significant financial disadvantage, his campaign was forced to depend on the Republican National Committee to supplement the $84.1 million he received from the federal treasury's election fund. His plan was to launch a coordinated advertising campaign with the national committee. Doing so, however, required that the combined ads promote national party

continued

BOX 7.2   PRESIDENTIAL CAMPAIGN STRATEGIES,
2004–2012 *continued*

candidates in addition to McCain. "Every time we said John McCain's name, we had to say congressional Republicans or congressional liberals as a match. . . . In half our ads, it looked like we were running against Harry Reid," said Sarah Simmons, McCain's director of strategy.[33] Moreover, the bulk of these "hybrid" ads had to be negative because of the low esteem in which Congress was held by the American people. Negative ads appeal more to partisans than to Independents. Thus they did not help McCain expand his base.[34]

By October, the people who advised McCain concluded that they needed a new campaign narrative if he was going to win. That narrative took the form of Joe the Plumber, a person who challenged Obama's economic policies at one of his campaign rallies. Joe became a symbol for middle-class workers who had lost their jobs and were angry about legislation that bailed out large financial firms that caused the problem but not average Americans who lost their jobs. Joe was a guy with whom regular folks could identify. Joe rallied Republicans but did not change the dynamics of the race. With the economy dominating the news, domestic terrorism less salient, and a Status of Forces Agreement reached with Iraq that would bring most U.S. forces home, there was little McCain could do to reverse the negative national political environment for the Republicans. His defeat was almost inevitable.

The 2012 Election
Barack Obama: Continue the Progress
Obama's reelection strategy was fashioned by the political consequences of the 2010 midterm elections and the nation's tepid recovery from the Great Recession. The victory of Tea Party candidates during the 2010 Republican primaries and congressional elections moved the GOP to the right, deadlocked policy making in Washington, and turned the economic focus to deficit spending, the growing national debt, and pending expiration of the Bush tax cuts. It provided Obama with the opportunity to claim the middle ground campaign much as Bill Clinton had done in his reelection campaign.

In his campaign, Obama described the electorate in terms of the haves and have-nots. He asked voters to reflect on which parties' policies would be likely to help them the most. The president's focus on the future of the middle class had another advantage. It shifted attention from the present to the years that were to follow, allowing him to point to the country's upward economic trajectory during his first term and mute Republican criticism that his economic policies were not working.

Defining his opponent early in the election cycle was also part of Obama's strategy. No sooner than the Republican nomination had been settled in early April, the Obama campaign launched its advertising, portraying Romney as a wealthy venture capitalist, more successful at making profits than keeping jobs for American workers. The Democratic campaign narrative cast him in the ideological mode of George W. Bush and Tea Party advocates.

Obama also used his symbolic and discretionary powers effectively as president. Helped by Hurricane Sandy, which hit the mid-Atlantic region a week before the election, he went to the distressed areas, empathized with those who suffered, and promised federal relief. People approved his handling of the disaster.[35]

BOX 7.2	PRESIDENTIAL CAMPAIGN STRATEGIES, 2004–2012 *continued*

Mitt Romney: Turning the Economy Around

Every reelection campaign is a referendum on the president's first term. The Republican strategy in the 2012 campaign emphasized the tepid economy and the inability of the Obama administration to turn it around in four years. Romney promised positive change. He said his private policy initiative would create six million more jobs. He criticized an expansive federal role, arguing that health care, education, and other social issues should be decided on a state-by-state basis. He did not emphasize Obamacare to which Republicans were strongly opposed; Romney had supported a similar health care initiative in Massachusetts when he was governor.

The Republican candidate also had to overcome the fuzzy image problem that most challengers face; his campaign had to learn what type of information voters wanted to know the most about him. They found the answer in public opinion surveys. People wanted to know what he would do as president. To provide this information, the campaign initiated a "Day One" advertising effort but had funds to run the ads in only four states; in fact, $20 million had to be borrowed just to stay on the air before the Republican convention. Super PACs that backed Romney did advertise during this period, but unable to coordinate their advertising with Romney's, they ran negative Obama ads, not positive Romney ones. As a consequence, Romney was not able to counter the negative image that the Democrats portrayed of him throughout the spring and summer of 2012.[36]

Although Romney's personal image improved a little, he still trailed Obama in likeability by 23 points before the Republican Convention and 12 points on election day. That Romney was unable to bridge the character gap worked to the president's political advantage.[37] Voters simply liked him more than Romney.

TACTICAL CONSIDERATIONS

STAGING

Orchestrating a campaign is not easy. The appearance of the stage, the timing of the event, the dignitaries invited and their seating positions, the recruitment and composition of the audience, the facilities for press coverage, the videotaping by professionals and other attendees, and, of course, the candidate's appearance, speech (and the sound bites written into it), and interaction with those present must be planned in detail and well ahead of the event. Nothing is left to chance.

Campaigns take steps to ensure friendly crowds and no hecklers if possible by distributing tickets to party workers, campaign volunteers, and political donors. Their own camera crews record the events and distribute video film clips to local, cable, and regional media as well as post them on their web sites and YouTube. Communication staff constantly twitter news about the event, the candidate's message, and the crowd's reaction to it. Knowing that their opponents and the press will focus on inconsistencies and slipups, candidates are warned to stick to the prepared script that has been pretested before groups of voters. Frequently, speechwriters will insert code words to generate a reaction from a particular group.

TIMING

In addition to what to say, how to say it, and to whom, timing is also important. Candidates naturally desire to build momentum as their campaigns progress. The 1996 Clinton campaign was one of the most successful in adhering to a timed plan for communicating various messages to the voters. In the year before the election, the president emphasized his centrist and moderate positions. As the Republican nomination got underway, he talked about family values and showcased himself in various presidential roles, in stark contrast to the Republican candidates, who were criticizing one another's qualifications for the presidency. During the general election campaign, Clinton remained on his presidential pedestal, emphasizing the accomplishments of his administration and his desire to build a "bridge to the future."

Running for reelection, Barack Obama followed a similar script. George W. Bush did not; instead, he emphasized his steadiness and presidential status while raising questions about his opponent's policy consistency and leadership skills. Challengers face a more condensed time frame, particularly after a competitive nomination and also when running against an incumbent. They have more things to do more quickly with fewer resources.

DAMAGE CONTROL

Opposition research is a critical campaign component, especially with the decline in the number of investigative reporters that work for major news organizations. In fact, the Pew Research Center's Project for Excellence in Journalism reported that midway through the 2012 general election campaign that candidates' staffs and the individuals and groups that supported them were the primary source of about half the news stories that were reported by the press.[38]

In addition to obtaining negative information "dug up" about one's opponents, candidates must defend ad lib comments they make or actions they take. Slipups inevitably occur; the electronic media has obliterated the line between private and public.

Denials are difficult in the face of evidence to the contrary. Explanations such as "I was quoted out of context" or "that's not what I meant" have become the standard responses.

To illustrate, in 2012, Romney told political contributors at a private event:

> There are 47 percent of the people who will vote for the president no matter what. All right, there are 47 percent who are with him, who are dependent upon government, who believe that they are victims, who believe the government has a responsibility to care for them, who believe that they are entitled to health care, to food, to housing, to you-name-it—that that's an entitlement. And the government should give it to them. And they will vote for this president no matter what. . . . These are people who pay no income tax. . . . [M]y job is not to worry about those people. I'll never convince them they should take personal responsibility and care for their lives.[39]

Unknown to him and his aides who attended the event, an attendee recorded his comments, and they went viral. Romney's remark reinforced the "wealthy, uncaring" image by which the Obama campaign and its Democratic supporters had described him.

Campaigns establish war rooms to respond quickly to unexpected statements and behavior from candidates and their surrogates, statements and behavior that the news media and political opponents highlight. The absence of a reaction is deemed to be an admission of guilt and becomes part of the story of the campaign. However, an overreaction can also be harmful if it keeps the item in the news as a subject of debate. So can an underreaction, such as Romney's to his 47 percent comments. He defended the substance of his remarks but acknowledged that they were not "eloquently" stated.

There are times, however, that ad lib comments can work to a candidate's advantage. When Republican vice presidential nominee Dan Quayle compared his Senate experience with John F. Kennedy's in his debate with Lloyd Bentsen, the Democratic candidate shot back, "I served with Jack Kennedy; I knew Jack Kennedy; Jack Kennedy was a friend of mine. Senator, you are no Jack Kennedy."[40] Quayle, shaken by Bentsen's blunt reply, remained on the defensive for the remainder of the debate.

OPERATIONS

Running a campaign is a complex, time-consuming, nerve-racking venture. Constant emergencies and unanticipated events must be dealt with as well as the numerous personal issues, heightened by the pace of work, the hours spent at it, and egos of the ambitious, mostly young people who get involved. Campaigns are hectic, fast-paced, and all-consuming experiences. Mistakes can be costly. Nonetheless, many of the people who work in political campaigns really enjoy the experience and expand their friends and acquaintances in the process.

ORGANIZATION

Presidential campaigns have become large and complex entities. They take months, even years, to design, structure, and staff. Figure 7.1 lists their basic operating units.

Within this basic structure, most strategic and major tactical decisions are highly centralized. There is a large headquarters out of which most of the principal advisers work. Since some have to travel with the candidate, attend to field operations, or just work out of their homes, the top people stay connected via conference calling, email, and Skype. Daily early morning and evening meetings are regularly held, often with the candidate on the line.

Obviously, grassroots activities have to be more decentralized. Some presidential campaigns organize, train, and run their own field offices and operations. Others are more dependent on state and local parties to do so. Until the 1970s, the Democrats had stronger state parties and a weaker national base and thus tended to rely on state parties to turn out the vote. In recent

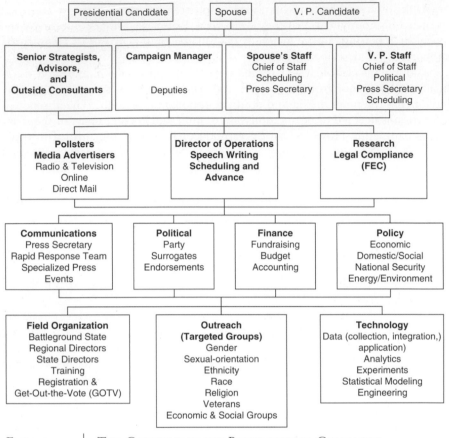

FIGURE 7.1 | THE CONTEMPORARY PRESIDENTIAL CAMPAIGN
ORGANIZATION

years, Republican presidential candidates have had to rely more on their
party's local and state organizations. Both McCain and Romney also used
the national Republican turnout organization that was built after the 2000
election to help identify supporters and get them to vote.

Sometimes, candidates circumvent their party when they do not trust the
establishment leaders to support their nominees enthusiastically. In 1964, Barry
Goldwater's backers were very leery of the backing they would receive from East
Coast Republicans. As a consequence, they built their own army of ideological
supporters from whom they solicited funds and voluntary campaign efforts.[41]

The same desire for control and for circumventing the party was evident
in Richard Nixon's reelection campaign in 1972. Completely separate from the
national party, even in title, the Committee to Reelect the President (known as
CREEP by its critics) raised its own money, conducted its own public relations
(including polling and campaign advertising), scheduled its own events, and
even had its own security division. It was this division, operating independently
from the Republican Party, which harassed the Democratic campaign of George
McGovern, heckling his speeches, spreading false rumors, and perpetrating

other illegal acts, including the attempted bugging of the Democratic National Committee headquarters at the Watergate Office Building. The excesses perpetuated by individuals in this group illustrate both the difficulty of overseeing all the aspects of a large presidential campaign and the risk of placing nonprofessionals in key positions of responsibility. Had the more experienced Republican National Committee exercised greater influence over the president's reelection, there might have been less deviation from accepted standards of behavior.

With the enactment of campaign finance legislation in the 1970s, separate presidential campaign organizations, distinct from the national party, have to be established to receive federal funds, file quarterly financial reports, and abide by the contributions and spending limits.

The George W. Bush campaign organizations of 2000 and 2004 and the Obama organizations of 2008 and 2012 are prototypes of well-run, well-coordinated operations. Each had highly experienced managers, pollsters, fund-raisers, and consultants. Each was hierarchical at the top and decentralized at the bottom. Each used the latest communication technologies to identify and persuade voters with each campaign more sophisticated than the previous one. Each campaign saw personal contact as the key to successful persuasion.

Karl Rove, who had overseen Bush's gubernatorial campaigns, masterminded the Republican grassroots effort. After the 2000 election, he became convinced that the older-style turnout instruments of mass market advertising, robo telephone calling, and direct mail were not sufficient to maximize the base vote.

To build their list of party leaners, Rove and other Republican leaders assembled a large data bank from conservative magazine subscribers, regular church-goers, listeners and viewers of certain radio and television stations, and people living in heavily Republican areas. The plan was simple: to identify "lazy Republicans," determine if they were registered to vote, contact them repeatedly during the campaign, and once they made their voting decision, get them to vote as soon as state laws permitted.

FIELD OFFICES

In 2008 and 2012, Obama mounted an even more sophisticated effort in the field and online. He had about 800 storefront offices in 2012, at least one per state, with most concentrated in the key battleground areas (see Table 7.1). In addition, the campaign had multiple staging areas (in homes of supporters) where canvassers would assemble, get their marching orders, and be directed to the locations they would be working. Volunteers could also get their assignments via cell, through an app, which gave them information on where to go, whom to call, and the odds of a person voting for Obama.

In contrast Romney's ground organization was smaller, less technologically advanced, and more dependent on local and state party organizations. Republicans claimed that they contacted 80.5 million people during the 2012 campaign, mostly in the major competitive states.[42] Romney had only 300 field offices, and most of them promoted other GOP candidates in addition to

Romney; almost all of Obama's offices were primarily devoted to his reelection.[43] The gap was greatest in Ohio (Obama had 131 offices compared to Romney's 40), in Florida (Obama had 106 compared to Romney's 47), and in Virginia, in which Obama had more than twice as many storefronts as Romney.[44]

BATTLEGROUND CONCENTRATION

In addition to the field offices, each campaign stages most of their events, candidate appearances, and advertising in the same battleground states. In 2012, the only other states to which the candidates traveled were those in which their wealthy donors lived and worked (mostly, California, Illinois, and New York, and Texas). Table 7.1 sums up these offices, activities, and advertising expenditures in the states in which they occurred.

TABLE 7.1 | FIELD OFFICES, CANDIDATE APPEARANCES, AND CAMPAIGN ADVERTISING IN THE KEY BATTLEGROUND STATES IN 2012

States	Field Offices		Candidate Appearances*		Advertising Expenditures (in Millions)†	
	Obama	Romney	Obama	Romney	Obama	Romney
Colorado	62	13	8	15	$36	$37
Florida	104	48	17	23	78	95
Iowa	67	14	11	16	27	30
Michigan	28	24	0	1	8	24
Minnesota	12	0	0	1	3	9
Nevada	26	12	6	7	26	29
New Hampshire	22	9	8	5	18	16
North Carolina	54	24	2	1	40	57
Ohio	131	40	28	45	72	78
Pennsylvania	54	25	0	5	11	20
Virginia#	61	29	10	26	21	25
Wisconsin	69	24	11	7	12	20
Total	690	262	101	152	$352	$440

* Includes vice presidential candidates Joe Biden and Paul Ryan.

† Money spent on advertising supporting Obama and Romney in the key states; a total of $404 million was spent on advertising by or for the Obama campaign and $492 million by and for the Romney campaign.

In addition to the expenditures spent in Virginia, the Democrats spent $34 million and the Republicans $41 million on advertising in the Washington, DC, metropolitan area, which includes Northern Virginia.

Sources: Field offices—Andrea Levien, "Tracking Presidential Campaign Field Operations," The Center for Voting and Democracy (fairvote.org), November 13, 2012. http://www.fairvote.org/research-and-analysis /blog/tracking-presidential-campaign-field-operations/

Candidate appearances—"Presidential Tracker," The Center for Voting and Democracy (fairvote.org). http://www.fairvote.org/research-and-analysis/presidential-elections/presidential-tracker/

Advertising expenditures—"Mad Money: TV Ads in the 2012 Presidential Campaign," *Washington Post.* http://www.washingtonpost.com/wp-srv/special/politics/track-presidential-campaign-ads-2012 /whos-buying-ads/

DIGITAL OPS

Obama's digital operation was also larger and more technologically advanced than his 2008 Internet campaign. In his first campaign, the Obama team had amassed millions of e-mail addresses, cell phone numbers, and zip codes but could not integrate data sources effectively. Thus, each operation from fundraising to canvassing to get-out-the-vote activities used its own data bank. The campaign had plenty of information, but it was collected from different sources that used different software and kept it in different data sets.[45]

The big advance in 2012 was digital integration. Beginning in 2011, the reelection campaign began to build its technological unit.[46] A group, Technology for Obama (T40), chaired by founders of Napster, Facebook, LinkedIn, Yelp, and Craigslist, raised money, identified and contacted experts that had the knowledge to consolidate the data, developed codes to use it, and designed outreach and innovative marketing campaigns.

The goal was to assemble a vast, consolidated data file in which detailed personal information on millions of people would be stored, integrated, and then provided to field staff and volunteers.[47] The technology group developed a new computing program, known *Narwhal*, named after an Arctic whale, which combined information the campaign collected from new and existing sources. *Narwhal* relied on Amazon's Simple Queue Service to process and store data.

Apps were built for the field operation to access the information needed to identify and register Obama voters in different geographical areas. A program known as *Dashboard* matched volunteers to their communities and directed their activities. It also provided the Obama campaign with data on canvassing: who had been contacted, how they had been contacted, and whether they were registered to vote.[48] Another app, *Call Tool*, provided volunteers with phone numbers to call and scripts to use if they desired.[49] The campaign claimed that it contacted 150 million people by personal telephone calls, and door-knocks.

Two groups were targeted: Democratically-oriented voters who were less likely to vote, and a smaller group of Independents who had not as yet decided for whom to vote. For the less likely voters, the problem the campaign had was how to reach them. Many were in the youngest voting age cohort, did not have a history of political involvement or association with the party or previous campaigns, or even a listed land-line phone. What they did have were politically active and connected friends. Obama's goal according to Teddy Goff, director of digital operations, was to get their friends to persuade them to vote for Obama.

> Of our GOTV [get-out-the-vote] targets, eighteen to twenty-nine years old, 50 percent of them we couldn't reach by phone. So they either don't have a land line, or we didn't have their cell number. . . . Of that group, 85 percent of them we could reach via a friend of Barack Obama.[50]

Facebook, which had quadrupled in number of users between 2008 and 2012, became the primary platform from which data were collected. Obama's supporters were urged to visit his web site, barackobama.com, through Facebook, thereby giving the campaign access to the personal information stored on their page as well as that of their friends' (through Facebook Connect). With this information, the campaign could also monitor the web activities of the users that had been identified. Added to the bank were data from state registration and voting lists, Democratic Party lists, Obama's 2008 campaign file as well as public opinion polls, broken down by demographic groups. By integrating the huge amounts of data, the campaign designed, directed, and personalized its appeals for money as well as for canvassing voters.

Romney could not match the size or sophistication of the Obama effort. He had a paid staff of 500 compared to Obama's 3,000; his data analytics team consisted of 4 techs; Obama's had over 50. Romney's automated turnout system for the key battleground states failed repeatedly on election day, in part because volunteers had not received the training they needed to use it.[51] Romney had fewer friends on Facebook (12.1 million on election day compared to Obama's 32.3 million), fewer Twitter and Google followers, and fewer volunteers making personal contacts with voters. [52]

Did Obama's field and digital operations make a difference? Most political observers and campaign operatives believe that they did,[53] that they helped the Obama campaign to expand the electorate in the key battleground states. [54] Political scientists John Sides and Lynn Vavreck's research indicated that Obama did better in counties in which he had field offices, but they also estimated that he would have won, albeit more narrowly, without them.[55]

SUMMARY

Throughout much of the nineteenth century, presidential campaigns were run by the political parties on behalf of their nominees. The goal of the campaign was to energize and educate the electorate with a series of public activities and events. Beginning in the 1840s, but accelerating in the 1880s, presidential candidates themselves became increasingly involved in the campaign. By the 1920s, they had become active participants, using radio, television, and the Internet to reach as many voters as possible.

Most presidential campaigns follow a general strategy based on the prevailing political attitudes and perceptions of the electorate, the reputations and images of the nominees and their parties, and the geography of the Electoral College. The strategy includes designing a basic appeal, creating a leadership image, dealing with incumbency (if appropriate), and allocating campaign resources in the key battleground states.

In projecting their basic appeals, Democratic candidates emphasize their party label and their familiar narrative that they are the party of average Americans, understand the problems people face in their everyday lives, and have designed policies that promote greater opportunities and less inequality for more people. Republicans stress the importance of individual initiatives, private ownership, and traditional family values. Since 1980, they have campaigned against large, intrusive, inefficient government that they claim creates dependency, saps energy, and discourages creativity in a free enterprise system.

Part of the strategy of every presidential campaign is to project an image of leadership. Candidates do this by trumpeting their own strengths and exploiting their opponent's weaknesses. They try to project those attributes that the public desires in their president, traits that are endemic to the office and resonate with the public mood at that time. Being president, making critical decisions, and exercising the powers of the office are evidence of the leadership skills that incumbents have displayed and challengers have to demonstrate.

An established record, particularly by presidents seeking reelection, shapes much of that leadership imagery. That record may contribute to or detract from a candidate's reelection potential. In good times, incumbents have an advantage; in bad times, they do not. When national security issues are salient, incumbents also tend to benefit. Public grievances must be deeply felt and broad-based to defeat a sitting president.

When allocating resources, the geography of the Electoral College must always be considered. Each party begins with a base of safe states. In the 1980s, that base was thought to be larger for the Republicans; today the Democrats are thought to have an advantage. In 2000 and 2004, the Electoral College was divided closely between red (Republican) and blue (Democratic) states, and there was stability in the states' voting preferences. In 2008, the Obama campaign made gains in the South and Southwest as well as in some of the traditional battleground states of the Midwest, inroads it mostly maintained in 2012.

The level of competition within states is another factor that affects campaign strategy and resource allocation. Only about twenty states have been perceived as truly competitive at the beginning of the race and usually less than ten at the end. Time, effort, and money are concentrated within the most competitive states; the rest of the country witnesses the campaign primarily in the news and by word of mouth; they do not see the candidates in person except perhaps at a fund-raiser or in an advertisement in one of the major media markets.

Advances in transportation and communications have made campaigns more complex, more expensive, and more sophisticated. Strategy and tactics are now more closely geared to the technology of contemporary politics and run by campaign professionals: pollsters, media consultants, direct mailers, grassroots organizers, lawyers, accountants, data collectors and analysts, and experts of the new media. Their inclusion in the candidate's organization has made the coordination of centralized decision making critical. It has also produced several complementary organizations and campaigns all operating at the same time: those of the candidates, the national and state parties, and outside, nonparty groups. When an incumbent is running, the White House is also involved.

The job of campaign organizations is to produce a unified and coordinated effort with centralized strategic decision making and a decentralized field operation. Since 2004, base mobilization has been the principal objective of both parties' presidential candidates. Large, integrated data banks are used to identify voters, script volunteers, and direct their canvassing efforts. Campaign communications are tested for impact prior to their delivery and then targeted to specific demographic, attitudinal, and interest groups.

Microtargeting is deemed to be more effective than mass marketing with personal contact the key to turning out voters. The name of the game is to persuade people to vote for a candidate on the basis of their preexisting values, beliefs, and interests.

WHERE ON THE WEB?

Many of the *Where on the Web* sites listed in Chapter 5 will be useful to study the general election as well.

- *Campaigns and Elections*
  www.campaignandelections.com
  A popular journal that focuses on campaigns and elections.

- 24-7 News Networks: CNN, Fox News, MSNBC
  www.CNN.com
  www.foxnews.com
  www.msnbc.com

  Contain news, investigatory, and feature stories on the presidential campaign.

- C-SPAN: The Road to the White House
  www.cspan.org
  Provides C-SPAN programming on the campaign as well as candidate appearances, speeches, student surveys, and political debates.

- Fivethirtyeight
  www.fivethirtyeight.com
  The web site of Nate Silver, a statistician and former *New York Times* analyst, examines polling data and predicts election outcomes.

- Gallup Poll
  www.gallup.com
  Contains the latest polling data on the campaign. Gallup is one of the country's premier polling organizations.

- Monkey Cage
  http://www.washingtonpost.com/blogs/monkey-cage/
  A blog of the *Washington Post* that contains interesting election commentary by political scientists, journalists, and others.

- *National Journal*
  www.nationaljournal.com
  Of the many news sources for following the presidential elections, the *National Journal*'s site is one of the best.

- *New York Times*
  www.nytimes.com
  > The *New York Times* prides itself on being a paper of record. You will find much information on the policy positions and speeches of the candidates in this newspaper and on its web site.

- *Politico*
  www.politico.com
  > An online news source that emphasizes politics and elections.

- *Real Clear Politics*
  www.realclearpoltics.com
  > Another online news source that emphasizes politics and elections.

EXERCISES

1. Indicate the initial geographic strategies of the major party candidates in 2008 and 2012 and how those strategies changed over the course of the campaign. Now compare these strategies to those you believe should or will be employed in 2016. Design a resource allocation memo for the candidate of your choice.

2. Assess how the candidates targeted their appeals in the most recent presidential election. What appeals did they direct toward their own partisans, especially to the principal groups within their party's electoral coalition, and how did they deal with Independents and others less interested in presidential politics?

3. How has the Internet changed the tactics and operations of presidential campaigns in recent years? To what extent has this new technology affected the democratic character of presidential elections?

4. Were you contracted, directly or indirectly, by a personal friend, party or nonparty group during the presidential campaign? If so, what arguments or campaign appeals did you find the most persuasive?

SELECTED READINGS

Campaign for President: The Managers Look at 2012. Lanham, MD: Rowman & Littlefield, 2013.

Doherty, Brendan J. *The Rise of the President's Permanent Campaign*. Lawrence, KS: University Press of Kansas, 2012.

Halperin, Mark, and John Heilmann. *Double Down: Game Change 2012*. New York: The Penguin Press, 2013.

Heilemann, John, and Mark Halperin. *Game Change*. New York: HarperCollins, 2010.

Issenberg, Sasha. "The Definitive Story of How President Obama Mined Vote Data to Win a Second Term," *MIT Technology Review* (2012). www.technologyreview.com/featuredstory/509026/how-obamas-team-used-big-data-to-rally-voters

Jamieson, Kathleen Hall, ed. *Electing the President 2012: The Insiders' View*. Philadelphia: University of Pennsylvania Press, 2013.

Melder, Keith. *Hail to the Candidate: Presidential Campaigns from Banners to Broadcasts*. Washington, DC: Smithsonian Institution Press, 1992.

Ornstein, Norman, and Thomas Mann, eds. *The Permanent Campaign and Its Future*. Washington, DC: AEI/Brookings, 2000.

Plouffe, David. *The Audacity to Win*. New York: Viking, 2009.

Popkin, Samuel L. *The Candidate: What It Takes to Win and Hold the White House.* Oxford, UK: Oxford University Press, 2012.

Sides, John, and Lynn Vavreck. *The Gamble; Choice and Chance in the 2012 Presidential Election.* Princeton, NJ: Princeton University Press, 2013.

Shaw, Daron R. *The Race to 270: The Electoral College and Campaign Strategies of 2000 and 2004.* Chicago: University of Chicago Press, 2006.

Tenpas, Kathryn Dunn. *Presidents as Candidates.* New York: Garland, 1997.

Troy, Gil. *See How They Ran: The Changing Role of the Presidential Candidate.* New York: Free Press, 1991.

White, Theodore H. *The Making of the President: 1960.* New York: Atheneum, 1988.

———. *The Making of the President, 1964.* New York: Atheneum, 1965.

———. *The Making of the President, 1968.* New York: Atheneum, 1969.

———. *The Making of the President, 1972.* New York: Atheneum, 1973.

———. *America in Search of Itself: The Making of the President, 1956–1980.* New York: Harper & Row, 1982.

Woodward, Bob. *The Choice.* New York: Simon & Schuster, 1997.

NOTES

1. Keith Melder, *Hail to the Candidate: Presidential Campaigns from Banners to Broadcasts* (Washington DC: Smithsonian Institution Press, 1992), pp. 70–74.
2. Ibid., p. 87.
3. Ibid., p. 88.
4. Marvin R. Weisbord, *Campaigning for President* (New York: Washington Square Press, 1966), p. 45.
5. Historian Gil Troy writes that Lincoln's avoidance of anything that smacked of political involvement was in fact a political tactic that he used throughout the campaign. Gil Troy, *See How They Ran: The Changing Role of the Presidential Candidate* (New York: Free Press, 1991), p. 66.
6. Weisbord, *Campaigning for President*, p. 5.
7. Melder, *Hail to the Candidate*, p. 104.
8. Ibid., p. 125.
9. Keith Melder, "The Whistlestop: Origins of the Personal Campaign," *Campaign and Elections*, 7 (May/June 1986), p. 49.
10. William Jennings Bryan, *The First Battle* (1896; reprint, Port Washington, NY: Kennikat Press, 1971), p. 618.
11. Melder, *Hail to the Candidate*, p. 129.
12. Weisbord, *Campaigning for President*, p. 116.
13. Franklin Roosevelt had been disabled by polio in 1921. He wore heavy leg braces and could stand only with difficulty. Nonetheless, he made a remarkable physical and political recovery. In his campaign, he went to great lengths to hide the fact that he could not walk and could barely stand. The press generally did not report on his disability. They refrained from photographing, filming, or describing him struggling to stand with braces.
14. Cabell Phillips, *The Truman Presidency* (New York: Macmillan, 1966), p. 237.
15. Stanley Kelley, *Professional Public Relations and Political Power* (Baltimore, MD: Johns Hopkins Press, 1956), pp. 161–162.
16. Danny Hayes, "Candidate Policies through a Partisan Lens: A Theory of Trait Ownership," *American Journal of Political Science*, 49 (Oct. 2005): 908–923.
17. Over the four-year period, negative economic evaluations and prognoses had declined; in fact, they were declining during the election campaign itself. In 2008,

58 percent evaluated economic conditions as fair or poor, 79 percent thought things were getting worse, and 86 percent were dissatisfied with the way things were going in the United States. Four years later, 35 percent described conditions as fair or poor, 50 percent thought they were getting worse, and 64 percent were dissatisfied with the way things were going in the country.

Gallup Poll, "Trends A-Z: Gallup Daily: U.S. Economic Conditions." http://www.gallup.com/poll/110821/Gallup-Daily-US-Economic-Conditions.aspx; "Gallup Daily: U.S. Economic Outlook." http://www.gallup.com/poll/110824/Gallup-Daily-US-Economic-Outlook.aspx; "Satisfaction with the United States." http://www.gallup.com/poll/1669/General-Mood-Country.aspx

18. David Axelrod, *Electing the President: 2012: The Insiders' View*, Kathleen Hall Jamieson, ed. (Philadelphia, PA: University of Pennsylvania Press, 2009), p. 68.

19. If he did not do well, however, the early debate would have given him more time to recover and still demonstrate his competence.

20. George W. Bush, "Acceptance Speech at the Republican National Convention" (August 3, 2000). www.presidency.ucsb.edu/ws/index.php?pid=25954.

21. Lee Atwater, architect of this strategy, noted: "When I first got into politics, I just stumbled across the fact that candidates who went into an election with negatives higher than 30 or 40 points just inevitably lost." Thomas B. Edsall, "Why Bush Accentuates the Negative," *The Washington Post* (Oct. 2, 1988), p. C4.

22. Obama was careful not to disparage McCain personally. He acknowledged his years of service and sacrifice to his country as a naval aviator and prisoner of war in Vietnam.

23. In his acceptance speech at the Democratic convention, Gore made a point of asking voters to support him on the basis of his policy goals, not Clinton's: "This election is not an award for past performance. I'm not asking you to vote for me on the basis of the economy we have. Tonight I ask for your support on the basis of the better, fairer, more prosperous America we can build together." Al Gore, "Acceptance Speech to the Democratic National Convention" (August 17, 2000). www.presidency.ucsb.edu/ws/index.php?pid=25963.

24. "The Final Days of the Media Campaign 2012," Pew Research Center's Project for Excellence in Journalism, November 19, 2012. http://www.journalism.org/files/legacy/Final%20Days%20Final.pdf

25. Gallup Poll, "Presidential Job Approval Center." http://www.gallup.com/poll/124922/Presidential-Approval-Center.aspx?ref=interactive

26. David Plouffe, *The Audacity to Win* (New York: Viking, 2009), pp. 249–258.

27. He won North Carolina and Indiana in 2008 but lost in 2012.

28. Ken Mehlman, *Campaign for President: The Managers Look at 2004* (Lanham, MD: Rowman and Littlefield, 2006), p.102.

29. In the words of Matthew Dowd, a senior strategist for the Bush campaign: "There were a lot of people who never knew if Kerry wanted to cut and run— they didn't know what he wanted to do. On Election Day, a lot of them questioned whether or not he had a different plan than the President. In the end, the majority of voters said, I trust the President more than John Kerry on Iraq." Matthew Dowd, *Campaign for President 2004*, p. 193.

30. Plouffe, *The Audacity to Win*, p. 249.

31. "Our response [to the statement] followed a standard formula. Insert a rebuttal to McCain's outrageous comment in Obama's next speech that day to create a back and forth, ensuring maximum coverage. Produce TV and radio ads for release by that afternoon and get them up in the states right away. Make sure all our volunteers and staff out in the states had talking points on this to drive home in their conversations with voters." Ibid., p. 332.

32. Christian Ferry, McCain's deputy campaign manager, stated: "She was a huge positive for our field operation. She generated incredible enthusiasm amongst our volunteers. Folks who probably were going to vote for McCain on election day were now saying, 'I am going to work very hard for McCain,' because of the type of affection they had not just for John McCain but for Sarah Palin."

33. Sarah Simmons, Ibid., p. 184.

34. McCain's suspension of his campaign also adversely affected his on-the-ground operations. According to Ferry, "There was a great deal of confusion. . . . Our volunteers weren't certain what exactly that meant for them. We had a period of ten days when our voluntary activity went way down." Christian Ferry, Ibid., p. 193.

35. Jeffrey M. Jones and Steve Ander, "Americans Praise Gov't Work on Natural Disasters, Parks," Gallup Poll, July 12, 2013. http://www.gallup.com/poll/163487 /americans-praise-gov-work-natural-disasters-parks.aspx

36. According to Romney's chief campaign strategist, Stuart Stevens, ". . . we did not have the ability to control the dialogue during the summer months. Our whole goal was to get to the debates alive. We realized that we were not in a position to win this thing until October, which is not unusual for a challenger."

37. When asked about the candidates' greatest strengths, 47 percent named some dimension of Obama's character compared with 23 percent naming a character trait for Romney. Lydia Saad, "Americans See Different Strengths in Obama and Romney," Gallup Poll, October 29, 2012. http://www.gallup.com/poll/158411 /americans-different-strengths-obama-romney.aspx

38. "Press Coverage of the Character of the Candidates Is Highly Negative, and Neither Obama Nor Romney Has an Edge," Pew Research Center's Project for Excellence in Journalism, August 23, 2012. http://www.journalism.org/2012/08 /23/2012-campaign-character-narratives/

39. YouTube, September 18, 2012. http://www.youtube.com/watch?v=M2gvY2wqI7M

40. Lloyd Bentsen, "Transcript of the Vice Presidential Debate," *The Washington Post* (Oct. 6, 1988), p. A30.

41. Karl A. Lamb and Paul A. Smith, *Campaign Decision Making: The Presidential Election of 1964* (Belmont, CA: Wadsworth, 1968), pp. 59–63.

42. Nick Judd, "Republican Party's Technology Revival Hopes Hinge on Data and Data Analysis," TechPresident.com, February 7, 2013. http://techpresident.com /news/23479/republican-partys-technology-revival-hinge-more-just-skype

43. Molly Ball, "Obama's Edge: The Ground Game That Could Put Him Over the Top," *The Atlantic*, October 24, 2012. www.theatlantic.com/politics/archive/2012 /obamas-edge-the-ground-game-that-could-put-him-over-the-top/264031

44. Ibid.

45. Tim Murphy, "Inside the Obama Campaign's Hard Drive," *Mother Jones*, October 2012. www.motherjones.com/politics/2012/10/harper-reed-obama -campaign-microtargeting; Gallagher, "Built to Win."

46. Ed Pilkington and Amanda Michel, "Obama, Facebook and the Power of Friendship: The 2012 Data Election," *The Guardian*, February 17, 2012. www.guardian .co.uk/world/2012/feb17/obama-digital-data-machine-facebook-election

47. Amanda Michel, "Obama Campaign to Break Ground with Tech Volunteer Office in San Francisco," *The Guardian*, March 22, 2012. www.guardian.co.uk /world/2012mar/22/obama-campaign-san-francisco-office/print

48. Steve Lohr, "The Obama Campaign's Technology Is a Force Multiplier," *New York Times*, November 8, 2012. http://bits.blogs.nytimes.com/2012/11/08/the-obama -campaigns-technology-the-force-multiplier/?_php=true&_type=blogs&_r=0

49. Sean Gallagher, "Built to Win: Deep Inside the Obama's Campaign Tech," *Ars Technica*, November 14, 2012. http://arstechnica.com/information-technology /2012/11/built-to-win-deep-inside-obamas-campaign-tech

50. Teddy Goff in Jamieson, ed. In *Electing the President 2012: The Insiders' View* (Philadelphia, PA: University of Pennsylvania Press, 2013), p. 129.

51. Sean Gallagher, "Inside Team, Romney's Whale of an IT Meltdown," ArsTechnica .com, November 9, 2012. http://arstechnica.com/information-technology/2012/11 /inside-team-romneys-whale-of-an-it-meltdown

52. Micah l. Sifry, "Presidential Campaign 2012, by the Numbers," Techpresident.com, November 26, 2012. http://techpresident.com/news/23178/presidential-campaign -2012-numbers

53. John Dickinson, "How Obama Won Four More Years," *Slate*, November 7, 2012; Alan Wirzbicki, "Obama Won Ohio with Ground Game," *Boston Globe*, November 9, 2012.

54. Neil Newhouse in Jamieson, ed. *Electing the President 2012*, p. 208.

55. John Sides and Lynn Vavreck, *The Gamble; Choice and Chance in the 2012 Presidential Election* (Princeton, NJ: Princeton University Press, 2013), pp. 220–221.

8 CHAPTER | MEDIA POLITICS

INTRODUCTION

Media and politics go hand in hand. The press has served as an outlet for divergent political views from the founding of the republic. When political parties developed at the end of the eighteenth century, newspapers became a primary means for disseminating their policy positions and promoting their candidates.

The early press was contentious and highly adversarial, but was not aimed at the masses. Written for the upper, educated class, newspapers contained essays, editorials, and letters that debated economic and political issues. It was not until the 1830s that the elitist orientation of the press began to change. Technological improvements, the growth in literacy, and the movement toward greater public involvement in the democratic process all contributed to the development of the so-called penny press, newspapers that sold for a penny and were directed at the general public.

THE MASS MEDIA AND ELECTORAL POLITICS: AN OVERVIEW

The penny press revolutionized American journalism. Newspapers began to rely on advertising rather than subscriptions as their primary source of income. To attract advertisers, they had to reach a large number of readers. To do so, newspapers had to alter what they reported and how they reported it. Prior to the development of the penny press, news was rarely "new"; stories were often weeks old before they appeared and were rewritten or reprinted from other sources. With more newspapers aimed at the general public, a higher premium was placed on gathering news quickly and reporting it in an exciting, easy-to-read manner.

PRINT MEDIA

Once newspapers became designed for the mass public, they began to help inform voting decisions for most of the electorate. The invention of the telegraph helped in this regard. The telegraph made it possible for an emerging Washington press corps to communicate information to the entire country. What was considered news also changed. Events replaced ideas; human interest stories supplemented the official proceedings of government; and drama and conflict were featured. Stories of crime, sex, and violence captured the headlines and sold papers, not essays and letters on public policy. Joseph Pulitzer's *New York World* and William Randolph Hearst's *New York Journal* set the standard for this era of highly competitive "yellow journalism."[1]

Not all newspapers featured sensational news. In 1841, Horace Greeley founded the *New York Tribune,* and ten years later, Henry Raymond began the *New York Times.* Both papers appealed to a more-educated audience interested in the political issues of the day. After a change in ownership, the *New York Times* became a paper of record. Operating on the principle that news is not simply entertainment but valuable public information, the *Times* adopted the motto "All the news that's fit to print." It published entire texts of important speeches and documents and detailed national and foreign news.

Toward the middle of the nineteenth century, newspapers began to shed their advocacy role in favor of more neutral reporting. The growth of news wire services, such as the Associated Press and United Press, and of newspapers that were not tied to political parties contributed to these developments.

As candidates became more personally involved in the campaign, they too became the subject of press attention. By the beginning of the twentieth century, the focus had shifted to the nominees, so much so that at least one candidate, Alton Parker, Democratic presidential nominee for 1904, angrily criticized photographers for their unyielding efforts to take pictures of him while he was swimming in the nude in the Hudson River.[2] Despite the intrusion into their personal lives, candidates began taking advantage of the press's interest in them, using "photo opportunities" and news coverage to project their images and extend their partisan appeal.

BROADCAST MEDIA

With the advent of radio in the 1920s and television in the 1950s, news media coverage of campaigns changed once again. Radio supplemented the print media. Although it did not provide regular news coverage, radio excelled at covering special events as they were happening. The 1924 presidential election was the first to be reported on radio; the conventions, major speeches, and election returns were broadcast live that year. During the 1928 election, both presidential candidates, Herbert Hoover and Alfred E. Smith, spent campaign funds on radio advertising.

Radio lost its national audience to television in the 1950s but remained a favorite communications medium of candidates seeking to target their messages to specific groups in specific locations and at specific hours. A cheap and accessible electronic medium, radio continues to be used extensively. The amount of time that people spend commuting in their automobiles has increased the importance of radio as a vehicle for information, advocacy, and debate.

The influence of television on presidential elections was first felt in 1952. The most important news event of that presidential campaign was a speech by General Dwight Eisenhower's running mate, Richard Nixon. Accused of obtaining secret campaign funds in exchange for political favors, Nixon defended himself in a television address. He denied accepting contributions for personal use, accused the Democratic administration of being soft on communism, criticized his campaign opponents, and vowed that he would never force his children to give up their dog, Checkers, who had been given to the Nixon family as a gift by political supporters. The emotion of the speech, and particularly the reference to Checkers, generated a favorable public reaction, ended discussion of the campaign funds, kept Nixon on the Republican ticket, and demonstrated the power of television for candidates in the political campaigns.

Paid television advertising by the major parties also first appeared in the 1952 presidential campaign. The major broadcast networks extended their evening news reports to half an hour in 1963, and by the end of the 1960s, television had become the principal source of election news for most Americans. Presidential campaigns in turn became made-for-television productions. Their public events were staged with television in mind. On-air interviews, talk-show participation, and even the entertainment format have become part and parcel of the modern electoral campaigns.

During the 1970s into the 1980s, the evening newscasts had the largest viewing audience, at its peak exceeding 75 million viewers. Today, it has about one-third of that amount. One of the reasons for the decline has been the growth of cable news networks. Cable and satellite technologies began to acquire more subscribers and all-news formats, thereby fragmenting the number of news sources.

Not only did cable news sources proliferate, but they have also led to the demise of the news cycle. In the age of newspapers, the cycle hinged on the time of day that the morning and afternoon papers had to go to press. During the era when most Americans received their news from the evening broadcast networks, it ended midafternoon, depending on whether visuals, pictures, or films were to be included. Video cameras, mobile trucks, and helicopters extended the deadlines, as has satellite technology. Cable news networks that were on 24-7 reduced still further the deadlines for reporting speeches and campaign events. Banner headlines and developing stories regularly appear.

Today, most houses are wired for cable or satellite coverage. Although the combined viewership of the 24-7 cable news networks is only about 3 million during prime viewing hours, that news is constantly updated and available at all hours. In addition, cable networks provide political dialogue, which is often heated, opinionated, and ideologically oriented, attracting like-minded viewers.[3]

THE INTERNET

The Internet has become an important primary and secondary source of news as well. In 2004, 21 percent cited the web as their principal source; by 2008, that percentage had risen to 36, with 58 percent of voters under thirty indicating that the Internet was their major source of information about the election.[4] Those percentages have continued to rise dramatically with almost half the public citing the Internet as one of their primary sources of election news in 2012 (see Table 8.1).

Besides being a relatively cheap and easy way to reach potential supporters, the Internet has become the most important way to identify and target younger voters who might otherwise not see as much of the campaign, receive much of the direct mail, or be contacted personally by a campaign worker.

Contemporary campaigns provide up-to-date information, including the latest speeches, forthcoming events, and all their news, advertising, and documentaries on their web sites. Social networking sites such as Facebook, Twitter, and web site blogs have been integrated into ongoing campaign communications. Internet advertising has also become standard.

The Internet has also made the contemporary news cycle rapid and continuous. Reporters are constantly updating their stories online. Rumors on the web seemingly move with the speed of lighting. The two-source rule that print reporters used to verify the accuracy of information has been abandoned in the interests of speed and competitiveness.

Table 8.1 lists the principal sources for election news.

TABLE 8.1 | PRINCIPAL SOURCES OF CAMPAIGN NEWS, 1992–2012

Question: How have you been getting most of your news about the presidential election campaign? From television, from newspapers, from radio, from magazines, or from the Internet? [Up to two answers were accepted.]

Main Source	1992	1996	2000	2004	2008	2012
Television	82%	72%	70%	76%	68%	67%
Broadcast				29	18	21
NBC				13	8	7
ABC				11	7	8
CBS				9	6	6
Cable				40	44	50
Fox				21	22	23
CNN				15	21	18
MSNBC				6	9	9
Local News				12	10	11
Newspapers	57	60	39	46	33	27
Radio	12	19	15	22	16	20
Magazines	9	11	4	6	3	3
Internet	–	3	11	21	36	47

Source: "Low Marks for the 2012 Election: Voters Pessimistic About Partisan Cooperation," Pew Research Center for the People and the Press (Nov. 15, 2012). http://www.people-press.org/2012/11/15/low-marks-for-the-2012-election

This chapter examines these developments and their impact on presidential electoral politics. The first section discusses the major news networks coverage of campaigns. It examines how they interpret political events and how candidates react to those interpretations. The second section describes the techniques that candidates have used in recent campaigns to circumvent the national press corps through news/entertainment programming. The third section turns to another news/entertainment feature—presidential debates. It describes the history of the debates and their structure, staging, and impact on the electorate. Political advertising is the subject of the fourth and final section. It describes some of the most successful commercials, the increasing emphasis on negativity, and the effect of mass marketing and microtargeting on voters.

TRADITIONAL HARD NEWS

The modus operandi of news reporting is to inform the public. But the press does so with its own professional orientation—one that affects what is covered and how it is covered.

HORSE RACE JOURNALISM

Political scientist Thomas E. Patterson argues that the dominant conceptual framework for election reporting is that of a game. The candidates are the players and their moves (words, activities, and images) are seen as strategic and tactical devices to achieve their principal goal, winning the election. Even their policy positions are frequently evaluated within this gaming framework; issue stands are described as calculated appeals to certain constituency groups. Although Patterson argues that the gaming aspect of electoral politics is most pronounced at the beginning of the presidential selection process, he also sees it as an organizing principle for the press throughout the entire election cycle.[5]

Why do the news media use the game metaphor ("horse race") as its primary one? The answer is entertainment. Races are exciting. Viewing elections as a game heightens viewers' interest. Heightened interest, in turn, increases the audience size and, of course, profits since advertising revenue is based on the estimated number of people watching or hearing a particular program or reading a paper.

There is another reason for employing the game format. It lends an aura of objectivity to reporting. Rather than presenting subjective accounts of the candidates' positions and their consequences for the country, the news media can present quantitative data on public opinion and the campaign. Polls are frequently reported as the dominant election story; at the very least, they share the spotlight with other campaign issues such as the candidates' character, strategies, and tactics.

Covering campaigns as if they were sporting events is not a new phenomenon. In 1976, Patterson found about 60 percent of television election coverage and 55 percent of newspaper coverage treated the campaign as if it were a contest between the candidates.[6] Michael J. Robinson's and Margaret Sheehan's analysis of the *CBS Evening News* during the 1980 election revealed that five out of six stories emphasized the competition.[7] The focus on the game of politics has continued in both the nomination and general election. According to the Pew Research Center's Project for Excellence in Journalism, 64 percent of the news stories during the 2012 Republican caucuses and primaries were framed on a variant of the horse race theme.[8] In 2008, it was 53 percent.[9] The race remains front and center throughout the general election. In 2012, 40 percent of all the election news stories were horse race oriented (see Table 8.2).

The problem with this type of journalism is that it diverts public attention from substance to strategy. Instead of examining the merits and limitations of a candidate's proposal, journalists explore the underlying political motivations for making the proposal, moving from the *what* to the *why* in the process. Such a perspective skews the information people receive; it heightens the partisan political component of elections and reduces the substantive policy debate to which most people are exposed. It also contributes to the amount and tone of the coverage, in both cases helping the candidate that is ahead.

In 2012, the amount of news coverage that Obama and Romney received was approximately equal until the final week of the campaign when the president, who was ahead in the polls and in the Electoral College math, got more.

TABLE 8.2 | NEWS COVERAGE OF THE PRESIDENTIAL CANDIDATES, AUGUST 27–NOVEMBER 5, 2012

| | Tone (Percentage) | | | | | |
| | Obama | | | Romney | | |
Type (Percentage)	Positive	Neutral	Negative	Positive	Neutral	Negative
Horse race (39%)	28	44	27	17	42	41
Advertising/ fund-raising (6%)	12	62	27	15	61	25
Voting laws and other political topics (8%)	27	47	27	24	45	30
Public record (6%)	19	48	33	14	48	38
Policy issues (21%)	12	53	35	7	54	39
Personal information (4%)	27	52	21	30	53	17
Other campaigns (6%)	23	61	17	16	57	27
Nonelectoral stories (10%)	3	68	29	4	81	15

Source: "Final Weeks in the Mainstream Press," Pew Research Center's Project for Excellence in Journalism, November 16, 2012. http://www.journalism.org/2012/11/16/final-weeks-mainstream-press/

He also received more positive coverage, particularly at the end, as the media tried to explain why he was ahead.[10] Naturally, more and better coverage help the frontrunner, particularly in the nomination stage when less is known about the candidates.[11] (Table 8.2 indicates the type and tone of coverage the candidates received in 2012.)

The orientation of cable news networks, particularly Fox and MSNBC, has contributed to the partisan spin on the coverage. Fox News directs its news programming toward conservatives and Republicans, gave Romney more favorable coverage whereas MSNBC, with a more liberal, Democratic orientation, was more positive toward Obama.

According to Professor Diana C. Mutz, the penchant of some news organizations to cast their reports within an ideological framework has fueled the partisan political divide in the United States. It has led to selective exposure, exposure that reinforces rather than challenges the political attitudes that people have.[12] Whereas partisan politics and selective exposure help clarify the issues for people with an ideological perspective, providing them with information to help support their beliefs, it also makes them less open to opposing views, simplifies policy problems, reduces common ground, and generates emotions that impede compromise.[13]

NEWSWORTHINESS: BAD NEWS IS 'GOOD' NEWS

The tone of election coverage tends to be negative. In 2012, 20 percent of the news stories on Obama were positive and 29 percent negative. Romney fared even worse. Only 15 percent of the stories on him were favorable compared to the 37 percent that were unfavorable. In the social media, the conversations were also more negative than positive.[14]

Why the negativity? Most academic experts see it as a consequence of several factors: the news media's watchdog role, the increasing negative tone of campaigns themselves, especially political advertising, and the press's concept of newsworthiness. Conflict is more newsworthy than consensus, emotion attracts more attention than passivity or even rational discourse; outcomes, particularly when they are unexpected, generate more interest than those that are anticipated.

A fresh face winning and an experienced candidate losing are news; an experienced one winning and an unfamiliar one losing are not. Similarly, the first time a candidate states a position, it may be newsworthy; the second time, it is old news; the third time, it is not news at all. Since candidates cannot give new speeches every time they make an address during a 6- to 9-month presidential campaign, the news media that cover the candidates look for other things to report.

Verbal slips, embarrassing incidents, quotes taken out of context, inconsistent statements, and mistakes often become the focus of attention. Kiku Adatto found that "only once in 1968 did a network even take note of a minor incident unrelated to the content of the campaign."[15] In recent elections, however, there is much more frequent reporting of trivial slips.[16] The news media's penchant for reporting slips of the tongue and off-color communications encourages the candidates not to be spontaneous, not to be candid, and, above all, not to make mistakes. It also encourages speechwriters to put in sound bites and applause lines that they want the press to highlight: "Where's the beef?" "It is morning in America," "Read my lips—No new taxes," "a bridge to the twenty-first century," "compassionate conservatism," the "war on terrorism," and "yes we can."

From the candidates' perspectives, the negative tone of the news is magnified by the fact that they are not given the opportunity to tell their own stories in their own words. Their responses are edited and shortened by the major news networks. The average length of a quotation from candidates on the evening news shows in 1968 was 42.3 seconds. Since 1988, it has been less than 10 seconds. Reporters and correspondents are on camera much longer than are the candidates, approximately seven times longer for most campaign stories;[17] on the news shows, they present the election to the voters, not the candidates themselves.

Television news has an additional bias. As an action-oriented, visual medium, its content must move quickly and be capable of projecting a strong screen image that emphasizes pictures and deemphasizes words; less attention is devoted to what candidates say and more to how people react to their words and images. News coverage of strident rhetoric has contributed to partisan incivility and passionate politics that characterizes today's political environment in America.[18]

THE STORY LINE

Frequently, the news is also fitted into a framework. According to Patterson, a dominant story line emerges and much of the campaign is explained in terms of it. He enumerates four generic media scenarios: the likely loser (McGovern 1972, Mondale 1984, and Dole 1988), the skillful front-runner (Reagan in 1984 and Clinton in 1996), the candidates who loses ground (Carter in 1980), and the opposite, the bandwagon effect (McGovern in the 1972 Democratic nomination, Carter in the 1976 nomination, and Reagan in the 1980 general election).

The story line in 2000 focused on the closeness of the race, attributed in part to the weaknesses of both candidates: Gore's personal shortcomings and Bush's lack of depth on the issues. A variant on the competition theme toward the end of the campaign was the spoiler scenario for Ralph Nader. In 2004, the focus was on leadership, Bush's leadership in the war against terrorism and the war in Iraq. In directing attention to the president, the news media made much of his polarizing candidacy to convey the hostile political climate in which the election was cast. Four years later, the story line was the failure of that leadership and which candidate would be best able to achieve policy and political change. In 2012, it was the political divide, two competing ideologies, and the president's small but steady lead.

Patterson's point is that the press fit the news of the campaign into the principal story rather than creating a new story from the changing campaign events. Naturally, the perceptions of the news media affect the electorate's understanding of what is happening.

Candidates try to create and maintain their own narrative. In this narrative, they present their goals, records, and accomplishments. The narrative is an explanation that leads to a conclusion, an argument for supporting them and opposing their challenger. Obama's narrative in 2008 was the need for change in politics and policies and his determination to achieve it. Four years later, it was to continue his leadership that had improved the economic and social conditions he inherited. He also contrasted the failed Republican policies that got the country into the recession with the Democratic programs that were getting the country out of it. Naturally Romney reversed blame and credit. His narrative contended that the tepid economic growth was the consequence of too much government spending and intrusion into the private sector and argued that his experience in the private and public sector gave him the know-how to fix it and improve the functioning of government.

Today, the presidential campaigns are better able to reduce press interference with their narrative. They have the ability to reach around the news media to contact voters directly. The revolution in communication technologies has enabled them to go viral. In 2004, blogs were first used by campaigns to communicate with voters, encourage them to participate, mobilize them, and turn them out to vote. In 2008, YouTube and Facebook enabled candidates to expand their viewership and multiply their personal contacts having supporters reach out to their friends. Twitter was just beginning to be used to convey information quickly to large numbers of people. In four years, the numbers of people that access these sites have quadrupled.

Moreover, with fewer investigative journalists, smaller news staffs, and the nonstop news coverage, reporters have become increasingly dependent on the campaigns for information about the candidates, their assertions, behavior, and biographies.[19] The strategists that orchestrate campaign communications have gained the upper hand.

IMPACT

The news media remain important for priming and framing the agenda by highlighting salient issues. They inform but do so critically in their watchdog role. They question the motives of candidates, compartmentalize their speeches into sound bites, highlight any slipups or inconsistencies, focus on character frailties, and provide criticism on policy stands.

In a highly polarized political environment, this negativity contributes to perceptions of bias. In surveys taken since 1992, the Pew Research Center for the People and the Press has found a growing correlation between partisan orientation and perception of fairness, with Republicans on a whole more critical of campaign press coverage than Democrats.

These perceptions have led the public to lose confidence in the news media. Thirty years ago, a majority of people thought that the news media got their facts right. Today, a majority believes that they do not, that the news media lack compassion, and that they are too negative. Confidence in the press (newspapers, television, and the Internet) has dropped more sharply than public confidence in other American institutions.[20] And it continues to decline.[21]

Yet even with all the negative coverage, most candidates conclude that critical coverage is still better than no coverage at all, particularly in the early phases of the nomination process and especially for the candidates who do not begin with national reputations. At the outset of the process, media attention conveys credibility; it is an indication that the press takes a candidate seriously. That is why candidates try their utmost to get coverage.

Although the news tends to be concentrated and focused on certain issues, events, and personal traits, the press does not speak in a single voice. The fragmentation of news sources and the orientations of news networks provide some balance to campaign coverage, although the self-selection process by which people choose the news outlets from which they get information tends to reinforce rather than challenge preexisting partisan and ideological orientations.

SOFT NEWS

The critical "gotcha" journalism of national news reporters and commentators encouraged candidates to find other formats for connecting with voters. Since the 1990s, one of the methods they have used increasingly has been to appear on talk-entertainment shows. Ross Perot pioneered this softer news format on television and Jerry Brown on radio.

For Perot, talk-show appearances constituted much of his "live" campaign, beginning with his announcement that he might run for president on *Larry King Live* in 1992 and again in 1996. Chris Dodd announced his candidacy for the 2008 Democratic nomination on *Imus in the Morning*. When asked why he chose that radio venue for making his announcement, Dodd said: "CBS said they would give me three minutes. I got 20 minutes on Imus."[22] And the appearances on news/entertainment shows have continued, even accelerated, in subsequent presidential campaigns. When Oprah Winfrey endorsed Barack Obama and traveled with him to rallies, it was considered an important news item and political endorsement.

The talk-entertainment format offers a much less hostile environment than interviews by national reporters and network anchors. The candidates are treated better, more like celebrities than politicians. They tend to be asked softball questions in comparison with the hardball, "gotcha" journalism of the national press corps. Candidates also have more time to answer the questions on these shows than the brief comments that are quoted by the news networks.[23]

The audience differences are also important. People who watch these shows tend to be less oriented toward partisan politics; thus, they may be more open to the information presented by the candidates who appear on these programs. Incidental learning occurs; candidate images improve as a consequence of the time and discretion they are given to talk about personal and family matters; they appear more lifelike and friendly, not the stereotypical politicians, the image that the press and their political opponents project.[24]

Variations of the talk-entertainment format are town meetings and call-in programs in which candidates answer questions posed by citizens. By interacting with everyday folks, presidential candidates can demonstrate their responsiveness, sincerity, and empathy. Bill Clinton was particularly effective in such a setting during his two presidential campaigns.

Another advantage of doing the news-entertainment circuit is that the candidates' appearances themselves may become newsworthy, thereby generating an even larger impact for the candidates when clips of their comments are rebroadcast or summarized on the news. Nor are the expenses associated with these appearances comparable to the costs of staging a major media event or even designing, testing, and airing an advertisement.

The diverse audience, the higher comfort level, and the greater ability of candidates to project their desired images by presenting seemingly spontaneous but often carefully crafted answers suggest that the soft news format will continue to be used by presidential campaigns to circumvent the national press corps and reach a portion of the general public directly.

Barack Obama on *The Daily Show* with Jon Stewart.

Local news outlets also offer candidates many of the same advantages that news/entertainment shows provide: more time, greater visibility, less invasive questioning, a different audience, interaction with local luminaries, and an opportunity to illustrate their personal side.

PRESIDENTIAL DEBATES

Debates constitute another important "informational" component of presidential campaigns, one which candidates, particularly those who are behind, find useful. They see debates as an opportunity to improve their own images and damage their opponents', a potential game changer. Unlike most of their campaign rhetoric—speeches, statements, and responses to questions—debates are live and unedited, although the formats, agreed to beforehand, limit the time for responses. Although the candidates' responses are usually prepared in advance, carefully crafted, and well rehearsed, they sound more authentic than prepared speeches read from a teleprompter. They also convey a more human dimension.

The news media like the debate format because it facilitates comparison. It fits into their game motif. It is a newsworthy event. Although debates draw a larger audience than does most news coverage of the election, they are not a source of revenue for the television networks because advertisements are not permitted during them.

The public likes debates because they are more exciting and "real" than staged events and canned stump speeches. They can be dramatic. They allow the electorate to evaluate the candidates at the same time and on the same stage. Debates provide voters with comparable information. They generate interest; they are a spectacle to be seen and heard. People learn from the debates, more so when information is not contested than when it is.[25]

HISTORY

The first series of televised debates occurred in 1960. John Kennedy used them to counter the impression that he was too young and inexperienced. Richard Nixon, on the other hand, sought to maintain his stature as Dwight Eisenhower's knowledgeable and experienced vice president and the obvious person to succeed his boss in office.

In the three elections that followed, Lyndon Johnson and then Nixon, both ahead in the polls, saw no advantage in debating their opponents and refused to do so. Gerald Ford, however, trailing Jimmy Carter in preelection polls, saw debates as his best opportunity to come from behind and win. The Carter camp, on the other hand, saw them as a means of shoring up Democratic support. In 1980, the rationale was similar. From Reagan's perspective, it was a way to reassure the electorate about himself and his qualifications for office. For Carter, it was another chance to emphasize the differences between Reagan and himself, their parties, and their ideological perspectives, issue positions, and personal attributes, including age and experience.

By 1984, presidential debates had become so much a part of presidential campaigns that even incumbents could not avoid them without making their avoidance a major campaign issue. Thus, Ronald Reagan was forced by public and press pressures to debate Walter Mondale, even though he stood to gain little and could have lost much from their face-to-face encounter. And in the 1992 election, George H. W. Bush's initial refusal to accept a plan for a series of campaign debates put forth by the Commission on Presidential Debates, a nonpartisan group that had organized the 1988 presidential and vice presidential debates, hurt him politically. Bill Clinton chided Bush repeatedly for his refusal to debate. Democrats dressed as chickens appeared at his campaign rallies. President Bush finally relented, telling his handlers, "I am tired of looking like a wimp."[26]

The issue in 1996 and again in 2000 was not whether to debate but whom to include. In 1992, Ross Perot and his running mate, Admiral James Stockdale, were invited to participate, and they did, to Perot's advantage but not to Stockdale's.[27] In 1996, Perot and his running mate, Pat Choate, were not asked. The Commission on Presidential Debates, composed of five Democrats and five Republicans, concluded that Perot's candidacy was not viable and that he had no chance of winning the Electoral College even though his name appeared on the ballot in all fifty states and the District of Columbia. The commission based its decision on Perot's standing in the polls, about 5 percent at that time, and on the judgment of a small number of political scientists and journalists, surveyed by the commission's staff and advisory council, who unanimously concluded that Perot not only could not win the election but would not carry a single state.[28]

The Commission on Presidential Debates has employed similar reasoning since then excluding third-party candidates. In doing so, it has established three criteria for inclusion in the debates in addition to the Constitution's eligibility requirement (be a natural-born citizen, thirty-five years of age or older, and a resident of the United States for at least fourteen years). Candidates have to be on the ballot in enough states to have a chance of winning a majority of the electoral votes, be organized in a majority of the congressional districts within the state, and demonstrate a sufficient level of electoral support by receiving an average of 15 percent or more in the preelection public opinion polls (to be calculated by averaging surveys of five different polling organizations). Not surprisingly, the only candidates to meet these criteria have been the Democratic and Republican presidential standard-bearers.

By bringing the candidates together on the same stage at the same time, the debates become a major news story, routinely covered by the news media. They attract more viewers than any other single event of the campaign. In 2008, an average of 60.5 million people watched the debates; in 2012, they averaged 64 million (see Table 8.3). The vice presidential debate has a smaller audience. Fifty-one million watched Joe Biden debate Paul Ryan in 2012; four years earlier, however, 70 million saw him debate Sarah Palin.[29]

TABLE 8.3 | PRESIDENTIAL DEBATES, 1960–2012

Year		Number of Debates	Average Estimated Size of the Television Audience (in Millions)	Percent of Households Watching
1960	Kennedy v. Nixon	4	77	60
1976	Carter v. Ford	4*	65	51
1980	Carter v. Reagan	1	81	59
1984	Mondale v. Reagan	3*	66	46
1988	Dukakis v. Bush	3*	66	36
1992	Bush v. Clinton v. Perot	4*	66	42
1996	Clinton v. Dole	3*	40	29
2000	Gore v. G. W. Bush	4*	40.6*	26
2004	G. W. Bush v. Kerry	4*	53.5†	36.3
2008	Obama v. McCain	4*	60.5†	37.6
2012	Obama v. Romney	4*	64.0†	44.3

*Includes one vice presidential debate.

†The average for just the three presidential debates.

Sources: Estimates of audience sizes for 1960–1992, "How Many Watched," *The New York Times* (Oct. 6, 1996), p. A25. Copyright © 1996 by the *New York Times*. Reprinted by permission. Estimates for 1996, "Debate Ratings Beat Baseball," Associated Press (Oct. 17, 1996). Copyright © 1996 by the Associated Press. Reprinted by permission. Estimates for 2000, 2004, 2008, and 2012 based on ratings by Nielsen Media Research. "Final Presidential Debate Draws 59.2 Million" (October 23, 2012). blog.nielsen.com/us /en/newswire/2012/final-presidential-debate-draws-59-2-million-viewers

Although presidential debates have now become part of the fabric of American presidential elections, their scheduling and format are still subject to arduous negotiation between the staffs of the major party candidates. In these negotiations, each side naturally wants to maximize its strengths. Candidates who are ahead in the polls when these negotiations occur, usually the incumbent, call the shots. The Commission on Presidential Debates hosts the events and both sides need to agree on the procedures for conducting them.

Sometimes, the agreement doesn't hold up, however. In 2004, for example, the rules specified that only the person talking would be seen on television; no cutaways to the other candidate would be permitted. The television networks, however, were not parties to the agreement and did not abide by it. Sometimes they showed one of the candidates and sometimes both. Kerry took notes when Bush was talking; Bush did not, however, when Kerry spoke. To some, the president appeared bored, tired, or irritated. Moreover, during the first debate, his suit jacket bulged in the middle of his back, suggesting to Democrats that he had a device feeding him the answers, an allegation that Bush's handlers vigorously denied. However, in the second and third debates, he wore a better-fitting suit.

PREPARATION

Despite the appearance of spontaneity, debates are highly scripted and carefully orchestrated events. The candidates are coached and rehearsed weeks, even months in advance. Planning for Romney's first October debate with President Obama began in June; during the Democratic convention, Romney's strategists held a debate camp in which the candidate participated. Five mock debates took place during this period and five more before the first debate was actually held.[30] The Obama campaign also began early planning, but not as early as Romney. There have been a few exceptions to the extensive preparation rule, the most notable being Richard Nixon's in his first debate with John Kennedy.[31]

To get ready, candidates go over briefing books that their aides prepare, view videos of their opponent, and engage in debates with stand-ins playing the role of their adversary. The objective is to anticipate the questions and provide thoughtful answers that are consistent with campaign speeches, press releases, political advertising, and the basic themes. It is also to ensure that no factual errors and ad-lib remarks are made.

In addition to their concerns about substance and rhetoric, campaign media consultants also consider style: how candidates look, how they dress, how they speak, and how they interact with the questioners and with their opponents. Kennedy and Carter talked faster than Nixon and Ford to create an action-oriented image in the minds of the viewers. Both tried to demonstrate their knowledge by citing many facts and statistics in their answers. Ford and Reagan spoke in more general terms. Reagan's wit and anecdotes in 1980, Bush's manner in 1988, and Perot's down-to-earth language and self-deprecating humor in 1992 conveyed a human dimension with which viewers could identify in contrast to their opponents' less empathetic responses. Dukakis was especially hurt by his reply to the question of whether he would favor an irrevocable death penalty for a person who raped and killed his wife. His matter-of-fact, rambling response sealed his technocratic, iceman image.

Challengers especially need to demonstrate their leadership credentials, their experience, their command of the issues, and their proposals for change. Incumbents need to defend their record and the progress they anticipate in the next four years. Both need to counter negative personal and partisan perceptions about themselves that have appeared in the news media coverage and their opponent's advertising. Naturally, they also have to magnify their positive attributes.

IMPACT

The first debate usually helps the challenger more than the incumbent. Just getting on the same stage with the president of the United States increases their stature. They have other initial advantages. Having gone through a competitive nomination process that included numerous debates should have been a learning process in which they have gained detailed knowledge of the issues, refined their arguments, and responded to personal and policy criticism. Incumbents, on the other hand, tasked with the continuous problems of governing, may be less focused, overconfident, and, as a result, seem less prepared.[32] In debate, it is offense that generates the most enthusiasm.

Incumbents usually have higher performance expectations, particularly in the eyes of the news media. Moreover, with the press hyping the debate, fitting it into its horse race storyline, and evaluating it in terms of the winner and loser, the leading candidate, more likely to be the incumbent than the challenger, is disadvantaged. A closer contest is more exciting and attracts a larger audience. But the challenger's advantage is usually short-lived.

The primary effect of debates is to shore up partisan support, particularly for the candidate whose electoral coalition has not coalesced as quickly. Mondale in 1984, Kerry in 2004, and Romney in 2012 gained such support from their first debate but could not extend it enough over the course of the debates, much less to election day.

In close races, debates can obviously make a difference. They can do so by increasing interest, clarifying issue positions, and shaping images. Potentially, they can convince the undecided for whom to vote and counter weak partisan preferences, but they do not usually do so.

To enhance their effect, debates need to have a cumulative impact, and again, they don't seem to have had such an effect. Incumbents tend to be better prepared and more energized in their second and subsequent debates. Their energy and performance rallies their base; the campaign in the final weeks returns public opinion and voting preferences to where they were before the debates were held.

The reason that debates rarely shift public opinion on a large scale is because most voters have their minds made up or at least have their partisan predilections intact before viewing the debates. In fact, they are attracted to the debates precisely because of their partisan orientations. In general, people who are more interested in the election are more likely to watch the debates; people who are more knowledgeable are more likely to learn from them; and people

Romney and Obama debate.

who have strong partisan inclinations are more likely to be convinced by them. They have what is called a confirmation bias. Partisans see the debate through a political lens and root for their own candidate. In situations in which information is contested, they tend to believe their candidate, not the opposition.[33]

As a result, a single poor performance, such as Reagan's in his first debate with Walter Mondale, Bush's in his first with John Kerry, and Obama's in the first debate with Romney, did not change the voting preferences of their most partisan supporters or shift the sentiment of most independent voters.[34] Table 8.4 indicates the results of Gallup surveys before and after the debates in the last six presidential elections.

TABLE 8.4 | THE IMPACT OF PRESIDENTIAL DEBATES ON ELECTORAL SUPPORT, 1992–2012

	1992			
Time Sequence	Bush	Clinton	Perot	Other/Undecided
Before the debates	33%	51%	10%	6%
After the debates	34	43	17	6

	1996		
Time Sequence	Clinton	Dole	Perot
Before the debates	52%	37%	5%
After the debates	54	41	5

continued

TABLE 8.4 | THE IMPACT OF PRESIDENTIAL DEBATES ON ELECTORAL
SUPPORT, 1992–2012 *continued*

2000

Time Sequence	Gore	Bush	Nader	Buchanan
Before the debates	49%	41%	2%	1%
After the debates	41	50	3	1

2004

Time Sequence	Bush	Kerry
Before the debates	52%	44%
After the debate	52	44

2008

Time Sequence	Obama	McCain
Before the debates	49%	44%
After the debates	50	43

2012

Time Sequence	Obama	Romney
Before the debates	48%	48%
After the debates	46	51

Sources: 1992 figures are based on the *Gallup Poll Monthly* (Sept. and Oct., 1992); 1996 figures are based on ABC News tracking poll of likely voters; 2000, 2004, and 2008 and 2012 figures from Gallup Poll of likely voters. (Gallup's final preelection poll of likely voters in 2012 was 49% Romney and 48% Obama.)

CAMPAIGN ADVERTISING

Candidates are marketed much like any commercial product. Political advertising is used to gain attention, make a pitch, leave an impression, generate an emotion, and ultimately to turn out and influence the vote.

Advertising allows candidates to state their policy positions in their own words, articulate the merits of their proposals, trumpet their qualifications, and criticize their opponents. More importantly, it allows them to reach people who are less interested in electoral politics, less likely to follow the campaign on a regular basis, and less knowledgeable about the candidates. It gives them information.

The trick is to make the commercials convincing. Candidate-sponsored ads are not unbiased, and the public knows it. To refine advertisements and improve the odds that they project the desired messages, which in turn produces the desired effects, ads are pretested before focus groups. When they are not, they can do more harm than good. Such was the case when Michael Dukakis's staff created a photo opportunity in which their candidate wore an army helmet and rode in a combat-ready tank. The objective of the advertisement was to demonstrate Dukakis's support for the military and for a strong national defense policy. The situation, however, looked so silly and contrived that the Republicans countered with a commercial of their own in which a scene from the Dukakis ad was featured along with information about the Democratic candidate's opposition to a long list of military programs and weapons systems.

Media consultants, specializing in political advertising, are hired to supplement regular campaign staff to design, produce, and target the advertisements as well as buy time on media markets in states on which the campaign is focusing. Campaigns normally retain an advertising firm to coordinate these activities. In his two presidential quests, Barack Obama used the Washington-based strategic communications firm GMMB to produce, place, and research its political advertising. Mitt Romney created his own media-buying group, American Rambler,[35] to work with the campaign's communication team to place its spots. Paid by salary rather than the usual commissions that media buyers receive, the Romney operation drew considerable criticism from Republican advertising establishment that claimed it was less efficient and more costly than private firms would have been.[36]

Designing and airing political commercials constitutes the principal expense of contemporary presidential campaigns, and those expenses have mushroomed in recent elections. In 2000, the total advertising by the candidates, parties, and nonparty groups on the race for the presidency amounted to $263 million; in 2004, the price tag was $620 million; in 2008, it was $603; and in 2012, it rose to $950 million. The increase in 2012 was a consequence of several factors: the closeness of the race, the passion and deep pockets of large donors, and their new vehicle for funding, Super PACs, with no contribution limits and, in many cases, their ability to mask their donors. The volume of ads in 2012 exceeded 1.4 million individual spots.[37]

Although approximately the same amount of money was spent on advertising by both sides in the 2012 presidential race, the Obama campaign got the biggest bang for its buck. The Obama team designed, ran, and targeted about two-thirds of its ads compared to only 36 percent for Romney's.[38] The rest of the pro-Romney, anti-Obama commercials were sponsored by party and especially, nonparty groups. By law, nonparty organizations cannot coordinate their campaign activities with the organizations of the presidential candidates. Thus, the Obama campaign could more closely meld its ads to its campaign narrative, sequencing strategy, geographic focus, and group targeting. And it could do all of this at less cost than the Republicans because the federal election law requires media outlets to sell advertising to the official campaigns organization at the lowest unit rate; outside groups pay more.

Format and Tone

Political commercials take many forms. Short ads, usually about 30 seconds, are interspersed with other commercials during regular programming while longer ones such as interviews, documentaries, and campaign rallies preempt scheduled programs and usually attract fewer viewers. One exception was Ross Perot's novel media campaign in 1992, which drew and maintained a large audience, averaging about 11.6 million viewers.

There are basically three types of political commercials: those that praise candidates and their accomplishments (positive ads), those that contrast candidates to the obvious advantage of the ad's sponsor (contrast ads), and those that just criticize opponents on the grounds of their policy preferences or personal attributes (negative ads). In most campaigns, candidates use all three types, although of late, the emphasis has been negative.

Positive commercials point to the strengths of a candidate. For presidents seeking reelection, or even vice presidents running for the top office, one of those strengths is clearly experience in high office, which incumbents always emphasize. One of Jimmy Carter's most effective commercials in 1980 showed him in a whirl of presidential activities ending as darkness fell over the White House. A voice intoned, "The responsibility never ends. Even at the end of a long working day, there is usually another cable addressed to the chief of state from the other side of the world where the sun is shining and something is happening." As a light came on in the president's living quarters, the voice concluded, "And he's not finished yet." Ronald Reagan in 1984 and George Bush in 1992 used a variation of the president-at-work ad.

Challengers need to stress their qualifications. They have to define themselves or risk having their opponents do it for them. Thus, the first task of most challengers or candidates who are not as well known is to present themselves to the American people, usually by designing and airing biographical videos that feature their life story in a positive and compelling way. They also contrast their skills, experience, and policy stands with their opponent's. In 1980, Reagan stressed his different kinds of solutions to the nation's old and persistent policy problems, as did Perot in 1992. In 2000, Bush emphasized his likeability and trustworthiness, and Gore, his knowledge and sensitivity to the problems of the working class. In 2012, Obama pointed to the economy's upward trajectory, while Romney emphasized its doldrums, especially high unemployment.

Negative ads exploit a candidate's weaknesses by focusing on character deficiencies, issue inconsistencies, and/or false leadership claims. They are not new. There has always been much negativity in American political campaigns. George Washington was called a philanderer and a thief; Andrew Jackson was accused of marrying a prostitute; at the outset of the Civil War, Abraham Lincoln was charged with being illegitimate and black; Theodore Roosevelt was said to be a drunkard; Herbert Hoover, a German sympathizer during World War I; and Franklin D. Roosevelt, a lecher, lunatic, and a closet Jew whose real name was Rosenfeldt.

What seems to be different today is the increasing emphasis placed on pure negativity. Data from the Wisconsin Advertising Project and its successor, the Wesleyan Media Project, indicate that 44 percent of the ads in 2004, 51 percent in 2008, and 64 percent in 2012 were of the attack, negative variety. Increased sponsorship of advertising by nonparty groups, primarily Super PACs, has contributed significantly to the negative tone. According to Professors Erika Fowler and Travis Ridout, the authors of the Wesleyan Media Project's report on the 2012 presidential election, 85 percent of the ads sponsored by these groups were negative; only 5 percent were positive.[39]

Super PAC negativity has some advantages for the candidates they support. It gets out the critical, potentially damaging information about an opponent without the candidate benefiting from the ad having to identify him- or herself and acknowledge approval of the ad. If the ad is too offensive, the candidate can ask the group sponsoring the ad to withdraw it; if it is effective, the candidate's organization can run supplementary ads on similar themes.

Another reason for the negativity is the attention the news media give to conflict. They are more apt to highlight negative attacks than positive attributes and claims. In short, the newsworthiness of the advertising is important.[40] Box 8.1 describes three famous examples.

BOX 8.1 | NOTORIOUS NEGATIVITY

In 1964, Lyndon Johnson ran as the peace candidate. He and his Democratic supporters suggested that Republican Barry Goldwater was a trigger-happy zealot who would not hesitate to unleash nuclear weapons against a communist foe and get the country into a nuclear war. This scary scenario was captured in the "Daisy Girl" ad in which a little girl is pictured in a meadow plucking petals from a daisy. She counts to herself softly. When she reaches nine, the picture freezes on her face, her voice fades, and a stern-sounding male voice counts down from ten. When he gets to zero there is an explosion, the little girl disappears, and a mushroom-shaped cloud covers the screen. Lyndon Johnson's voice is heard: "These are the stakes—to make a world in which all of God's children can live, or go into the dark. We must either love each other, or we must die." The ad ended with an announcer saying, "Vote for President Johnson on November 3. The stakes are too high for you to stay home."

The commercial was run only once. Goldwater supporters were outraged and protested vigorously, but their protestations actually kept the issue alive. Parts of the ad were reshown on television newscasts. The Democrats had made the point, and the news media made it stick.

continued

BOX 8.1 | NOTORIOUS NEGATIVITY *continued*

Courtesy of the Democratic National Convention

A still from the "Daisy Girl" anti-Goldwater ad.

The second infamous ad, "Willie Horton," featured a mug shot of an African American prisoner who had raped a white woman while on a weekend furlough from a Massachusetts jail. Aimed at those who were fearful of crime, and especially of African American males, the ad, sponsored by a PAC supporting George H. W. Bush in 1988, was supplemented by other prisoner ads designed by the Bush campaign. The cumulative impact of these ads left the impression that Dukakis was a liberal do-gooder. By the end of the 1988 presidential campaign, 25 percent of the electorate knew who Willie Horton was, what he did, and who furloughed him; 49 percent thought Dukakis was soft on crime.[41]

The third ad that became news was run in August 2004, right after the Democratic Convention in which Kerry had emphasized his Vietnam military record in his acceptance speech. He had been awarded two Purple Hearts and a Bronze Star for his valor in commanding a navy gunboat under attack. A group consisting of some Vietnam veterans, calling themselves Swift Boat Veterans for Truth, disputed Kerry's claims and brought attention to his antiwar efforts after his release from active duty. Shown in August during the lull between major party conventions, the ad captured national attention. The decision of the Kerry campaign not to respond to the charge gave the ad credibility and undermined the image that the Democrats were trying to project about Kerry.

The reach and potential impact of the first Swift Boat ad, which was shown in just seven small media markets (Charleston, Dayton, Green Bay, La Crosse, Toledo, Wausau, and Youngstown), was enormous. The Swift Boat Veterans gave over 1,000 interviews on talk radio, appeared on network newscasts, and raised $19 million, which they used to run other anti-Kerry ads. Although news reporters raised questions about the validity of the allegations, the attention that the press gave to the charges actually extended and may have enhanced the ad's impact.

EMOTIVE CONTENT

Ads have emotive content. They can generate or exacerbate feelings that moti-vate political participation.

Positive ads are "feel good" ads. They may be designed to make people feel proud or patriotic. They can convey feelings of warmth, empathy, and sensitivity. A good example of this type of ad pictured President George W. Bush giving a big hug to Ashley, a little girl whose mother died in the terrorist attacks at the World Trade Center in New York City. He said, "I know that's hard. Are you all right?" Ashley replied, "He's the most powerful man in the world and all he wants to do is make sure I'm safe." Ashley's father added: "What I saw was what I want to see in the heart and in the soul of the man who sits in the highest elected office in our country."[42]

Twenty million dollars was spent on the air buys for "Ashley." There were 7,000 showings in Ohio alone. Seventy percent of the people polled in that state remember seeing the ad.[43] Said Kerry's media adviser, Bob Strum, "'Ashley' was real, was human, people could relate to it. 'Ashley' probably cost us Ohio and cost us the presidency!"[44]

Many times ads are designed to enhance character. Make people feel better about the person for whom they are voting. Take this excerpt for a 2008 ad for Senator John McCain:

> Shot down, bayoneted, tortured. Offered early release, he said, "No." He'd sworn an oath. Home, he turned to public service. His philosophy: before party, polls and self—America. A maverick, John McCain tackled cam-paign reform, military reform, spending reform. . . . a man who has al-ways put his country and her people before self, before politics. . . . Don't hope for a better life. Vote for one. McCain.[45]

Negative ads convey unpleasant emotions; fear, repulsion, anger. The Daisy Girl and Willie Horton ads generated fear. In the 2004 election, the Bush campaign played on the fear produced by the terrorist attacks. One ad, titled "Risk," included pictures of terrorist attacks, frightened children, and a warning:

> After September 11, our world changed. Either we fight terrorists abroad or face them here. John Kerry and liberals in Congress have a different view. They opposed Reagan as he won the Cold War, voted against the first Gulf War, voted to slash intelligence after the first Trade Center at-tack, repeatedly opposed weapons vital to winning the war on terror. John Kerry and his liberal allies: Are they a risk we can afford to take today?[46]

The Swift Boat ads conveyed feelings of deceit and perhaps anger that Kerry wasn't what he claimed to be, a war hero. In 2012, the Obama cam-paign ran an ad that showed Mitt Romney singing "America the Beautiful" with graphics that suggested he had sent jobs overseas, sought tax havens for his income, and stowed family wealth in Swiss bank accounts. After his comments that 47 percent of Americans don't pay taxes, are dependent on government, and believe that they are entitled to food, housing, and health, the Obama campaign ran an ad that simply showed the video of Romney making these remarks.

THEMES AND TARGETS

Advertising must be coordinated with strategy. The 2012 Obama campaign began with several advantages. It had more time and money. It also had the status of the presidency, the personal popularity of president, the ideological positions that his opponent had to take to win the Republican nomination, and the criticism Romney had to endure from his primary opponents.

There were four key components of Obama's advertising message: the problems he inherited, the progress he had made, the insensitivity of Romney to the problems most Americans faced, and the policy choices that voters had in the 2012 election. During the campaign, at different points and with different emphases, each of these components was stressed.

The initial focus was on Romney. Beginning in April and continuing through early summer, Obama's advertising defined him as a failure as governor, out of touch with average citizens, and pursuing a Republican policy that not only failed in the past but was responsible for the Great Recession. An excerpt from an early Obama ad sums up the anti-Romney argument:

> When Mitt Romney was governor, Massachusetts lost 40,000 manufacturing jobs—a rate twice the national average—and fell to 47th in job creation, fourth from the bottom. Instead of hiring workers from his own state, Romney outsourced call-center jobs to India. He cut taxes for millionaires like himself, while raising them on the middle class. And left the state $2.6 billion deeper in debt … Romney economics. It didn't work then, and it won't work now.[47]

Another ad, focusing on the choice voters had, aired from the late summer throughout the remainder of the campaign with Obama himself, the principal narrator:

> Over the next four months you have a choice to make. Not just between two political parties or two people. It's a choice between two very different plans for our country. Governor Romney's plan would cut taxes for the folks at the very top, roll back regulations on big banks; and he says if we do our economy will grow and everyone will benefit. But you know what? We tried that top-down approach. It's what caused the mess in the first place. I believe the only way to create an economy built to last is to strengthen the middle class; asking the wealthy to pay a little more, so we can pay down our debt in a balanced way. So that we can afford to invest in education, manufacture, and home-grown American energy. For good, middle class jobs. Sometimes politics can seem very small. But the choice you face? It couldn't be bigger.[48]

The challenge for Romney was to present a picture of a failed economy, a president unable to fix it, and to show what he would do differently. Here's an excerpt from one of his "Day 1" ads.

> What would be different about a Romney presidency? From day one President Romney focuses on the economy and the deficit, unleashes America's energy resources and stands up to China on trade. President Romney's leadership puts jobs first. But there's something more than Legislation or new policy, it's the feeling we'll have that our country is back, back on the right track. That's what will be different about a Romney Presidency.[49]

Other Romney ads presented the election as a referendum on the "failed" Obama presidency.

The advertising is directed toward the most competitive states. In their tracking of advertising expenditures in the 2012 presidential election, the Center for Voting and Democracy found that the Obama campaign spent 99.6 percent of its advertising budget and the Romney campaign 99.9 percent of its in just 10 states.[50] Within the competitive states, campaigns are targeted to specific groups, differentiated by the areas in which they live, the networks they prefer, the programs they watch, and the times of the day they watch them. The Obama campaign used data that identified persuadable voters, their viewing habits, as well as TV scheduling, including reruns and new programming, and ratings to reach potential supporters.

ACCURACY AND IMPACT

The public has become more leery of political advertising. Its hyperbole and shrill accusations, exaggeration and false claims, and its overwhelming volume have contributed to public skepticism, even numbness. A research report by the Annenberg Public Policy Center at the University of Pennsylvania estimated that more than 25 percent of the expenditures of nonparty groups were spent on television ads that contained at least one deception.[51] The center operates a web site (factcheck.org) that monitors the accuracy of ad claims, candidate statements, and press releases. It highlights the biggest whoppers. In the 2012 campaign, they included Obama's claim that Romney would raise taxes by $2,000 on middle-income taxpayers and Romney's that Obama would raise them by $4,000 on the same group. Also disputed was Romney's assertion that Obama would drop work requirements for welfare recipients and Obama's that Romney favors legislation that would prevent all abortions, even in cases of rape and incest.[52] Major news organizations also engage in fact checking, but their impact is usually limited to a single story, while the ads are continuous; hence, they reach more people more often.

How important is the advertising in affecting turnout and voting behavior? Most voters say that it is not, that they are not influenced by the advertising. Surveys taken by the Pew Research Center following the last five presidential elections found only a small percentage of the electorate admitting that political commercials were very or somewhat helpful in determining their vote. That percentage ranged from a low of 24 percent in 2012 to a high of 38 percent in 1992; In contrast, 72 percent in 2012 and 66 percent in 2008 said that they were not too or at all helpful. Presidential debates were evaluated more positively by about two-thirds of the voters.[53]

Communications consultants and campaign strategists obviously disagree about the importance of advertising. They claim the ads provide information, frame the debate, and motivate voting. Political scientists, however, see activation and reinforcement of preexisting partisan beliefs as the primary effect, particularly of negative ads.[54] They have become an important component of the base-maximizing strategy of recent presidential campaigns. But negative advertising also increases cynicism, decreases feelings of efficacy, and can turn off independent and less partisan voters.[55]

SUMMARY

The mass media have a profound effect on presidential elections: on the organization, strategy, and tactics of the campaign, the distribution of resources, and directly or indirectly on the electorate's voting decisions. That is why so much of a presidential campaign is devoted to media-related activities.

First newspapers, then radio and television, and more recently, the Internet have provided the primary communication channels through which information flows to and from voters. The multiplication of news networks on cable and news sites on the Internet, the increasing importance (and length) of local news shows, and the entertainment/news format have provided additional, and, for the most part, more favorable outlets for candidates to reach the electorate than they had when the broadcast news networks monopolized campaign reporting. The news cycle has evolved into one of almost instantaneous and continuous coverage from multiple sources.

The news media see and report the election as a game, fitting statements, events, and activities into various story lines. Their schema highlights drama and gives controversial statements and events the most attention but also downplays in-depth discussions of policy issues. Campaign coverage also plays up personalities and gives disproportionate attention to blunders, factual errors, personal exaggerations, and slips of the tongue; reporters focus on conflict and emphasize the contest, particularly its human dimensions rather than its policy consequences.

Candidates naturally try to present their own narrative and maintain it in the face of unanticipated events, opponent's attacks, and critical news media coverage. They do so by planting stories, leaking their own opposition research, scripting their speeches with sound bites, orchestrating events with the mass media in mind, minimizing spontaneity to prevent embarrassing words or situations, and creating good visuals. But even with all this preparation and staging, the news of their campaign may not be accurate or complete, and from the candidates' perspective, it is never good enough.

For this reason, candidates also try to circumvent the national news media to reach the voters directly. They can now do so more easily with digital communications technology. Social networking, blogging, twittering, and videoing on YouTube have become standard fare today. Internet technology also facilitates the collection, integration, and analysis of great quantities of data to reach a broader electorate in a more personalized manner.

Do new technologies facilitate a more democratic electoral process? They do in the sense that they provide more information to more people. They have helped the campaigns reconnect to voters on a more personal level. They have revived grassroots politics. There are more small donors, more volunteers, and more friends communicating with one another. But there is also no evidence that the electorate is more knowledgeable, that big donors are less important, that the campaigns are less manipulative, and that voters are more rational or less cynical.

People also like to be entertained, so candidates resort to various popular news/entertainment formats to convey a message, project an image, energize their supporters and make them feel part of the campaign. These formats reach many of those less interested in national politics, people who do not watch election news on a regular basis.

Presidential debates also provide large-audience opportunities for candidates to reiterate appeals, look presidential, and expand and excite their partisan base. Debates, especially, facilitate candidate comparisons that initially work to the advantage of challengers who need to present themselves as the equal of their incumbent opponents. The news media play a role here as well, covering the debates and often participating in them by asking questions and reporting the candidates' responses, the public's reaction, and their own evaluations of the winners and losers. They then integrate the debate into the ongoing storylines of the campaign.

In a very close race, debates can make a difference although they have not usually changed public opinion or reversed anticipated election results. Partisans disproportionately comprise the debate audience; they tend to root for *their* candidates and believe in the information that their candidate presents. Handlers from the campaigns and significant others try to "spin" the results to their political advantage. As a consequence, bounces from the debates tend to be short-lived and fade into the political environment that helps shape the election outcome.

Since campaign news may disrupt or deviate a candidate's basic themes and leadership imagery, campaigns try to reinforce their appeals through simplification, repetition, and emotion, using mass-marketing techniques and microtargeting messages to do so. Designed to win over undecided voters and energize supporters, political ads utilize both positive and negative arguments and graphics to highlight the merits of supporting a particular candidate and opposing the others. Since 2004, the amount of negativity has increased. Negative ads capture press attention and mobilize the base.

Voters have become increasingly leery about the claims of these ads, in part because of their obvious bias, stridency, and slickness. News organizations and nonpartisan public policy institutes also evaluate the accuracy of the ads, their hyperbole and exaggeration. But media consultants and politicians believe they have an impact. They believe that the ads contribute to the public knowledge, that they frame and clarify the debate, that they extend the campaign to people who might otherwise tune out, and that they reinforce partisan loyalties.

 ## WHERE ON THE WEB?

In addition to the media outlets mentioned in previous chapters, here are some others to explore.

- **Associated Press**
  www.ap.org
  > The largest news service in the United States provides fast-breaking information on its wire service and web site.

- **Commission on Presidential Debates**
  www.debates.org
  > Plans the debates, selects the cities, decides which candidates can participate, and moderates the discussion format between the principal candidates. The commission also provides transcripts of past and present presidential debates.

- **The Freedom Forum**
  www.freedomforum.org
  > Provides information on freedom of the press issues, with links to the Newseum, the Media Studies Center, and the First Amendment Center, all sponsored by the Gannett news organization.

- **FactCheck.org**
  www.factcheck.org
  > A nonpartisan, nonprofit group organized by the Annenberg Public Policy Center at the University of Pennsylvania that evaluates the accuracy of political advertising. A sister web site, FlackCheck.org, engages in political parody and humor to mock false and deceptive advertising.

- **Living Room Candidate**
  www.livingroomcandidate.org
  > An online site for televised presidential candidate commercials since 1952.

- ***New York Times***
  www.nytimes.com
  > A paper of record, the *New York Times* is the newspaper most likely to carry the transcripts of the candidate's major speeches.

- **The Pew Research Center for the People and the Press**
  www.people-press.org
  > A nonpartisan research organization sponsored by the Pew Charitable Trusts that surveys public opinion on politics and the media.

- **Pew Research Center's Project for Excellence in Journalism**
  www.journalism.org
  > The Center monitors the amount and tone of news coverage of the election; it also surveys online communications.

- **Political Communication Lab at Stanford University**
  http://pcl.stanford.edu/
  > Contains most presidential campaign advertisements and speeches from 2000 to the present.

- *Politico*
  www.politico.com
  > An online publication devoted to national politics.

Washington Post

www.washingtonpost.com
> A good source of information about the campaign and the mind set of the candidates. The *post* tracks the flow of money, advertising, and campaign appearances.

EXERCISES

1. Follow the campaign on the source from which you receive most of your election news. Do you feel that the news coverage was balanced? Was there media bias? Compare your perceptions on the amount and tone of coverage with the surveys conducted by the Pew Research Center's Project for Excellence web site (journalism.org).

2. Indicate the principal narratives of the campaign as articulated by the major party candidates and by the news media. Which of these narratives did you find most compelling?

3. View one of the presidential debates and note the principal policy positions of the candidates. Which of these policies are apt to be the easiest to achieve if elected and which would be the most difficult? (Transcripts and videos of the debates can be found on the web site of the Commission on Presidential Debates. www.debates.org.)

4. Contrast the advertisements of the presidential candidates on the basis of their messages, presentations, and targeted groups. These ads should also be available on the candidates' web sites. Then check the accuracy of these ads on Factcheck .org. Which seem to be the most accurate, the most persuasive, and the most interesting?

5. Follow the blogs of the principal candidates' web sites. Which of them seem to convey the most enthusiasm among their supporters?

SELECTED READINGS

Denton, Robert E., Jr. *The 2012 Presidential Campaign: A Communication Perspective*. Lanham, MD: Rowman & Littlefield, 2014.

Farnsworth, Stephen J., and S. Robert Lichter. *The Nightly News Nightmare: Network Television Coverage of Presidential Elections, 1988–2008*. Lanham, MD: Rowman & Littlefield, 2010.

Fowler, Erika Franklin, and Travis N. Ridout. "Negative, Angry, and Ubiquitous: Political Advertising in 2012." *The Forum*, 10 (Feb. 2013): 51–61.

Geer, John G. *In Defense of Negativity: Attack Ads in Presidential Campaigns*. Chicago: University of Chicago Press, 2006.

————. "The News Media and the Rise of Negativity in Presidential Campaigns." *PS: Political Science and Politics*, 45 (July 2012): 422–427.

Goldstein, Ken, and Paul Freedman. "Campaign Advertising and Voter Turnout: New Evidence for a Stimulation Effect." *The Journal of Politics*, 64 (Aug. 2002): 721–740.

Huber, Gregory, and Kevin Arceneaux. "Identifying the Persuasive Effects of Presidential Advertising." *American Journal of Political Science*, 51 (Oct. 2007): 957–977.

Jamieson, Kathleen Hall, ed. *Electing the President 2012: The Insiders' View.* Philadelphia, PA: University of Pennsylvania Press, 2013.

Kenski, Kate, Bruce W. Hardy, and Kathleen Hall Jamieson. *The Obama Victory: How Media, Money, and Message Shaped the 2008 Election.* Oxford, UK: Oxford University Press, 2010.

Lau, Richard R., Lee Sigelman, and Ivy Brown Rouver. "The Effects of Negative Political Commercials: A Meta-Analytic Reassessment." *Journal of Politics*, 69 (Nov. 2007): 1176–1209.

Mutz, Diana C. "How the Mass Media Divide Us," in *Red and Blue Nation? Characteristics and Causes of America's Polarized Politics*, Pietro S. Niola and David W. Brady, eds. Washington, DC: Brookings/Hoover, 2006, pp. 223–262.

Napoli, Philip M. *Audience Evolution: New Technologies and the Transformation of Media Audiences.* New York: Columbia University Press, 2011.

Patterson, Thomas E. *Out of Order.* New York: Knopf, 1993.

West, Darrell M. *Air Wars: Television Advertising and Social Media in Election Campaigns, 1952–2012.* 6th ed. Washington, DC: CQ Press, 2013.

NOTES

1. The term "yellow journalism" comes from the comic strip "The Yellow Kid," which first appeared in Joseph Pulitzer's *New York World* in 1896. The kid, whose nightshirt was colored yellow in the paper, was an instant hit in the black-and-white newspapers of the day and sparked a bidding war for the comic strip between Pulitzer and William Randolph Hearst. Although the strip's popularity lasted only a few years, the competition between these two media titans continued for decades.

2. David Stebenne, "Media Coverage of American Presidential Elections: A Historical Perspective," in Martha FitzSimon, ed., *The Finish Line: Covering the Campaign's Final Days* (New York: Freedom Forum Media Studies Center, 1993), p. 83.

3. "State of the News Media: 2014," Pew Research Center's Project for Excellence in Journalism, March 26, 2014. http://www.journalism.org/2014/03/26 /state-of-the-news-media-2014-key-indicators-in-media-and-news/

4. "High Marks for the Campaign, a High Bar for Obama," Pew Research Center for the People and the Press, November 13, 2005. www.people-press.org /report/?pageid=1429

5. Thomas E. Patterson, *Out of Order* (New York: Knopf, 1993), pp. 53–133.

6. Thomas E. Patterson, "Television and Election Strategy," in Gerald Benjamin, ed., *The Communications Revolution in Politics* (New York: Academy of Political Science, 1982), p. 30.

7. Michael J. Robinson and Margaret A. Sheehan, *Over the Wire and on TV: CBS and UPI in Campaign '80* (New York: Russell Sage Foundation, 1983), p. 148.

8. Tom Rosenstiel, Mark Jurkowitz, and Tricia Sartor, "How the Media Covered the 2012 Primary Campaign," Pew Research Center's Project for Excellence

in Journalism, April 23, 2012. http://www.journalism.org/2012/04/23/romney-report/

9. "Winning the Media Campaign," Pew Research Center's Project for Excellence in Journalism, October 22, 2008. http://www.journalism.org/2008/10/22/winning-media-campaign/

10. "The Final Days of the Media Campaign 2012," Pew Research Center's Project for Excellence in Journalism, November 19, 2012. http://www.journalism.org/2012/11/19/final-days-media-campaign-2012/

11. John Sides and Lynn Vavreck, *The Gamble* (Princeton, NJ: Princeton University Press, 2013), p. 43.

12. Diana C. Mutz, "How the Mass Media Divide Us," in Pietro S. Nivola and David W. Brady, eds., *Red and Blue Nation? Characteristics and Causes of America's Polarized Politics* (Washington, DC: Brookings/Hoover, 2006), pp. 224–240.

13. Kathleen Hall Jamieson and Bruce Hardy, "What Is Civil Engaged Argument and Why Does Aspiring to It Matter?" *PS: Political Science and Politics*, 45 (July 2012): 412–415.

14. "The Final Days of the Media Campaign 2012," Pew Research Center's Project for Excellence in Journalism, November 19, 2012. http://www.journalism.org/2012/11/19/final-days-media-campaign-2012/

15. Kiku Adatto, "The Incredible Shrinking Sound Bite," *New Republic* (May 28, 1990), p. 22.

16. Roger Ailes, media director for George Bush's 1988 campaign and head of Fox News, explained this phenomenon in the following manner:

> Let's face it, there are three things that the media are interested in: pictures, mistakes, and attacks. That's the one sure way of getting coverage. You try to avoid as many mistakes as you can. You try to give them as many pictures as you can. And if you need coverage, you attack, and you will get coverage.
>
> It's my orchestra pit theory of politics. If you have two guys on stage and one says, "I have a solution to the Middle East problem," and the other guy falls in the orchestra pit, who do you think is going to be on the evening news?
>
> Roger Ailes in David R. Runkel, ed., *Campaign for President: The Managers Look at '88* (Dover, MA: Auburn House, 1989), p. 136.

17. "Journalists Monopolize TV News," Center for Media and Public Affairs, p. 21; Patterson, *Out of Order,* p. 106.

18. Mutz, "How the Mass Media Divide Us," p. 246.

19. In its analysis of the principal narratives of the 2012 election, the Pew Research Center's project for Excellence in journalism reported, "Reporters and (talk-show personalities) account for about half as many of the assertions about the candidates' character and biography as they did 12 years ago—27% versus 50% in 2000." "The Master Character Narratives in 2012," Pew Research Center's Project for Excellence in Journalism, August 23, 2012. http://www.journalism.org/2012/08/23/2012-campaign-character-narratives/

20. "Topics A–Z: Confidence in Institutions," Gallup Poll, 2014. http://www.gallup.com/poll/1597/Confidence-Institutions.aspx#2

21. Andrew Dugan, "Americans' Confidence in News Media Remains Low," Gallup Poll, June 9, 2014. www.gallup.com/poll/17174/amricans-confidence-news-media-remains-low.aspx?version=print

22. Chris Dodd quoted in Dan Balz, "Democratic Senator Dodd Enters Presidential Race," *The Washington Post* (Jan. 12, 2007), p. A6.

23. In his initial quest for the presidency in 2000, George W. Bush spoke for thirteen minutes on a single appearance on the *Late Show with David Letterman*—longer than the total time he appeared on the evening news of three television broadcast networks during the *entire* month of October. Similarly, Gore appeared on Letterman's show in September for more time than he appeared on the three evening news shows during that whole month combined. "Journalists Monopolize TV Election News," Center for Media and Public Affairs, October 30, 2000, p. 27. http://www.cmpa.com/wp-content/uploads/2013/10/prev_pres _elections/2000/2000.10.30.Journalists-Monopolize-TV-Election-News.pdf

24. Matthew A. Baum, "Talking the Vote: Why Presidential Candidates Hit the Talk Show Circuit," *American Journal of Political Science,* 49 (April 2005): 213–234.

25. Jeffrey A. Gottfried, Bruce W. Hardy, Kenneth M. Winneg, and Kathleen Hall Jamieson, "All Knowledge Is Not Created Equal: Knowledge Effects and the 2012 Presidential Debates," *Presidential Studies Quarterly*, 44 (Sept. 2014): 407.

26. Peter Goldman, Thomas M. DeFrank, Mary Miller et al., *Quest for the Presidency: 1992* (College Station: Texas A&M Press, 1994), p. 535.

27. Admiral Stockdale had not been briefed by Perot's handlers prior to the debate. He was unable to answer questions about Perot's policy positions. At one point when the moderator asked him a question, he said that he could not hear it because his hearing aid was not on. Viewers did not come away with confidence that he could be an effective vice president, much less president.

28. Perot complained bitterly, first appealing to the Federal Communications Commission and then instituting legal action to prevent the debates from being held if he could not participate. Although he failed to stop the debates, he used his exclusion to emphasize one of his campaign themes—the self-serving nature of the two-party system and the need to reform it. The reason that Perot was so agitated was that participating in the debates was part of his 1996 campaign strategy. He had boosted his popularity significantly in 1992 by his performance in the presidential debates and hoped to do so again in 1996.

29. "51.4 Million Viewers Tune into Biden and Ryan's Vice Presidential Debate," Nielsen Company, October 12, 2012. www.blog.nielsen.com/51-4-million -viewers-tune-into-biden-ryans-vice-presidential-debate.htm

30. Beth Myers, in Kathleen Hall Jamieson, ed., *Electing the President 2012: The Insiders' View* (Philadelphia: University of Pennsylvania Press, 2013), pp. 98–100.

31. Nixon had closeted himself alone in a hotel before his first debate with Kennedy and received only a ten-minute briefing. Moreover, he had bumped his knee on a car door going into the television studio and was in considerable pain. Theodore H. White, *The Making of the President, 1960* (New York: Atheneum, 1988), p. 285.

32. In his first debate with Romney, President Obama appeared worn, distracted, and defensive.

33. Jeffrey A. Gottfried et al., "All Knowledge Is Not Created Equal," pp. 407–408.

34. Normally, the vice presidential debate is not nearly as consequential as the presidential one. Fewer people watch it since that debate involves the number two players on the teams. But the debate can still raise or allay doubts about the vice president's capacity to fill in if something were to happen to the president. In 1988, the vice presidential debate worked to Dan Quayle's disadvantage when his performance confirmed rather than challenged the impression that he was not up to the job. In 1992, Admiral James Stockdale, Perot's running mate, seemed unprepared, which left doubts in voters' minds whether he (and by implication, Perot) were qualified for the country's top two jobs. In 1996, Jack Kemp

floundered on foreign affairs. No such concerns were evident about either vice presidential nominee during their one debate in 2000, 2004, 2008, or 2012.

35. The group was named for the car that American Motors produced when Romney's dad headed the company.

36. Tom Hamburger, "Romney Spent More on TV Ads but Got Much Less," *Washington Post*, December 11, 2012. www.washingtonpost.com/politics/romney-campaigns-tv-ad-strategies-criticized-in-election-postmortems/2012/12/11/a2855aec-4166-11e2-bca3-aadc9b7e29c5_story.html.

37. Erika Franklin Fowler and Travis N. Ridout, "Negative, Angry, and Ubiquitous: Political Advertising in 2012," *The Forum*, 10 (February 2013): 51–61. www.degruyter.com/view/j/for.2012.10.issue-4/forum-2013-0004/forum-2013-0004.xml?format=INT

38. John C. Tedesco and Scott W. Dunn, "Political Advertising in the 2012 Presidential Election," in Robert E. Denton, Jr., ed., *The 2012 Presidential Campaign: A Communication Perspective*. Lanham, MD: Rowman & Littlefield, 2014, p. 80.

39. Fowler and Ridout, "Negative, Angry, and Ubiquitous," p. 59.

40. John G. Greer, "The News Media and the Rise of Negativity in Presidential Campaigns," *PS: Political Science and Politics*, 43 (April): 422–427.

41. Edwin Diamond and Adrian Marin, "Spots," *American Behavioral Scientist*, 32 (March/April 1989): 386.

42. "Ashley's Story," Living Room Candidate.org. www.livingroomcandidate.org/commercials/2004/ashleys-story.

43. The poll was conducted by Public Opinion Strategies. L. Patrick Devlin, "Contrast in Presidential Campaign Commercials of 2004," *American Behavioral Scientist* 49 (Oct. 2005), p. 296.

44. Bob Strum, "Contrasts in Presidential Campaign Commercials of 2004," p. 296.

45. "Love 60," Living Room Candidate.org. www.livingroomcandidate.org/commercials/2008/love-60.

46. Lynda Lee Kaid, "Videostyle in the 2004 Presidential Advertising," in Robert E. Denton, Jr., ed., *The 2004 Presidential Campaign: A Communication Perspective* (Lanham, MD: Rowman & Littlefield, 2005), p. 292.

47. Jim Margolis, "We've Heard It All Before," in Kathleen Hall Jamieson, ed., *Electing the President 2012: The Insiders' View*, pp. 137–138.

48. "The Choice," Political Communication Lab, Stanford University. www.pcl.stanford.edu/campaign/2012/?adv=The+Choice+-+BarackObama+-+Sep+12

49. Stuart Stevens, Jamieson, ed., *Electing the President 2012*, p. 158.

50. "Presidential Tracker," Center for Voting and Democracy. http://www.fairvote.org/research-and-analysis/presidential-elections/presidential-tracker/

51. "Annenberg Public Policy Center Calculates Dollars Spent by Third-party Groups on Deceptive TV Ads Attacking or Supporting the Presidential Candidates," Annenberg Public Policy Center, September 25, 2012. http://www.annenbergpublicpolicycenter.org/appc-calculates-dollars-spent-by-third-party-groups-on-deceptive-tv-ads-attacking-or-supporting-the-presidential-candidates

52. "Whoppers of 2012: The Biggest Falsehoods from the Presidential Campaign, "Annenberg Public Policy Center, October 31, 2012. http://www.factcheck.org/2012/10/whoppers-of-2012-final-edition

53. "The Final Days of the Media Campaign 2012," Pew Research Center's Project for Excellence in Journalism, November 19, 2012. http://www.journalism.org/2012/11/19/final-days-media-campaign-2012/

54. Ken Goldstein and Paul Freedman, "Campaign Advertising and Voter Turnout: New Evidence for a Stimulation Effect," *Journal of Politics* 64 (Aug. 2002): 122–123. See also Steven Finkel and John Geer, "A Spot Check: Casting Doubt on the Demobilizing Effect of Attack Advertising," *American Journal of Political Science,* 42 (June 1988): 573–595; Paul Freedman and Ken Goldstein, "Measuring Media Exposure and the Effects of Negative Campaign Ads," *American Journal of Political Science,* 43 (Sept. 1999): 1189–1208; Kim Fridkin Kahn and Patrick Kenney, "Do Negative Campaigns Mobilize or Suppress Turnout? Clarifying the Relationship between Negativity and Participation," *American Political Science Review,* 93 (Dec. 1999): 877–890; Martin Wattenberg and Craig Brians, "Negative Campaign Advertising: Demobilizer or Mobilizer?" *American Political Science Review,* 93 (Dec. 1999): 891–900; John G. Geer, *In Defense of Negativity: Attack Ads in Presidential Campaigns* (Chicago: University of Chicago Press, 2006).

55. Stephen Ansolabehere and Shanto Iyengar, *Going Negative: How Political Advertisements Shrink and Polarize the Electorate* (New York: Free Press, 1995), pp. 147–150.

THE ELECTION: ITS MEANING AND CONSEQUENCES

9 CHAPTER | UNDERSTANDING PRESIDENTIAL ELECTIONS

INTRODUCTION

Predicting and assessing the results of the election is a favorite American pastime in which politicians, journalists, academics, and the politically engaged public participate. Presidential campaigns are newsworthy, both informative and entertaining. Forecasting election outcomes, monitoring and analyzing public opinion, and anticipating the effect on governance and public policy is fair game, consistent with democratic debate but also with commentary that accompanies sporting events.

Predictions and assessments of the vote are based on elaborate equations, predicated on past elections, current survey data, and the wisdom of those who study elections: political scientists, historians, and communication scholars; politicians and media consultants; and of course, reporters and other political pundits. Their analyses provide important information to candidates running for office and to those who have been elected. For the people running campaigns, surveys of public opinion indicate the issues that can be effectively raised and those that should be avoided, which audiences should be targeted and what messages should be communicated, even the words and expressions that are apt to produce the most desired effect. For public officials, analyses of voter preferences, opinions, and attitudes provide an interpretation of the vote, indicate the range and depth of concerns on the key issues, and signal the amount of support and opposition newly elected presidents are likely to receive on them when they begin their term in office.

This chapter discusses the presidential vote from these perspectives. The first anticipates the vote by examining the environment and public opinion as the election approaches. There are many ways to assess the electoral environment. The first part of this section looks at how political scientists have tried to do so, the models they have used, and the success that they have had in predicting the vote. The focus then shifts to the public, its attitudes, beliefs, and opinions. Here we look at snapshots of the public over the course of the election campaign. This part of the chapter discusses national opinion polls, describes their methodologies, and evaluates their predictive success. We then turn to the news media's election forecasts and analyses based on the large exit poll that is taken primarily on election day as voters leave the precincts in which they have cast ballots.

The second section turns to an explanation of the vote itself. After discussing election day surveys, it reports on the American National Election Studies (ANES), which have been conducted since 1952 by researchers at the University of Michigan and, since 2005, Stanford University. These studies, which interview voters before and after the election, provide basic data that scholars have used to analyze elections and understand voting behavior and how the campaign affected the vote. The principal findings of these analyses are summarized for each presidential election since 1952.

The final section of the chapter turns to the relationship between campaigning and governing, between issue debates and public policy making, and between candidate evaluations and presidential style. How do campaign promises shape the new agenda and leadership expectations impact on performance evaluations? Does the projected or perceived image of the candidates affect the tone of the presidency or the actions of the winner in office? Can an electoral coalition be converted into a governing coalition?

PREDICTING PRESIDENTIAL ELECTIONS

Political scientists have had a long-running debate about how much campaigns really matter. Do they dictate, influence, or have relatively little impact on the outcome of the election?

There are several principal schools of thought. One argues that campaigns usually do not matter all that much and that the environment in which elections occur shapes the electorate's judgment and augurs the outcome of the vote; another suggests that it is the preexisting political views that matter; a third alternative is that campaigns can be decisive, particularly when the electorate is closely divided. These contending points of view are not necessarily inconsistent with one another, but they do reflect differences in the perceptions of what the most important influences on voting are—economic, social, and political conditions; political attitudes, salient issues, the personalities of the candidates, or the conduct of the campaign itself.

STATISTICAL MODELS

Those in the environment-conditions-the-outcome school have constructed formal models by which they forecast the popular vote. They identify critical variables that have influenced past elections; assess them within the current economic, social, and political environment; quantify them for the purpose of analysis; and then place them in an equation intended to predict the percentage of the two-party vote that the winning candidate will receive. They then test the model on the basis of how successfully it would have predicted previous presidential elections.

The components of most models include economic and political variables. Since economic performance is a major criterion by which the electorate evaluates the party in power and its candidates for office, especially if the incumbent is running for reelection, almost all the election models contain measures of the economy; some modelers also try to anticipate how the economy will perform in the year of the election and how the public thinks it will perform. They use indicators such as the gross national product (GNP), gross domestic product (GDP), rate of economic growth, level of unemployment, number of new jobs created since the previous election, rate of inflation, consumer confidence index, and forecasts about the country's economic future. Conditions change, so the closer to election that they factor these variables into their model, the more accurate their predictions are apt to be.

Forecasters face another problem. The actual state of the economy and perceptions of it may differ. The economic conditions that the press highlights, the diverse effect of the economy on different people in different areas at different times, and partisan views that shape how many people evaluate the economy can exacerbate the gap between public perceptions and economic analysis although it is possible to anticipate what public perceptions may be on the basis of current economic conditions.[1] To capture these campaign-related variables, the modelers frequently have to incorporate polling data into their equations.

A second set of variables concerns the political environment: the partisan disposition of the electorate, the public's approval of the current president, and the length of time that president's party has been in control of the White House.

Partisanship has become a more important influence on voting, so important that it has lessened the independent impact of nonpolitical factors on the outcome. Many of these nonpolitical factors are evaluated through a partisan lens. The fact that the parties have been at or near parity for the last three decades, however, has made the popular vote in presidential elections since 2000, with the exception of 2008, very close. The margin of victory has not exceeded four percent in national elections although competitiveness between the major parties within many of the states varies more.

The division between the red and blue states has remained remarkably steady. Only three states switched their presidential vote from 2000 to 2004 and two from 2008 to 2012. Changing demographics, especially the increase of minorities in the electorate, help explain the shifts in the states that have gone from red to blue.

Another factor that affects the political environment is incumbency. Incumbents, whose party has just won the White House, usually get reelected. Only Carter failed to do so in 1980. After retaining control of the White House, however, for a period of 8 to 12 years, the "time-for-a-change" variable kicks in. Grievances mount and public discontent is directed toward the party in power and its candidates.

Challengers face another disadvantage if they have to go through a very competitive nomination process to become the party's standard-bearer. As we have mentioned previously, competitive primaries and caucuses can damage personal images of the winners, decrease their financial resources, and deepen the divide within a party, hurdles that must be overcome to win the general election. In recent times, the influence of party activists on nomination process has forced candidates to take more extreme policy positions that may adversely impact them in the presidential election.

The third set of factors is election specific. Events that occur during the campaign, such as the financial crisis of 2008 or even Hurricane Sandy, can affect voters' opinions and their behavior at the polls as well as the campaign itself: disproportionate resources, more effective outreach, a series of politically incorrect or ill-conceived statements or actions, and personal health issues may influence the outcome, particularly if the country is closely divided politically and/or the economy mixed and its future trajectory unpredictable.

To identify which of these variables is likely to be most important, and in what combination with one another, forecasters turn to history. They calculate the relationship of these factors to past election outcomes. In doing so, they make an assumption that those factors that best predicted the vote in the past will continue to do so in the future. There are several problems with this assumption, however, changing conditions, opinions, even beliefs. Take the views on gender-orientation, for example, or the longer-term, psychological consequences of the Great Recession.

The longer the time period from the date of the forecast to the vote of the public can also affect its accuracy. If the forecast is made early, if the variables that are analyzed are based on data from previous years or months before the election, if the impact of the campaign itself is not considered—either because one group of economic or political factors is so dominant or because the modelers assume that the campaigns will cancel each other out—then forecasts may be inaccurate because models are incomplete or the assumptions on which they were based are incorrect. So with all these difficulties, why do political scientists forecast election outcomes long before they occur? One reason is that they believe environments matter, in some cases more than campaigns themselves, that most people make retrospective judgments that shape their political outlook and voting behavior. And these judgments tend to be predictable. They assume that when an accumulation of factors point in one direction, the die has been cast.

How accurate have the forecasters been? In 2000, well before the election, all the modelers predicted a Gore victory over Bush from 52.8 percent to 60.3 percent of the popular vote. They did so on the basis of a booming economy, the absence of a national security threat, the U.S. status as a superpower, and President Bill Clinton's high job approval ratings. Gore actually received 48.4 percent of the total vote and 50.2 percent of the two-party vote.[2]

In 2004, the modelers did better. They all forecast that Bush would win the popular vote, receiving anywhere from 49.9 percent to 57.6 percent of the two-party vote. The average forecast was 53.8 percent; Bush actually received 50.7 percent of the total vote and 51.2 percent of the two-party vote.[3]

The outcome of the 2008 presidential election was not hard to predict, particularly after the financial crisis of mid-September of that year. But even before that crisis, a Democratic victory seemed probable with economic growth declining; an unpopular, two-term president in the White House; and a war in progress that a majority of Americans had come to believe was a mistake. Most of the political science forecasters predicted an Obama victory by an average of 52 percent of the two-party vote.[4] He won 52.9 of the total vote and 53.7 of the two-party vote.

In 2012, the forecasters were divided. Of the 13 who published their prediction before the election, eight said Obama would win and five Romney. Their estimates ranged from 53.8 percent for Obama to 53.1 percent for Romney.[5] The average forecast of the two-party vote was 50.4 percent for Obama. He actually won 52 percent of that vote and 51.1 percent of all the votes cast.[6]

PUBLIC OPINION POLLS

If campaigns matter, if opinions change, then forecasters and analysts need to follow the polls. So do journalists who rely on them to describe the race, anticipate the outcome, and explain the opinions and behavior of the voters. Polls also are thought to contribute to the objectivity of reporting although descriptions of who's ahead tend to affect the tone of presidential election coverage.[7]

Sometimes proprietary, campaign polls are given to the press to try to affect media coverage. Obviously, campaigns want to release data most favorable to their candidate. Nate Silver, chief polling analyst for the *New York Times* in 2012, contends that these internal polls tend to be less accurate not only because of their selective release of information but also because pollsters hired by the campaign do not want to provide bad news that undermines the morale of fellow campaigners and could result in fewer polls being authorized and thus less business for them.[8]

There are hundreds of public opinion surveys at the state and national levels. In 2012, *Real Clear Politics*, an online political news organization, listed the results from 68 post–Labor Day, 203 for the entire election year, and 299 for the two-year cycle.[9] Pollster.com tracked 589.[10]

A Brief History of Election Polling

Although the number of polls has mushroomed in recent years, polling itself is not a new phenomenon. There have been nationwide assessments of public opinion since 1916. The largest and most comprehensive of the early surveys were the straw polls conducted by the *Literary Digest,* a popular monthly magazine. The *Digest* mailed millions of ballots and questionnaires to people who appeared on lists of automobile owners and in telephone directories. In 1924, 1928, and 1932, the poll correctly predicted the winner of the presidential election. In 1936, it did not: a huge Alfred Landon victory was forecast, and a huge Franklin Roosevelt victory resulted.

What went wrong? The *Digest* mailed 10 million questionnaires over the course of the campaign and received 2 million back. As the ballots were returned, they were tabulated. This procedure, which provided a running count, blurred shifts in public opinion that may have been occurring during the campaign. But that was not its only problem. The principal difficulty with the *Digest*'s survey was that the sample of people who responded to the survey was not representative of the voting public. Automobile owners and telephone subscribers were simply not typical voters in 1936, since most people did not own cars or have telephones. This distinction mattered more in 1936 than it had in previous years because of the Great Depression. There was a socioeconomic cleavage within the electorate. The *Literary Digest* sample did not reflect this cleavage; thus, its results were wrong.

While the *Digest* was tabulating its 2 million responses and predicting that Landon would be the next president, a number of other pollsters were conducting more scientific surveys and correctly forecasting Roosevelt's reelection. The polls of George Gallup, Elmo Roper, and Archibald Crossley differed from the *Digest*'s in two major ways: they were considerably smaller, and their samples were more representative of the population as a whole, allowing more accurate generalizations to be made.

The *Digest* went out of business, but Gallup, Roper, and Crossley continued to poll and to improve their sampling techniques. In 1940, Gallup predicted Roosevelt would receive 52 percent of the vote; he actually received 55 percent. In 1944, Gallup forecast a 51.5 percent Roosevelt vote, very close to his actual 53.2 percent. Other pollsters also made predictions that closely approximated the results. As a consequence, public confidence in election polling began to grow.

The confidence was short-lived, however. In 1948, all major pollsters forecast a victory by Republican Thomas E. Dewey. Their errors resulted from poor sampling techniques, from the premature termination of polling two weeks before election day, and from incorrect assumptions about how the undecided would vote.

In attempting to estimate the population in their samples, the pollsters had resorted to filling quotas. They interviewed a certain number of people with different demographic characteristics until the percentage of these groups in the sample resembled that percentage in the population as a whole. Simply because the percentages were approximately equal, however, did not mean that the sample was representative of people in these groups. For example, interviewers avoided certain areas in cities, and their results were consequently biased.

Moreover, the interviewing stopped several weeks before the election. In mid-October, the polls showed that Dewey was ahead by a substantial margin. Burns Roper, son of Elmo Roper, polling for *Fortune* magazine, saw the lead as sufficiently large to predict a Dewey victory without the need for further surveys. A relatively large number of people, however, were undecided. Three weeks before the election, Gallup concluded that 8 percent of the voters had still not made up their minds. In estimating the final vote, Gallup and other pollsters assumed that the undecided would divide their votes in much the same manner as the electorate as a whole. This assumption turned out to be incorrect. Most of those who were wavering in the closing days of the campaign were Democrats. In the end, most of them voted for Truman or did not vote at all.

The results of the 1948 election once again cast doubt on the accuracy of public opinion polls. Truman's victory also reemphasized the fact that surveys reflect opinion at the time they are taken, not necessarily days or weeks later. Opinion and voter preferences may change.

Polling Accuracy

To improve their monitoring of shifts within the electorate, pollsters changed the method of selecting people to be interviewed. They developed a more effective means of anticipating who would actually vote and polled continuously to and through election day to identify more precisely and quickly shifts in public sentiment and reactions to campaign events. Obviously, polls conducted closer to the day on which people vote are more likely to forecast the actual results more accurately than polls taken months before.[11]

Aggregating the results of different polls conducted over the same period is more likely to reflect public opinion. But polls remain time bound; they are valid only for the period during which they were taken. To mirror changes in public opinion over time, survey researchers use rolling polls in which about one-third of the sample changes daily.

These refinements in polling have produced better and more accurate results, particularly as the election approaches, but the predictions have not been perfect. In 1980, the size of Reagan's victory was substantially underestimated in some nationwide polls; in 1992 and 1996, Clinton's margin was overestimated. In 2012, Obama's was underestimated by every major national pollster in its final preelection poll (see Table 9.1). Two major survey organizations, Rasmussen Reports and the Gallup Poll, had Romney ahead.[12] What's the problem? Box 9.1 describes some of the problems pollsters face today.

ELECTION NIGHT FORECASTS AND POST-ELECTION ANALYSES

Forecasts continue right to the end, until all the votes are tabulated. The final projections and vote analyses are presented by the major television broadcast and cable news networks during the night of the election as well as the

| BOX 9.1 | THE PROBLEMS WITH POLLS |

There are both substantive and methodological problems that pollster encounter. Some are merely statistical. Every poll has a sampling error that varies with the size of the poll. Most of the major national surveys vary between +/– 2 to 3.5 percent. They also have a level of confidence that the results will be within this error range. Most have a confidence level of 95 percent.

Other more recent problems have to do with the declining response rate, the changing technologies to communicate with the public, and the screens for determining likely voters.[13]

The proportion of the population that are contacted by pollsters, that agree to be interviewed, and that complete the interview has declined markedly in the last 15 years according to a study by the Pew Research Center. Of those randomly selected to be included, only 9 percent in 2012 were willing to complete the interview, a figure that compares to 36 percent in 1997, 28 percent in 2000, and 21 percent in 2009.[14] The proliferation of telephone surveys during the evening and the introduction of caller ID have contributed to the lower response rate.

The accuracy problem has been aggravated by the proliferation of cell phones and the decreasing portion of people with landlines. Cell phone calling is more expensive because the law prohibits random digit dialing of cell phone numbers. Moreover, exclusive cell phone users tend to be younger, more urban, more mobile, and more likely to be racial and ethnic minorities with lower incomes than online users. Undersampling cell users decreases the representative quality of the overall survey.[15]

Another problem results from respondents providing the politically correct but not necessarily a truthful answer to the question, do you intend to vote? Since more people surveyed indicate that they will vote than actually do vote, pollsters have to identify likely voters. They ask a series of questions designed to determine a person's likelihood of voting: Are you registered? Did you vote in the last election? By the way, where do people vote around here? The potential for a respondent voting is calculated on the basis of these and other questions that measure interest in the election, concern about the outcome, and strength of their partisan allegiances.

There are also election-specific factors that can affect voting. Underestimating Obama's 2012 vote was consequence of several of them: the extent of early voting (about 30 percent), the changing demographics of the electorate, and the competitiveness of some states, all of which offset the stronger, more intense anti-Obama views of Republicans.

Other responses that can affect the accuracy of polls include information that people may not want to reveal, such as racial, religious, ethnic, or gender-orientation bias. In 2008 with an African American running for president, pollsters feared the so-called "Bradley effect." In 1982, California polls predicted that Los Angeles mayor Tom Bradley, an African American, would be elected governor of California. But they were wrong. Bradley lost a close election. Similarly, other state polls overestimated the vote African American candidates would receive for mayor of Chicago in 1983, governor of Virginia in 1989, and mayor of New York City in 1989. Since the 1990s, there has been less evidence of such an effect, a hidden anti-minority vote.[16]

That the major pollsters in 2012 were less accurate than in the past presidential election is likely to modify the methodology, assumptions, and estimates they use in future elections.[17] There will probably be increased use of online polling, which was more accurate than the live telephone surveys and much more accurate that automated telephone polling.[18]

TABLE 9.1 | ACCURACY OF THE FINAL 2012 PREELECTION POLLS

Poll	Dates	Obama	Romney	Spread
Actual Results		51.1	47.2	Obama +3.9
Real Clear Politics	10/31–11/5	48.8	48.1	Obama +.7
Politico/GWU	11/4–11/5	47	47	Tie
Rasmussen	11/3–11/5	48	49	Romney +1
IBD/TIPP	11/3–11/5	50	49	Obama +1
CNN/Opinion Research	11/2–11/4	49	49	Tie
Gallup	11/1–11/4	49	50	Romney +1
ABC/Washington Post	11/1–11/4	50	47	Obama +3
Monmouth/SurveyUSA	11/1–11/4	48	48	Tie
NBC/Wall Street Journal	11/1–11/3	48	47	Obama +1
Pew	10/31–11/3	50	47	Obama +3

Source: "General Election: Romney vs. Obama," Real Clear Politics. http://www.realclearpolitics.com /epolls/2012/president/us/general_election_romney_vs_obama-1171.html

following day. They are also made available by the Associated Press and major newspapers such as *Los Angeles Times*, *The New York Times*, *Wall Street Journal*, and *Washington Post*. In reporting the results, the news media have three principal objectives: to report the actual vote, forecast the winners ahead of the vote tabulation, and analyze the results. They want to do so quickly and accurately.

Beginning in the 1960s, the major networks and news services established a consortium, the News Election Service (NES), to pool their resources in reporting the vote count. Thousands of reporters were assigned to precincts and county election boards around the country to relay the presidential, congressional, and gubernatorial votes as soon as they were tallied by local and state officials.

If all the news media wanted to do was simply report the actual vote, this type of reporting would have sufficed. But they also want to analyze the vote and explain its meaning. Thus, they need to know who voted for whom and why. The best way to obtain this information is to get it from the people themselves right after they exit the voting precincts.

Exit Polling

The first exit poll was conducted for CBS News in 1968. Other news networks followed. But this type of polling is expensive and requires large numbers of people who have to be trained for one day's work. It also requires sophisticated computer programming as well as considerable historical data on state precincts and their voting trends. To save money, the major news organizations formed a consortium to collect the data, project the winners, and explain the outcomes.

Initially, the participating organizations made their own election calls on the basis of the data they were receiving. The desire to be first resulted in several incorrect projections. After a failed attempt to overhaul their combined election day polling operations, the networks contracted with an outside firm, Edison Research, to do it for them.

Here's how exit polling works. A large number of precincts across the country are randomly selected, 350 in 2012, plus telephone interviews are used to capture the preferences of early voters. The random selection of polling locations is made within states in such a way that principal geographic units (cities, suburbs, and rural areas), size of precincts, and their past voting records are taken into account. Several thousand representatives of the polling organization administer the poll to voters who are chosen in a systematic way (for example, every third, fourth, or fifth person) as they leave the voting booths. Voters are asked to complete a short questionnaire (thirty to forty items) that is designed to elicit information on their voting choices, political attitudes, and evaluations of the candidates, as well as their own demographic characteristics. Several times over the course of the day, the questionnaires are collected, tabulated, and their results telephoned to a central computer bank where they are analyzed using various statistical measures.

A variety of models are used to compare the returns from the precincts to those of past elections and to returns from other parts of the state. The sequence of the votes, the order in which they are received, is also considered in the analysis. Then, after most or all of the voting in a state has been completed, the findings of the exit poll are made public by the news media. Over the course of the evening, the networks adjust the exit poll data to reflect the actual vote as it is tabulated.

The exit poll is usually very accurate. Because it is conducted over the course of the day, there may be a little bias that would underrepresent or overrepresent certain types of voters who cast their ballots at different times of the day. By the end of the day, however, this bias should be eliminated.

Only voters are sampled and in large numbers, thereby reducing the error to much less than that of the national surveys conducted before the election. In addition, the exit poll provides a sample of sufficient size to enable analysts to discern the attitudes, opinions, and choices of smaller groups and subgroups within the electorate. In 2012, the sample size of the national exit poll was 26,565. This figure included 4,408 telephone interviews of early voters[19] (see Table 9.3 later in this chapter). In addition, Edison did additional interviews in designated states to provide data for state-based elections.

Early Vote Projection Controversies

Early projections of the winner on election night based on exit polling have generated considerable criticism, primarily on the grounds that they discourage turnout and affect voting in states in which the polls are still open. This controversy was heightened in 1980. When the early returns and polls conducted for the networks and major newspapers all indicated a Reagan landslide, the broadcast news networks projected his victory early in the evening while voting was still occurring on the West Coast and in Hawaii. At 9:30 PM Eastern Standard Time (EST), President Jimmy Carter appeared before his supporters and conceded defeat. Almost immediately, Carter's early announcement incurred angry protests, particularly from defeated West Coast Democrats, who alleged that the president's remarks discouraged many Democrats from voting. It is difficult to substantiate their claim, however.[20] Researchers who have studied the impact of the 1980 television projections on voting have found a small reduction in turnout in the West but little evidence of vote switching or turnout bias toward or against the projected winner as a result of the early projections.[21]

The minimal effect of the election reporting on the outcome of the election seems to be related to the fact that relatively few people watch the broadcasts and then vote. Most people vote first and watch the returns later in the evening. Perhaps this pattern of voting and then watching or listening to the returns explains why George H. W. Bush's projected victory on the networks in 1988 before the polls closed on the West Coast did little to change the results in three out of four Pacific states (Washington, Oregon, and Hawaii) that voted for Michael Dukakis. Nonetheless, sensitivity to the criticism that early returns affect turnout and voting behavior led the networks to agree prior to the 1992 election not to project winners in any state until its polls had closed. In states with different time zones, a majority of its polls have to close before winners would be projected.

The networks amended their pledge to make a national prediction in 1996 even as people were voting on the West Coast. Promptly at 9 PM EST, they forecast a Clinton victory. In anticipation of this early forecast, Republicans bitterly criticized the practice of "calling" the election before the polls had closed and warned of possible legislation to prevent it from happening again. No such legislation has been enacted, however, although congressional hearings were held.

Another early prediction controversy in which speed and accuracy collided occurred in 2000. Early in the evening of the election (7:50 PM EST), the television broadcast networks forecast a victory for Al Gore in Florida on the basis of exit polls even though residents in the central time zone living in the Florida Panhandle were still voting. The announcement elated Democrats. However, as the evening wore on, a discrepancy became evident between the actual returns and the exit polls. On the basis of this discrepancy, CNN retracted its prediction of a Gore victory. The other networks quickly followed suit. At 2:16 AM EST, the Fox News channel declared Bush the winner on the basis of tabulated returns. Again, the other networks quickly followed.

Hearing the news, Vice President Gore called Governor George W. Bush to concede the election and was on his way to make a public announcement to his supporters. Before he did so, however, he learned that the election was still too close to call. Gore then telephoned Bush again and retracted his concession while the networks retracted their prediction of a Bush victory.[22] In the end, the closeness of the Florida vote, combined with the voiding of thousands of improperly punched ballots, precluded a valid exit poll prediction.

The first release of the exit polling data in 2004 (at 12:59 PM) showed Kerry with a small but statistically insignificant lead. By midafternoon, however, his lead had jumped to 3 percent, a percentage that was statistically significant. Democrats were gleeful; Republicans were puzzled. A subsequent analysis of the polling data found that in the morning, Democrats, especially women, were more willing to complete the survey than were men, skewing the results in Kerry's favor. His lead, however, diminished as the day wore on. The completed poll confirmed Bush's popular and Electoral College wins.

There were no major exit poll controversies in 2012 although some Republican commentators had difficulty believing the accuracy of the poll data the networks were receiving. (Table 9.3 reports the results of the exit polls in the past four presidential elections.)

INTERPRETING THE ELECTION RESULTS

In addition to predicting the results, the television networks and major news organizations also provide an instant analysis of results on election night and the days after. This analysis, based primarily on exit poll data, relates voting decisions to the issue positions, ideological perspectives, and partisan preferences of the electorate. Patterns among demographic groups, issue stands, and electoral perceptions and choices are noted and used to explain why people voted for particular candidates.

Although the exit poll provides a portrait of the electorate, it does not provide an explanation of how the campaign has affected the vote. To understand changes in public attitudes and opinions during the campaign, it is necessary to survey people over the course of the election cycle, asking the same questions. The nationwide polls conducted by major commercial polling organizations do so but not with the same respondents.

Generic trends are informative but do not explain individual voting behavior. To find out why people vote as they do, you need to ask the same people, preferably before and after the election. Since 1948, the American National Election Studies (ANES) have done so. They have utilized an interview/reinterview model, conducted in homes, to collect data on issue preferences, political attitudes, and voting decisions. These data have been utilized by political scientists and others to explain why individuals vote as they do.

MODELS OF VOTING BEHAVIOR

There are two basic theoretical models that electoral scholars have proposed: the *prospective*, which emphasizes the issues and looks to the future, and the *retrospective*, which evaluates the candidates and their parties on the basis of their past behavior in office.[23]

Prospective Voting
In the prospective voting model, voters compare their beliefs and policy preferences with those enunciated by the parties and their nominees. They make

a determination of which party and which candidates espouse positions that are closer to their own and thus would more likely pursue those positions if elected. In other words, voters make a judgment on the prospects of obtaining future policies they desire based on the current positions of the candidates and their parties and the policies they promise to redeem if elected.

To make a prospective judgment, voters must have discernible beliefs and opinions of their own; they must also have enough information to differentiate the candidates' beliefs and opinions from one another; and finally, they must be able to make a judgment about which party and candidate's views are closer to their own on issues they deem most important.

If people were only concerned with a single issue, the choice might be easy. But alas there are usually multiple issues upon which the candidates and parties take positions. To simplify the task for voters, the issues are frequently bundled together by the parties and their nominees and given an ideological label. Since the 1980s, voters have no difficulty discerning the Democratic Party as more liberal and the Republican Party as more conservative. The issues have changed but the ideological orientation of the parties has not. In fact, that orientation has become clearer. Thus, people who think of themselves as conservative and would like the next government to pursue conservative policies tend to vote Republican, and people who identify themselves as liberal tend to vote Democratic. Exit poll data in Table 9.3 indicate a high correlation between perceived ideology and voting behavior.

Not everyone has strong ideological convictions, however. There are many people who think of themselves as moderate, a plurality of people according to the most recent exit poll. In fact, today, most people see leaders of both parties as more extreme in their beliefs than they themselves are. People who do not have strong ideological inclinations or whose views fall between the positions of the major-party candidates need to consider other factors in deciding how to vote. But what choice do they actually have if the major party's candidates present such consistent and diverse policy stands? Professor Morris Fiorina argues that they have little, that elected partisan leaders have sorted the options in such a way that forces moderate voters to support ideologically extreme candidates.[24]

Retrospective Voting

Another way to make a voting decision is to evaluate current economic, social, and political conditions and determine which party is primarily responsible for them. People who determine how they are going to vote in this manner are making a retrospective judgment. History serves as a prologue for the future. Unlike the prospective voters who compare their policy preferences with those of the candidates running for office, retrospective voters make a decision on the basis of who was in power, what they achieved, and whether the outcome was favorable or unfavorable for them and the country.

If the economy is strong, society harmonious, and the nation secure and at peace, people assume that their leaders, particularly the president, must be doing a good job. If conditions are not good, then the president gets much of the blame.[25] Thus, the key question that voters ask themselves when making a retrospective evaluation is "Am I and my country better off now than before the party now in power and its presidential and vice presidential candidates won control of the White House?"

In 2012, Romney asked voters to make a retrospective judgment on President Obama and his inability to turn the economy around quickly enough. Obama admitted that more needed to be done even though the economic trajectory was going in the right direction. He asked voters to make a prospective judgment on which policies, his or the ones that Romney proposed, were more like to help more Americans.

In both the prospective and retrospective models, partisanship is apt to be an important influence on the evaluations people make in arriving at their voting decision. In the retrospective model, partisanship itself is the consequence of evaluations of the past performance of parties. It therefore functions as a summary judgment of how the parties and the candidates have done and as a basis for anticipating how they will do in the future.[26] Partisans who make a retrospective evaluation are more apt to rate presidents of their party more favorably before, during, and after the election and those of the other party less favorably. They also tend to see themselves as closer to the positions of their candidate and party, positions they support.

Since the identification people have with political parties is the most stable and resilient factor affecting the voting decision, it is considered to be the single most important long-term influence on voting, both direct and indirect. Ideology has worked to reinforce this influence. In other words, the partisan prism through which most voters view the election is more compelling today than it was two or three decades ago. That prism exerts more influence on their evaluation of the candidates, the issues, and, subsequently, the voter's electoral choice.

EXPLAINING CONTEMPORARY PRESIDENTIAL ELECTIONS: 1952–2012

Although party is a stabilizing force, the candidates and the issues vary from election to election. These variations affect voting decisions and the election outcomes, particularly during periods of partisan parity, periods that have characterized the American political climate since the mid-1980s.[27] The next section briefly discusses the interaction of partisan support, candidate images, and salient issues from the election of 1952 to the present.

1952–1956: The Impact of Personality
In 1952, the Democrats were the majority party, but the Republicans won the presidential election and gained control of both houses of Congress. The issues of that election—the fear of communism at home and abroad, the presence of corruption in high levels of government, and the U.S. involvement in the Korean War—benefited the GOP, as did the popularity of its presidential

candidate, former general Dwight D. Eisenhower. These short-term factors offset the Democrats' longer-term, partisan advantage.[28]

The Republicans lost their congressional majority two years later, but the president remained popular. Personality trumped partisanship in the presidential vote in 1956, but the Democrats maintained their partisan advantage within the body politic.

1960–1972: The Increasing Importance of Issues

Beginning in 1960, the issues of the campaign seemed to play a more important role in the election's outcome than they had since the New Deal realignment. In general, noneconomic issues contributed to the defection of Democrats from their party's presidential candidates in 1960, 1968, and 1972 and to defections by Republicans (and southern Democrats) in 1964.

John Kennedy's Catholicism was a primary concern to many voters in 1960 and helps explain the closeness of the presidential election as a whole. Despite the Democrats' dominance within the electorate, Kennedy received only 115,000 more votes than Richard Nixon, 0.3 percent more of the total vote. Kennedy's Catholicism cost him votes in the heavily Protestant South. Outside the South, Kennedy actually picked up Democratic votes because of the massive support he received from Catholics and the concentration of this religious group in the cities in the large industrial states.[29]

Although Kennedy barely won in 1960, Lyndon Johnson won by a landslide four years later. Short-term factors contributed to the magnitude of the Johnson victory.[30] Barry Goldwater was perceived as a minority candidate within a minority party, ideologically to the right of most Republicans. Moreover, he did not enjoy as favorable public image as Johnson did. Policy attitudes also favored the Democrats, even in foreign affairs. Goldwater's militant anticommunism scared many voters. They saw Johnson as the peace candidate.

Two groups of voters began to change their voting preferences and eventually their partisan orientations in the mid-1960s. White southern Democrats, opposed to their party's civil rights initiatives, cast a majority of their votes for Goldwater, and moderate, northern Republicans, who disagreed with Goldwater's conservative policy positions, voted for Johnson. For the first time since the New Deal, five states in the solid Democratic South (plus Goldwater's home state of Arizona) went Republican, auguring the major regional realignment in the elections that followed.

In addition to civil rights, a new set of foreign policy issues also split the Democrats in 1968. The Vietnam War and the unrest and protests it generated on college campuses increased Democratic defections as that party's share of the vote declined by 19 percent. The Republican vote, however, increased by only 4 percent. The third-party candidacy of George Wallace accounted for much of the difference. Wallace's popular support was issue based. Although he did not have much personal appeal, his policy positions did, particularly among white southerners, young new voters, and some blue-collar workers.[31] Had Wallace not run, the Republican presidential vote undoubtedly would have been larger because Nixon was the second choice of most Wallace voters.

The results of the 1968 presidential election thus deviated from the partisan alignment of the electorate. A significant number of voters had grievances against the Democratic Party and against Lyndon Johnson's prosecution of the Vietnam War. The party's candidate, Hubert H. Humphrey, suffered accordingly. A decline in the intensity of partisanship and a growth in the number of Independents contributed to issue voting during this period. Had it not been for the Democrats' large partisan advantage and the overwhelming African American vote that Humphrey received, the presidential election would not have been nearly so close.

The trend away from partisan voting for the majority party's presidential candidate continued in 1972. With a nominee who was ideologically and personally unpopular, the Democrats suffered their worst presidential defeat since 1920. Richard Nixon enjoyed a better public image than George McGovern. Nixon was seen as the stronger of the two presidential candidates. These perceptions, positive for Nixon and negative for McGovern, contributed to Nixon's large victory in the 1972 election. More of the electorate saw the Republican standard-bearer as closer to their policy positions than the Democratic candidate. McGovern was perceived as liberal on all issues and ideologically to the left of his own party. Democrats defected in considerable numbers; Republicans stayed with their nominee.[32] The Democrats retained control of Congress, however.

1976–1996: The Evaluation of Performance

Issue differences narrowed in 1976. Neither Gerald Ford nor Jimmy Carter emphasized the social and cultural concerns that played a large role in previous presidential contests. Both focused their attention on trust in government and on domestic economic matters. In the wake of Watergate and a recession that occurred during the Ford presidency, it is not surprising that these issues worked to the Democrats' advantage. Carter was also helped by a slightly more favorable personal assessment than voters gave Ford.[33] The latter's association with the Nixon administration, reinforced by his pardon of the former president, his difficult struggle to win his own party's nomination, and his seeming inability to find a solution to the country's economic woes adversely affected his presidential image although being president probably helped him more than it hurt him.

With sociocultural issues muted and the Vietnam War over, economic concerns divided the electorate along partisan lines. This division put the candidate with the most partisan support back in the driver's seat. Carter won primarily because he was a Democrat and secondarily because his personal evaluation was more favorable than Ford's. Carter was also helped by being a southerner. He received the electoral votes of every southern state except Virginia. In an otherwise divided Electoral College, this southern support proved to be decisive.

When Carter sought reelection four years later, being a Democrat, an incumbent, and a southerner was not sufficient to win. Poor performance ratings overcame the advantage that incumbency normally brings to a first-term president. In 1976, Carter was judged on the basis of his potential *for* office, and he beat Ford. In 1980, Carter was judged on the basis of his performance *in* office, and he lost badly to Ronald Reagan. Economic conditions—high inflation, large-scale unemployment, and the decreasing competitiveness and productivity of American industry—worked to the advantage of the party out of power. For the first time in many years, the Republicans were seen as the party better able to invigorate the economy, return prosperity, and lower inflation; the partisan divide was narrowing.

In addition, dissatisfaction with the conduct of foreign affairs culminating in frustration over the Soviet Union's invasion of Afghanistan, and especially in the failure of the United States to obtain the release of American hostages held in Iran, contributed to Carter's defeat and to changing public attitudes toward defense spending and foreign affairs. In 1980, most Americans supported increased military expenditures, a position with which Reagan was closely identified, combined with a less conciliatory, tougher, international posture. The voters made a negative retrospective evaluation of Carter's presidency and he lost. His opponent appeared to offer greater potential for leadership.[34]

Four years later, voters rewarded President Reagan for a job well done with a huge victory. It is interesting to note that ideology did not work to Reagan's advantage in either 1980 or 1984. It was conditions more than Reagan's positions on the issues that apparently influenced the electorate's judgment. A resurgent economy, strengthened military, and renewed feelings of national pride brought the president broad support. Although voters agreed with his opponent's policy positions on many of the specific problems confronting the nation, they viewed Reagan's leadership skills more highly. It was a retrospective vote. The electorate supported Reagan primarily for his performance in office. In other words, they voted *for* him in 1984 just as they had voted *against* Carter four years earlier.

The trend of retrospective voting continued in 1988 with the election of Reagan's vice president, George H. W. Bush. Bush won because the electorate evaluated the Reagan administration positively, associated Bush with that administration, and concluded that he, not Michael Dukakis, would be better able and more likely to maintain the Reagan revolution and the good times people associated with it.[35] That Bush was not as favorably evaluated as Reagan had been four years earlier partially accounts for his narrower victory.[36] From a partisan perspective, the electorate was almost evenly divided, but it had also become more conservative.

In 1992, with the economy in recession, budget and trade deficits rising, and layoffs of white-collar managers and blue-collar workers dominating the news, Bush was judged on his own performance in office, and that judgment was negative. Although he was credited with a successful foreign policy, especially the reversal of Iraq's invasion of Kuwait, the lower salience of foreign policy issues in 1992 undercut the president's achievements within that policy realm and even served to highlight his inattention to domestic matters. The economy was the principal issue and Clinton its principal beneficiary. With slightly more Democrats in the electorate than Republicans, Clinton received the votes of three out of four Democrats. For the first time since 1964, Republican defections actually exceeded those of Democrats. Turnout, traditionally seen to advantage the Republicans, was neutralized in 1992 with Democratic turnout up and Republican turnout down. Still, Clinton's partisan advantage could have been offset by a lopsided vote of Independents against him, but they divided their support among the three candidates (the third being Ross Perot), giving Clinton a plurality of their vote (38 percent) with Perot and Bush splitting the rest.[37]

By 1996, domestic concerns were still dominant, but the economy was stronger, crime had decreased, and the nation remained at peace—all conditions that favored the incumbent. Despite misgivings about some aspects of the president's personal character, voters saw him as more caring, more in touch with the times, and more visionary than his Republican opponent, Robert Dole, and they responded accordingly, reelecting the Democratic president but also the Republican congressional majority.

2000–2012: Partisanship, Ideology, and Incumbency

Although the 2000 election could have been another referendum on the Clinton presidency (as many perceive the 1988 election was on the Reagan presidency), it was not. Vice President Al Gore sought to distance himself from the scandals of the Clinton years; he emphasized the policy differences between himself and Governor George W. Bush rather than contrasted the economic, social, and international conditions at the end of 2000 with those of 1992, the last time the Republicans were in control of the White House.

Encouraging voters to make more of a prospective choice than a retrospective judgment turned out to be a poor strategic decision for the vice president. Gore's proportion of the Democratic vote dropped below Clinton's. By severing his ties with the Clinton administration, Gore hurt his own candidacy.[38] He won the popular vote but not the Electoral College vote.

Although third-party candidates Ralph Nader and Pat Buchanan attracted much less attention and support than Perot, the closeness of the 2000 election enhanced their influence, especially Nader's.[39] Had Nader not been on the Florida ballot, Gore would have probably won that state and thereby the Electoral College. In the exit polls conducted on election day, 70 percent of those who said that they voted for Nader indicated that they would still have voted had he not run. Of this group, Gore was preferred over Bush by a margin of two to one.

The election of 2004 extended and reinforced most of the cleavages within the body politic that had been evident since the late 1980s; the major parties were at parity and deeply divided by ideology. President George W. Bush was viewed as a highly polarizing figure: Republicans overwhelmingly supported him, and Democrats overwhelmingly disapproved of his presidency. The electoral strategies of the presidential candidates changed with both parties trying to maximize their base vote. The ability of the president to focus public attention on the terrorism issue combined with perceptions of his strong leadership following the attacks on September 11, 2001, worked to his advantage, solidifying his base. The Republicans bested the Democrats in the turnout contest in the key battleground states; Republican partisans were slightly more loyal to their party's nominees than were Democrats to theirs. Nonetheless, the popular vote was close and the red state–blue state division persisted. Only three states—Iowa, New Hampshire, and New Mexico—switched their presidential vote between 2000 and 2004.

After the election, the Bush administration ran into trouble. The president's domestic initiative to privatize Social Security failed; his administration's response to Hurricane Katrina was late and inadequate; public opinion turned against the war in Iraq; and the economy was faltering and the budget deficit was getting larger. During the 2008 election, there was a major financial crisis. The president's approval ratings dropped dramatically. On election day, 72 percent of the population disapproved of the job he was doing.

Beginning in 2006 and continuing through 2008, a majority of Americans believed that the Democrats would do a better job than the Republicans of keeping the country prosperous.[40] Democratic partisans increased by 3 percent during this period. A larger proportion of people also identified as Independents while the Republican base shrank.[41] All of these factors helped the Democrats. The grassroots support Obama was able to muster, the large war chest he had raised, and the more disciplined, thematic campaign he mounted led to his large electoral victory. Obama won 52.9 percent of the popular vote and 67.8 percent of the electoral vote.

Although the 2008 election was described as historic because the first African American was elected president, trends evident in past elections persisted. Partisan and ideological voting patterns continued although conservatives voted slightly more Democratic in 2008 than in the two previous presidential elections. The religious division remained; a majority of Protestants voted for the Republican candidate while Catholics, closely divided in 2000 and 2004, voted more heavily Democratic due in large part to the increase of Hispanics in the electorate. Obama won the votes of moderates and Independents.

The gender gap, which had been 11 percent in 2000 and 5 percent in 2004, expanded to 13 percent in 2008, with 56 percent of women voting for Obama. Younger voters favored the Democratic candidate by more than two to one. The Republican lock on certain states' electoral vote was also broken by Democratic victories in Virginia, North Carolina, Colorado, and Indiana. Obama won all the competitive battleground states with the exception of Missouri.

In 2008, the electorate made a retrospective judgment. More than three out of four voters thought that the country was "seriously off on the wrong track" and most blamed the Bush administration for the unsatisfactory conditions. People wanted change; they saw Obama as the candidate most likely to achieve it.

There was some prospective voting. The electorate was closer to McCain than Obama on many issues; however, the high level of dissatisfaction and the deteriorating economy proved to be more influential on the election outcome than policy preferences.[42] Those preferences, however, were to become a problem for Obama when he pursued his government-oriented domestic agenda.

The economic recession and its aftermath plagued the Obama administration throughout the next four years. Although the Democrats controlled both Houses of Congress by large margins in 2009 and 2010 and succeeded in enacting a $787 billion stimulus package of government spending and state grants, their impact on the economy was slow and uneven. Unemployment remained high, over 8 percent throughout most of the election cycle; job creation lagged; income levels stagnated; the gap between rich and poor increased; and most people's evaluation of the economy remained fair or poor. A majority of Americans still thought the country was on the wrong track.

Although the president was personally popular, his policies were not. With the Republicans gaining seats in the Senate and a majority in the House in the 2010 midterm elections, cooperation between Congress and the White House declined; the president's legislative agenda stalled. Each party blamed the other for the impasse. President Obama advocated issue stands that coincided with the help-the-middle-class theme that he was to articulate in his reelection campaign; Republican candidates took conservative stances that appealed to partisan activists likely to determine the 2012 nomination's outcome.

Obama used his personal appeal to his advantage. The final exit poll in 2012 indicated that 10 percent more voters perceived him to be more in touch with the people like themselves and more likely to pursue policies that favored the middle class than Romney[43] (see Table 9.2). Not only did voters see the president to be more empathetic but also more competent and honest. The negative attacks on Romney's character that stereotyped him as a profit-driven business executive, a conservative ideologue in the tradition of George W. Bush, and a candidate of, by, and for the wealthy made an impact, particularly on Independents.[44] Romney's much quoted reference to the 47 percent of Americans that didn't pay taxes and were dependents on government welfare programs reinforced the Democrats' critique of him.

Only on the attribute of economic leadership did Romney lead Obama but only barely. Voters also saw president as *almost* as likely as Romney to fix the economy, undercutting the principal argument of the Romney campaign that Obama's economic policies had failed (and implicitly, would continue to do so).

On most of the policy issues, voters evaluated Obama more highly than Romney. Surprisingly, the Affordable Care Act to which Republicans in general and congressional Republicans in particular were so critical also benefited the president. Of the 18 percent who saw health care as most important, 75 percent said they voted for Obama; those who deemed the budget deficit as most important (15 percent) voted two to one for Romney. With the war in Iraq over and troops being withdrawn from Afghanistan, foreign policy was not a major concern in the 2012 presidential election, but to the extent people saw it as important, Obama benefited (see Table 9.2).

In summary, with the electorate divided over which candidate would provide stronger economic leadership, Obama won the personal attribute and policy issue debates, contributing to his victory in a country that was divided politically and viewed the economy more negatively than positively.

TABLE 9.2 | PERSONAL QUALITIES AND ISSUE VOTING IN THE 2012
PRESIDENTIAL ELECTION

Percent of Voters		Obama	Romney
Most important personal qualities			
21	Cares about people like me	81	18
18	Is a strong leader	38	61
27	Shares my values	42	55
29	Has a vision for the future	45	54
Most important issues			
59	Economy	47	51
18	Health care	75	24
15	Budget deficit	32	66
5	Foreign policy	56	33

Source: National exit poll conducted by Edison Media Research for most national news organizations and found on their web sites.

Familiar voting patterns within the body politic continued through the 2012 election cycle. Partisanship and ideology correlated highly with voting. More than 90 percent of self-identified partisans supported their party's nominee. Ideological trends also remained strong with more than 80 percent of liberal and conservatives voting Democratic and Republican, respectively; moderates (41 percent of those who identified their ideological preference in the exit poll) preferred Obama by 15 percent.

In an age of partisan parity, the outcome of the 2012 election hinged on the turnout of the electorate. Obama's campaign increased the pool of likely voters by maximizing participation of ethnic and racial minorities that tend to vote Democratic. The president received 71 percent of the Hispanic vote that increased to 10 percent of the total electorate; it had been 9 percent four years earlier. He also got 73 percent of the Asian American vote that also increased in size. Obama's vote among African Americans was larger than it was in 2008. For the first time, African American turnout exceeded that of the white majority.

Obama did better among younger, poorer, and less well-educated voters; Romney's support came from people that were older, had higher incomes, and achieved higher education levels—with one exception, the voters with the most education, those with postgraduate degrees, preferred Obama. There was also a large gender gap in 2012, a 16-point difference between the votes of men and women. Young, unmarried women, in particular, were supportive of the president; older white men were much more likely to vote for Romney. Religiosity continued to help the Republicans—the more religious activities in which people were engaged, the more likely they were to vote Republican. However, the proportion of the population participating in these activities may be declining. Twenty percent of the voters identified their religious beliefs as some other than Protestant, Catholic, or Jewish or none at all.

TABLE 9.3 | PORTRAIT OF THE AMERICAN ELECTORATE, 2000–2012 (IN PERCENTAGES)

Percentage of 2012 Electorate		2000			2004			2008			2012		
		Bush	Gore	Nader	Bush	Kerry	Other	Obama	McCain	Other	Obama	Romney	Other
	Total vote	48%	48%	3%	51%	48%	1%	53%	46%	1%	51%	47%	2%
Gender													
47	Men	53	42	3	55	44	1	49	48	3	45	52	3
53	Women	43	54	2	48	51	1	56	43	1	55	44	1
Race and ethnicity													
72	Whites	54	42	3	58	41	1	43	55	2	39	59	2
13	Blacks	9	90	1	11	88	1	95	4	1	93	6	1
10	Hispanics	35	62	2	44	53	3	67	31	2	71	27	2
3	Asians	41	55	3	44	56	–	62	35	3	73	26	1
2	Others							66	31	3	58	38	2
Marital status													
60	Married	53	44	2	57	42	1	47	52	1	42	56	2
41	Unmarried	38	57	4	40	58	1	65	33	2	62	35	3
Age													
19	18–29 years	46	48	5	45	54	1	66	32	2	60	37	3
27	30–44 years	49	48	2	53	46	1	52	46	2	52	45	3
38	45–64 years	49	48	2	52	47	1	50	49	1	47	51	3
16	65+ years	47	50	2	52	47	0	45	53	2	44	56	–

continued

TABLE 9.3 | PORTRAIT OF THE AMERICAN ELECTORATE, 2000–2012 (IN PERCENTAGES) *continued*

Percentage of 2012 Electorate		2000			2004			2008			2012		
		Bush	Gore	Nader	Bush	Kerry	Other	Obama	McCain	Other	Obama	Romney	Other
Education													
3	Not H.S. grad	38	59	1	49	50	0	63	35	2	64	35	1
21	H.S. grad	49	48	1	52	47	1	52	46	2	51	48	1
29	Some college	51	45	3	54	46	0	51	47	2	49	48	3
29	College grad	51	45	3	52	46	1	50	48	2	47	51	2
18	Postgraduate	44	52	3	44	55	1	58	40	2	55	42	3
Religion													
53	Protestant*	56	42	2	59	40	0	45	54	1	42	57	3
25	Catholic	47	50	2	52	47	1	54	45	1	50	48	2
2	Jewish	19	79	1	25	74	–	78	21	1	69	30	1
Labor unions													
18	Union household	37	59	3	40	59	1	59	39	2	58	40	2
Income†													
20	Under $15,000	37	57	4	36	63	1	73	25	2	63	35	2
21	$15,000–$29,999	41	54	3	42	57	1	60	37	3	56	42	
31	$30,000–$49,999	48	49	2	49	50	1	55	43	2	46	52	
	$50,000–$74,999	51	46	2	56	43	1	48	49	3			
	$75,000–$99,999	52	45	2	55	45	0	51	48	1			
21	$100,000–$149,999	54†	43†	2†	57	42	1	48	51	1	52		
	$150,000–$199,999				58	42	0	50	50	2	44	54	2
7	$200,000+				63	35	1	52	46	2	44	54	

Family's financial situation is

Better today	25	36	61	2	80	19	1	37	60	2	84	15	1
Same today	41	60	35	3	49	50	1	45	53	2	58	40	2
Worse today	33	63	33	4	20	79	1	71	28	1	18	80	2

Party

Republicans	32	91	8	1	93	6	1	9	90	1	6	93	1
Independents	29	47	45	6	48	49	3	52	44	4	45	50	5
Democrats	38	11	86	2	11	89	0	89	10	1	92	7	1

Ideology

Liberals	25	13	80	6	13	85	2	89	10	1	86	11	3
Moderates	41	44	52	2	45	54	1	60	39	1	56	41	3
Conservatives	35	81	17	1	84	15	1	20	78	2	18	82	3

Employment status

Work full-time for pay	60	48	49	2	53	45	1	55	44	1	49	49	2
Do not work full-time	40	48	47	3	51	49	0	50	48	2	53	45	2

*Includes all Protestants; about half of them indicated that they were evangelical, fundamentalist, and/or "born again" Christians. *This half voted heavily for Romney,* about three-quarters of them.

†For the 2000 election, these numbers represent the response for "Income $100,000 or more," as the last three income categories were not differentiated at that time.

Source: General Exit Poll in 2000 conducted by VNS, a consortium of the major news organizations—ABC, CBS, CNN, FOX, NBC, the Associated Press; General Exit Poll in 2004–2012 conducted by Edison Media Research for the National Election Pool and found on the web sites of major news organizations following the election.

CONVERTING ELECTORAL CHOICE INTO PUBLIC POLICY

It is not unusual for the meaning of the election to be ambiguous. The reasons that people vote for presidents vary. Some do so because of their party affiliation, some because of issue stands, and some because of their assessment of the candidates' potential and their past performance. For most people, a combination of factors contributes to their voting decision. That combination makes it difficult to discern exactly what the electorate means, desires, or envisions by its electoral choice.

THE PRESIDENT'S IMPRECISE MANDATE

The president is rarely given a clear mandate for governing. For a mandate to exist, the presidential candidates must take discernible and different policy positions and the electorate must vote for them primarily because of these positions. Moreover, the results of the election must be consistent. If there is a discrepancy between the popular and the electoral vote, or if one party wins the White House and another wins the Congress, it is difficult for a president to claim an electoral mandate (much less govern).

Few elections meet the criteria for a mandate. Presidential candidates usually take a range of policy stands, sometimes waffle on a few highly divisive and emotionally charged issues, may differ from their party and its other candidates for national office in their priorities and even on some of their issue stands, and rarely have coattails long enough to sweep congressional candidates into office. In fact, the presidential candidates tend to run behind the congressional candidates of their own party in those candidates' legislative districts.

Mandates may not exist, but that has not prevented presidents from claiming them. They do so mainly for political reasons. Winning a large popular and electoral vote and gaining control of Congress creates opportunities that a newly elected president might want to seize.

Professor Patricia H. Conley argues that the elections of 1952, 1964, and 1980 encouraged the winners to claim a policy mandate. Eisenhower's campaign promise to go to Korea, Goldwater's opposition to Johnson's domestic legislative program, and Reagan's rejection of Democratic liberalism provided the electorate with a clear choice of which policy direction it preferred. The winners' sizable victories were interpreted as mandates for these presidents to pursue their policy goals and the initiatives designed to achieve them.[45]

The election of 2008 might also been seen as a mandate, a mandate for change. President George W. Bush was extremely unpopular; a majority of Americans opposed the war in Iraq, and both presidential candidates promised to transform policies and politics. Obama and his fellow Democrats had designed a legislative package of economic and social reforms even before assuming office and succeeded in getting them enacted into law within the administration's first two years in office.

Obama's legislative policy successes, however, failed to produce the discernible economic, social, and political changes he desired and the public expected within the period before the next election. With Republicans becoming even more critical, presidential job approval declining, and support for his health care initiative waning, Democrats lost control of the House of Representatives and seats in the Senate in the 2010 midterm elections. Obama's window of opportunity had closed very quickly as had Clinton's in 1994 and Bush's in 2006.

Even if they occur, mandates are short-lived. In an era of party unity and parity, mandates take on a partisan coloration with success tied to relatively quick, tangible results.

Much of a president's governing problems stem from the campaign itself; candidates may become their own worst enemy. They make more promises than they can deliver and may not establish priorities clearly. Nor do they usually discuss the costs of their proposals, the tradeoffs that may be necessary to achieve them, much less how long it will take for the policy to have an effect on negative conditions.

But candidates do try to redeem most of their campaign promises. They do so because they believe in them, need to maintain their personal and partisan credibility, want to be reelected, and desire a tangible legacy. In a study of campaign promises and presidential performance between the years 1964 and 1984, political scientist Jeff Fishel found that presidents submitted legislative proposals or signed executive orders that were broadly consistent with about two-thirds of the promises they made during their campaign.[46] Of the 532 promises Obama made in his two presidential campaigns, he has kept 45 percent by the end of the sixth year of his presidency, compromised on 25 percent, broken 22 percent, and had the rest stalled or in the works according to the *Tampa Bay Times* web site, politifact.com.[47]

EXPECTATIONS AND LEADERSHIP

There is another problem. When campaigning, candidates also try to create an aura of leadership, conveying such attributes as assertiveness, decisiveness, compassion, and integrity. Kennedy promised to get the country moving, Johnson to continue the New Frontier–Great Society programs, Nixon to "bring us together," and George H. W. Bush to maintain the Reagan policies that produced peace and prosperity for the eight previous years but do so in "a kinder and gentler" way. In 1992, Clinton pledged policy change in a moderate direction and an end to gridlock between Congress and the presidency; in 1996, he promised to build a bridge to the twenty-first century. In 2000, George W. Bush promised to defuse the strident partisan political climate in Washington, and in 2004, to "do whatever it takes" to win the war on terror. Barack Obama promised to change policy and politics in his 2008 campaign and continue his efforts to promote greater opportunities and improve conditions for middle-class Americans in 2012.

This imagery also shapes performance expectations. In the 1976 election, Jimmy Carter heightened these expectations by his constant reference to the strong, decisive leadership he intended to exercise as president. His decline in popularity stemmed in large part from his failure to meet these leadership expectations. After George W. Bush, reelected in large part because voters saw him as a stronger leader than his Democratic opponent, did not exercise such leadership in the aftermath of Hurricane Katrina, his job approval suffered significantly. Barack Obama was thinking of the expectations and the short time he would have to meet them in his speech on the night of his 2008 election victory when he said, "The road ahead will be long. Our climb will be steep. We may not get there in one year or even one term, but America—I have never been more hopeful than I am tonight that we will get there."[48]

All new administrations, and, to some extent, most reelected ones, face diverse and often contradictory demands. By their ambiguity, candidates encourage voters to see what they want to see and believe what they want to believe. Disillusionment naturally sets in once a president begins to make decisions. Political scientist John E. Mueller has referred to the disappointment that people may experience with a president as "the coalitions of minorities variable." In explaining declines in popularity, Mueller notes that presidents' decisions inevitably alienate parts of the coalition that elected them. This alienation usually produces a drop in popularity over the course of an administration.[49]

THE ELECTORAL COALITION AND GOVERNING

Not only does the selection process inflate performance expectations and create a set of diverse policy goals but also it may decrease the president's power to achieve them. Moreover, the anti-Washington, antigovernment mood of the electorate, evident since the 1980s, has given outsiders, who are less experienced in national politics and may as a result be less knowledgeable about the demands of the office when they first assume it, an electoral advantage. Carter in 1976, Clinton in 1992, and Obama in 2008 made much of the fact that they did not owe their nomination to the power brokers within their own party.

But even an experienced Washington hand would face difficulties. The political muscle of the White House has been weakened by the growth of autonomous state and congressional electoral systems; the proliferation of well-organized, well-funded, and well-led interest groups; the decentralization and compartmentalization of power within the government; and divided governement combined with the polarized political environment.

Presidential candidates begin their quest for office largely on their own. They essentially designate themselves to run. They create their own organizations, choose professionals to run them, mount their own campaigns, and make their own promises. So do most members of Congress. Moreover, the coattails that tied party partisans to the winning presidential candidate have all but dissipated. Members of Congress can choose to follow the president's lead or choose not to do so; either way, it is their constituency that will decide their fate, not the president's national popularity.

To win elections, presidential candidates have to mobilize a broad constituency. Nonparty groups play a large role in that mobilization process; they run campaigns within campaigns—contributing and spending money, communicating with their members and sympathizers, and trying to turn out the vote. But they do so with strings attached. They encourage candidates to take policy positions they favor and, if elected, to pursue policies they advocate. They maintain their access to decision makers. Critics argue that interest group leaders "buy" their access with their political contributions and their group's electoral activities. Presidents who deviate from their campaign agenda do so at the risk of alienating these groups.

Presidential campaigns encourage candidates to promise new programs and project an image of leadership. Normally, candidates indicate what they will do if elected, but rarely do they add the caveat "if Congress is willing to do so, if the bureaucracy follows my lead, or if the courts deem it constitutional." There is a disconnect between the campaign promises and leadership images of those who run for the presidency and the reality of the American constitutional system, which divides powers to prevent any one institution from dominating and dictating public policy on its own.

Transitioning to Government

The organization of presidential campaigns, the key players in that organization, and their relationship to the candidate all have important implications for government. A campaign organization reflects the candidate's management style: his or her willingness to take advice, to delegate to others, and to make decisions and adhere to them or adjust them if the situation changes. Reagan's reliance on his campaign staff, his reluctance to second-guess his advisers, augured his White House staffing arrangement and his passive administrative style. Similarly, George W. Bush's hands-off style of management suggested the type of CEO approach he took in his presidency. In contrast, Clinton's penchant for getting into the details of operations and policy matters represented the other extreme. Moreover, his constant desire to assess the public mood before, during, and after he voiced his policy preferences was also reflected in the way in which he did business as president. Obama's emphasis in 2008 on his role as a policy visionary, not bureaucratic manager, has mirrored his style as president, especially his tendency to delegate the formulation and implementation of his public policy goals to others.

A second way in which campaigns affect governance is through the personnel. Presidents tend to hire their campaign workers not only to reward them for their efforts but also because they can depend on their loyalty and work ethic. Many of the principals in the campaign end up in the White House in administrative, policy, and public relations positions. The Center for Responsive Politics regularly identifies public officials who engage in "revolving door" politics, moving in and out of government and using their expertise and contacts in public sector to help them in the private sector and vice versa.[50]

The relationship between the candidate's organization and the party's organization also impacts on governance. Candidates who circumvent their party and its elected officials in the planning and conduct of their presidential campaigns, as Richard Nixon did in 1972, Jimmy Carter in 1976, and, to a lesser extent, Bill Clinton in 1992, find it more difficult to mobilize the necessary political support in Congress.

SUMMARY

Americans are fascinated by presidential elections. They want to know who will win, why the successful candidate has won, and what the election portends for the next four years. Their fascination stems from four interrelated factors: elections are dramatic, decisive, participatory, and affect future leadership and public policy.

Using past elections as a guide, political scientists have tried to construct models to anticipate how the electorate will react to economic, political, and social conditions. The models provide formulas for calculating the percentage of the popular vote the winning candidate is likely to receive on the basis of a combination of quantifiable economic and political variables. They have been reasonably accurate, although they overestimated the size of Gore's popular vote in 2000 and Bush's in 2004 and underestimated Obama's in 2012.

But the United States does not elect a president by direct popular vote. And campaign strategies are based on the politics of the Electoral College. Campaigns matter, especially in the battleground states, so long as an accumulation of factors within the political environment do not overwhelmingly favor one candidate.

To discern how campaigns affect the electorate, researchers constantly monitor public opinion. They do so by analyzing data from national and state opinion polls. The key is to identify likely voters. The electorate is not the public. It is a little more than half the eligible citizenry in a presidential election, around 40 percent or less in a midterm congressional election (in 2014, it was only 36 percent), and as little as 15 percent in a primary.

Polls are also an important instrument for messaging: deciding what to emphasize and how to prioritize, articulate, and target their policy and personal appeals. National opinion polls can be fairly accurate measures of the public mood and candidate preferences at the time the polls are taken. They also provide data, especially the large national exit poll and the American National Election Studies, to help explain the meaning of the election: the issues that are most salient, the positions that are most popular, and the hopes and expectations for the newly elected leaders of government.

The personality of the candidates, the issues of the campaign, and, most importantly, the partisanship of the electorate influence turnout and voting behavior. Singularly and together, these factors, as seen through the prism of partisanship, explain the outcome of the vote. Since 2000, the electorate has been at or near partisan parity. The presidential campaign is concentrated in the most competitive Electoral College states.

Changing demographics have shifted the map of the Electoral College to the Democrats' favor. More red states have become blue states than the reverse. To offset this trend, the Republicans need to expand their electoral base among younger voters and racial and ethnic minorities. To do so they need to upgrade their technology, modify their ideology, and take policy positions that are more appealing to a growing multicultural and racial society.

Where on the Web?

Public Opinion

Access the latest polls about the election from the following sites:

- **Fivethirtyeight.com**
  www.fivethirtyeight.com
- **Gallup Organization**
  www.gallup.com
- **CBS News Poll**
  www.CBSNews.com
- **The Pew Research Center for the People and the Press**
  www.people-press.org
- **Pollingreport.com**
  www.pollingreport.com
- **Roper Center for Public Opinion Research at the University of Connecticut**
  www.ropercenter.uconn.edu
- ***Real Clear Politics***
  www.realclearpolitics.com

Election Results

The web sites of most major news organizations will have the unofficial results as collected by the Associated Press as the election day vote is tabulated. The official results take longer and are reported by the Federal Election Commission several months later after each state has provided the Commission with its total vote including absentee ballots and provisional votes.

Election Analysis

Most major news organizations usually carry the final exit poll in whole or in part on their web sites. In addition, data from the American National Election Studies (www.electionstudies.org) are made available to faculty and students at universities and colleges that are members of the Inter-University Consortium for Political and Social Research beginning about six months after the election is completed.

Exercises

1. Look at polls over the course of the election, and try to explain opinion shifts on the basis of events in the campaign or in the country as a whole. You can obtain a graph of Gallup polling over the course of the election at that organization's web site (www.gallup.com). Other excellent sources are www.realclearpolitics.com and www.fivethirtyeight.com.

2. Look at the results of several national polls at different points in the election cycle to determine how they contrast and compare to one another. If the polls show different results for the same period, try to ascertain which groups were being sampled and their responses reported (the general public, the electorate, registered voters, or most likely voters), whether the same questions were being asked, how many people were surveyed, and the extent to which the results were within the margin of the sampling error.

3. After the election has concluded, access the large exit poll that will appear on the web sites of most major news networks. In your analysis, note how major demographic groups voted, what the primary issues were, how important partisanship and ideology seemed to be, and the feelings voters had toward the candidates and their parties. Are the divisions, evident in past elections, continuing, or do you see changes in the voting patterns of the American electorate?

4. On the basis of the results of the presidential election, write a memo for the winning candidate explaining the meaning of the election: the policy agenda that should be pursued, and the president's chances for achieving it, given the outcome of the congressional elections.

SELECTED READINGS

Abramson, Paul R., John H. Aldrich, and David W. Rohde. *Change and Continuity in the 2012 Elections*. Washington, DC: CQ Press, 2015.

Campbell, James. ed. "Symposium: Forecasting the 2012 American Election." *PS: Political Science and Politics*, 45 (Oct. 2012): 591–668.

"Changing Face of America Helps Assure Obama Victory," Pew Research Center for the People and the Press, November 7, 2012. http://www.people-press .org/2012/11/07/changing-face-of-america-helps-assure-obama-victory/

Conley, Patricia Heidotting. *Presidential Mandates: How Elections Shape the National Agenda*. Chicago: University of Chicago Press, 2001.

Dahl, Robert A. "Myth of the Presidential Mandate." *Political Science Quarterly*, 105 (Fall 1990): 355–372.

Fiorina, Morris. *Retrospective Voting in American National Elections*. New Haven, CT: Yale University Press, 1981.

Jacobson, Gary C. "How the Economy and Partisanship Shaped the 2012 Presidential and Congressional Elections." *Political Science Quarterly*, 128 (Spring 2013): 1–38.

Lewis-Beck, Michael S., and Mary Stegmaier, eds. "Symposium: U.S. Presidential Election Forecasting." *PS: Political Science and Politics*, 47 (April 2004): 284–328.

Lopez, Mark Hugo. "Latino Voters in the 2012 Election," Pew Research Center's Hispanic Trends Project, November 7, 2012. http://www.pewhispanic .org/2012/11/07/latino-voters-in-the-2012-election/

Miller, Arthur H., and Martin P. Wattenberg. "Throwing the Rascals Out: Policy and Performance Evaluations of Presidential Candidates, 1952–1980." *American Political Science Review*, 79 (1985): 359–372.

Panagopoulos, Costas, and Jeffrey E. Cohen, eds. "Symposium on 2012 Presidential Election." *Presidential Studies Quarterly*, 44 (Sept. 2014): 384–521.

Sabato, Larry J., ed. *Barack Obama and the New America*. Lanham, MD: Roman and Littlefield, 2013.

Sides, John, and Vavreck, Lynn. *The Gamble: Choice and Chance in the 2012 Presidential Election.* Princeton, NJ: Princeton University Press, 2013.

Weiner, Marc D., and Gerald M. Pomper. "The 2.4% Solution: What Makes a Mandate?" *The Forum,* 4 (2006). www.bepress.com/forum/vo4/iss2/art4

Winneg, Kenneth, Kathleen Hall Jamieson, and Bruce W. Handy. "Party Identification in the 2012 Presidential Election." *Presidential Studies Quarterly,* 44 (March 2014): 143–155.

NOTES

1. Michael S. Lewis-Beck and Charles Tien, "Proxy Models and Nowcasting: U.S. Presidential Elections in the Future," *Presidential Studies Quarterly,* 44 (Sept. 2012): p. 541.

2. Some critics attributed the incorrect estimates of the final popular vote to ideological bias. They see political scientists as liberal-leaning and Democrats—hence more favorable to Gore than Bush. Others, however, contended that the 2000 election was unique, or at least different from previous elections. Bill Clinton's personal digressions may also have been a factor that none of the models included. Perhaps the economy didn't help the Democrats as much as in the past because the prosperity had lasted too long and people had become complacent.

3. For a discussion and synopsis of the 2004 model forecasts, see Alan I. Abramowitz, James E. Campbell, Robert S. Erikson, Thomas M. Holbrook, Michael S. Lewis-Beck, Helmut Norpoth, Charles Tien, and Christopher Wiezien, "Forecasting the 2004 Presidential Election," *PS: Political Science and Politics,* 37 (Oct. 2004): pp. 733–767.

4. James E. Campbell, ed., "Symposium: Forecasting the 2008 National Elections," *PS: Political Science and Politics,* 41 (Oct. 2008): pp. 679–707.

5. James Campbell, ed., "Symposium: Forecasting the 2012 American National Elections," *PS: Political Science and Politics,* 45 (Oct. 2012): pp. 591–668. Others who participated in the symposium include Alan Abramowitz, Michael Bednarczuk, Michael Berry, Kenneth Bickers, James Campbell, Alfred Cuzan, Robert Erikson, Douglas Hibbs, Thomas Holbrook, Florian Hollenbach, Bruno Jerome, Veronique Jerome-Speziari, Carl Klarner, Michael Lewis-Beck, Brad Lockerbie, Jacob Montgomery, Helmut Norpoth, Charles Tien, Michael Ward, and Christopher Wiezien.

6. "Federal Elections 2012: Election Results for the U.S. President, the U.S. Senate and the U.S. House of Representatives," Federal Election Commission, July 2013. http://www.fec.gov/pubrec/fe2012/federalelections2012.pdf

7. "The Final Days of the Media Campaign 2012," Pew Research Center's Project for Excellence in Journalism, November 19, 2012. http://www.journalism. org/2012/11/19/final-days-media-campaign-2012/

8. Nate Silver, "When Internal Polls Mislead, a Whole Campaign May Be to Blame," *New York Times,* December 1, 2012. http://fivethirtyeight.blogs.nytimes .com/2012/12/01/when-internal-polls-mislead-a-whole-campaign-may-be-to -blame/?_php=true&_type=blogs&_r=0

9. "Polling Data," *Real Clear Politics.* www.realclearpolitics.com/epolls/2012 /president/us/general_election_romney_vs_obama-1171.html

10. Costas Panagopoulos and Benjamin Farrer, "Preelection Poll Accuracy and Bias in the 2012 General Elections," *Presidential Studies Quarterly,* 44 (June 2014): p. 353.

11. However, pollster Nate Silver also notes that polls conducted over the final three weeks of the campaign are more apt to be accurate than the final poll an organization conducts if that organization changes its assumptions and methods to conform to the results that other polls are getting. Nate Silver, "Which Polls Fared Best (and Worst) in the 2012 Presidential Race," *New York Times*, November 10, 2012. www://fivethirtyeight.blogs.nytimes.com/2012/11/10/which-polls-fared -best-and-worst-in-the-2012-presidential-race/?_php=true&_type=blogs&_r=0

12. Gallup, perhaps the country's best-known polling organization, also overestimated Obama's 2008 vote and the Republicans' 2010 congressional vote.

13. In the early polls, personal interviews were held in people's homes, a method that put respondents at ease. Establishing a personal relationship with the people being interviewed was thought to contribute to the truthfulness of their responses. But home interviewing was slow and costly for polling organizations. During the 1980s, telephone interviews replaced personal visits; random-digit dialing was used to reach both listed and unlisted numbers.

    Automated dialing, recorded messages, and eventually computerized calling greatly increased the number of phone calls people received, especially in the evening when they returned home from work. Complaints about being constantly disturbed by callers, particularly telemarketers, led Congress to enact legislation that allowed people to place their phone numbers on the Federal Communication Commission's "Do Not Call List." Survey researchers, nonprofit organizations, bill collection agencies, and companies with whom a person had done business were exempted from the call prohibition. These exceptions encouraged some telemarketers to pretend they were conducting a survey in order to gain information about respondents and also to sell a product to them. As the calls persisted, the "hang up" rate and number of noncompleted surveys rose.

14. "Assessing the Representative of Public Opinion Surveys," Pew Research Center for the People and the Press, May 15, 2012. http://www.people-press .org/2012/05/15/assessing-the-representativeness-of-public-opinion-surveys

15. Sometimes pollsters try to compensate weighting the demographic characteristics of their online sample with those of the population as a whole. Such a process decreases but does not remove the bias. Silver, "Which Polls Fared Best."

16. Daniel J. Hopkins, "No Wilder Effect, Never a Whitman Effect: When and Why Polls Mislead about Black and Female Candidates," *Journal of Politics*, 71 (2009, No. 3): pp. 769–781.

17. "Gallup 2012 Presidential Election Polling Review," Gallup Poll, June 4, 2013. http:// www.gallup.com/poll/162887/gallup-2012-presidential-election-polling-review.aspx

18. Silver, "Which Polls Fared Best."

19. Tom Webster, "Edison Successfully Conducts the 2012 National Election Exit Polls," Edison Research, November 10, 2012. http://www.edisonresearch.com /edison-successfully-conducts-the-2012-national-election-exit-polls/.

20. In general, turnout declined more in the East and Midwest than it did in the West in 1980. Even if there was a decline after Carter's concession, there is little evidence to suggest that Democrats behaved any differently from Republicans and Independents. Hawaii, the last state to close its polls, voted for Carter.

21. Raymond Wolfinger and Peter Linquiti, "Tuning In and Turning Out," *Public Opinion,* 4 (Feb./March 1981): pp. 57–59; Harold Mendelsohn and Irving Crespi, *Polls, Television, and the New Politics* (Scranton, PA: Chandler, 1970), pp. 234–236.

22. Sandra Sobieraj, "The Story Behind the Near-Concession." Associated Press, (Nov. 8, 2000). www.ap.org

23. Morris P. Fiorina, *Retrospective Voting in American National Elections* (New Haven, CT: Yale University Press, 1981).

24. Morris P. Fiorina, Samuel J. Abrams, and Jeremy C. Pope, *Culture War: The Myth of a Polarized America*, 3rd ed. (New York: Longman, 2010).

25. Presidents will not be blamed for natural disasters or even acts of terrorism over which they have no control, but they will be evaluated on how quickly and effectively they react to cataclysmic events, empathize with the victims, and provide the help to them. The Bush administration's late and ineffective response to Hurricane Katrina significantly and negatively affected public perceptions of the president's management style while Obama's rapid and personal response to Hurricane Sandy, which occurred a week before the 2012 election, helped him.

26. It can also be seen as a social identity and value. Partisans vote on the basis of their identities and beliefs.

27. For a very interesting article on the impact of emotions on learning, perceptions, and voting, see George E. Marcus and Michael B. Mackuen, "Anxiety, Enthusiasm, and the Vote: The Emotional Underpinnings of Learning and Involvement During Presidential Campaigns," *American Political Science Review*, 87 (Sept. 1993): pp. 672–685.

28. The electorate saw the Republicans as better able to deal with the problems of fighting communism, promoting efficiency in government, and ending the war than the Democrats and evaluated Eisenhower's leadership skills more highly than Stevenson's. For an analysis of the components of the 1952 presidential election, see Angus Campbell, Philip E. Converse, Warren E. Miller, and Donald Stokes, *The American Voter* (New York: Wiley, 1960), pp. 524–527.

29. Kennedy's Catholicism may have enlarged his Electoral College total by 22 votes. See Ithiel de Sola Pool, Robert P. Abelson, and Samuel Popkin, *Candidates, Issues, and Strategies* (Cambridge, MA: MIT Press, 1965), pp. 115–118.

30. For a discussion of the 1964 presidential election, see Philip E. Converse, Aage R. Clausen, and Warren E. Miller, "Election Myth and Reality: The 1964 Election," *American Political Science Review*, 59 (June 1965): pp. 321–336.

31. Philip E. Converse, Warren E. Miller, Jerrold G. Rusk, and Arthur C. Wolfe, "Continuity and Change in American Politics: Parties and Issues in the 1968 Election," *American Political Science Review*, 63 (Dec. 1969): p. 1097.

    Wallace claimed that there was not "a dime's worth of difference" between the Republican and Democratic candidates and their parties. He took great care in making his own positions distinctive. The clarity with which he presented his views undoubtedly contributed to the issue orientation of his vote. People knew where Wallace stood and liked him or didn't like him because of his policy positions.

32. Arthur H. Miller, Warren E. Miller, Alden S. Raine, and Thad A. Brown, "A Majority Party in Disarray: Policy Polarization in the 1972 Election," *American Political Science Review*, 70 (Sept. 1976): pp. 753–778.

33. Arthur H. Miller and Warren E. Miller, "Partisanship and Performance: Rational Choice in the 1976 Presidential Elections," paper presented at the annual meeting of the American Political Science Association, Washington, DC, September 1–4, 1977.

34. Warren E. Miller, "Policy Directions and Presidential Leadership: Alternative Interpretations of the 1980 Presidential Election," paper presented at the annual meeting of the American Political Science Association, New York, September 3–6, 1981.

35. J. Merrill Shanks and Warren E. Miller, "Alternative Interpretations of the 1988 Election," paper presented at the annual meeting of the American Political Science Association, Atlanta, Georgia, August 31–September 3, 1989, p. 58.

36. Paul R. Abramson, John H. Aldrich, and David W. Rohde, *Change and Continuity in the 1988 Elections* (Washington, DC: CQ Press, 1990), p. 195.

37. Had Perot not run, it is unlikely that the results of the election would have been any different. Exit polls of Perot voters indicate that they would have divided their votes fairly evenly between Clinton and Bush, although the number of people casting ballots would undoubtedly have declined.

38. Gore's advisers contended that they had no choice. Their surveys indicated that Clinton was a liability, that he turned off swing voters, and that the electorate was tired of his scandal-plagued administration and wanted a change. What they did not calculate was the extent to which Clinton energized the Democratic base.

39. For an excellent discussion on the influence of third-party candidates, see Samantha Luks, Joanne M. Miller, and Lawrence R. Jacobs, "Who Wins? Campaigns and the Third Party Vote," *Presidential Studies Quarterly,* 33 (March 2003): pp. 9–30.

40. "Topics from A–Z: Party Images," Gallup Poll (2010). www.gallup.com /poll/24655/Party-Images.aspx#2

41. Kenneth Winneg and Kathleen Hall Jamieson, "Party Identification in the 2008 Presidential Election," *Presidential Studies Quarterly,* 40 (June 2010): pp. 205–251.

42. Paul R. Abramson, John H. Aldrich, and David W. Rohde, *Change and Continuity in the 2008 Elections* (Washington: DC: CQ Press, 2010), p. 168.

43. Andrew Kohut, "Misreading Election 2012," *Wall Street Journal,* November 13, 2012. http://www.wsj.com/articles/SB10001424127887323894704578113231375465160.

44. David B. Holian and Charles Prysby, "Candidate Character Traits in the 2012 Presidential Election," *Presidential Studies Quarterly,* 44 (Sept. 2014), p. 503.

45. Patricia Heidotting Conley, *Presidential Mandates: How Elections Shape the National Agenda* (Chicago: University of Chicago Press, 2001), pp. 77–115.

46. Jeff Fishel, *Presidents and Promises* (Washington DC: CQ Press, 1994), pp. 38, 42–43.

47. "Obamameter," *Tampa Bay Times.* http://www.politifact.com/ (accessed January 7, 2015)

48. Barack Obama, "Victory Speech," *Huffington Post,* November 4, 2008. www.huffingtonpost.com/2008/11/04/obama-victory-speech_n_141194.html

49. John E. Mueller, *War, Presidents, and Public Opinion* (New York: Wiley, 1973), pp. 205–208, 247–249.

50. Midway through President Obama's second term, the center identified 557 individuals who had moved from the administration to the private sector. The implication was that their public access, information, and contacts work to enhance their own private interests and those of the organizations that employ them.

REFORMING THE ELECTORAL SYSTEM

CHAPTER 10

INTRODUCTION

The American political system has evolved significantly since the second half of the twentieth century. Party rules, finance laws, and media coverage are now very different from what they were before the 1960s. The composition of the electorate has changed as well, with the expansion of suffrage to all citizens eighteen years of age or older and the continuing modification of legal procedures for voting. Some of these procedures have made it easier to vote such as simplifying registration procedures, obtaining absentee ballots, and extending the time for voting, and some have made it harder, such as requiring a government issued photo identification in order to vote or shortening the period in which votes can be cast. Campaigning for president has changed as new communication technologies have enabled the parties and their nominees to measure public opinion, focus resources in the most competitive states, and target and personalize appeals to specific groups of potential voters.

Have these changes been beneficial or harmful? Have they improved the democratic character of the political system? Have they made the elections more efficient, more representative, and more legitimate in the eyes of voters?

These questions have elicited a continuing, and sometimes spirited, debate, but no consensus.

Critics allege that the electoral process is too long, too costly, too burdensome, too error prone, and too easily subject to discretionary decisions by state election officials and to manipulation by the parties, candidates, and their supporters. They claim that it wears down candidates and numbs voters and that it results in too many personal accusations and too little substantive discussion, too much name-calling and "sound bite" rhetoric, and too little real debate on the issues. They have said that many qualified people are discouraged from running for office; much of the electorate is uninformed, uninterested, and uninvolved; and a sizable proportion of the citizenry still do not vote.

Other criticisms are that the system benefits the wealthy and the special interests; encourages factionalism; weakens the party's control over the campaign of its presidential and vice presidential candidates; overemphasizes personality and underemphasizes policy; encourages deceptive claims, exaggerations, and allegations; and is unduly influenced by news media motivated more by audience size and economic gain than public service.

In contrast, proponents argue that the political system is seen as more legitimate and operates more democratically than ever before. There are relatively few disputed elections; people abide by the results; and the number of people voting has increased, particularly in presidential elections. Candidates, even lesser-known ones, now have an opportunity to run for office and in the process demonstrate their competence, endurance, motivation, and leadership skills. Parties remain important as vehicles through which the system operates and by which governing is accomplished. Those who defend the electoral system believe voters do receive as much information as they desire and enough to make informed and reasoned judgments. Most voters believe that as well according to postelection surveys conducted by the Pew Research Center for the People and the Press.[1]

The old adage "where you stand influences what you see" is applicable to the debate about electoral reform. No political process is completely neutral. There are always winners and losers. To a large extent, the advantages that some enjoy are made possible by the disadvantages that others encounter. Rationalizations aside, much of the debate about the system—about equity, representation, and responsiveness—revolves around a very practical, political question: Who benefits, and who does not?

Proposals to change the system need to be assessed in the light of this question. They should also be judged on the basis of how such changes would affect the operation of the electoral system, the agenda and composition of government, and the public policies made by elected officials. This chapter discusses some of these proposals and the effect they could have on the road to the White House. The chapter is organized into two sections: The first deals with the more recent developments and proposed modifications of party rules, campaign finance regulations, and media coverage; and the second examines the long-term, democratic issues of citizen participation, representation, and equity in the electoral process. Throughout this discussion, basic questions central to a democratic electoral process are addressed.

MODIFYING RECENT CHANGES IN PARTY RULES

Of all the changes that have recently occurred, the reforms in the nomination process, particularly the selection of delegates, have engendered the most controversy and resulted in the most persistent fine-tuning. Designed to encourage grassroots participation and broaden the base of representation, these reforms have also extended the nominating period, made the campaign more expensive, and the need for early money more critical. They have also generated candidate-based organizations, weakened the influence of some state and local party leaders, converted conventions into coronations, and loosened the ties between the parties and their nominees. All of these consequences have made governing more difficult.

Since 1968, when the Democrats began to rewrite their rules for delegate selection, the parties have suffered from unintended repercussions of their rules changes. Each succeeding presidential election has seen reforms to the reforms, modifications that have attempted to reconcile expanded participation and representation with the traditional need for party unity and campaign oversight and with the goal of successfully pursuing a partisan agenda in government. Although less reform-conscious than the Democrats, the Republicans have also tried to steer a middle course between greater rank-and-file involvement and more equitable representation on the one hand and the maintenance of successful electoral and governing coalitions on the other.

How to balance these often competing goals has been a critical concern. Those who desire greater public participation have lauded the trend toward having more primaries and a larger percentage of delegates selected in them. Believing that the reforms have opened up the process and made it more democratic, participatory advocates favor the continued selection of delegates based on the proportion of the popular vote that they or the candidate to whom they are pledged receive. In contrast, those who believe that greater control by state and national party leaders is desirable argue that the reforms have gone too far and that extended nomination campaigns have fractionalized the parties and disadvantaged their standard-bearers in the general election. They would prefer fewer primaries, a smaller percentage of delegates selected in them, more unpledged delegates and party leaders participating in the nominating conventions, and a larger role for state and national party organizations during the entire presidential campaign.

WHO SHOULD PARTICIPATE IN THE CAUCUSES AND PRIMARIES?

Party rules have consistently sought to limit participation in its primary elections to registered or self-declared partisans, although such restrictions are difficult to enforce in practice. The participation of Independents and crossover voting by the partisans of the other party has remained a contentious issue and a strategic choice that candidates for the nomination must consider. Do they direct their appeals to Independents as John McCain and Barack Obama did in 2008 or appeal primarily to their own party partisans as Hillary Clinton did in 2008 and most Republican candidates did in their party's 2012 nomination process?

From the party's perspective, the issue of allowing nonpartisans to participate dilutes the influence of party regulars and creates the possibility of selecting a nominee who does not best reflect the interests, needs, or ideological views of most of the party's rank and file. A special fear is that adherents of the other party will cross over to vote for the weaker opposition candidate in order to enhance their own nominee's chances in the general election.

On the other hand, from the perspective of the citizenry, a primary closed to all but registered partisans precludes much of the population from participating and reduces the incentive for nonparticipants to become informed and get involved during the election cycle. Moreover, it allows party elites, interest group leaders, and a relatively small number of wealthy people to extend their influence over the process and the outcome; it also permits partisan activists, who tend to have the strongest ideological convictions, to exercise disproportionate influence on the candidates, encouraging them to adhere to the beliefs and issue positions of a narrower group of partisans rather than a broader cross section of the party and the electorate. Political parties can benefit from an open primary system if it leads to the recruitment of more active supporters or makes their nominees more electable.

HOW SHOULD THE VOTES BE ALLOCATED?

Another rules issue concerns the allocation of votes in primaries. Since 1992, the Democrats have used a straight proportional voting system that allocates pledged delegates according to the percentage of the popular vote they or the candidate to whom they are committed receives. The Republicans have permitted the states to decide on the method of allocation, which could be proportional or winner-take-all within districts or on an at-large basis; in 2012, new GOP rules required states that held their contests before April to select convention delegates on the basis of a proportional vote; this requirement was modified for 2016 but remains in effect for states that hold their contests from the official opening of the calendar, March first, until the middle of that month. After that, states can decide how they wish to allocate their delegates.

Proportional voting more closely reflects the view of a state's primary electorate, but it also could have the effect of extending the nomination, delaying a consensus on the eventual nominee, and costing more money, as it did in 2008 for the Democrats and in 2012 for the Republicans.[2] The more divided the party going into its nominating convention, the weaker its candidates are likely to be in the general election, or so the thinking has been within the national leadership of both major parties. The election of Barack Obama, after an extended and highly competitive nomination process, has not reversed this judgment.

The elimination of unpledged superdelegates by the Democrats has made a potential undemocratic outcome to their selection process much less likely.

SHOULD THE NOMINATION PROCESS BE SHORTENED?

Some people have urged that the period during which presidential nominations occur be condensed. Professor Thomas E. Patterson has argued that an extended nomination "disrupts the policy process, discourages the candidacies of responsible officeholders, and wears out the voters."[3] It also diverts public attention from issues of government to campaign-related controversies and does so many months before the general election campaign begins. Moreover, Patterson notes that a long election cycle generates more negative news about the candidates as the campaign progresses, thereby souring voters on the choices they have on primary day and creating image problems for the candidates in the general election.[4]

Several proposals have been made for addressing the issue of excessively long campaigns. Some have even been introduced in the form of legislation in Congress. A simple change would be to limit the period during which caucuses and primaries can be scheduled to two or three months and perhaps also shorten the period during which candidates can raise money for their nomination campaigns. As noted in previous chapters, the invisible primary starts for most candidates and the news media before or during the year preceding the election. A second proposal would cluster primaries and caucuses, forcing states in designated regions or groups to hold their elections on the same day. A third plan, which is already in effect, provides incentives for states to schedule their contests later in the spring, but there have been few takers. A fourth idea is to create a national primary.

Spreading out the caucuses and primaries reduces the impact of frontloading. It gives more candidates a better chance to demonstrate their qualifications. It provides more time for voters to evaluate the candidates. It also weakens the news media's influence on public opinion, which is greatest at the beginning of the nomination process when less is known about the candidates.

Both major parties have attempted to frame their nomination process by specifying the time frame in which primaries and caucuses can be held. But getting states to adhere to that time frame is difficult. The threat of reducing or eliminating their convention delegation has not prevented states, such as Michigan and Florida, in recent nominations from holding their contests before the parties' imposed window for scheduling caucuses and primaries officially opens. If conventions were decision-making bodies, if the winning candidate did not care about unifying the party, and if the states that violated party rules were not seen as critical in the general election, then a party's sanctions might be sufficient to bring recalcitrant states in line. But alas, they have not been.

As a consequence, both Democratic and Republican party rules now permit four states (Iowa, New Hampshire, Nevada, and South Carolina) to hold their nomination contests before others may do so. The parties have also tried to schedule the starting date for caucuses and primaries later in the calendar year but with only partial success. Holding them later may increase public awareness, but it may also provide more time for raising and spending money. What seems probable, however, is that the first day that all states are allowed to hold their caucus or primary, the first Tuesday in March 2016, will have a disproportionate number of contests; it will be Super Tuesday.

CAN FRONT-LOADING BE PREVENTED?

Front-loading, which has continued to be a problem, creates inequities. It gives greater influence to those states that hold their contests earlier and less to those that hold them later. To the extent that voters in the early states are not representative of the party's rank and file, much less the electorate as a whole, they can generate momentum for a candidate who may not be the first or most acceptable choice for the party and may as a consequence be disadvantaged in the general election.

Front-loading helps well-known and well-financed candidates. Conversely, it hurts long shots that must raise more money more quickly and must also enter more contests to demonstrate their electoral viability if they have the staff and resources to do so. If not, they must make strategic choices of where to campaign. Without a strong on-the-ground effort, lesser-known candidates must rely on mass media to reach voters in large states. In short, a compressed calendar of caucuses and primaries reduces the likelihood that a non-front-runner can win the party's nomination.

From the perspective of a democratic political system, perhaps the most negative aspect of front-loaded campaigns is that the decisive stage of the nomination process occurs before most people are paying attention to electoral politics. By the time the party's electorate tunes in during and after the Iowa caucuses and the New Hampshire primary, the field has already thinned out. Moreover, there is little incentive for the public to stay attentive or even turn out to vote in later contests once the nominee has been effectively determined. Add to this problem the fact that front-loading presidential caucuses and primaries so early also may separate them from the nomination contests of other party candidates within the state, thereby reducing the link between the party's presidential standard-bearer and other nominees seeking elective office.

SHOULD REGIONAL PRIMARIES BE INSTITUTED?

The nomination process could be regionalized, with states in different regions required to hold their caucuses and primaries on the same day. Since the 1980s, there have been voluntary agreements among states in some regions to do so. The case for regional primaries is based on the assumption that such a system would be more equitable for the states, providing more focus for the candidates and, ultimately, benefits for the region.

As long as the regions adopted some plan to rotate their nomination dates, which they do not do at present, each of them over time would be able to exercise approximately equal influence in the selection of a party's nominee. Moreover, candidates would be forced to address regional concerns and appeal to regional interests. A nomination that extended to the four regional primaries would probably ensure that the winning candidate had broader-based geographic support, the kind of support that is necessary to win in the Electoral College.

But regionalization is not without its critics, who fear that it would exacerbate sectional rivalries, encourage local or area candidates, and produce more candidate organizations to rival those of the state and national parties. Moreover, like straight proportional voting, a regional primary system could impede the emergence of a consensus national candidate, thereby extending the process to the convention and increasing, not decreasing, burdens on the nominees in the general election. In addition, regional primaries help the best-organized and best-financed candidates in the region and require more resources be devoted to the mass media.

SHOULD A NATIONAL PRIMARY BE HELD?

Another option, and the one that represents the most sweeping change, would be to hold a national primary. The heavily front-loaded schedule in recent presidential nominations has created a *de facto* jumbo primary on Super Tuesday, the first Tuesday when all states are permitted to hold nominating elections, much to the dismay of the leaders of both major parties that object to the concentration of so many contests on the same day.

Congress has been cool to idea of a national primary, but the general public seems to favor it. The most recent Gallup Poll on the issue conducted in July 2013 indicated that 58 percent of the public favors such a proposal to the present patchwork system, 33 percent were opposed.[5] Most proposals for a national primary call for it to be held in the late spring or early summer, followed by party conventions. Candidates who wanted to enter their party's primary would be required to obtain a certain number of signatures. Any aspirant who won a majority of that party's vote would automatically receive the nomination. In some plans, a plurality would be sufficient, provided it was at least 40 percent of the total vote. In the event that no one received 40 percent, a runoff election could be held several weeks later between the top two finishers, or the national nominating convention could choose from among the top two or three candidates. In any event, nominating conventions would continue to be held to select the vice presidential candidates, to decide on the platforms, and to determine party rules.

A national primary would be consistent with the "one-person, one-vote" principle that guides most aspects of the U.S. electoral system and a democratic selection process. All participants would have an equal vote in the selection.[6] No longer would voters in the states that held the early caucuses and primaries exercise more influence.

It is also likely that a national primary would stimulate turnout. It would give more people more incentive to get involved, to work for the candidates, and to vote. A national primary would probably result in an outcome more representative of the party's electorate than is currently the case.

A single primary election for each party would accelerate a nationalizing trend. Issues that affect the entire country would be the primary focus of attention, forcing candidates to address the problems they would most likely debate in the general election and initially confront as president.

Moreover, the results of the election would be clear-cut. The person with the most votes would be the winner. The media could no longer interpret primaries and caucus returns as they see fit. An incumbent's ability to garner support through the timely release of grants, contracts, and other spoils of government might be more limited in a national contest, but it would not be eliminated entirely. The president would continue to have an organizational, financial, and status advantage.

On the other hand, such an election would undoubtedly discourage challengers who lacked national reputations. No longer could an early victory catapult a relatively unknown aspirant into the position of serious contender or jeopardize a president's chances for renomination. In fact, lesser-known candidates, such as George McGovern, Jimmy Carter, Michael Dukakis, and even Bill Clinton in 1992, might find it extremely difficult to raise money, build an organization, and mount a national campaign. Barack Obama would certainly have had a harder time beating Hillary Rodham Clinton in 2008 without his victory in Iowa.

From the standpoint of the major parties, a national primary might further weaken the ability of party leaders to influence the selection of the nominees. Moreover, a post-primary convention could not be expected to tie the nominee to the party, although it might tie the party to the nominee, at least through the general election and longer, if that nominee were victorious.

Whether a national primary winner would produce the party's strongest candidate is also open to question. With a large field of contenders, those with the most devoted or ideological supporters might do best. On the other hand, candidates who do not arouse the passions of the diehards, but who are more acceptable to the party's mainstream, might not do as well. Everybody's second choice might not even finish second, unless systems of approval voting or cumulative voting were used.[7] Approval or cumulative voting systems, however, complicate the election, confuse the electorate, and lead some to question the validity of the results, undercutting the legitimacy of the electoral process.

A national primary would lessen the ability of states to determine when and how their citizens would participate in the presidential nomination process, although they would still be responsible for holding caucuses and primaries for other candidates for federal and state office.

Finally, a national primary would in effect produce two presidential elections every four years. Could public attention be maintained throughout the entire election cycle? Could sufficient money be raised? If so, by which candidates—those who are personally wealthy or have reputation and position to attract such support? Could the candidates' grassroots organizations handle such a task, not once but twice? These questions have tempered widespread support within the parties for a national primary despite the general appeal of the idea to the public.

Recently, several political scientists have proposed a combination of rotating small-state primaries followed by a national primary.[8] Their plan calls for randomly selecting about one dozen small states and allowing them to hold their contests—caucuses or primaries—in which candidates would compete. Later in the spring or early summer, a national primary would be held in which voters in all states would be able to participate.[9] The parties could limit the number of candidates based on their success in the small-state contests or allow anyone to enter. If no one received a majority, a runoff election could be held or the national nominating convention could decide among the top candidates.

The architects of this plan believe that partisans of both the small and large states would benefit. The small states would essentially narrow down the field, and people in all the states could then decide on the nominee. This idea reverses the logic of delegates at the Constitutional Convention in 1787 who thought that the large states, with the most electoral votes, would choose the top candidates, but in all likelihood, no one, other than George Washington, would have the required Electoral College majority. Thus, the House of Representatives, voting by states, would select the president and vice president.

The merits of combining a state and national vote are that it might contribute to a more representative selection process in which partisans in both small and large states would exercise more equal influence over the selection of the nominee than occurs in the current nomination process. Not only would a national primary encourage more people to participate but it might also put them in a position to select the most qualified candidate based on candidate performance in the small-state elections.[10]

There are several problems with this hybrid selection process, however. Would the small states, such as Iowa and New Hampshire, agree to a selection lottery? Would the large states be willing to allow the small states to participate twice? Would a combined process save money or be more expensive? Would it extend or shorten the nomination process? Would it favor front-runners or provide greater opportunities for non-front-runners than currently exist? Would it make for a more enlightened public choice? Would people that register as Independents be able to vote in a national primary or would that vary, as it currently does, from state to state?

THE PERILS OF CAMPAIGN FINANCE

Closely related to the delegate selection process are the laws governing campaign finance. These laws were first enacted in the 1970s in reaction to the secret and sometimes large illegal bequests to candidates, the disparity in contributions and spending among the candidates, and the spiraling costs of modern campaigns, particularly television advertising. The finance laws were designed to improve accountability and transparency, reduce spending, subsidize nominations, and fund the general election. Some of these objectives have been partially achieved; others have not, but unintended and what many consider to be undesirable consequences have also resulted from the laws and Supreme Court decisions on them.

The laws have taken campaign finance out of the back rooms and put much of it into the public spotlight. They have also, however, created a nightmare of compliance procedures and reporting requirements. Detailed records of practically all contributions and expenditures of the presidential campaign organizations must now be kept and periodically reported to the Federal Election Commission.[11] Accountants and attorneys, specializing in election law, are now as necessary as pollsters, image makers, mass marketers, grassroots organizers, and experts in digital technologies.

CAN CAMPAIGN CONTRIBUTIONS AND EXPENDITURES BE EFFECTIVELY LIMITED?

The hard-money, soft-money, independent-spending conundrum remains. The Supreme Court has said that corporations, and by inference, labor unions, candidate-oriented groups, and individuals may engage in free speech without limits imposed on their election giving and spending. Although some of these groups remain subject to the disclosure provision of the Bipartisan Campaign Reform Act (BCRA), they can circumvent these provisions by donating money to intermediaries—nonparty groups—which spend some or all of it on political activities during election campaigns and even after them.

Can these loopholes be closed? Yes, say some members of Congress who introduced legislation to limit spending by corporations that receive $50,000 or more in government contracts or corporations that are owned or controlled by foreigners. The legislation, known by its acronym DISCLOSE (Democracy Is Strengthened by Casting Light on Spending in Elections), would have also increased disclosure requirements. Enacted by the House of Representatives in 2010, when the Democrats were in control, the bill died in the Senate.

Soft money, given to 527s and 501c groups, continues to be an issue although not as much of a problem in recent elections after Super PACs were allowed to raise and spend unlimited amounts. The prohibition on nonparty groups coordinating their spending with parties and candidates remains but has led to confusion by voters and complaints by candidates that they are unable to control the information, imagery, and political discourse in their election campaigns even though many of them hire the same political consulting firms as their Super PAC supporters. Most nonparty group expenditures are used for negative advertising, ads that can mislead and may turn off voters, but seem to energize partisans.

One fear that has not come to pass, however, is that the ban on the national parties soliciting soft money would hurt their fund-raising. Since 2004, the major parties have raised more in hard money than they had in hard money and soft money combined previously. And in 2008 and 2012, Barack Obama in the general election raised record amounts for his campaign. The ability to do so from private donors has rendered the public funding provisions of campaign finance laws obsolete for the principal candidates of the major parties.

CAN PUBLIC FUNDING BE SAVED?

Despite the benefits of public funding that made presidential elections more equitable, broadened the field of potential contenders, increased competition at the beginning of the process, lessened to some extent dependence on large contributions from wealthy donors, and at least initially reduced the amount of time candidates had to spend raising funds, there has been little public outcry about its demise. Suspicion of politicians, opposition to federal "give-away programs," and fear of tax increases and larger government expenditures that would be required to replenish the treasury's campaign fund have lessened public support for federal funding. In 2012, only 6 percent of taxpayers checked off the box on their tax form that allows $3 of their taxes to go to the national campaign fund.[12] And that percentage is expected to decline even further in the years ahead.

Can public funding be saved? Perhaps, the question is how. Several recommendations have been proposed:

- Raise the limits on spending for candidates that accept federal funds;
- Provide matching grants for candidates that qualify for them earlier in the nomination process rather than waiting until the calendar year of the election to do so;
- Allow candidates to supplement their public funds with private contributions.

The Obama campaigns in 2008 and 2012 have demonstrated that Internet solicitation can generate a large number of small but steady contributors.

Alternatively, Congress could follow the lead of several European countries by prohibiting private contributions entirely and providing the parties or their candidates with a larger amount of money with which to campaign, but there seems to be little support for such a proposal at this time in the United States.

The campaign finance quandary at its most basic level is one of competing values: The freedom to spend on behalf of one's interests, beliefs, and opinions versus the equality of citizens in affecting campaign issues, debate, and election outcomes. In a democratic political system in which the vote and presumably the voice of all citizens should be equal, the wealthy should not have an advantage, but in a free and open society, everyone should be able to voice their opinions and spend their personal resources as they see fit. Here is the problem: how to ensure that candidates have sufficient funds, that freedom of speech is protected, that political equality is promoted, and that the public has sufficient information to make an informed judgment. No wonder campaign finance reform has proven to be so difficult, so controversial, and seemingly insoluble.

PUBLIC AWARENESS AND KNOWLEDGE

For the electorate to make an enlightened judgment, people must have sufficient and accurate information about the candidates and parties, their policy positions, and campaign promises. They also must have some knowledge about the candidates' past experience and the parties' record while governing. Past performance is a criterion for anticipating future behavior.

Is the amount and type of information available in contemporary campaigns sufficient for people to make an informed judgment when voting? As we previously noted, most voters continue to answer "yes" to this question, but political scientists and other students of election behavior are not so sure. Almost everyone agrees that the more information people have about the candidates, issues, and parties, the better able they will be to cast an enlightened vote. But how much information is necessary and desirable to do so? And what type of information does the electorate currently receive?

Changes in communication technology have made more information available and accessible, but surveys do not indicate that the public is more knowledgeable about electoral politics than in the past.[13] Selective exposure to a partisan news media combined with personalized and microtargeted campaign appeals provide voters with information most likely to reinforce their beliefs and opinions. Massive advertising directed toward the competitive states echoes and exaggerates campaign themes. Fact checks receive much less attention.

What can be done to enhance the quantity and quality of information about the election that the public receives? Would providing candidates with free time on the news media to respond to allegations and claims made by their opponents help? Some claim that it would,[14] but getting or requiring news media organizations to give free time to all candidates would be difficult, given the media costs, their first amendment rights, and profit motives.

IS CAMPAIGN NEWS COVERAGE SATISFACTORY?

Critics say "no," pointing to news media bias and spin and to the emphasis on the horse race, campaign strategy, and personal behavior at the expense of more substantive discussion of policy issues.

To augment public knowledge, scholars have suggested that the major news networks and wire services assign special correspondents to cover the policy issues of the campaign, much as they assign people to report on its color, drama, and personal aspects. Others have suggested that the press place greater emphasis on campaign coverage, that they assess the accuracy of the statements and advertising claims of the candidates, and that they indicate the potential costs and benefits of the policy proposals the candidates offer.

In addition to criticizing press coverage of the campaign, academicians and others have called into question the amount and accuracy of election reporting. Other than requiring fairness, preventing obscenity, and ensuring that public service commitments are met, there is little the government can do to regulate the news media without impinging on the First Amendment that protects freedom of the press. The news media can choose which elections and candidates to cover, what kind and how much coverage to provide them, how to interpret the results of primaries and caucuses, and even predict who will win before the election is concluded. These choices, however, tend to be exercised by the news networks with public preferences in mind. Not only do corporations that own media affiliates engage in constant private polling to discern the interests of their viewers, listeners, and readers, but people "vote" every day when they turn on a particular program on radio or television or buy a particular newspaper or magazine.

There is much that candidates can do, however, to affect the coverage they receive. If their words are unreported or not reported correctly, or if their ideas are misinterpreted or their motives suspected, they can seek other mass media formats to reach the general public, as they have done by using the entertainment and talk shows, maintaining their own web sites, and through social networking. They can also employ satellite technology to reach local and regional audiences directly and thereby circumvent the national networks and news services. Unfortunately, candidates can also restrict press access to them, make unsubstantiated claims and accusations about an opponent, and provide or leak negative and inaccurate information to the news media. The reduction of news staffs by the major news organizations has also reduced their investigative capacities and made journalists more dependent on information they receive from others involved in the campaigns, including candidate organizations.

DOES EARLY EXIT POLL REPORTING AFFECT VOTING DECISIONS AND ELECTION OUTCOMES?

Another media-related issue is the election-night predictions based on exit polling data that the networks air before all voting has been completed. Beginning in 1984, the networks promised not to forecast the results in any state until a majority of its polls had closed, although they violated that promise in reporting the exit poll results and projecting the winner in Florida in 2000.

Are early-night forecasts really a problem? After all, public opinion polls on the election's probable outcome are being reported right up to election day. People watch the early returns, to learn the outcome to celebrate or commiserate with their friends and family accordingly. Although political scientists have found that the early forecasts may depress turnout in states in which the polls are still open, they have found little evidence that these predictions affect overall results of the vote.[15] Nonetheless, the perception that a problem exists is itself a problem, one that has forced Congress on several occasions to hold hearings on the matter and the news organization to abide by their promise not to "call" an election within a state until a majority of its polls have closed.

SHOULD ELECTION-NIGHT REPORTING BE CHANGED?

Americans are glued to their television sets on election night. They want to know who has won. The national news networks with their anchors and well-known reporters provide a running account replete with victory and concession statements by the candidates, remarks by campaign aides, and commentary by political experts. Exit poll data are often reported, usually more to predict outcomes than to understand who voted for whom and why. Viewers and listeners have to trust that the data are accurate and that the sample is sufficiently large and properly weighted to permit generalizations—assumptions that are not always true. Local stations are given a few minutes to report local results, but the major networks focus on the presidential election and, to a lesser extent, that of Congress. The print media, especially the major national newspapers, can do a more comprehensive job.

What is not provided in election-night coverage is in-depth analyses of the policy implications of the election outcome for the country. In addition to a demographic analysis, who voted for whom and why, the public would benefit from a more sophisticated understanding of what public perceptions were at the time of the election, the policy preferences of the newly elected public officials, the new administration's legislative and executive priorities, the compatibility of the people who were elected with one another and those who remain in the government, and the likelihood of the newly elected or reelected president and Congress being able to form governing coalitions along partisan, issue, or ideological lines. But whether reporters, weary of the campaign and eager to end the election story, are in a position to provide such information and the electorate is willing to absorb it is another matter.

ENHANCING THE DEMOCRATIC CHARACTER OF PRESIDENTIAL ELECTIONS

How can the structure and conduct of presidential elections be more consistent with a democratic electoral process? Increasing voter turnout, improving the quantity and quality of information that is available to the electorate, and having the results reflect public opinion more closely would help promote democratic values and produce a more democratic electoral process.

IS NONVOTING A PROBLEM IN U.S. ELECTIONS?

Many political scientists would say "yes."[16] They would point to the gap between those eligible to vote and those who actually do so. This gap, which will always exist in a system that does not compel voting, widened during the last forty years of the twentieth century. In 1996, for the first time since 1920, more than half of those eligible chose not to vote; in 2012, 42 percent of the eligible citizenry and 46 percent of the voting-age population did not do so;[17] in the 2014 midterm elections, about 64 percent of people who were eligible did not vote.[18]

Low turnout in a free and open electoral system has been a source of embarrassment to the United States and of concern to its political leaders for several reasons. It weakens their credibility when promoting democracy abroad if it is practiced so lackadaisically at home. Moreover, the demographic differences between voters and nonvoters—those in the electorate are more educated with higher incomes than the general population—increase the influence gap within the political arena, advantaging the advantaged. Those with more education and higher incomes regularly exercise more influence over the outcome of elections, the agenda of government, and its public policy decisions. Disparities in political participation reinforce and even widen the division between the "haves" and "have-nots." The income gap between the rich and poor is increasing.

If nonvoting is considered a problem in a democratic electoral process, then what can and should be done about it? Should people be encouraged to vote? Should they be forced to do so?

How Can More Citizens Be Encouraged to Vote?

The national government and some of the states have been trying to make it easier for people to vote. We have discussed some of the ways in which Congress has tried to facilitate voting.

Ease Government-Imposed Regulations

The enactment of the "motor-voter" bill in 1993 has made registration easier. The Help America Vote Act (HAVA) in 2002 provided money to computerize and consolidate state voter registration lists, make voting more accessible to the disabled and to non-English-speakers, protect the integrity of the voting process, and permit provisional voting by people whose registration is challenged at the time they vote. The law also created the U.S. Election Assistance Commission (EAC) to oversee its implementation. Thus far, the law has helped improve the accuracy of registration lists, provided money for new voting machines, and reduced the number of incidences of voter intimidation and fraudulent voting practices.

More needs to be done, however, according to the Commission on Federal Election Reform, which studied voting problems and electoral issues following the 2004 election. The commission recommended a series of measures: a universal system of voter registration for the entire country, uniform procedures for counting provisional ballots and determining voter eligibility, a country-wide system of voter identification, and civic education programs for the general public. It also urged states to restore voting rights to ex-felons who have served their sentences.[19] Other suggestions include electronic voting machines with a paper ballot backup system.[20]

After his reelection, President Obama appointed a Bipartisan Voting Commission to examine problems of voter access and to improve the administration of elections. In a letter to the president dated January 2014, the commissioners recommended:

- modernization of the registration process through continued expansion of online voter registration and expanded state collaboration in improving the accuracy of voter lists;
- improved access to the polls through expansion of the period for voting before the traditional election day, and through the selection of suitable, well-equipped polling place facilities, such as schools;

- state-of-the-art techniques to assure efficient management of polling places, including tools the Commission is publicizing and recommending for the efficient allocation of polling place resources;
- reforming the standard-setting and certification process for new voting technology to replace soon-to-be antiquated voting machines and encourage innovation and the adoption of widely available off-the-shelf technologies.[21]

Although both commissions' proposals would improve the integrity of voting in the United States, might make it easier for people to vote, which, in turn, could decrease the economic discrepancies between voters and nonvoters, it is unlikely that the reforms would eliminate these problems entirely or vastly increase turnout. Making it easier to vote is not the same thing as encouraging people to vote. Congress has not acted on these reports.

Other suggestions to make registration automatic, as it is in many European countries and in the state of Oregon, or to extend it to election day itself, as is already permitted in a few states, have also been advanced. Counties or states that have facilitated registration in these ways have considerably higher levels of turnout than those that have not. But whether these states are better governed and/or their elections are perceived as fairer and more reflective of popular choice has become a debatable issue.

Over the past decade, a number of states have established new voter identification requirements to prevent fraudulent voting. Democrats contend that these requirements disproportionately affect minorities who are less likely to have the needed ID credentials, such as a driver's license or passport. The Supreme Court has upheld the right of states to require voter IDs, but many of the laws have continued to be challenged in federal court.

Make Election Day a Holiday or Nonworkday

Another idea to enhance turnout would be to make election day a national holiday or move it to Veterans Day, which comes later in the month. Presumably, either change would prevent work-related activities from interfering with voting as much as they currently do for a large number of would-be voters. Many countries follow the practice of holding their elections on a holiday or Sunday.

There are problems with each of these proposals, however. An additional national holiday would cost employers millions of dollars in lost revenue and productivity, with no guarantee that turnout would increase. Moreover, veterans would probably object to having politics obscure the meaning for which the Veterans Day holiday was intended—to honor those who served and sacrificed for their country. For workers in certain service sectors, Sunday or a national holiday might still be a workday.

Some states have extended the period for voting up to twenty-one days prior to the election to increase the number of voters.[22] Others have enacted a "no-fault" absentee ballot system for those who find it difficult or inconvenient to get to the polls on election day. Under a liberalized absentee voting procedure, any eligible voter can obtain an absentee ballot with no questions asked. A majority of states currently provide one or both of these options. Oregon and Colorado have gone so far as to institute a mail ballot, and turnout in those states now exceed the national average.

Extending the voting period and balloting by mail are not without their costs, however. Fear of fraud if the ballots get into the wrong hands is one concern. Voting without all pertinent information is another. People who vote early do so without knowing what may be revealed or happen after they cast ballots but before the campaign has ended. They may, in effect, be overly influenced by a candidate's targeted advertising and grassroots activity, make a spur-of-the-moment decision, and then, if state law permits, be asked to vote. Candidates who lack the money, digital technology, and field organization to match their opponents, such as Kerry in Ohio in 2004 and McCain and Romney in several of the close competitive states in 2008 and 2012, have been disadvantaged by early voting. In the last two presidential elections, about 30 percent of the electorate voted before election day.

Conduct Citizen Education Campaigns

Educating the people on the merits of participating and the responsibilities of citizenry might also generate greater involvement and a higher turnout. If the public better understood what difference it makes who wins, if people had greater confidence that elected officials would keep their promises and that government would address salient issues, then more citizens might vote.

Professor Heather Gerken, an elections expert at Yale Law School, has suggested that turnout could be increased if states and local governments measured how democratic their elections systems actually were by using an index based on the proportion of eligible voters who were registered, who actually voted, and the accuracy of the vote count itself. She is counting on the competitive spirit of state and local governments to increase their electoral democracy.[23] Gerken's proposal would not require national legislation, although it might require additional funding to collect the data necessary for the local and state indexes.

But invigorating the electoral environment and encouraging more people to vote are not easy tasks. If they were, they would have already been accomplished. It is difficult to convince people who are not that interested in politics and do not see what difference it makes to them who wins to educate themselves, participate in campaigns, and turn out to vote.

If, however, more people voted on a regular basis, the parties and candidates would have to broaden, not narrow, their appeals. They would have to address the needs and desires of all the people and not concentrate on those who are most likely to vote for their candidates, partisans and independent leaners. Those who have not participated as frequently in the current voluntary system of voting—the poorer, less educated, and younger—would receive more attention not only from candidates but also from elected officials. More equitable public policies from the perspective of these groups might result.

Encourage Grassroots Campaigns
Another way to increase turnout is for party and nonparty groups to continue to devote more resources to get-out-the-vote activities as they have done in recent elections. Turnout has increased, particularly in the competitive battle-ground states. In the nonbattleground states, however, the increase has been more modest. Nonetheless, by maximizing their base vote and appealing to new voters as well as Independents, Bush in 2004 and Obama in 2008 and 2012 helped enlarge their electorate. But too much emphasis placed on maxi-mizing a partisan base also further divides the electorate into warring camps, gives party activists and interest group leaders more influence, and polarizes the political environment, which in turn results in the election of public offi-cials that may be less prone to compromise. In such an environment, shifts in party control of government are also apt to be more disruptive and produce more changes in public policy.

Change the Electoral System Entirely
The Electoral College does not encourage turnout in the noncompetitive states. Neither does having noncompetitive, single-member districts for the election of members of Congress. Replacing the Electoral College with a direct popular vote and either making single-member districts more competitive or converting them into multimember districts in which congressional candidates would be chosen on the basis of the proportion of the vote that they or their party receive would increase turnout.

But systemic reforms are difficult to accomplish. They upset the estab-lished political order and are likely to generate opposition from those who fear the changes would adversely affect them. Some of these proposals would re-quire a constitutional amendment, which is always harder to enact than legis-lation. As a consequence, major alterations of the election system in the United States are not likely to be implemented in the short run or in the absence of a major political upheaval or crisis.

Require Voting as an Obligation of Citizenship
Another proposal would be to compel people to vote as an obligation of citizenship. Penalties could be imposed on those who refused to do so. A num-ber of countries require their citizens to vote, and their turnout is high.

One obvious problem with forcing people to vote is the compulsion itself. Some people may be physically or mentally incapable of voting. Others may not care, have little interest, and have very limited political knowledge. They might not even know the names of the candidates. Would the selection of the best-qualified person be enhanced by the participation of uninformed, unin-terested, and uncaring voters? Might demagogy be encouraged or even slicker and more sophisticated advertising designed and targeted to a dumbed-down electorate? Would government be more responsive and more popular, or would it be more prone to what British philosopher John Stuart Mill referred to as "the tyranny of the majority"?

Finally, is it democratic to force people to vote? If the right to vote is an essential component of a democratic society, then what about the right not to vote—isn't that an important right that should be protected as well? In short, the turnout issue is a difficult one to resolve. There are costs and benefits in enlarging the electorate as well as in the ways that this enlargement is achieved. Greater participation would probably produce a more representative election outcome but not necessarily a more informed or enlightened one. It would reduce the bias that now exists between the voters and nonvoters, but it might also result in a more contentious political environment that spills over into the operation of government. It would probably result in a more representative government but not necessarily a more efficient one nor one capable of making better public policy decisions.

Should the Electoral College be Modified or Abolished?

In addition to the problem of who votes, another source of contention is how the votes should be aggregated. Theoretically, the Constitution allows electors chosen by the states to vote as they please. In practice, most votes are cast for the popular-vote winner of the state. Electors are chosen for their partisan allegiances and are expected to vote for their party's nominees.

This *de facto* system has been criticized as undemocratic, unrepresentative of minority views within states, and potentially unreflective of the nation's popular choice. Most Americans want to abolish it according to polls taken over the last two decades.[24] Candidate strategies to win the Electoral College vote focus on the key battleground states in which less than one-third of the population lives.[25]

The campaign's concentration on the competitive states not only excludes most Americans from seeing the presidential candidates up close or even in television advertising, but it also skews the campaign away from the issues in the noncompetitive states, discourages people in the nonbattleground states from voting, creates the false impression that the results of the election represent a countrywide judgment, and correspondingly gives the winner a national mandate.

Over the years, there have been numerous proposals to alter the presidential voting system. The first was introduced in Congress in 1797. Since then, there have been more than 500 others. In urging changes, critics have pointed to the Electoral College's archaic design, its electoral biases, geographic unevenness, and the undemocratic results it can produce and did in 2000 (see Chapter 1).

Eliminate the Electors
The electors in the Electoral College have been an anachronism since the development of the party system. Their role as partisan agents is not and has not been consistent with their exercising an independent political judgment. In fact, twenty-nine states plus the District of Columbia prohibit such a judgment

by requiring electors to cast their ballots for the winner of the state's popular vote. The Supreme Court has upheld such laws in its decision in the case of *Ray v. Blair* 343 U.S. 214 (1952) but has not ruled on the penalties that these laws prescribe for faithless electors, which are usually quite modest, such as a small fine.

One proposal is to simply do away with the electors entirely and the danger that they may exercise their personal preferences rather than the preferences of the people who elected them. First proposed in 1826, this suggestion has received substantial support, including the backing of Presidents John Kennedy and Lyndon Johnson. The Automatic Plan, as it is called, keeps the Electoral College intact but eliminates the electors. Electoral votes are automatically given to the candidate who has received the most popular votes in the state.

Other than removing the potential problem of faithless or unpledged electors, which has not been a major problem to date, the plan would do little to change the system as it currently operates. There have in fact been only a few faithless electors who failed to vote for their party's nominees—eight since 1948.[26] In 2000, one District of Columbia elector submitted a blank ballot to protest the District's lack of voting representation in Congress. Four years later, one Democratic elector from Minnesota made a mistake and voted for John Edwards for president and John Kerry for vice president.[27] In short, faithless electors have not been much of a problem, not one of sufficient magnitude to justify a constitutional amendment.

Apportion the Electoral Vote to the Popular Vote

Electing the entire slate of presidential electors has also been the focus of considerable attention. If the winner of a state's popular vote takes all the electoral votes, the impact of the dominant party is increased. As noted previously, the presidential candidates give more attention to the more competitive states.

From the perspective of the other major party and minor parties within the state, this winner-take-all system is neither desirable nor fair. In effect, it does not provide representation for people who do not vote for the winning candidate. And it does more than that: It discourages a strong campaign effort by a party that has little chance of winning the presidential election in that state, such as Democrats in Utah or Alaska or Republicans in Hawaii or Rhode Island. Naturally, the success of other candidates of that party in those states is affected as well. The winner-take-all system reduces voter turnout in noncompetitive states.

One way to rectify this problem would be to have proportional voting. Such a plan has been introduced on a number of occasions in Congress; in 2004, it appeared as an initiative on the Colorado ballot. But the voters of that state wisely rejected it because it would have reduced Colorado's influence in the Electoral College. A proportional voting system only makes sense for individual states if *all* states adopt such a system. Under a proportional system, the electors would be abolished, the winner-take-all principle would be eliminated, and a state's electoral vote would be divided in proportion to the popular vote the candidates received within the state. A majority of votes in the Electoral College would still be required for election. If no candidate obtained a majority, most proportional voting plans call for a joint session of Congress to choose the president from among the top two or three candidates.

Proportional state voting for president would have a number of major consequences if adopted on a nationwide basis. It would decrease the influence of the most competitive states and increase the relative importance of the less competitive ones. Having the electoral vote proportional to the popular vote provides an incentive to all the parties, not simply the dominant one, to mount a more vigorous campaign and establish a more effective on-the-ground organization. This incentive could strengthen the other major party within the state, but it might also encourage third party and independent candidates as well, thereby weakening the two-party system. Ross Perot, who received no electoral votes under the present winner-take-all system, would have received approximately 102 under the proportional plan in 1992 and 49 in 1996. Bill Clinton would not have received a majority of the electoral votes in 1992 or 1996 if they had been determined on the basis of the proportion of the vote he received in individual states (see Table 10.1).

A proportional state electoral vote would give third-party candidates, such as Perot and Nader, potentially more influence to effect the outcome of the election by instructing their electors to vote for one of the major party candidates or less likely, cast their vote for the candidate they prefer and thereby force the House of Representatives (controlled by one of the major parties) to determine the winner.

Selection by the House weakens a president's national mandate and might encourage the major party candidates to make promises or grant favors to legislators in exchange for their support (such as what was done in 1876). Such actions could decrease presidential influence during the initial period of an administration and reward regional or state interests at the expense of the national interest. And what happens if the leading candidate is of one party and a majority of state delegations in the House of Representatives is of the other? Would legitimacy of the result be enhanced under that arrangement?

Operating under a proportional plan would probably make the Electoral College vote much closer, thereby reducing the claim of a broad mandate most presidents want to make. George H. W. Bush would have defeated Michael Dukakis by only 43.1 electoral votes in 1988, Jimmy Carter would have defeated Gerald Ford by only 11.7 in 1976, and Richard Nixon would have won by only 6.1 in 1968. The election of 2000 would have been even closer, with Bush winning by less than 1 electoral vote; in 2004, he would have won by 16.9. And in at least one recent instance, a proportional electoral vote in the states might have changed the election results. Had this plan been in effect in 1960, Richard Nixon would probably have defeated John Kennedy by 266.1 to 265.6 (see Table 10.1).

TABLE 10.1 | VOTING FOR PRESIDENT, 1956–2012: FOUR METHODS FOR AGGREGATING THE VOTES

Year	Electoral College	Proportional Plan	District Plan	Direct Election (Percentage of Total Votes)
1956				
Eisenhower	457	296.7	411	57.4
Stevenson	73	227.2	120	42.0
Others	1	7.1	0	0.6
1960				
Nixon	219	266.1	278	49.5
Kennedy	303	265.6	245	49.8
Others (Byrd)	15	5.3	14	0.7
1964				
Goldwater	52	213.6	72	38.5
Johnson	486	320.0	466	61.0
Others	0	3.9	0	0.5
1968				
Nixon	301	231.5	289	43.2
Humphrey	191	225.4	192	42.7
Wallace	46	78.8	57	13.5
Others	0	2.3	0	0.6
1972				
Nixon	520	330.3	474	60.7
McGovern	17	197.5	64	37.5
Others	1	10.0	0	1.8
1976				
Ford	240	258.0	269	48.0
Carter	297	269.7	269	50.1
Others	1	10.2	0	1.9
1980				
Reagan	489	272.9	396	50.7
Carter	49	220.9	142	41.0
Anderson	0	35.3	0	6.6
Others	0	8.9	0	1.7
1984				
Reagan	525	317.6	468	58.8
Mondale	13	216.6	70	40.6
Others	0	3.8	0	0.4

Year	Electoral College	Proportional Plan	District Plan	Direct Election (Percentage of Total Votes)
1988				
Bush	426	287.8	379	53.4
Dukakis	111	244.7	159	45.6
Others	1	5.5	0	1.0
1992				
Bush	168	203.3	214	37.5
Clinton	370	231.6	324	43.0
Perot	0	101.8	0	18.9
Others	0	1.3	0	0.6
1996				
Clinton	379	262.0	345	49.2
Dole	159	219.9	193	40.7
Perot	0	48.8	0	8.4
Others	0	7.3	0	1.7
2000				
Gore	266[*]	259.9[†]	250	48.4
Bush	271	260.3	288	47.9
Nader/Others	0	17	0	2.7
2004				
Kerry	251[‡]	258.3	221	48.3
Bush	286	275.2	317	50.7
Nader	0	4.5	0	1.0
2008				
Obama	365	283.4	296	52.9
McCain	173	246.9	242	45.7
Others	0	8.5	0	1.4
2012				
Obama	332	271.18	264	51.06
Romney	206	257.94	274	47.21
Others	0	8.88	0	2.73

[*] One Democratic elector in the District of Columbia cast a blank electoral vote to protest the District's absence of voting representation in Congress.

[†] If the vote were divided just between the two major candidates in 2000, the electoral vote would have been 268.77 for e Gore and 269.23 for Bush.

[‡] A Minnesota elector mistakenly voted for Edwards for president and Kerry for vice president.

Sources: Figures on proportional and district vote for 1952–1980 were supplied to the author by Joseph B. Gorman of the Congressional Research Service, Library of Congress. Calculations from 1984 to the present were made by the author on the basis of data reported in the *Almanac of American Politics* (Washington, DC: National Journal, annual), *America Votes* (Los Angeles, CA: Sage/CQ Press, annual) and by the Federal Election Commission.

Choose Electors in the Same Way as Members of Congress
Another proposal aimed at reducing the effect of winner-take-all voting is to choose electors in the same way a state chooses its members of Congress. Instead of selecting the entire slate on the basis of the statewide vote for president, only two electoral votes would be decided in this manner. The remaining votes would be allocated on the basis of the popular vote for president within individual districts (probably congressional districts). Maine and Nebraska currently employ such a district voting system.

In 2008, one of Nebraska's congressional districts, the one that included the city of Omaha and surrounding areas, voted for Obama while the other two congressional districts and the state overall voted for McCain, giving the Republican candidate four of the state's five electoral votes; in 2012, they all went for Romney. Under this plan, a majority of the electoral votes would still be necessary for election. If the vote in the Electoral College were not decisive, then most district plans call for a joint session of Congress to make the final selection.

For the very smallest states, those with three electoral votes, all three electors would have to be chosen on a statewide basis. For others, however, the combination of district and at-large selection would probably result in a split electoral vote, especially in the larger states. On a national level, this change should make the Electoral College more reflective of the partisan division of the newly elected Congress rather than of the popular division of the national electorate.

The losers under such an arrangement would be the large, competitive states and, most particularly, the cohesive, geographically concentrated groups within those states. The winners would include small states. Third parties, especially those that are regionally based, might also be aided to the extent that they were capable of winning specific legislative districts.

Republicans would benefit more from such an arrangement than Democrats. If the 1960 presidential vote were aggregated on the basis of one electoral vote to the popular-vote winner of each congressional district and two to the popular-vote winner of each state, Nixon would have defeated Kennedy 278 to 245, with fourteen unpledged electors, and in 2012, Romney would have defeated Obama, 274 to 264. In 1976, the district system would have produced a tie, with Carter and Ford receiving 269 votes each (see Table 10.1).

Elect the President by Direct Popular Vote
Of all the plans to alter or replace the Electoral College, the direct popular vote has received the most attention and public support. Designed to eliminate the College entirely and count the votes on a nationwide basis, it would elect the popular-vote winner provided the winning candidate received a certain percentage of the total national vote. In most plans, 40 percent of the total vote would be necessary.[28] In some, 50 percent would be required. In the event that no one got the required percentage, a runoff between the top two candidates would be held to determine the winner.[29]

A direct popular vote would, of course, remedy a major problem of the present system—the possibility of electing a nonplurality president. It would better equalize voting power both among and within the states. The large competitive states would lose some of their electoral clout by the elimination of the winner-take-all system. Party competition within the states and perhaps even nationwide would be increased. A direct election would force the candidates to campaign in population centers, appeal to urban and suburban voters, and would give them more justification for claiming a national mandate.

Critics, however, see a direct popular vote, particularly a close one, as more likely to nationalize and thereby aggravate problems, such as meeting the eligibility requirements, fraudulent voting practices, and tabulation errors like the ones that Florida experienced in 2000. A national election would probably cost more and the campaign might be longer. Less populated, rural areas, particularly in the mountain states, Hawaii, and Alaska, might be neglected. An election decided primarily by voters concentrated on the Atlantic and Pacific coasts would not provide the geographic balance that reflects the system's federal design. Finally, a plurality winner might not receive an Electoral College majority. In seven out of the twenty-five elections in the twentieth century and one out of four in the twenty-first century, the winner did not receive 50 percent of the popular vote.

A direct election, however, might also encourage minor parties to enter and compete more vigorously, which could weaken the two-party system. The possibility of denying a major party candidate 50 percent of the popular vote might be sufficient to entice a proliferation of third-party and independent candidacies and produce a series of bargains and deals in which support might be traded for favors and appointments in new administration which might even look more like a multiparty coalition than one in which one party controls the executive branch.

The organized groups that are geographically concentrated in the large industrial states would have their votes diluted by a direct election. Jewish voters, for example, highly supportive of the Democratic Party since World War II, constitute less than 2.5 percent of the total population but 14 percent in New York, one of the larger states. Thus, the impact of the New York Jewish vote is magnified under the present Electoral College arrangement, as is that of Hispanic voters in Florida, Texas, and other southwestern states, and California, and that of Christian fundamentalists and evangelicals in the South.[30]

There are partisan issues as well. Republicans perceive that they would be disadvantaged in a direct popular vote. The only Republican to win a popular majority since 1988 has been George W. Bush who received 50.7 percent of the 2004 vote. Looking into the future, Republicans are also nervous about demographic trends: the increase in racial and ethnic minorities as well as younger voters, groups that have voted heavily Democratic in recent elections.

A very close popular vote could also cause problems in a direct election. The winner might not be evident for days, even months. Voter fraud could have national consequences. Under such circumstances, large-scale challenges by the losing candidate would be more likely and would necessitate national recounts rather than confining such recounts to individual states, as the current Electoral College system does.

The provision for the situation in which no one received the required percentage of the popular vote has its drawbacks as well. A runoff election would extend the length of the campaign and add to its cost. Considering that some aspirants begin their quest for the presidency even before the start of the two-year election cycle, a more protracted process might unduly tax the patience of the electorate and produce an even greater numbing effect than currently exists. Moreover, it would also reduce an already short transition period for a newly elected president and would further drain the time and energy of an incumbent seeking reelection.

There is still another difficulty with a contingency election. It could reverse the order in which the candidates originally finished. This result might undermine the ability of the eventual winner to govern successfully. It might also encourage spoiler candidacies. Third parties and Independents seeking the presidency could exercise considerable power in the event of a close contest between the major parties. Imagine Perot's influence in a Bush–Clinton runoff in 1992 or Nader's in a Gore–Bush runoff in 2000. Nonetheless, the direct election plan is supported by public opinion and has been ritualistically praised by contemporary presidents. Gallup polls have indicated that a sizable majority favoring a direct popular vote to the current electoral system.[31]

In 1969, the House of Representatives actually voted for a constitutional amendment to directly elect the president and vice president, but the Senate refused to go along. Despite public support, it seems unlikely that sufficient impetus for a change that requires a constitutional amendment will occur until the issue becomes salient to more people and states that believe they currently have an advantage with the Electoral College system decide to forgo their perceived advantage in the interest of a larger democratic objective. Don't hold your breath!

With the likelihood of a constitutional amendment remote, proponents of a direct popular vote have come up with another idea to achieve the same goal—an interstate compact in which states would agree to join together to pass identical laws that award all of their electoral votes to the presidential candidate who won the most popular votes in the country as a whole regardless of which candidate won the state's popular vote. The compact would not take effect, however, until it was agreed to by states that constitute a majority of the Electoral College. Otherwise, there would be no assurance that the candidate with the most popular votes would win in the Electoral College.[32]

The practical merit of such a plan is that it would not require a constitutional amendment; it would also allow states to retain their authority for choosing their electors and for deciding how they should vote. Ten states and the District of Columbia with a total of 165 electoral votes had formally agreed to join such a compact, although other states are also considering it.[33]

SUMMARY

There have been changes and continuities in the way we select a president. In general, the changes have made the system more democratic. The continuities link the system to its constitutional roots and its republican past.

The nomination process has been affected more than the general election. Significant modifications have occurred in the rules for choosing delegates, the laws and judicial decisions regarding them, and the ways candidates communicate with voters.

Supporters of the parties' rules changes contend that they have taken the nomination out of the back rooms and into the public arena, provided more opportunities for more candidates to compete, and given partisans a greater voice in choosing their party's nominees. Critics allege that the party rules still favor nationally recognized candidates, allow activists to exercise more influence, and do not encourage participation in the states that hold their contests later in the process after the nominee has been effectively determined.

The campaign finance system has also been problematic. Many of the undemocratic features of the private funding system remain even though the size of individual and group contributions to federal candidates and parties have been limited, spending restrictions have been imposed on federally funded candidates, public funding has provided greater opportunities for more candidates to run for their party's nomination, helped for a time to equalize campaign expenditures, and increased public disclosure of campaign contributions and expenditures. Inequities have persisted, however; loopholes in the law have permitted groups to skirt the federal public contributions limits; Supreme Court decisions have allowed unlimited independent spending by individuals, nonparty groups, and now corporations, labor unions, and candidate-oriented Super PACs; public funding is now jeopardized by candidates' abilities to raise large amounts of private money without spending limits; and each presidential campaign is more expensive than the previous one, often by significant amounts.

The public's ability to make an informed, enlightened judgment has also been called into question by the amount and quality of the communications received from the candidates and parties and coverage by the news media. The channels of communication have increased, but the bulk of the communication is skewed toward specific groups that receive appeals designed to gain their attention and mobilize their support. This information is often incomplete and one-sided. Candidates with the most money have the loudest voice, which they can use to drown out their opponents' claims and accusations.

In addition to being highly targeted, political commercials have become increasingly negative and emotionally charged. The news media seem more concerned with reporting the race, strategies of the candidates, and their personal and professional behavior than educating the public on the principal issues of the day, the way candidates would deal with these issues, and the impact of their policies on the country in the short and long term.

Have these changes been beneficial or harmful? Have they functioned to make the system more efficient, more responsive, and more likely to result in the choice of a well-qualified candidate? Politicians, journalists, and political scientists disagree in their answers.

Who votes and how votes should be aggregated continues to prompt debate and elicit concern. The expansion of suffrage has made the election process more democratic in theory, but the actual rates of participation have reduced this theoretical gain. Although the failure to vote of a substantial portion of the adult population has been a source of embarrassment and dismay to proponents of a democratic electoral process, there is also little agreement on how to deal with this problem in a federal system that values individual initiative, civic responsibility, and states' rights simultaneously.

Finally, the equity of the Electoral College has also been challenged, but none of the proposals to alter or abolish it, except the direct election of the president, have received much public backing. With no outcry for reform, Congress has been reluctant to alter the system by initiating an amendment to the Constitution and seems unlikely to do so until another electoral crisis and/or unpopular result creates sufficient public pressure to force its hand. Proponents of direct election have thus recommended that states form an interstate compact and agree to have their electors support the national popular-vote winner, but thus far, not enough states have done so to implement the plan.

Does the electoral process work? Yes. Can it be improved? Of course, it can. Will it be changed? Probably, but if the past is any indication, there is no guarantee that legally imposed changes will produce only, or even, their desired effect. If politics is the art of the possible, then success is achieved by those who can adjust most quickly to the changes in the legal and political environment and turn those changes to their electoral advantage.

 ## WHERE ON THE WEB?

Public Interest Groups

- **Center for Responsive Politics**
  www.opensecrets.org

- **The Center for Voting and Democracy**
  www.fairvote.org

- **Common Cause**
  www.commoncause.org

- **League of Women Voters**
  www.lwv.org

- **National Popular Vote**
  www.nationalpopularvote.com

- **Public Citizen**
  www.citizen.org

Think Tanks

- **The American Enterprise Institute for Public Policy**
  www.aei.org
  A moderate, Republican-leaning institute interested in public policy.

- **The Brookings Institution**
  www.brookings.org
  Washington's oldest think tank; it has a moderate, centrist orientation.

- **Cato Institute**
  www.cato.org
  A libertarian-oriented institute that examines contemporary public policy issues.

- **Center for American Progress**
  www.americanprogress.org
  A liberal-oriented, Democratic-leaning think tank that examines contemporary issues and provides reports and op-ed articles.

- **Heritage Foundation**
  www.heritage.org
  A conservative group concerned with salient public policy issues.

- **Joint Center for Political and Economic Studies**
  www.jointctr.org
  A liberal-oriented think tank specializing in issues of particular concern to minority groups.

- **Urban Institute**
  www.urban.org
  A nonpartisan institute for the study of domestic public policy.

Government Sources

- **Congress**
  www.thomas.gov or www.house.gov and www.senate.gov

- **Presidency**
  www.whitehouse.gov

EXERCISES

1. From the perspective of American democracy, explain what you consider to be the major problems facing the presidential electoral system today and why you think they are problems. Then describe whether (and, if so, how) liberal, moderate, and conservative groups as well as the Democratic, Republican, and minor parties see the issue you have identified and indicate any solutions they have proposed to fix it. Which of their proposals do you think is best and why? If you do not think any of their proposals will be effective then propose one of your own.

2. Examine the legislation Congress has enacted in the twenty-first century to reform the electoral system. Indicate the major provisions of the legislation and how they have been implemented to date. What else do you think that Congress can and should do?

3. From the perspective of the presidential candidates, what is the most odious feature of the current presidential electoral system? Under the existing law, advise the candidates how to deal with this problem and/or propose reforms to reduce or eliminate it.

SELECTED READINGS

Bennett, Robert W. *Taming the Electoral College.* Stanford, CA: Stanford University Press, 2006.

Center for Voting and Democracy. *The Shrinking Battleground: The 2008 Presidential Election and Beyond.* www.fairvote.org/shrinking

Coleman, Kevin J., R. Sam Garrett, and Thomas H. Neale. "Contemporary Developments in Presidential Elections." Congressional Research Service, Library of Congress, January 9, 2012. http://fpc.state.gov/documents/organization/180682.pdf

Corrado, Anthony J., Michael J. Malbin, Thomas E. Mann, and Norman J. Ornstein. *Reform in an Age of Networked Campaigns: How to Foster Citizen Participation Through Small Donors and Volunteers.* Washington DC: A Joint Project of the Campaign Finance Institute, the American Enterprise Institute, and the Brookings Institution, 2010.

Edwards, George C., III. *Why the Electoral College Is Bad for America.* 2nd ed. New Haven, CT: Yale University Press, 2011.

Gerken, Heather K. *The Democracy Index: Why Our Election System Is Failing and How to Fix It.* Princeton, NJ: Princeton University Press, 2009.

Issacharoff, Samuel, Pamela S. Karlan, and Richard H. Pildes. *When Elections Go Bad: The Law of Democracy and the Presidential Election of 2000.* New York: Foundation Press, 2001.

Koza, John R., et al. *Every Vote Equal: A State-Based Plan for Electing the President by National Popular Vote.* Los Altos, CA: National Popular Vote Press, 2006.

Neale, Thomas H. "The Electoral College: How It Works in Contemporary Presidential Elections." Congressional Research Service, Library of Congress, October 22, 2012. http://fpc.state.gov/documents/organization/28109.pdf

Panagopoulos, Costas. "Are Caucuses Bad for Democracy?" *Political Science Quarterly,* 125 (Fall 2010): 425–442.

Polsby, Nelson W. *Consequences of Party Reform.* New York: Oxford University Press, 1983.

Schumaker, Paul D., and Burdett A. Loomis, eds. *Choosing a President: The Electoral College and Beyond.* New York: Chatham House, 2002.

Tolbert, Caroline J., Amanda Keller, and Todd Donovan. "A Modified National Primary: State Losers and Support for Changing the Presidential Nominating Process." *Political Science Quarterly,* 125 (Fall 2010): 393–424.

Tolbert, Caroline J., and Peverill Squire, eds. "Reforming the Presidential Nomination Process." *PS: Political Science and Politics,* 42 (Jan. 2009): 27–79.

Wayne, Stephen J. *Is This Any Way to Run a Democratic Election?* 5th ed. Washington, DC: Sage/CQ Press, 2014.

NOTES

1. "Low Marks for the 2012 Election," Pew Research Center for the People and the Press, November 15, 2012. http://www.people-press.org/2012/11/15 /low-marks-for-the-2012-election/

2. Romney won the nomination in 2016 five weeks later in the election cycle than McCain in 2008 even though Romney was competing against what most observers considered a weaker group of candidates.

3. Thomas E. Patterson, *Out of Order* (New York: Knopf, 1993), p. 210.

4. Ibid.

5. Jeffrey M. Jones, "Americans in Favor of National Referenda on Key Issues: Majority Also Backs Shorter Presidential Campaigns and National Primary," Gallup Poll, July 10, 2013. http://www.gallup.com/poll/163433/americans -favor-national-referenda-key-issues.aspx

6. They would not have an equal voice, however, because of the disparities in resources among the candidates and their supporters.

7. Approval voting allows the electorate to vote to approve or disapprove each candidate who is running. The candidate with the most approval votes is elected. In a system of cumulative voting, candidates are rank-ordered, and the ranks may be averaged to determine the winner.

8. Caroline J. Tolbert, Amanda Keller, and Todd Donovan, "A Modified National Primary: State Losers and Support for Changing the Presidential Nominating Process," *Political Science Quarterly*, 125 (Fall 2010): pp. 393–424.

9. Ibid., 421. The small states that held preprimary contests could allocate half their delegates to their early election and half to the national primary or they could allocate all of them to either election if they were to choose to do so. It would be up to the state.

10. Ibid.

11. It normally takes the Federal Election Commission up to two years to complete an audit of the expenses and determine which of them may not have been in compliance with the law.

12. R. Samuel Garrett, "Proposals to Eliminate Public Financing of Presidential Campaigns," Congressional Research Service, Library of Congress, December 9, 2013. http://assets.opencrs.com/rpts/R41604_20131209.pdf

13. "Public Knowledge of Current Affairs Little Changed by News and Information Revolutions: What Americans Know: 1989–2007," Pew Research Center for the People and the Press, April 15, 2007. http://www.people-press.org/2007/04/15 /public-knowledge-of-current-affairs-little-changed-by-news-and-information -revolutions/

14. Kate Kenski, Bruce W. Hardy, and Kathleen Hall Jamieson, *The Obama Victory: How Media, Money, and Message Shaped the 2008 Election* (Oxford, UK: Oxford University Press, 2010).

15. "Eleven Recommendations for Improving Election Night Television," Cambridge, MA: The Joan Shorenstein Center on the Press, Politics, and Public Policy, Kennedy Institute, Harvard University (2004).

16. APSA Task Force on Inequality and American Democracy, "American Democracy in an Age of Rising Inequality," *Perspectives on Politics*, 2 (Dec. 2004): pp. 647–690.

17. Michael P. McDonald, "November 2012 General Election Turnout Rates," updated Sept. 3, 2014. www.electproject.org

18. Michael P. McDonald, "November 2014 General Election Turnout Rates," updated Dec. 30, 2014. www.electproject.org
19. Excluded would be those convicted of a capital crime and sex offenders. "Building Confidence in U.S. Elections," Report of the Commission on Federal Election Reform (Sept. 2005).

    In forty-eight states, incarcerated prisoners cannot vote. In eleven states, ex-felons are permanently barred from voting. The prohibitions against felons apply to about 5.85 million people living in the United States. "U.S. Felons Disenfranchisement Laws by State," The Sentencing Project. http://www .sentencingproject.org/template/page.cfm?id=133
20. There have been accuracy and security problems with electronic voting. Computer scientists contend that the current system is vulnerable to hidden programming by the designers of such systems as well as to outside hacking. A small error in the programming could switch hundreds, if not thousands, of votes. They also claim that the voting machines have not been adequately tested, a claim that the Election Assistance Commission supported when it decertified the main company testing the machines in 2007 on the grounds that it did not adequately document the tests it was doing on the equipment. Christopher Drew, "Citing Problems, U.S. Bars Lab from Testing Electronic Voting," The New York Times (Jan. 4, 2007), pp. A1, A14.

    Another issue has been the absence of a paper trail to use when determining the accuracy of electronic machines in tabulating the vote. Without such a trail, it is difficult to check whether all the votes have been properly recorded and tabulated.

    Voting on the Internet is even more suspect. Problems with security prompted the Department of Defense to cancel the implementation of a web-based system to allow members of the armed forces stationed abroad to vote via the Internet.
21. The Presidential Commission on Election Administration, January 2014. https://www.supportthevoter.gov/files/2014/01/Amer-Voting-Exper-final -draft-01-09-14-508.pdf
22. A few states have begun reducing the time frame for early voting, essentially to save money.
23. Heather K. Gerken, The Democracy Index: Why Our Election System Is Failing and How to Fix It (Princeton, NJ: Princeton University Press, 2009).
24. Lydia Saad, "Americans Call for Term Limits, End to Electoral College," Gallup Poll, January 18, 2013. http://www.gallup.com/poll/159881/americans-call -term-limits-end-electoral-college.aspx
25. The Center for Voting and Democracy reported in 2006 that more than 30 percent of the nation's white population lived in the battleground states compared to just 21 percent of African Americans and Native Americans, 18 percent of Latinos, and 14 percent of Asian Americans. "Presidential Election Inequality: The Electoral College in the 21st Century," A Report by the Center for Voting and Democracy (Takoma Park, MD: Center for Voting and Democracy, 2006), p. 13.
26. According to Fairvote.org, a group that wants to replace the Electoral College with a direct popular vote or, in the absence of a constitutional amendment, an agreement among the states to have their electors vote for the national popular-vote winner regardless of how their state votes, there have been 157 faithless electors. Seventy-one changed their votes because the candidate for whom they were going to vote died before they were to cast their votes. In the other cases,

the electors simply decided on their own not to vote for their party's designated candidate. www.archive.fairvote.org/index.php?page=973

27. The same problem occurred in 1988, although in that case, the reversal of names for the presidential and vice presidential votes was done on purpose by a Democratic West Virginia elector.

28. Abraham Lincoln was the only plurality president who failed to attain the 40 percent figure. He received 39.82 percent in 1860, although he probably would have received more had his name been on the ballot in nine southern states.

29. Other direct election proposals have recommended that a joint session of Congress decide the winner. The runoff provision was contained in the resolution that passed the House of Representatives in 1969. In 1979, a direct election plan with a runoff provision failed to win the two-thirds Senate vote required to initiate a constitutional amendment.

30. John Kennedy carried New York by approximately 384,000 votes. He received a plurality of more than 800,000 from precincts that were primarily Jewish. Similarly, in Illinois, a state he carried by less than 9,000, Kennedy had a plurality of 55,000 from the so-called Jewish precincts. Mark R. Levy and Michael S. Kramer, *The Ethnic Factor* (New York: Simon & Schuster, 1972), p. 104.

31. Lydia Saad, "Americans Call for Term Limits, End to the Electoral College," Gallup Poll, January 18, 2013. http://www.gallup.com/poll/159881/americans -call-term-limits-end-electoral-college.aspx

32. *Every Vote Equal: A State-based Plan for Electing the President* (Los Angeles: National Popular Vote Press, 2006), pp. 243–274.

33. For the latest information on the number of states that have agreed to this compact see www.nationalpopularvote.com.

INDEX